T0382668

Technological Prospects and Social Applications of Society 5.0

This book provides readers to the vision of **Society 5.0**, which was originally proposed in the fifth Basic Science and Technology Plan by Japan's government for a technology-based, human-centered society, emerging from the fourth industrial revolution (Industry 4.0). The implementation of AI and other modern techniques in a smart society requires automated data scheduling and analysis using smart applications, a smart infrastructure, smart systems, and a smart network.

Features

- Provides an overview of basic concepts of Society 5.0 as well as the main pillars that support the implementation of Society 5.0.
- Contains the most recent research analysis in the domain of computer vision, signal processing, and computing sciences for facilitating smart homes, buildings, transport, facilities, environmental conditions and cities, and the benefits these offer to a nation.
- Presents the readers with practical approaches of using AI and other algorithms for smart ecosystem to deals with human dynamics, the social objects, and their relations.
- Deals with the utilization of AI tools and other modern techniques for smart society as well as the current challenging issues and its solutions for transformation to Society 5.0.

This book is aimed at graduate and postgraduate students, researchers, academicians working in the field of computer science, artificial intelligence, and machine learning.

Technological Prospects and Social Applications of Society 5.0

Edited by
Lavanya Sharma
P. K. Garg

CRC Press
Taylor & Francis Group
Boca Raton London New York

CRC Press is an imprint of the
Taylor & Francis Group, an **informa** business

A CHAPMAN & HALL BOOK

Front cover image: Lightspring/Shutterstock.

First edition published 2024
by CRC Press
2385 NW Executive Center Drive, Suite 320, Boca Raton, FL 33431

and by CRC Press
4 Park Square, Milton Park, Abingdon, Oxon, OX14 4RN

CRC Press is an imprint of Taylor & Francis Group, LLC

© 2024 selection and editorial matter, Lavanya Sharma and P. K. Garg; individual chapters, the contributors

Library of Congress Cataloging-in-Publication Data
Names: Sharma, Lavanya, editor. | Garg, Pradeep K., editor.
Title: Technological prospects and social applications of society 5.0 /
edited by Lavanya Sharma, Pradeep Garg.
Description: Boca Raton : Chapman & Hall/CRC Press, 2023. |
Includes bibliographical references and index. |
Identifiers: LCCN 2022060069 (print) | LCCN 2022060070 (ebook) |
ISBN 9781032347592 (hardback) | ISBN 9781032349770 (paperback) |
ISBN 9781003324720 (ebook)
Subjects: LCSH: Society 5.0. | Technological innovations–Social aspects.
Classification: LCC T14.5 .T43959 2023 (print) | LCC T14.5 (ebook) |
DDC 303.48/3–dc23/eng/20230301
LC record available at https://lccn.loc.gov/2022060069
LC ebook record available at https://lccn.loc.gov/2022060070

ISBN: 978-1-032-34759-2 (hbk)
ISBN: 978-1-032-34977-0 (pbk)
ISBN: 978-1-003-32472-0 (ebk)

DOI: 10.1201/9781003324720

Typeset in Times
by codeMantra

Dedicated to my Dada Ji (Late. Shri Ram Krishan Choudhary Ji)

Dr. Lavanya Sharma

Dedicated to my Parents (Late Shri Ramgopal Garg and Late Smt Urmila Garg)

Prof. Pradeep K. Garg

Contents

Part I   Introduction to Society 5.0

Part II   Tools & Technologies for Society 5.0

Part III   Smart Society-based Applications

Part IV   Challenges, Opportunities and Novel Solutions

Preface

Society 5.0 may have multiple components, such as the natural systems (e.g., Physics, Chemistry, and Biology), the cognitive systems (e.g., neurosciences, psychology, and artificial intelligence) and the service systems. The quality of human lives can be improved through smart services which still needs the most development. It is also called service science or service engineering, wherein service always involves either a human-human interaction or human-no-human, such as with robotics. Almost any engineering systems involve human operators and human beings, and in that sense, human–machine interaction or human–environment interaction are evolving into the smart services space. The **AI**-related technologies may be useful for supporting human interaction with other agents. Optimal results are obtained by various approaches and algorithms, including **AI**, which exceed far beyond the capabilities of humans, and these results are fed back to the physical space. This process brings new values to business and society in ways not previously possible. The implementation of **AI** in a smart society, in which the analysis of human habits is mandatory, requires automated data scheduling and analysis using smart applications, a smart infrastructure, smart systems, and a smart network.

The proposed book provides readers to the vision on upcoming cities, facilities, and metropolitan lives in connection with **Society 5.0**, which was originally proposed in the fifth Basic Science and Technology Plan by Japan's government for a technology-based, human-centered society, emerging from the fourth industrial revolution (Industry 4.0). The **AI** has the ability to predict and automate the pre-defined sets of tasks using, and in some cases generating data, over a specific task. In smart society, a dedicated method is required to manage and extract the massive amount of data and the related data mining techniques. The methods and approached used provide near-zero-failure advanced diagnostics for smart management, which is exploitable in any context of Society 5.0, thus reducing the risk factors at all management levels and ensuring quality and sustainability.

This book comprises four different parts and provide detailed description of various components and pillars of Society 5.0. It would highlight the current challenging issues and their solutions by utilizing of AI, IoT, and cloud tools and techniques for smart society, such as Industry 4.0, digital innovations, emergency departments, intelligent traffic systems (ITS), visual surveillance, automotive industry, environmental monitoring, mobility, smart infrastructure, smart health care system, smart security and surveillance system, smart energy motion-based object detection and tracking for real-time applications, cybersecurity, Fintech, and many more. In summary, this book seeks to be a contribution to a more informed society, shaped by the digital data in the social dynamics.

Overall this publication *Technological Transformation Towards Society 5.0* helps the readers to understand Technologies value to individuals as well as homes and organizations. In addition, it provides future insights to undertake research work in future challenging areas.

Acknowledgments

I am especially grateful to my dada ji, my parents, my husband, and my beautiful family for their continuous support and blessings. I would like to thank my husband Dr. Mukesh for his continuous motivation and support throughout this project. Apart from his busy schedule, he always motivated and supported me. I owe my special thanks to Mrs. Samta Choudhary ji and Late Shri Pradeep Choudhary ji for their invaluable contributions, cooperation, and discussions. I am very much obliged to Prof. Pradeep K Garg, the editor of this book, for his motivation and support. This book would not have been possible without the blessings and valuable guidance of Prof. Garg. . Above all, I express my gratitude to Almighty God.

Dr. Lavanya Sharma

The author sincerely acknowledges the valuable contributions of the authors of various chapters as well as Dr Lavanya Sharma, editor of the book to make the contents and subject matter more meaningful. I am extremely grateful to my family members; Mrs Seema Garg, Dr Anurag Garg, Dr Garima Garg, Mr Hansraj Aggrawal, Ms Pooja Aggrawal and Master Avyukt Garg, and all relatives & friends for their understanding, continuous encouragement, moral support and well-wishes. Above all, I express my gratitude to Almighty God for offering all blessings and giving me enough strength to work hard to complete the Book on time, as planned. Finally, I like to express our sincere thanks to the publisher, M/s CRC Press whose have cooperated to publish this book in a timely manner.

(Pradeep K Garg)
Professor
Civil Engineering Department
Indian Institute of Technology Roorkee
& Former, Vice Chancellor
Uttarakhand Technical University, Dehardun

Editors

Lavanya Sharma is an Assistant Professor, Amity Institute of Information Technology at Amity University UP, Noida, India. She did her M.Tech (Computer Science & Engineering) in 2013 at Manav Rachna College of Engineering, affiliated to Maharshi Dayanand University, Haryana, India. She did her Ph.D at Uttarakhand Technical University, India, as a full time Ph.D Scholar in the field of Digital Image Processing and Computer Vision in April 2018, and received *TEQIP* scholarship for the same. Her research work is on Motion based Object Detection using Background Subtraction Technique for Smart Video Surveillance. She is a recipient of several prestigious awards during her academic career. She has about more than 30+ research papers to her credit including Elsevier (SCI Indexed), Inderscience, IGI Global, IEEE Explore, and many more. She has authored six books including five books with Taylor & Francis, CRC Press. Dr. Sharma has done various courses from IIRS (ISRO dehradun, India). She has guided about more than 50 PG and UG projects. She also contributed as Organizing Committee member Springer's Springer and IEEE conferences. She is an Editorial Member/Reviewer of various journals of repute and active program committee member of various IEEE and Springer conferences. Her primary research interests are Digital Image Processing and Computer Vision, Artificial Intelligence, Mobile Ad-hoc networks, and Internet of Things. Her vision is to promote teaching and research, providing a highly competitive and productive environment in academic and research areas with tremendous growing opportunities for the society and her country.

P. K. Garg worked as a Vice Chancellor, Uttarakhand Technical University, Dehradun. Presently, he is a Professor in the Department of Civil Engineering, IIT Roorkee. He has completed B.Tech (Civil Engg.) in 1980 and M.Tech (Civil Engg) in 1982 at the University of Roorkee (now IIT Roorkee). He is a recipient of Gold Medal at IIT Roorkee to stand first during M.Tech programme, Commonwealth Scholarship Award for doing Ph.D. from University of Bristol (UK), and Commonwealth Fellowship Award to carry out post-doctoral research work at University of Reading (UK). He joined the Department of Civil Engg at IIT Roorkee in 1982 and gradually advancing his career rose to the position of Head of the Department in 2015 at IIT Roorkee.

Prof. Garg has published more than 300 technical papers in national and international conferences and journals. He has undertaken 26 research projects and provided technical services to 83 consultancy projects on various aspects of Civil Engineering, generating funds for the Institute. He has authored three text books on *Remote Sensing, Theory and Principles of Geoinformatics*, and *Introduction to Unmanned Aerial Vehicles*, and produced two technical films on Story of Mapping. He has developed several new courses and practical exercises in Geomatics Engineering. Besides, supervising a large number of undergraduate projects, he has guided about 72 M.Tech and 27 Ph.D. Thesis. He is instrumental in prestigious MHRD funded projects on e-learning; Development of Virtual Labs, Pedagogy and courses under NPTEL. He has served as experts on various national committees, including Ministry of Environment & Forest, EAEC Committee, NBA (AICTE) and Project Evaluation Committee, DST, New Delhi.

Prof. Garg has reviewed a large number of papers for national and international journals. Considering the need to train the human resource in the country, he has successfully organized 42 programmes in advanced areas of Surveying, Photogrammetry, Remote Sensing, GIS and GPS. He has successfully organized 10 conferences and workshops. He is a life member of 24 professional societies, out of which he is a Fellow member of 8 societies. For academic work, Prof. Garg has travelled widely, nationally and internationally.

Contributors

Anuj Kumar Atrish
Department of Civil Engineering, Master of Technology
Manav Rachna International Institute of Research and Studies
Faridabad, India

Surendiran Balasubramanian
Department of Computer Science and Engineering
National Institute of Technology
Puducherry, India

Tushar Bharadwaj,
Geomatics Engineering, Department of Civil Engineering
Indian Institute of Technology
Roorkee, India

Thierry Bouwmans
MIA Lab
University of La Rochelle
La Rochelle, France

Dharmendra Carpenter
Department of Anaesthesiology & Critical Care
Narayana Multispecialty Hospital
Jaipur, India

Mukesh Carpenter
Department of General and Laparoscopic Surgery
Alshifa Multispecialty Hospital
Okhla, India

Haobam Derit Singh
Department of Civil Engineering, Faculty of Engineering and Technology
Manav Rachna International Institute of Research and Studies
Faridabad, India

Joe Dhanith
School of Computer Science and Engineering
Vellore Institute of Technology
Chennai, India

P. K. Garg
Civil Engineering Department
Indian Institute of Technology
Roorkee, India

Rahul Dev Garg
Geomatics Engineering Group, Department of Civil Engineering
Indian Institute of Technology
Roorkee, India

Yaman Hooda
Department of Civil Engineering
Manav Rachna International Institute of Research and Studies
Faridabad, India

Vinod Kumar Jangid
Department of Respiratory Medicine
Medical College
Kota, India

V. Jokanović
Institute of Nuclear Science "Vinča"
ALBOS doo
Beograd, Serbia

Sujithra Kanmani
School of Computer Science and Engineering
Vellore Institute of Technology
Chennai, India

Siddhartha Khare
Geomatics Engineering, Department of Civil Engineering
Indian Institute of Technology
Roorkee, India

Vallidevi Krishnamurthy
School of Computer Science and Engineering
Vellore Institute of Technology
Chennai, India

Vedant Kulshrestha
Department of Forensic Medicine &
    Toxicology
Uttar Pradesh University of Medical Sciences
Saifai, India

Abhishek Kumar
Department of General and Laparoscopic
    Surgery
Venkateshwar Hospital
Dwarka, India

Akash Kumar
Geomatics Engineering, Department of Civil
    Engineering
Indian Institute of Technology
Roorkee, India

Shamita Kumar
Institute of Environment Education and
    Research
Bharati Vidyapeeth Deemed University
Pune

Satyam Mishra
School of Computing science and Engineering
Galgotias University
Greater Noida, India

Millie Pant
Mehta Family School of Data Science and
    Artificial Intelligent
Indian Institute of Technology
Roorkee, India

Wieke Prummel
MIA Lab
University of La Rochelle
La Rochelle, France

Ravi Saraswat
School of Computing Science and Engineering
Galgotias University
Greater Noida, India

Sudhriti Sengupta
School of Computing Science and Engineering
Galgotias University
Greater Noida, India

Lavanya Sharma
AIIT, Amity University
Noida, India

Mayank Sharma
Geomatics Engineering Group, Department of
    Civil Engineering
Indian Institute of Technology
Roorkee, India

Meenu Singh
Department of Applied Mathematics and
    Scientific Computing
Indian Institute of Technology
Roorkee, India

Anastasia Zakharova
MIA Lab
University of La Rochelle
La Rochelle, France

Part I

Introduction to Society 5.0

1 The Emergence of Society 5.0

P. K. Garg
Indian Institute of Technology

CONTENTS

1.1 INTRODUCTION

Worldwide, over the past decade, the society and economy have faced acute pressure due to economic, political, and environmental changes. Japan, an East-Asian country, has a developed economy with a high human development index value despite the country has faced specific problems and challenges. Several polices have been developed by the nation to bring advancements in the country. The Industry Revolution 4.0 (IR 4.0) addresses the need of adopting digital transformation in the manufacturing processes (i-scoop, 2018). Society 5.0 is based on the same concept that aims to minimize the problems being faced by Japan. Japan, one of the world's "innovation nations," planned to implement the innovation strategies to develop globally competitive expertise in several areas, such as semi-conductors, mobile internet, consumer electronics, video games, smart energy, LED lighting systems, and many other commercially viable areas.

In 2016, in the Fifth Science and Technology Basic Plan, Keidanren (Japan Business Federation, 2016) published a document on *Toward realization of the new economy and society- Reform of the economy and society*, which defined Society 5.0 as *a modern vision for sustainable development of society*. In January 2016, Japanese Government formally introduced a new concept of Society 5.0 (i.e., Super Smart Society). The conceptual model of Society 5.0 was proposed by the Japanese Government's Council of Science, Technology and Innovation for the future society. It defines Society 5.0 as

> a society that is capable of providing the necessary goods and services to the people who need them at the required time and in just the right amount; a society that is able to respond precisely to a wide variety of social needs; a society in which all kinds of people can readily obtain high-quality services, overcome differences of age, gender, region, and language, and live vigorous and comfortable lives.

It is expected to be a creative society, where modern technologies incorporate the creativity of people to find solutions of social problems and improve the quality of life (Garg et al., 2022). Keidanren (2017) defined Society 5.0 as *a human-centered society that balances economic advancement with the resolution of social problems by a system that highly integrates cyberspace and physical space*. This human-centered society is characterized by the fusion of cyberspace and physical space to provide goods and services that bring the economic development, resolve the social problems of individuals and ensure suitable infrastructure for sustainable living of people in

DOI: 10.1201/9781003324720-2

3

a modern society. A cyber-physical system (CPS) is basically *a computer system in which mechanisms are controlled and monitored by algorithms.* In a CPS, physical and software components are integrated at different spatial and temporal scales (Figure 1.1). Some examples of CPS include smart grid, autonomous automobile systems, medical monitoring, industrial control systems, robotics systems and automatic pilot avionics. The modern society will bring economic growth and offer solutions to global and local challenges.

According to Keidanren (2017), Society 5.0 is a future society where the Internet of Things (IoT), Artificial Intelligence (AI), robots, sensors, and other innovative technologies will play a lead role not only to optimize the needs of individuals but also the society as a whole (Harayama, 2018). The Keidanren is a major stakeholder in Society 5.0 which identifies that the use of these technologies will contribute to Japan's economic benefits and provide cutting-edge solutions to the challenges being faced, such as an aging society and combating the natural disasters.

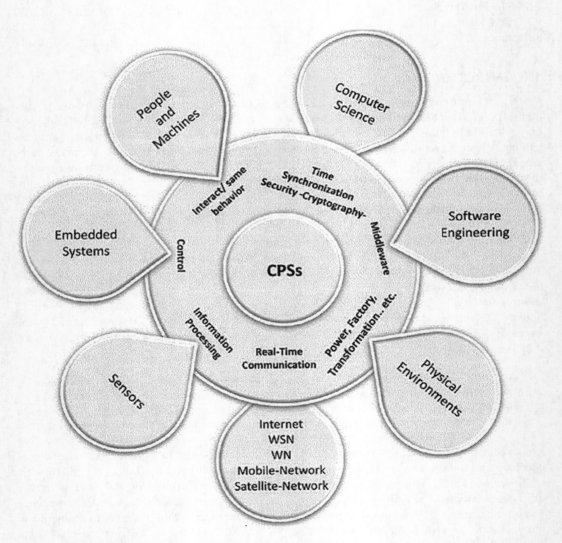

FIGURE 1.1   CPS and its parts and characteristics (Aldosari, 2017).

1.2 THE SOCIETY 5.0

In April 2016, in the G7 Business Summit, the leaders of G7 countries and the EU discussed various issues, such as world economy, trade and investment, digital revolution and global issues, where Society 5.0 was the key concept discussed to bring digital revolution and was accepted by international leaders. With a concept to shifting from "solving social issues" to "creating a better future," Society 5.0 proposed a model for Japan that also combined Germany's "Industrie 4.0" vision. It was Japan's original initiative. Germany, one of the leading nations, promotes such reforms nationally, adopting the concept of "Industrie 4.0," announced in 2010 as High-Tech Strategy (2020). Thereafter, besides Germany, many other nations, such as the US and Singapore, have adopted the concept to bring changes in the society.

The term Society 5.0 denotes the fifth stage of society, following the Hunting society (Society 1.0), Agrarian society (Society 2.0), Industrial society (Society 3.0), and Information society (Society 4.0), as shown in Figure 1.2. Moving from the Hunting society to the Agrarian society, humans have enhanced the food productivity to meet their hunger (Narvaez Rojas et al., 2021). In the Industrial society, the production capabilities and mobility were increased by adopting the power. In the Information society, the capacity of telecommunications and information processing was enhanced by IT, which increased the access to information and communications, and exploring internet-based services. The earlier revolutions, including the agricultural and industrial revolutions, have made significant technological advances and structural changes in the society.

Societies 3.0 and 4.0 focused on efficient mass production and consumption to enhance material wealth in society. In Society 5.0, the digital technologies will attempt to meet the diverse needs of people. In addition, people will have imagination and innovation to identify the needs and challenges in society, which will help them to convert into businesses. However, in Society 4.0,

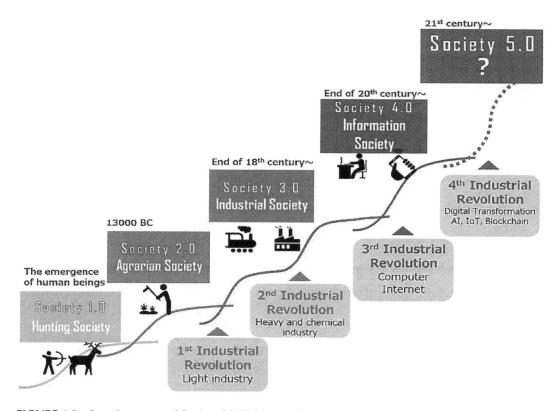

FIGURE 1.2 Japan's concept of Society 5.0 (Keidanren, 2017).

the wealth and information were with the handful of people that widened the gap, but in Society 5.0, wealth and information will be distributed and decentralized throughout the society. Thus, there will not be any disparity and all will get the opportunities to participate anytime and anywhere. The information generated will be shared by various users, not accessible to only few selected companies. In Society 4.0, vulnerabilities increased, e.g., rapid deterioration of large quantities of infrastructure, heavy damages caused by earthquakes and floods, increasing disparity, growing social anxiety about terrorism and other crises, and damages caused by cyber-attacks (Narvaez Rojas et al., 2021). In Society 5.0, modern social infrastructure will reduce the unemployment and poverty and enhance the resilience to disasters, which can lead to sustainable development. Citizens will be safe and secured, especially against terrorism and disasters in physical spaces and attacks in cyber space. Top class medical care will be available to all, regardless of their location, and the medical facility will continue even during the disasters. Society 5.0 will pay more attention in the areas susceptible to various types of disasters. In Societies 3.0 and 4.0, people were dependent on systems requiring greater utilisation of resources. In Society 5.0, the use of data will enhance the energy efficiency, as traditional energy networks would not only be the sources but alternate sources shall also be utilized. Advanced approaches of water supply and waste management will be practiced. Other than the big cities, alternatives will be provided for living in regions of harmony with nature. As the economy develops, organic food better for health will serve the larger community, minimizing the food wastage.

1.3 THE AIMS OF SOCIETY 5.0

In Society 5.0, all individuals can contribute with their imagination and creativity to live a happy lifestyle to achieve Sustainable Development Goals (SDGs), as presented in Figure 1.3. Society 5.0 for SDGs will solve creative problems using digital transformation. It will bring major changes to individual's life.

Innovation is the key parameter to the success of Society 5.0. Figure 1.4 shows the linkages between Society 5.0, sustainability and innovation. Several strategies may require digital innovation, and digital technology. Digital innovations in a super-intelligent society aim to improve the quality of life of people (Ferreira and Serpa, 2018). This insight seeks a strong linkage between Society 5.0 and digital social innovations. Digital social innovation requires integration of innovation process, social world and digital ecosystem. The focus of social innovation is to address the important social challenges and not just the technology itself.

Society 5.0 can greatly impact the society to improve quality of life and sustainability. The sustainability is an important element for innovation focusing on economic, environmental, and social dimensions. The economic dimension of sustainability is directly related to the profit, economic

FIGURE 1.3   Characteristics of Society 5.0.

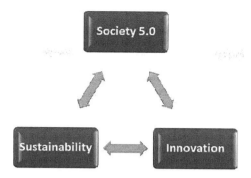

FIGURE 1.4   Linkages between Society 5.0, sustainability and innovation.

growth, efficient use of resources and the financial viability of firms. The environmental dimension concerns on reducing the pollution and the optimum use of resources. The social dimension focuses issues, such as equal opportunities, distribution of wealth, ethical behavior, equity, and justice (Savaget et al., 2019).

Japan plans to take the lead worldwide for achieving a smart society with better future. Society 5.0 will contribute to sustainable development of global economy by adopting the approach in other countries. It will promote the activities with the help and support a several partners, including governments/municipalities, universities, R&D institutes, and companies. Society 5.0 will also promote public–private projects in areas that will support to the cause. In addition, it capitalizes on creativity of "disruptive innovation" and "innovation based on social issues", and "invisible manufacturing" (e.g., software),

1.4   KEY ISSUES OF SOCIETY 5.0

Society 5.0 is an imperative strategy for revitalizing Japan. It provides several options to resolve social issues using reliable and quality data, and such approach can also be applied to solving global social problems. In Society 5.0, Japanese has identified to get solution of several national issues, such as less number of children, shortages of labor-type workers, super-aging society, natural disasters, cyber-attacks, and environmental considerations.

Keidanren (2017) identified five priority areas: cities, regions, infrastructure, cyber-space and goods, products and services, as shown in Figure 1.5. For each area, the plan consists of three

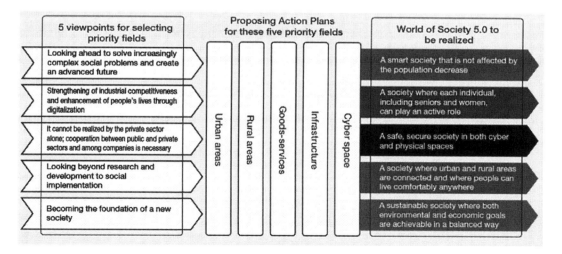

FIGURE 1.5   Five priority areas in Society 5.0 (Keidanren, 2017).

objectives and three core initiatives. In the cities section, for example, the objectives included reducing financial pressures through public–private partnerships; minimizing traffic jams, continuation of distribution of power during disasters; enhancing global participation with women and senior citizens; and attracting greater investment in Japan. Cities in Society 5.0 would mainly require (i) developing sensor networks that enable constant, instantaneous visualization of urban activities; (ii) establishing infrastructure for urban management catering to individual's requirements, and (iii) establishing systems and structures ensuring effective database urban management. As cities' functions are represented in 3D and as Digital Twins, geospatial data will serve as the backbone. In future, the advanced geospatial tools will solve the specific needs and challenges of the urban environment.

Regions in Society 5.0 involve (i) establishing infrastructure that will use smart technology to support agriculture, leading to cutting in labor requirements, (ii) application of cutting-edge technology for comprehensive regional care, such as transport for patients, services for children with illness, etc., and (iii) establishing disaster prevention/mitigation infrastructure for all-time energy supply and infrastructure monitoring.

Infrastructure in Society 5.0 would need (i) developing smart construction and production systems, (ii) developing asset management system through AI technology, and (iii) establishing "virtual Japan" platform that will provide relevant information for urban development. Globally, the infrastructure and construction projects and smart city operation have given a rise to availability of products, services and solutions for the urban environment.

Cyber space in Society 5.0 will require (i) developing data distribution platforms, (ii) developing digital twin platforms, (iii) developing systems that promote the distribution and use of data, (iv) solving problems arising due to increased use of cyber space, and (v) developing security platforms. Society 5.0 would focus on (i) developing a platform for goods, products, and services, (ii) prioritizing basic technologies in growth fields, and (iii) developing an environment to have global competitiveness for all sized enterprises.

Aging of people has been posing greater challenges in Japan, and Society 5.0 plans to take up such issues while providing high quality health care. Japan with its limited resource has been facing various social issues due to declining birth rate and increasing aging people and reduced research. The innovations in Society 5.0 will resolve the challenges of an aging population, energy shortages, environmental degradation, changing nature of work, and many others. Developing a trend toward a human-centered society, health care will increase the life expectancy of citizens (Garg et al., 2022). It proposes a new model for Japan that would prevent from illnesses and help in achieving SDGs and resolving global issues.

Society 5.0 puts the efforts on innovation in Japan by giving priority to societal needs. It consists of two important elements: "digital transformation" and "imagination and creativity of diverse people", which will reform the organizational structure for individual's imagination and creativity using digital transformation. The aim is to have a society where varied social challenges are resolved by incorporating the concepts of the IR 4.0 (e.g., IoT, Big data, AI, robot, and economy) into industry and socially (Narvaez Rojas et al., 2021). Thus, Society 5.0 will be equipped with new technologies that plans to make individual's life more comfortable and healthy. In addition, it with modern technologies would make an attempt to solve many social issues for sustainable development (Savaget et al., 2019).

In all, Society 5.0 must realize the following:

a. Unaffected by population decrease
b. Individuals, including the elderly and women, are able to participate
c. Safe and secure cyberspace and physical space
d. Possible to live comfortably in cities and regions, and
e. Sustainable balancing the economy and environment

1.5   PROBLEMS AND CHALLENGES IN SOCIETY 5.0

At present, Japan's society is facing several challenges, such as an increased aged population, gender disparity, and energy and environmental threats. To realize Society 5.0, many difficulties will be faced. Although it can prove to be a game changer for economy and society, it has some drawbacks and challenges. For example, it may lead to huge unemployment, which will hamper social and political tranquility. In addition, it tends to digital divide, rising inequality, and alienation and separation of family and society. It also requires skilled and qualified manpower to use ICT and associated technologies to its full potential (Garg et al., 2022). It requires huge infrastructure and funding, which itself is a big question mark. Cybercrime and digital security is major concern.

There are several adverse effects from Society 5.0, like-

1. Unemployment will rise because all things are done by machines
2. Machines will replace human jobs
3. Humans will become more dependent on machines
4. Can weaken our knowledge because the task/activities will be replaced by a machine
5. Less jobs for people as they are replaced by machines, and therefore welfare/prosperity will threaten
6. Consumptive culture will become high
7. Our cultural roots will be eroded and lost
8. Decrease of social life so that the sense of need for others is increasingly absent
9. The need for each other will disappear because there is someone who helps (AI/Robot)
10. There will not be a mutual greeting between people but greet with machines
11. The interaction with humans will decrease, but more interaction with machines
12. Crimes will become more because unemployment rises, and
13. Cyber-crime will become high

In April 2016, Keidanren listed five obstacles (or "Walls") that are to be removed for the success. It is important to break through these "five walls" – the wall of ministries and agencies, wall of the legal system, wall of technologies, wall of human resources, and wall of social acceptance as well as the wall of industry itself (Harayama, 2018).

1. **Wall of Ministries and Agencies:** The national strategies are to be designed and developed by ministries and agencies in addition to industry and academia to promote these strategies.
2. **Wall of the Legal System:** It is important to develop the rules for promoting the applications of data. Existing regulations may create in developing innovative technologies, such as next-generation automobiles, unmanned aerial vehicles (UAVs), and robots; thus, further reform is required considering the feedback from citizens.
3. **Wall of Technologies:** It is to be ensured that government invests some percentage of GDP in R&D. It is essential not only to encourage the innovative government R&D projects, such as Cross-ministerial Strategic Innovation Promotion Program (SIP) and Impulsing Paradigm Change through Disruptive Technologies Program (ImPACT) but also to reform the innovation system for social implementation of new technologies.
4. **Wall of Human Resources:** The human resources are essential to contribute to the development of Society 5.0, both nationally and internationally, based on educating the human resource and large-scale joint research projects. It is necessary to provide education and IT literacy at primary and secondary levels to bring creativity and promote life-long education. Another important issue is to train human resources, especially for cyber-security, data science and international standardization, which are essential factors to implement Society 5.0. The government should also make a plan to retain highly-skilled manpower.

5. **Wall of Social Acceptance:** A social binding is essential among the stakeholders based on their ethical, legal and social implications. Understanding the benefits, global expansion of Society 5.0 incorporating the cultures and regional characteristics of the country is required to be promoted by industry, academia, and the government.

6. **Wall of Industry:** Industry has the most important role to play in Society 5.0, and thus increased global competitiveness of industries is required to achieve the development of industries as well as success in Society 5.0.

1.6   THE POSSIBLE SOLUTIONS

Human and social capital is essential for the development of innovative methods of a smart society. Society 5.0 advocates the use of modern technologies and tools to connect the people and things and share information and knowledge for the development of society. Creating new industries is essential to the prosperity. The basic purpose is to modify the manufacturing processes for the upgradation of data process, services and products to suit the given environment and human needs, along with the smart systems and infrastructures.

Keidanren mentioned that the key to success is data. The data utilization can (i) improve the competitiveness in the industry, (ii) improve quality of life of people, and (iii) provide solutions to tackle the social issues. These data could be available from various sources; personal data from public and private sectors, public data from various governments (e.g., land and water maps, traffic volumes, disasters, climate, etc.), cadastral land data (e.g., land titles, mutation, cost of the land, etc.), health-related information (e.g., medical expenses, special medical check-up, health care data, etc.), business-related data (e.g., trades, customers, loss-profit, log data, etc.), sensor data (e.g., machinery and infrastructure data), and so on. As we face the challenges of hyper-aging in the society, the industries will come forward to develop a modern healthcare system keeping the privacy and security intact.

Society 5.0 intends to apply modern technologies for managing social system and issues by relaxing various social constraints (Nakanishi, 2019). The AI would gather information from physical space in cyber space, making the data analysis faster. The ICT in manufacturing industry will bring automation, making the production efficient, flexible, cost-effective and intelligent. These systems would integrate various data and methods used for digitalization, networking, and application of AI, such as smart applications, smart infrastructure, smart systems and a smart network. The processes will be used to create a knowledge-based society to meet human needs as well as achieve social, environmental, and economic sustainability.

The IT has been used in businesses, but technological growth in IoT, AI, sensors, robots, blockchain, and smartphones is increasing the innovations and generating new businesses rapidly. The use of science and technology, supported by IT and innovations, can be used to bring prosperity to citizens, irrespective of age, caste, gender, language or region, and change the social structures. The IT is the main tool to integrate cyber space and physical space and create a new value from Big data (Garg et al., 2022).

Society 5.0 was launched as a new vision for a sustainable society that uses modern technologies to ultimately achieve the economic development, on the basis of SDGs established by the United Nations (Zengin et al, 2013). It will provide solutions to relevant social problems (Keidanren, 2017), as shown in Figure 1.6. A total of 17 SDGs have been identified in relation to various activities which are to be completed by 2030. With each activity, there are more than one SDGs linked, as shown in Table 1.1. Vision of Society 5.0 defines the importance of technologies for solving the current social problems for the survival of humankind and society (Higashihara, 2018).

Many activities of organizations require innovations for creating new products and services that would fulfil the needs of people and developing the technologies which are significantly better than the previous one (OCED, 2005). This advancement would require large investment in developing the necessary infrastructure. The technologies used in Society 5.0 will attempt to minimize the use

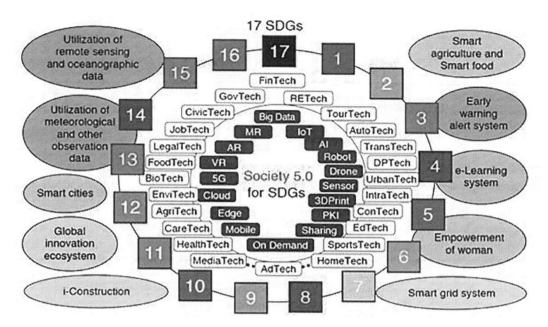

FIGURE 1.6   Society 5.0 for achieving the SDGs (Zengin et al, 2013).

TABLE 1.1
Activities Linked with Various SDGs

Activity	Correlated with SDG
Sustainable infrastructure systems	SDG 9, SDG11 and SDG12
Smart agriculture and food	SDG1, SDG2, SDG12, SDG14, and SDG15
e-learning system	SDG4, SDG5, SDG8, SDG10, SDG16, and SDG17
Early warning systems	SDG3, SDG9, SDG11, SDG13, SDG14, SDG15, SDG16, and SDG17
Empowering women	SDG4, SDG5, SDG8, and SDG10
Sustainable energy	SDG7, SDG11, SDG12, and SDG13
Remote sensing and oceanographic data	SDG6, SDG7, SDG13, SDG14, and SDG15

of natural resources, especially for reduction of greenhouse gas emissions, increased productivity, reduced wastage of food, etc. Several advanced technologies, such as AI and data mining, have proved cost-effective in solving the resources issues. The use of Society 5.0 concept for achieving SDGs requires the active participation of various stakeholders, and their roles are shown in Figure 1.7. The success of 5.0 would however depend on infrastructure, technologies, human values and knowledge (Higashihara, 2018).

1.7   CONCLUSION

Society 5.0 is a human-centered society. In comparison to Society 4.0, Society 5.0 is concerned with the problem solving, data value creation, diversity, decentralization, resilience to disasters and sustainability. In Society 5.0, everyone can create value anytime, and anywhere, without any constraints. It is aiming to solve burning social problems of the society, focusing on longer

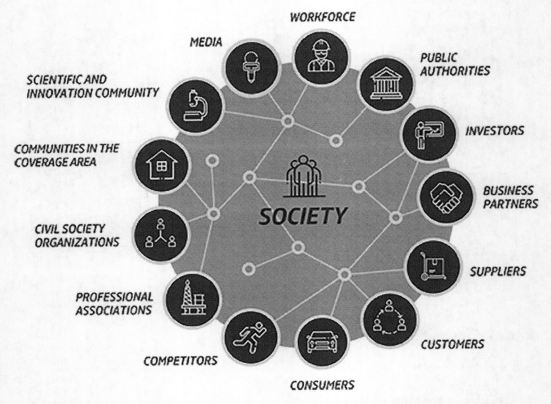

FIGURE 1.7   Role of stakeholders for the success of Society 5.0 (Higashihara, 2018).

lifespan, aging societies, concentration of wealth and regional imbalances (Nakanishi, 2019). It also explores the possibility for solving of individual's social problems through organizational activities and creating guidelines for advancement of societies, internationally. Society 5.0 is not going to happen automatically, but it would be created by participation from various stakeholders, and not just by the technology alone. Diverse people can create diverse values with varied imagination and creativity. Japan wishes to take this concept globally, in partnership with the countries.

The concept of Society 5.0 and its initiative is relatively new. It may take a bit longer to expect rapid results from digital transformation. But, it is promising to realize that Society 5.0 is progressing steadily. In this society, everyone can participate and develop diverse creativity to derive new values useful to the society. It is to be understood that Society 5.0 will not just create products or services, but it is amalgamations of technologies, products and services, which is still at a developmental stage. The foundation of Society 5.0 is the cutting-edge technologies that can bring the great reform.

REFERENCES

Aldosari, Fahd. (2017). Security and privacy challenges in cyber-physical systems, *Journal of Information Security*, 8, 285–295. https://doi.org/10.4236/jis.2017.84019.

Ferreira, C. M., and Serpa, S. (2018). Society 5.0 and social development: Contributions to a discussion. *Management and Organizational Studies*, 5(4), 26. https://doi.org/10.5430/mos.v5n4p26.

Garg, P. K., Tripathi, Nitin, Kappas, Martin, and Gaur, Loveleen (Eds.). (2022). *Geospatial Data Science in Healthcare for Society 5.0*. Springer Nature, Singapore.

Harayama, Yuko. (2018). Society 5.0: Aiming for a new human-centered society Japan's science and technology policies for addressing global social challenges. *Hitachi Review*, 66, 6, 556–557.

Higashihara, T. (2018). *A Search for Unicorns and the Building of "Society 5.0"*. World Economic Forum, Davos.

High-Tech Strategy (2020) Implementation of an Industry 4.0 strategy – the German Platform Industrie 4.0. Technical report, Secretary General of the Platform Industrie 4.0, Germany. https://www.bmwk.de/Redaktion/EN/Dossier/industrie-40.html.

i-scoop. (2018). From Industry 4.0 to Society 5.0: The big societal transformation plan of Japan. https://www.i-scoop.eu/industry-4-0/society-5-0/.

Japan Business Federation (2016) Toward Realization of the New Economy and Society—Reform of the Economy and Society by the Deepening of "Society 5.0", Japan Business Federation, Japan.

Keidanren. (2017). *Revitalizing Japan by Realizing Society 5.0: Action Plan for Creating the Society of the Future ~Overview*. February 14, 2017, Japan Business Federation (Keidanren), Tokyo.

Nakanishi, H. (2019). Modern society has reached its limits. Society 5.0 will liberate us. *World Economic Forum*. https://www.weforum.org/agenda/2019/01/modern-society-hasreached-its-limits-society-5-0-will-liberate-us/.

Narvaez Rojas, C., Alomia Peñafiel, G. A., Loaiza Buitrago, D. F., and Tavera Romero, C. A. (2021). Society 5.0: A Japanese concept for a superintelligent society. *Sustainability 2021*, 13, 6567. https://doi.org/10.3390/su13126567.

OCED. (2005). *Annual Report-2005*. The Organisation for Economic Co-Operation and Development (OECD), Paris.

Savaget, P., Geissdoerfer, M., Kharrazi, A., and Evans, S. (2019). The theoretical foundations of sociotechnical systems change for sustainability: A systematic literature review. *Journal of Cleaner Production*, 206, 878–892.

Zengin, Yunus, Naktiyok, Serkan, Kaygin, Erdogan, Kavak, Onur, and Topeuoglu, Ethem. (2013). An investigation upon industry 4.0 and society 5.0 within the context of sustainable development goals. *Sustainability*, 13, 2682. https://doi.org/10.3390/su13052682.

2 Foundation and Pillars of Society 5.0 and Their Roles

Lavanya Sharma
AIIT, Amity University

CONTENTS

2.1 INTRODUCTION

Society 5.0 is a "human-centred" society that balances commercial advancement with the resolution of social challenges by a system that extremely integrates cyberspace or virtual reality and physical space. This society is also known as super smart society. This concept was first proposed in **the fifth Science and Technology Basic Plan by cabinet office** as a future society that Japan be supposed to aim. It is technologically described as a system of systems (SoS) where various systems such as energy management systems (EMSs), transport systems are connected through internet to achieve certain global requirements such as reduction in carbon emissions [1–14]. It basically follows the listed societies:

- Society 1.0 (hunting and gathering society)
- Society 2.0 (agricultural society)
- Society 3.0 (industrial society)
- Society 4.0 (information society)

Society 1.0 deals with groups of persons hunting, congregating in balanced coexistence with environment. In Society 2.0, groups were created based on agricultural cultivation, growing business, and nation-building, whereas Society 3.0 is a society that encourages industrialization through industrial revolution, making people in a large group. Society 4.0 is meta-community society that recognizes the urgent requirement to improve the value systems and social agreements to support innovative society. In Society 5.0, several systems are interconnected with each other through Internet for knowledge and information sharing with each other as shown in Figure 2.1. Thus, technically Society 5.0 can be defined as a system of system (SoS) where systems are connected to each other to form a large network-based system [1,5,12–15].

DOI: 10.1201/9781003324720-3

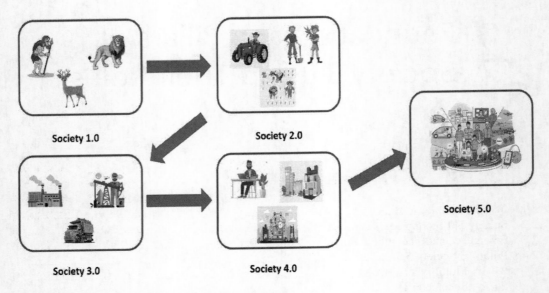

FIGURE 2.1   Transition of Society 1.0 to Society 5.0.

In Society 5.0, multiple systems are connected through the Internet, through which they communicate and interact with each other. Thus, Society 5.0 is technologically defined as a SoS where multiple systems form a large networked system. In a SoS, several heterogeneous systems communicate with each other and cooperatively act to accomplish a universal requirement. For example, an EMS and a road transport (RTS) system consist of various systems that can be connected to form a SoS to reduce emission of carbon. In several cases like the above, a SoS has a hierarchical structure. Figure 2.2 shows an example of a SoS of an EMS and a transport system [15–30].

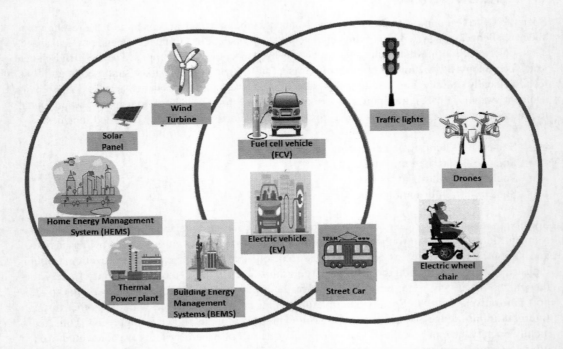

FIGURE 2.2   A system of systems (SoS) of an Energy management system and Transport system.

2.2   SOCIETY 5.0 TECHNOLOGIES

In Society 5.0, cyberspace is formed with the combination of both virtual and physical spaces. In this system, sensors are present in the physical space, and data is collected in the cyberspace using these sensors using internet. Here, cyberspace is also termed as cloud server. Then, the data collected using sensors can be analysed by efficient Artificial intelligence (AI) algorithms. Then, we act upon the ecosystem by distributed actuators allocated in the real space. This complete system is a feedback system, and its stability feedback can be measured. In Society 5.0, both machines and human beings are in the feedback loop [30–40]. They consist of a social system through their smart devices such as smart watches, smartphones, and smart vehicles. To control this system, a new control theory, such as game theory, has to be applied. Key technology for Society 5.0 are distributed optimization, Artificial intelligence (AI), machine learning (ML), deep learning (DL), game theory, sensor network, security, and global network control [25,31,41].

2.3   EMERGENCE AND THEORETICAL FRAMEWORK OF SOCIETY 5.0

Society 5.0 emerged as a "Japanese government" program where government plans to develop to better, smart, and more affluent human-centred society using technological advancements. This program also aims to recover the economy of the country. In Europe, the similar program is known as "Industry 4.0". or "Fourth Industrial revolution". In the USA, it is known as "Industrial Internet". The concept of Society 5.0 is based on the socio-technological outcomes of Industry 4.0. In this period, approximately from 2011 to 2030, technological advancements are empowered to transform a service-oriented society to a society where individual is at the centre. Society 5.0 imagines a supportable **social-class** system where human power is no longer required for the analysis and data collection, but Big Data, AI, IoT, ML and robotic technologies are used. This society is aware of limited human productivity - so it is looking for resources that will break through the present idea of immobility and generate a modern society [8]. Industry 4.0 brought two major concepts which play a significant role in the development of Society 4.0 and that unveil the basic concepts of the future Society 5.0 [25–40,42–45].

- **Smart Factory**: This is based on the ecological mutual interaction between machines and human beings. A future smart factory is very close to the model of "Society 5.0". Its vision is to create a human-centred society where products and services are intended to gather basic needs and lessen the gaps, such as region, generation, and ethnicity. According to the Japanese AI Technology Strategy, it presents the vital technology for the emergence of Society 5.0.
- **Smart Urbanization:** According to the present discourse about urban development scheme is based on sustainable urbanization which consists of advanced technological outcomes that enable the transformation of the cities into smart cities.

2.4   PILLARS OF SOCIETY 5.0

The convergence of AI, big data, IoT and other technologies aim to develop supportive solutions to effectively impact all dimensions also known as digital pillar of society by entirely changing the way of living [3,10,12,25–49]. There are five digital pillars of Society 5.0 which are listed below:

1. Mobility
2. Sustainability
3. Government
4. Finance
5. Healthcare

2.4.1 MOBILITY

Urban transportation is profiting from high-level IT developments. In the last few decades, there is a boom in transit standardization and data. As a result, cities are able to provide real-time data to offer an ideal combination of public transport to get from one place to another. In the case of airport system, biometric technologies also provide accurate and efficient identification process. Advancement in digital technologies provides a wide range of solutions for better driving experience through autonomous driving mode, less maintenance, and remote monitoring. In the case of external driving experience such as vehicle-to-vehicle (V2V) communication, navigation system, and many more [10–27].

2.4.2 SUSTAINABILITY

It is the ability to exist constantly, and the utilization of resources, orientation of technological development, investments, and institutional variations are all in harmony and improve both present and future ability to meet human requirements and desire. For all of the above reasons, this digital pillar is very important, as it has consequences in all other pillars [12–33].

2.4.3 GOVERNMENT

Digital government is a crucial element of a successful economy of a country. To achieve successful transition, governments should work in collaboration with private trades to provide 5G networks and data centres. It also promotes digital awareness among citizens and also enable reliable access to data and services through AI-based identification systems such as biometrics. Developing a digital transformation ecosystem and innovative digital economy creates innovative business models and services [13,28–39].

2.4.4 FINANCE

It includes various manufactured goods, applications, methods, and various models that are based on cloud computing, big data, AI, and ML that transformed conventional banking and financial system into modern system. Digital transformation has empowered financial organizations to drastically reduce paperwork involved in processes such as customer care work, identification, transaction process, and risk management. Now, service providers can customize value-added services more securely using Blockchain [1,4,13,18,34–40,42–46].

2.4.5 HEALTHCARE

Advancement in technologies reduce the healthcare worker workload by reducing he human errors, optimizing systems, improvement of the patient outcome, low hospital cost, better care, and better and early diagnosis. These tech innovations play an important in healthcare system. AI-enabled devices, electronic health records (EGRs), and telemedicine are a few examples of digital solutions that are completely reforming how we access healthcare, how decisions can be made about health issues, appropriate treatment plans, and how data is shared among healthcare and insurance providers, and government [40–53].

2.5 SOCIETY 5.0 IN INDIA

This concept integrates with Hitachi's vision of a "Sustainable Society" where every person can have a safe life. Using digital solutions and integrated methodologies, Hitachi is prepared to work with the Indian government in order to develop a robust framework for an easy transition to current

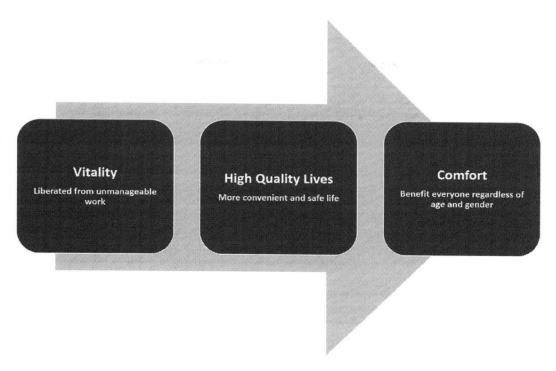

FIGURE 2.3   Society 5.0: Collaboration of Hitachi and India.

scenario to Society 5.0 [41,50–54]. It can also help resolve several social challenging issues through advanced technologies. A leading partner to the government's "Digital India" initiative, this company collaborates with the government in various sectors such as railways, finance, agriculture, urban development, and e-governance to drive India to become a nation well equipped to meet requirements of Society 5.0 in the future [9] as shown in Figure 2.3. In India, this company is contributing to Society 5.0 by providing comprehensive IT x OT solutions In India, Society 5.0 can have various advantages because it can address several listed issues:

- Agricultural issues can be solved with mixed agriculture, mechanization, and automation.
- Using new technologies and innovation, civilians can access various services such as healthcare
- Block chain technology can ensure good governance.
- Big data, Robotics, AI, CV, and ML can solve the traffic issues, healthcare problems, and productivity of industries and service sector.

2.6   SOCIETY 5.0 CHALLENGING ISSUES

Society 5.0 can be a game changer for Indian economy and society, but it has some challenging issues such as:

- It leads massive unemployment that will slow down social and political tranquillity.
- A huge amount of funding and infrastructure to establish smart society in India
- Cyber-crime and digital security are also major concern.

2.7 CONCLUSION

Society 5.0 is a "human-centred" society and can be a gamechanger for Indian society. This chapter presents the emergence, and theoretical framework Society 5.0 such as smart factories and smart urbanization. This chapter also summarizes the concepts and technologies of Society 1.0, Society 2.0, Society 3.0, and Society 4.0. Furthermore, this chapter presents the five digital pillars such as mobility, sustainability, government, finance, and healthcare. Finally, this chapter deals with the open challenging issues and future of Society 5.0 in India.

REFERENCES

1. Society 5.0 Overview. Available at: https://www.ingentaconnect.com/contentone/sil/impact/2020/00002020/00000002/art00002?crawler=true&mimetype=application/pdf [accessed on 15 July 2022].
2. Pillars of Society 5.0. Available at: https://www.thecairoreview.com/essays/society-5-0-and-the-future-economies/ [accessed on 15 July 2022].
3. Society 5.0 Overview. Available at: https://ijarsct.co.in/Paper2762.pdf [accessed on 15 July 2022].
4. Pillars of Society 5.0. Available at: https://sg.nec.com/en_SG/campaign/society5.0/pages/pillar.html [accessed on 15 July 2022].
5. Society 5.0 Overview. Available at: https://www8.cao.go.jp/cstp/english/society5_0/index.html [accessed on 15 July 2022].
6. Society 5.0 Technologies. Available at: https://encyclopedia.pub/entry/123 [accessed on 15 July 2022].
7. Society 5.0 Roadmap. Available at: https://techcrunch.com/2019/02/02/japans-society-5-0-initiative-is-a-roadmap-for-todays-entrepreneurs/ [accessed on 15 July 2022].
8. Society 5.0 Overview. Available at: https://encyclopedia.pub/entry/2084 [accessed on 15 July 2022].
9. Society 5.0 India. Available at: https://social-innovation.hitachi/en-in/knowledge-hub/viewpoint/society-5-0/ [accessed on 15 July 2022].
10. L. Sharma, M. Carpenter (Eds.), *Computer Vision and Internet of Things: Technologies and Applications* (1st ed.), Chapman and Hall/CRC, 2022. https://doi.org/10.1201/9781003244165.
11. Lavanya Sharma, "Computer-aided lung cancer detection and classification of CT images using convolutional neural network", *Computer Vision and Internet of Things: Technologies and Applications*, Taylor & Francis, CRC Press, pp. 247–262, 2022.
12. Lavanya Sharma, "Analysis of machine learning techniques for airfare prediction", *Computer Vision and Internet of Things: Technologies and Applications*, Taylor & Francis, CRC Press, pp. 211–231, 2022.
13. Lavanya Sharma, "Innovation and emerging computer vision and artificial intelligence technologies in coronavirus control", *Computer Vision and Internet of Things: Technologies and Applications*, Taylor & Francis, CRC Press, pp. 177–192, 2022.
14. Lavanya Sharma, "Self-driving cars: Tools and technologies", *Computer Vision and Internet of Things: Technologies and Applications*, Taylor & Francis, CRC Press, pp. 99–110, 2022.
15. Lavanya Sharma, "Computer vision in surgical operating theatre and medical imaging", *Computer Vision and Internet of Things: Technologies and Applications*, Taylor & Francis, CRC Press, pp. 75–96, 2022.
16. Lavanya Sharma, "Preventing security breach in social media: Threats and prevention techniques", *Computer Vision and Internet of Things: Technologies and Applications*, Taylor & Francis, CRC Press, pp. 53–62, 2022.
17. Lavanya Sharma, Mukesh Carpenter, "Use of robotics in real-time applications", *Computer Vision and Internet of Things: Technologies and Applications*, Taylor & Francis, CRC Press, pp. 41–50, 2022.
18. Lavanya Sharma et al., "An overview of security issues of internet of things", *Computer Vision and Internet of Things: Technologies and Applications*, Taylor & Francis, CRC Press, pp. 29–40, 2022.
19. Lavanya Sharma, "Rise of computer vision and internet of things", *Computer Vision and Internet of Things: Technologies and Applications*, Taylor & Francis, CRC Press, pp. 5–17, 2022.
20. Lavanya Sharma, "Human detection and tracking using background subtraction in visual surveillance", *Towards Smart World: Homes to Cities using Internet of Things*, Taylor & Francis, CRC Press, pp. 317–329, 2020.
21. Lavanya Sharma, "The rise of internet of things and smart cities", *Towards Smart World: Homes to Cities using Internet of Things*, Taylor & Francis, CRC Press, pp. 1–19, 2020.

22. Lavanya Sharma, "The future of smart cities", *Towards Smart World: Homes to Cities using Internet of Things*, Taylor & Francis, CRC Press, pp. 1–19, 2020.

23. Lavanya Sharma, Nirvikar Lohan, "Internet of things with object detection", *Handbook of Research on Big Data and the IoT, IGI Global*, pp. 89–100, 2019. ISBN: 9781522574323, https://doi.org/10.4018/978-1-5225-7432-3.ch006.

24. Lavanya Sharma, "The rise of the visual surveillance to internet of things", *From Visual Surveillance to Internet of Things*, Taylor & Francis, CRC Press, 2019.

25. Lavanya Sharma, P K Garg, "Block based adaptive learning rate for moving person detection in video surveillance", *From Visual Surveillance to Internet of Things*, Taylor & Francis, CRC Press, 2019.

26. Lavanya Sharma, P K Garg, "Smart E-healthcare with internet of things: Current trends challenges, solutions and technologies", *From Visual Surveillance to Internet of Things*, Taylor & Francis, CRC Press, 2019.

27. Lavanya Sharma, P K Garg, Naman Agarwal, "A foresight on e-healthcare trailblazers", *From Visual Surveillance to Internet of Things*, Taylor & Francis, CRC Press, 2019.

28. Lavanya Sharma, P K Garg, "IoT and its applications", *From Visual Surveillance to Internet of Things*, Taylor & Francis, CRC Press, 2019.

29. Lavanya Sharma, P K Garg, "Future of internet of things", *From Visual Surveillance to Internet of Things*, Taylor & Francis, CRC Press, 2019.

30. G. Jha, L. Sharma, S. Gupta, "Future of augmented reality in healthcare department", In: Singh P.K., Wierzchoń S.T., Tanwar S., Ganzha M., Rodrigues J.J.P.C. (eds), *Proceedings of Second International Conference on Computing, Communications, and Cyber-Security. Lecture Notes in Networks and Systems*, vol. 203. Springer, Singapore, 2021. https://doi.org/10.1007/978-981-16-0733-2_47.

31. G. Jha, L. Sharma, S. Gupta, "E-health in internet of things (IoT) in real-time scenario", In: Singh P.K., Wierzchoń S.T., Tanwar S., Ganzha M., Rodrigues J.J.P.C. (eds), *Proceedings of Second International Conference on Computing, Communications, and Cyber-Security. Lecture Notes in Networks and Systems*, vol. 203. Springer, Singapore, 2021. https://doi.org/10.1007/978-981-16-0733-2_48.

32. S. Sharma, S. Verma, M. Kumar, L. Sharma, "Use of motion capture in 3D animation: Motion capture systems, challenges, and recent trends", *2019 International Conference on Machine Learning, Big Data, Cloud and Parallel Computing (COMITCon)*, pp. 289–294, 2019, https://doi.org/10.1109/COMITCon.2019.8862448.

33. S. Kumar, P. Gupta, S. Lakra, L. Sharma, R. Chatterjee, "The zeitgeist juncture of "Big Data" and its future trends", *2019 International Conference on Machine Learning, Big Data, Cloud and Parallel Computing (COMITCon)*, pp. 465–469, 2019, https://doi.org/10.1109/COMITCon.2019.8862433.

34. S. Makkar, L. Sharma, "A face detection using support vector machine: Challenging issues, recent trend, solutions and proposed framework", In: Singh M., Gupta P., Tyagi V., Flusser J., Ören T., Kashyap R. (eds), *Advances in Computing and Data Sciences. ICACDS 2019. Communications in Computer and Information Science*, vol. 1046. Springer, Singapore, 2019. https://doi.org/10.1007/978-981-13-9942-8_1.

35. Lavanya Sharma Ayush, Deepa Gupta, "Motion based object detection based on background subtraction: A review", In *3rd IEEE International Conference on Electronics Communication and Aerospace Technology, ICECA 2019*, Coimbatore, India, 12–14 June 2019.

36. Lavanya Sharma, Sudhriti Sengupta, Birendra Kumar, "An improved technique for enhancement of satellite images", *Journal of Physics: Conference Series*, 1714, 012051, 2021, https://doi.org/10.1088/1742-6596/1714/1/012051.

37. Supreet Singh, Lavanya Sharma, Birendra Kumar, "A machine learning based predictive model for coronavirus pandemic scenario", *Journal of Physics: Conference Series*, 1714, 012023, 2021.

38. Gunjan Saraogi, Deepa Gupta, Lavanya Sharma, Ajay Rana, "Un-supervised approach to backorder prediction using deep autoencoder", *Recent Patents on Computer Science, Bentham*, 14, 8, 2021.

39. Lavanya Sharma, Nirvikar Lohan, "Performance analysis of moving object detection using BGS techniques in visual surveillance", *International Journal of Spatiotemporal Data Science, Inderscience*, 1, 22–53, 2019.

40. Anubhav Kumar, Gaurav Jha, Lavanya Sharma, "Challenges, potential & future of IOT integrated with block chain", *International Journal of Recent Technology and Engineering*, 8, 2S7, 530–536, 2019, https://doi.org/10.35940/ijrte.B1099.0782S719.

41. Lavanya Sharma, Pradeep K Garg, *From Visual Surveillance to Internet of Things*, Taylor & Francis, CRC Press, 2019. ISSN: 9780429297922.

42. Ujwal Chopra, Naman Thakur, Lavanya Sharma, "Cloud computing: Elementary threats & embellishing countermeasures for data security", *International Journal of Recent Technology and Engineering*, 8, 2S7, 518–523, 2019, https://doi.org/10.35940/ijrte.B1097.0782S719.

43. Gauri Jha, Pawan Singh, Lavanya Sharma, "Recent advancements of augmented reality in real time applications", *International Journal of Recent Technology and Engineering*, 8, 2S7, 538–542, 2019, https://doi.org/10.35940/ijrte.B10100.0782S719.

44. Akshit Anand, Vikrant Jha, Lavanya Sharma, "An improved local binary patterns histograms techniques for face recognition for real time application", *International Journal of Recent Technology and Engineering*, 8, 2S7, 524–529, 2019, https://doi.org/10.35940/ijrte.B1098.0782S719. ISSN: 2277-3878.

45. Lavanya Sharma, Annapurna Singh, Dileep Kumar Yadav, *Fisher's Linear Discriminant Ratio Based Threshold for Moving Human Detection in Thermal Video*, Infrared Physics and Technology, Elsevier, 2016 (SCI impact factor: 1.58, Published).

46. Lavanya Sharma, Dileep Kumar Yadav, "Histogram based adaptive learning rate for background modelling and moving object detection in video surveillance", *International Journal of Telemedicine and Clinical Practices, Inderscience*, 2016, ISSN: 2052-8442, https://doi.org/10.1504/IJTMCP.2017.082107.

47. L. Sharma, M. Carpenter (eds), *Computer Vision and Internet of Things: Technologies and Applications* (1st ed.). Chapman and Hall/CRC, 2022. https://doi.org/10.1201/9781003244165.

48. Lavanya Sharma, Pradeep K Garg "Artificial intelligence: Challenges, technologies and future", Wiley (In production), 2021.

49. Lavanya Sharma, *Towards Smart World: Homes to Cities using Internet of Things*, Taylor & Francis, CRC Press, 2020 (ISSN: 9780429297922).

50. Lavanya Sharma, *Object Detection with Background Subtraction*, LAP LAMBERT Academic Publishing, SIA OmniScriptum Publishing Brivibas gatve 197, Latvia, European Union, 2019 (ISBN: 978-613-7-34386-9).

51. A.G. Pereira, T.M. Lima, F.C. Santos, "Industry 4.0 and society 5.0: Opportunities and threats", *International Journal of Recent Technology and Engineering*, 8, 5, 3305–3308, 2020.

52. C. Narvaez Rojas, G.A. Alomia Peñafiel, D.F. Loaiza Buitrago, C.A. Tavera Romero, "Society 5.0: A Japanese concept for a superintelligent society", *Sustainability* 13, 12, 6567, 2021.

53. Y. Li, Q. Liu, "A comprehensive review study of cyber-attacks and cyber security; emerging trends and recent developments", *Energy Reports*, 1, 7, 8176–8186, 2021.

54. M. Fukuyama, "Society 5.0: Aiming for a new human-centered society", *Japan Spotlight*, 27, Society 5.0, 47–50, 2018.

3 Insights of Smart Society
An Overview of Trends, Benefits and Application Areas

Meenu Singh and Millie Pant
Indian Institute of Technology

CONTENTS

3.1   INTRODUCTION

The idea of "Society 5.0 (S5.0)" or "Smart Society" was conceptualised by the Government of Japan in the 5th Science and Technology Basic Plan on Jan 2016 (Rojas et al. 2021). The idea was to project a vision of a future society to industry and public to overcome the chronic social and economic changes and to ensure that all the citizens are leading a high-quality, comfortable and vital life. This concept was an outcome of the countless discussions held among specialists from diverse sectors and was based on extensive research into socio-technology development throughout history and contemporary global trends. It is expected that this concept will expand the transformation beyond industry and create a super-smart society where new ideas and values are constantly developed to support both social progress and economic growth.

There are many factors that lead to the vision of super smart society or S5.0, and availability of huge amount of digital data is one of them. This in turn is due to the super advancement in the area of information and communications technology (ICT) in recent years and the expansion of cyberspace. Since the last few decades, our private and professional lives have been saturated with this progress, transforming the industrial society into a manufacturing society where data is the leader. This has also altered the process of developing new ideas for innovation, resulting in the emergence of a new global information society. i.e, S5.0, where data collection, its processing, and its transmission are one of their goals at various stages to promote social and economic welfare.

In other words, S5.0 can be thought of as a model that combines the physical space (real space) and cyberspace, where cyberspace is the digital or virtual environment where data from the actual

DOI: 10.1201/9781003324720-4

world is gathered, transformed into information, and then processed to generate answers (Deguchi et al. 2020). Big data analytics, the Internet of Things (IoT) and artificial intelligence (AI) are a few examples of research and development technologies embedded in our daily lives. IoT makes it possible to collect a wide range of data in cyberspace, whereas AI can evaluate the massive volumes of data collected, construct a cyber model that mimics real-world behaviour and help reshape the world.

The chapter is further divided into four sections. Section 3.2 explores the emergence of S5.0, followed by the explanation of sustainable developments goals in Section 3.3. Section 3.4 presents the applications of technologies in various services areas that can assist in driving the development of smart societies. Finally, some concluding remarks are provided in Section 3.5.

3.2   THEORETICAL BACKGROUND

The development of a society is based on the human needs and the availability of resources. Looking back one can observe the evolution of a society from the hunting point of view to industry point of view and now to human point of view. S5.0 is a direct outcome of the Fourth Industrial Revolution (Industry 4.0 or I4.0) and shares many characteristics with it. S5.0 mainly tries to enhance the features of I4.0 by enhancing or by adding new components to it (Rojas et al. 2021).

3.2.1   INDUSTRIAL REVOLUTIONS

The First Industrial Revolution (I1.0, 1780 to 1820) is known for three significant developments: (i) machines inventions, (ii) energy generation options such as steam technology and (iii) labour organisation forms. In human history, I1.0 is regarded as the most significant social, economic and technological transformations. The period of Second Industrial Revolution (I2.0) was started from 1870, when the word entered into an era of globalisation. This era boosted the generation of novel energy options such as electricity, automatic machineries, oil generated sources, development of land and air transportation and means of communication systems.

The Third Industrial Revolution (I3.0) began after 1914, which highlighted the development of new ICT, such as the Internet, which was based on the invention of the microprocessor and transistor.

The Fourth Industrial Revolution began in the 1980s, where the attention was towards digitalisation (I4.0). Sensors and information systems, IoT, big data, cloud computing, robotics and augmented reality were used to develop a wide range of new factory technologies for complete manufacturing automation. IoT and AI have had a direct impact on society by creating new modes of transportation and communication as well as creating value and opportunities.

The Fifth Industrial Revolution (I5.0) is already predicted by several technological pioneers and even business innovators that I5.0 will feature autonomous manufacturing with AI as the primary backbone of the technology, along with incorporation of human intelligence (Breque, De Nul, and Petridis, 2021). Figure 3.1 depicts the industrial revolution from I1.0 to I5.0.

3.2.2   EMERGENCE OF S5.0

S5.0 has emerged in recent years, attempting to expose the digital transformation of information society (in business and private life) of I4.0. It is a futuristic super-smart society introduced by Japanese government policies, where everyone will be benefitted from the concept of smart living enhanced by scientific and technological innovations. It seeks to create a human-centred society by fusing cyberspace and physical space, thereby facilitating economic development and ensuring a high quality of life for all citizens (Fukuda, 2020; Potočan, Mulej and Nedeljko, 2020). This was primarily defined and developed during the Fourth Industrial Revolution in order to address current societal issues more effectively and efficiently (Rojas et al. 2021).

Figure 3.2 depicts the phase transition of societies from being hunter–gatherer societies to information societies under the influence of scientific and technological innovation. Initially, in the very

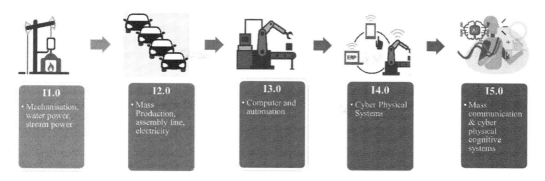

FIGURE 3.1   Overview of industries transformation from I1.0 to I5.0.

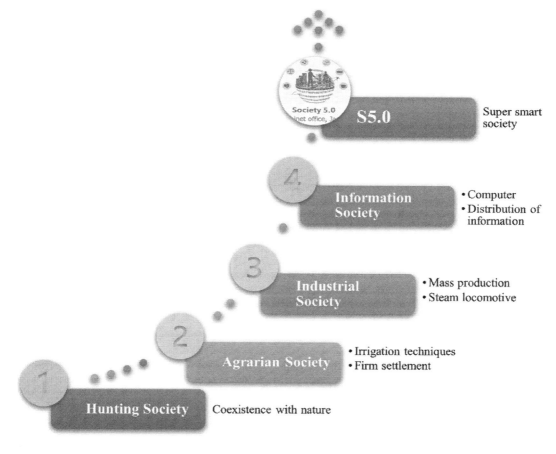

FIGURE 3.2   Overview of societies transformation from S1.0 to S5.0.

beginning the main aim of mankind was survival – protection from wild animals and natural calam-
ities and gathering food. This phase transitioned into an agrarian society, where the man started the
process of agriculture. During this phase, irrigation techniques and various agriculture tools were
developed and also the society became more civilised and proper settlements were created. As the
level of comfort increased, more innovations came into the picture, more developments took place
and now the focus was on machines and production. Little later, with the invention of computers and

TABLE 3.1

Details of Societal Revolutions

	S1.0	S2.0	S3.0	S4.0	S5.0
Society	Hunting	Agrarian	Industrial	Information	Super-smart
Material	Stone, Soil	Matel	Plastic	Semiconductor	Material 5.0
Transport	Foot	Ox, horse	Motor car, boat, plane	Multimobility	Autonomous driving
City ideas	Viability	Defensiveness	Functionality	Profitability	Humanity
Form of settlement	Nomadic, small settlement	Fortified city	Linear (industrial) city	Network city	Autonomous decentralised city
Productive approach	Capture/Gather	Manufacture	Mechanisation	ICT	Merging of cyberspace and physical space

communication technologies, the focus was on the distribution of information. Observing the above transitions one can easily see the strong correlation between the technological development and the societal development. In general, social changes follow industrial revolutions. Table 3.1 depicts the evolution of society from S1.0 to S5.0 in detail (Deguchi et al. 2020; Fukuda 2020).

3.3   SUSTAINABLE DEVELOPMENTS GOALS AND S5.0

The concept of S5.0 emerged as a part of V Science and Technology Basic plan framework (2016–2021) (Rojas et al. 2021). Its actions and goals are in line with the Sustainable Developments Goals (SDGs), which is defined as "a universal call for poverty ending, protect the planet and ensure prosperity for all[1]", according to the United Nations Development program. The 17 UN Sustainable Development Goals (SDGs) are shown in Figure 3.3.

These SDGs objectives are expected to be met by the end of 2030 under S5.0. Since then, most of the countries have begun their research strategies and investment toward S5.0, which is designed to achieve sustainable development objectives from the start, taking into account advances in infrastructure and technology, with the goal of improving industrialisation and the environment (Aquilani et al. 2020; Fukuda 2020; Hayashi et al. 2017; Záklasník and Putnová 2019). Specific SDG goals for each sector are summarised and presented below in Figure 3.4 (Mourtzis, Angelopoulos, and Panopoulos 2022).

3.3.1   ROLE OF DATA IN S5.0

S5.0 is conceptualised as a super smart, human-centric society which largely depends on the availability of data and the methods to analyse that data. This is where Big data analytics, data science, machine learning (ML) and AI are critical Research and Development (R&D) technologies will play an essential role to achieve the objectives of S5.0 (Melnyk et al. 2019). These goals require an advanced fusion of physical and cyberspaces, for which data must be gathered from numerous sensors situated in the physical world and then synthesised using the IoT (Fukuyama 2018). Figure 3.5 shows the most critical technologies, networks and devices required to establish the S5.0 environment (Peraković et al. 2020).

3.4   IMPLEMENTATION OF TECHNOLOGIES

The opportunities provided by scientific and technological advancements are huge. This has had an impact on industrial transformation, international trade, personal and private lifestyle choices

---

[1]   https://www.nzog.com/sustainability/community/sdgs/ Accessed 15 Sept 2022.

FIGURE 3.3 17 UN sustainable developments goals (SDGs).

and consumer behaviours. Many international research institutions have examined alteration in future job requirements due to the development of AI, Big Data, cloud computing and other technologies. However, there has been little research into how these technologies drive smart societies' development and application. This section aims to highlight some of the sectors that have immense potential for the application of various technologies and that will lead to the development of S5.0. Figure 3.6 represents the implementation of S5.0 in four major areas.

3.4.1 Healthcare

S5.0 in digital health care presents a viewpoint where technology supports and improves health care systems to ensure a high quality of life. By implementing technology, data insights can be used to forecast and prevent diseases based on immediate and remote health care services. Researchers have used AI, ML and deep learning technologies to detect breast cancer and brain tumours (Amin et al. 2021; Bai et al. 2021; Zebari et al. 2021; Soomro et al. 2022).

Healthcare professionals are increasingly using technology devices to help provide better healthcare. Many healthcare-related organisations in the nations like the United States and India are shifting to the intelligent management and service provided by novel technologies for: (i) storing the medical data in cloud for tracking health status of their population; (ii) gathering patient information via a data registration process; (iii) storing each patient's medical history for improved healthcare (Jin and Kim 2018; Lin, Lin, and Huang 2018; Peng and Goswami 2019; Verma and Sood 2018; Hayashi et al. 2017).

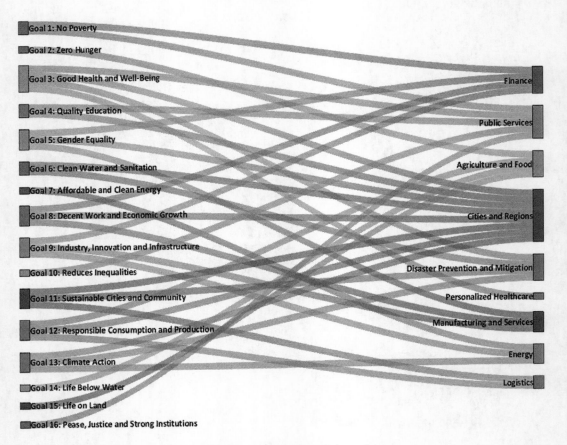

FIGURE 3.4   Summary of 17 UN SDG goals as per each sector in society.

3.4.2   EDUCATION

New S5.0 technologies have recently impacted education, resulting in significant structural changes. Face-to-face instruction in the classroom is no longer necessary as more students can be reached simultaneously using videoconferencing and virtual reality equipment than can physically fit in a classroom.

A thorough educational system at all levels is necessary, and professionals must develop and gain skills connected to data management and processing. Universities must develop adaptive learning programmes, digital resources for lecturers and students, collaborative teaching and learning technology and online learning materials for all students (Carayannis and Morawska-Jancelewicz 2022). This would result in greater researchers' mobility between organisations, industries and disciplines. As there is still a significant gap between universities and business, which must be encouraged to generate knowledge.

The educational S5.0 system must promote the design of training processes that facilitate the development of competencies not only for work but also for cultural consumption, adaptation to constantly changing environments, ownership of basic concepts, interaction with our environment and others, as well as social and personal development (Rojas et al. 2021).

In 2010, Germany demonstrated a significant change in several educational institutions when the IoT is used to convert education to digital formats and is used for fostering distance learning and achieving a technological vision of privacy (Takakuwa, Veza, and Celar 2018).

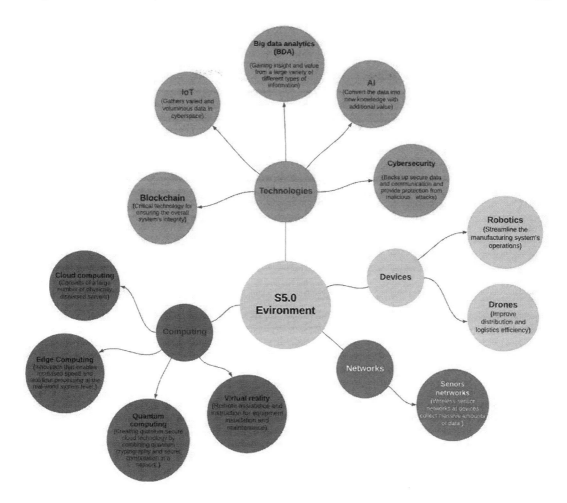

FIGURE 3.5 Details of the most critical technologies, networks and devices needed to establish the S5.0 environment.

3.4.3 Finance

The support and spread of big data and AI has been inextricably linked to the rapid development of financial technology in recent years. The transition from "data" to "big data" reflects the fact that, with the widespread use of the internet, humans have entered the era of "data economy."

According to relevant statistics, there were 4.1 billion internet users worldwide, and the widespread use of network technology resulted in a significant increase in data output (Hernandez et al. 2016). Face and image recognition, speech recognition, big data analysis, machine translation and deep learning are among AI's core developments and future applications (Lu et al. 2015; Najafabadi et al. 2015). Some new innovation technologies, such as Blockchain technology, have the potential to address trust issues in financial transactions by removing the need for trading partners to implement mechanisms to signal or convey trust (Anon 2015). Blockchain technology is being used in finance services to help improve trust relationships by (i) improving the security of transactions and data exchanges, (ii) enabling the expression of benevolence, (iii) improving the efficiency and quality of communication and (iv) increasing transparency (Kowalski, Lee, and Chan 2021; Pal, Tiwari, and Behl 2021).

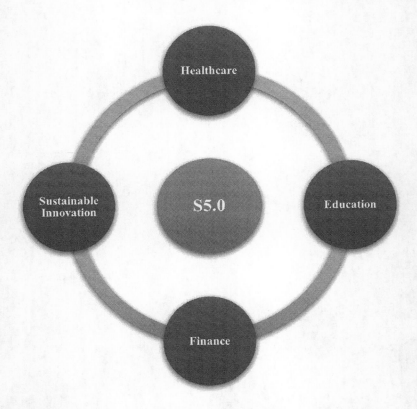

FIGURE 3.6   Implementation of S5.0 in four major areas of society.

3.4.4 SUSTAINABLE INNOVATION

Sustainable innovation is regarded as a fundamental concept in the S5.0 development process. Sustainable innovation is defined as the incorporation of long-term environmental, social and financial considerations into organisational systems. This type of integration results from ideas to R&D and the subsequent commercialisation of results. Products, services, technologies and new business and organisational models are the end results.

Sustainability is a key concept for the innovation processes presented by S5.0 due to its deep relevance in economic, social and environmental dimensions. In the economic context, sustainability is linked to profit, with issues such as economic growth, resource efficiency and the financial viability. In the context of the environment, it focuses on pollution control as well as the efficient and appropriate use of natural resources. In a social context, sustainability refers to issues such as opportunity equality, equity in wealth distribution, ethical behaviour, equity and impartiality. In this way, it aims to achieve a more competitive economy, which creates long-term economic growth with more and better jobs, as well as social stability and inclusive growth (Rojas et al. 2021).

In Japan, a study was conducted to examine the effect of S5.0 practices in accordance with the SDG goals. This helped in highlighting the low-density goals that needed attention. More studies are needed to understand the effectiveness of SDG goals (Zengin et al. 2021).

3.5   CONCLUSIONS AND FUTURE SCOPE

This chapter gave an overview of the S5.0, a super smart, human centric society where the focus is on the comfort and satisfaction of mankind. This chapter provided an overview of the phase transition from one form of society to another and discussed various factors that are lead to the concept of S5.0. Few concluding remarks that can be made based on the above observations are as follows:

1. **Technology and Society**: Technological and social developments go hand-in-hand and development in one area have a tremendous effect on the other. Societal development is a direct outcome of the technical developments. However, while technology is driven more by the inventions, society is driven more by regional economies, culture and political developments.
2. **Role of Data in S5.0**: Data is going to be the lead player in the implementation of S5.0. The quantum of data available is unimaginable, thanks to the development of various ICTs, but management of such huge amount data is still a challenge. Despite the availability of sophisticated tools and techniques for data curation and management, much work is still to be done to analyse the data in the favour of the society.
3. **Major Areas of Implementation of S5.0**: Four sectors where the implementation of S5.0 is going to lay a major role are: Health Care, Education, Finance and Sustainable Innovations. These are the pillars which lay the foundation of a smart society which is healthy, educated and financially stable and is sustainable.

3.5.1 Future Scope

a. The concept of S5.0 or a human centric society is a very interesting concept but is more centred towards the developed countries. It will be an interesting study to see how the concepts of S5.0 can be implemented for developing countries like India.
b. The present study talks of technical and societal developments but has not considered the ethical issues. No society is complete without following the ethical norms and guidelines and therefore thoughts should be put in this direction as well and can be a part of some future study.

REFERENCES

Amin, Javaria, Muhammad Sharif, Anandakumar Haldorai, Mussarat Yasmin, and Ramesh Sundar Nayak. 2021. "Brain Tumor Detection and Classification Using Machine Learning: A Comprehensive Survey." *Complex & Intelligent Systems* 8(4):3161–3183. doi: 10.1007/S40747-021-00563-Y.

Anon. 2015. "Blockchain: The next Big Thing." *Economist (United Kingdom)* 411(8933). doi: 10.1007/S42354-018-0001-X.

Aquilani, Barbara, Michela Piccarozzi, Tindara Abbate, and Anna Codini. 2020. "The Role of Open Innovation and Value Co-Creation in the Challenging Transition from Industry 4.0 to Society 5.0: Toward a Theoretical Framework." *Sustainability* 12(21):8943. doi: 10.3390/SU12218943.

Bai, Jun, Russell Posner, Tianyu Wang, Clifford Yang, and Sheida Nabavi. 2021. "Applying Deep Learning in Digital Breast Tomosynthesis for Automatic Breast Cancer Detection: A Review." *Medical Image Analysis* 71:102049. doi: 10.1016/J.MEDIA.2021.102049.

Breque, Maija, Lars De Nul, and Athanasios Petridis. 2021. *Industry 5.0- Publications Office of the EU.*

Carayannis, Elias G., and Joanna Morawska-Jancelewicz. 2022. "The Futures of Europe: Society 5.0 and Industry 5.0 as Driving Forces of Future Universities." *Journal of the Knowledge Economy* 1–27. doi: 10.1007/S13132-021-00854-2/FIGURES/5.

Deguchi, A., Hirai, C., Matsuoka, H., Nakano, T., Oshima, K., Tai, M., & Tani, S. 2020. *Society 5.0: A People-Centric Super-Smart Society.* Tokyo, Japan: Springer.

Fukuda, Kayano. 2020. "Science, Technology and Innovation Ecosystem Transformation toward Society 5.0." *International Journal of Production Economics* 220:107460. doi: 10.1016/J.IJPE.2019.07.033.

Fukuyama, Mayumi. 2018. "Society 5.0: Aiming for a New Human-Centered Society." *Japan Spotlight* 6(August):47–50.

Hayashi, Hisanori, Hisashi Sasajima, Yoichi Takayanagi, and Hirco Kanamaru. 2017. "International Standardization for Smarter Society in the Field of Measurement, Control and Automation." *2017 56th Annual Conference of the Society of Instrument and Control Engineers of Japan, SICE 2017*, 263–66. doi: 10.23919/SICE.2017.8105723.

Hernandez, Kevin, Becky Faith, Pedro Prieto Martín, and Ben Ramalingam. 2016. *The Impact of Digital Technology on Economic Growth and Productivity, and Its Implications for Employment and Equality: An Evidence Review.*

Jin, Wenquan, and Do Hyeun Kim. 2018. "Design and Implementation of E-Health System Based on Semantic Sensor Network Using IETF YANG." *Sensors* 18(2):629. doi: 10.3390/S18020629.

Kowalski, Michał, Zach W. Y. Lee, and Tommy K. H. Chan. 2021. "Blockchain Technology and Trust Relationships in Trade Finance." *Technological Forecasting and Social Change* 166:120641. doi: 10.1016/J.TECHFORE.2021.120641.

Lin, Yi Chun, Yen Ting Lin, and Po Sen Huang. 2018. "Future Prospects of Artificial Intelligence and How It Drive to Smart Society." *2018 International Conference on Orange Technologies, ICOT 2018.* doi: 10.1109/ICOT.2018.8705920.

Lu, Jie, Vahid Behbood, Peng Hao, Hua Zuo, Shan Xue, and Guangquan Zhang. 2015. "Transfer Learning Using Computational Intelligence: A Survey." *Knowledge-Based Systems* 80:14–23. doi: 10.1016/J.KNOSYS.2015.01.010.

Melnyk, Leonid, Oleksandr Kubatko, Iryna Dehtyarova, Oleksandr Matsenko, and Oleksandr Rozhko. 2019. "The Effect of Industrial Revolutions on the Transformation of Social and Economic Systems." *Problems and Perspectives in Management* 17(4):381–391. doi: 10.21511/PPM.17(4).2019.31.

Mourtzis, Dimitris, John Angelopoulos, and Nikos Panopoulos. 2022. "A Literature Review of the Challenges and Opportunities of the Transition from Industry 4.0 to Society 5.0." *Energies* 15(17):6276. doi: 10.3390/en15176276.

Najafabadi, Maryam M., Flavio Villanustre, Taghi M. Khoshgoftaar, Naeem Seliya, Randall Wald, and Edin Muharemagic. 2015. "Deep Learning Applications and Challenges in Big Data Analytics." *Journal of Big Data* 2(1):1–21. doi: 10.1186/S40537-014-0007-7.

Pal, Abhinav, Chandan Kumar Tiwari, and Aastha Behl. 2021. "Blockchain Technology in Financial Services: A Comprehensive Review of the Literature." *Journal of Global Operations and Strategic Sourcing* 14(1):61–80. doi: 10.1108/JGOSS-07-2020-0039/FULL/PDF.

Peng, Cong, and Prashant Goswami. 2019. "Meaningful Integration of Data from Heterogeneous Health Services and Home Environment Based on Ontology." *Sensors* 19(8):1747. doi: 10.3390/S19081747.

Peraković, Dragan, Marko Periša, Ivan Cvitić, and Petra Zorić. 2020. "Information and Communication Technologies for the Society 5.0 Environment." (December). doi: 10.37528/ftte/9788673954318/postel.2020.020.

Rojas, Carolina Narvaez, Gustavo Adolfo, Alomia Peñafiel, Diego Fernando, Loaiza Buitrago, Carlos Andrés, Tavera Romero, Pedro Verga Matos, Tania Pereira Christopoulos, and G. A. A. P. Co. 2021. "Society 5.0: A Japanese Concept for a Superintelligent Society." *Sustainability* 13(12):6567. doi: 10.3390/SU13126567.

Soomro, Toufique A., Lihong Zheng, Ahmed J. Afifi, Ahmed Ali, Shafiullah Soomro, Ming Yin, and Junbin Gao. 2022. "Image Segmentation for MR Brain Tumor Detection Using Machine Learning: A Review." *IEEE Reviews in Biomedical Engineering.* doi: 10.1109/RBME.2022.3185292.

Takakuwa, Soemon, Ivica Veza, and Stipe Celar. 2018. "'Industry 4.0' in Europe and East Asia." *Annals of DAAAM and Proceedings of the International DAAAM Symposium* 29(1):0061–0069. doi: 10.2507/29th.daaam.proceedings.009.

Verma, Prabal, and Sandeep K. Sood. 2018. "Cloud-Centric IoT Based Disease Diagnosis Healthcare Framework." *Journal of Parallel and Distributed Computing* 116:27–38 doi: 10.1016/J.JPDC.2017.11.018.

Záklasník, Martin, and Anna Putnová. 2019. "Digital Society - Opportunity or Threat? Case Studies of Japan and the Czech Republic." *Acta Universitatis Agriculturae et Silviculturae Mendelianae Brunensis* 67(4):1085–1095. doi: 10.11118/ACTAUN201967041085.

Zebari, Dilovan Asaad, Dheyaa Ahmed Ibrahim, Diyar Qader Zeebaree, Habibollah Haron, Merdin Shamal Salih, Robertas Damaševičius, and Mazin Abed Mohammed. 2021. "Systematic Review of Computing Approaches for Breast Cancer Detection Based Computer Aided Diagnosis Using Mammogram Images." *Applied Artificial Intelligence* 35(15):2157–2203. doi: 10.1080/08839514.2021.2001177.

Zengin, Yunus, Serkan Naktiyok, Erdoğan Kaygın, Onur Kavak, and Ethem Topçuoğlu. 2021. "An Investigation upon Industry 4.0 and Society 5.0 within the Context of Sustainable Development Goals." *Sustainability* 13(5):2682. doi: 10.3390/SU13052682.

Part II

Tools & Technologies for Society 5.0

4 Role of Geospatial Data, Tools and Technologies in Society 5.0

P. K. Garg
Indian Institute of Technology

CONTENTS

4.1 INTRODUCTION

In the 21st century, the innovations backed by technology offer solutions to the political, economic and social models and greatly improve the workflow efficiency and productivity. Society 5.0 is a modern concept that provides guidance for the social development, impacting the societies at all fronts (Hayashi et al., 2017). It strengthens the citizen-technology relationship for the improvement of quality of life of people through a super smart society. It, also known as the "Creative society", relies on the digital transformation. The digital transformation through the use of data, advanced digital technology and data analysis will change the components of the society, such as public administration, industrial setup and job opportunities. In such society, digital transformation integrated with the creativity and imagination of people plays an important role to solve the social issues and improve the quality of life. Society 5.0 provides a strong bonding between the modern technology and digital information, focusing largely on the sustainable development of society (Sułkowski et al., 2021). It focusses on two types of relationships: between the technology and society, and between the individuals and society.

According to the 5th Science and Technology Basic Plan, Japan aims to become *the most innovation-friendly country in the world* (Garg et al., 2022). Society 5.0 is a new guiding principle for innovation. The world is facing a greater change in industries and societies with inclusion of technologies, such as AI, Internet of Things (IoT), sensors, cloud, robotics, Augmented Reality (AR),

DOI: 10.1201/9781003324720-6

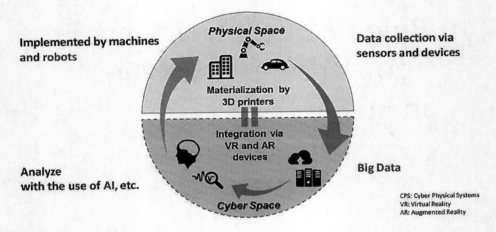

FIGURE 4.1   Integration of physical space with the cyberspace in Society 5.0 (Keidanren, 2017).

Virtual Reality (VR), 3D printing, blockchains and quantum computing (Sharma and Garg, 2021). Companies, such as Google, Amazon, Facebook and Apple, are already using these technologies. Society 5.0 requires a fusion of these technologies for physical, digital and biological activities in a country (Figure 4.1).

With geo-location facility, time and place have become important attributes in providing the answer of what, where, when, how and why of things. Decisions can be made and problems solved with the use of data, technologies and people connected through the internet. The geospatial sector is at the core of this digital ecosystem.

4.2 DATA-DRIVEN SOCIETY

There are three essential elements of Society 5.0 that will enhance the innovation: data, information and knowledge, as given in Table 4.1. The raw data collected becomes useful as it is converted to information, and then the information is transformed into knowledge. In general, data relates to the activities in the physical world that is represented either as numerals, names, text, etc. Information is made meaningful by synthesis of data for a specific purpose or action. Information is converted to knowledge when it is comprehended and analysed. Knowledge helps us making a right decision. It can take the form of generalised observations which are derived from individual cases. Knowledge helps determine the causes of a problem, which can be used to derive solutions while addressing these causative factors. The more the knowledge, the more the judicious decision.

TABLE 4.1
Data, Information and Knowledge

Data *Simple Observations about the State of World*	Information *Data with Relevance and Purpose*	Knowledge *Interpretation, Reflection and Synthesis of Data and Information*
Easily structured	Requires unit of analysis	Difficult to structure
Easily obtained by machines	Requires consensus about the meaning	Difficult to capture on machines
Often quantified	Requires human mediation	Often tacit
		Difficult to transfer, Requires action and creation by the people

A knowledge-based society can be helpful to create a new infrastructure to transform the society. In such a society, universities and businesses can also be very helpful to create new value by comprehending knowledge (Zengin et al., 2013).

The data and its strategic value have a great relevance in today's digital age. In a data-driven society, the Cyber Physical Space (CPS) is applied to various sectors of a society through networking using IoT. The gathered data is converted into information and implemented to the real-world for making positive changes. So, in a data-driven society the data gathered by IoT networks is converted into information and knowledge to be used to "drive" or "move" the real-world.

In the 21st century, the spatial and non-spatial data are most valuable assets to plan economic growth, initiate research, create innovation and derive enhanced socioeconomic benefits, helping create approximately USD 5.4 trillion annual economic value. The data economy would certainly enhance the working of governments, organisations, departments and citizens by using data analytics to enhance efficiency, develop innovative models, increase revenue growth and achieve sustainability. In addition, the data economy will trigger more research and innovation, business opportunities and knowledge base to solve global challenges. The innovations coming out of trends and relationships of different datasets, known as data-driven innovations, would act as interface for enhancing the growth and productivity. Data capture from a variety of sources, data maintenance, data management and data integration; all have been benefitted with the development of new technological tools.

Digitalisation of data is important for the advancement of technology-based innovations. Analogue to digital data conversion helps several economic sectors of the world. Both spatial and non-spatial data, and other data gathered from various sources are playing an important role to the technology. Thus, in the context of Society 5.0, data-driven innovations are helping to arrive at solutions leading to sustainable development. This requires optimum utilisation of resources for the betterment of society. Data-driven technology and market innovations, as well as R&D activities can significantly impact the economy of society.

There are various sources of data to be used in Society 5.0, as briefly discussed below:

4.2.1 BIG DATA

As a result of technology development, huge amount of data is being gathered in the field, called Big data. Big data is growing rapidly with time, therefore the conventional data management tools can't be used to store it or process it, efficiently. Big data may be available as structured, unstructured or semi-structured (Garg, 2020). It can be gathered from various sources, such as the Internet, Facebook, Instagram, Twitter, etc. The non-spatial data may be collected from social media sources, text, tables and demographic and economic data, whereas the spatial data may be collected from geospatial tools and technologies and sensor networks. Big data is represented by four V's: volume, velocity, veracity and variety, but it may also bring significant "value" through its processing, which is also known as the fifth V. This data requires modern techniques to extract the useful information. As more and more real-time observations are collected from IoT-based sensors, modern technologies, such as edge analytics and fog computing can also be used effectively for faster pattern recognition and interpretation (Sharma and Garg, 2021).

4.2.2 GEOSPATIAL DATA

The evolution of geospatial information started between the 1970s and 1980s, with the development of computers and software for digital mapping, which later on automated the traditional map-making process and "overlay" of maps. Geospatial technology providing geospatial data can be broadly divided into four categories; Global Navigation Satellite System (GNSS), GIS and Spatial Analytics, Earth Observation (satellite, aerial and street imagery) and Scanning Technologies (LiDAR, RADAR).

The geospatial data can take many forms and types, such as building addresses, geographic areas, forest, water bodies or the location of people (Garg, 2020). It is available at different accuracy levels; ranging from millimetres to hundreds of metres. In addition, the availability of smartphones and other digital devices has given a way for mobile applications. The geospatial data collection processes may include-

a. Optical-mechanical instruments to carry out detailed land surveys
b. Digitisation and scanning of analogue maps
c. Satellites, airplanes and drones to collect earth observation images
d. GNSS to collect navigational and positional data
e. Radar and LiDAR systems to assess the position of objects and
f. Location sensors in-built in several connected devices, including mobile handsets and vehicles, to provide locational data

The geospatial infrastructure of any nation consists of data, technology, policy and people. It uses geospatial data and services to develop the plans for the future. Geospatial infrastructure integrates the data, information, technology, processes and socioeconomic aspects at a common reference frame. It may be used to derive knowledge-driven innovations and services so that various stakeholders can make the correct decision for action plans.

Geospatial data/information is essential for the development of infrastructure, economic activities and development of society. Many sectors are already integrating geospatial data in their work plans and deriving the economic benefits, so there is an increased demand of geospatial data in economic sectors. The traditional sectors contributing to the economy of a nation require data with high positional accuracy, but many new sectors, such as navigation, businesses, financial services, telematics and tourism may need data of positional accuracy 10 m or more. The use of GNSS, satellite images, laser scanners, smartphones, UAVs and underground mapping tools, such as Ground Penetrating Radar (GPR), has increased manifolds over the past to collect the data/information with required precision. Today, the geospatial data, information and technology are utilised in many fields, such as defense and intelligence, disaster management, land administration, urban development and infrastructure development. Looking at its potential benefits, it has also been applied to other sectors, such as banking and finance, retails, supply chain and logistics, real-estate, agriculture, etc.

With the growth of online and location-based services (e.g., Uber, Tripadvisor and Airbnb), maps have become important for many businesses. Public is not only the users of spatial tools and related services but also the creators of large amount of geospatial data. For example, the global businesses, like Google, have made digital maps accessible globally. Companies, like Uber, integrate geospatial data, positional data, transport network and other similar information to provide solutions and services that are data-driven. Similarly, Mapbox has emerged as a biggest mapping platform in the world, providing live location data. Several such industries are utilising geospatial data and technologies to provide various services to their users. Although the service industries are using geospatial data and technology successfully for offerings various services to their customers, but it seems that public sectors are far behind in utilising these new business models.

Geospatial data and information can provide spatial and temporal solutions to the social, economic and environmental challenges for sustainable development (Garg et al., 2022). Combining spatial and non-spatial data is critical to make the strategic decisions. The modern technologies, such as Blockchain, IoT, AI and ML provide ample avenues for developing the innovations and solutions to take up such challenges, as given in the Sustainable Development Goals (SDGs) for prosperity (Figure 4.2). These data-driven innovations will bring economic growth, better well-being and sustainability (Zengin et al., 2013).

Figure 4.3 shows a framework of data for sustainable development, as identified to develop the national geospatial information system under the National Spatial Data Infrastructure (NSDI). The NSDI will work in association with other national information systems for data integration, analysis, modeling, aggregation, fusion, communication across various disciplines and organisations. In addition, it will provide analysis tools for developing evidence-based decision-making policy. The NSDI, supported by good quality geospatial data, can offer solutions for many national issues, including SDGs.

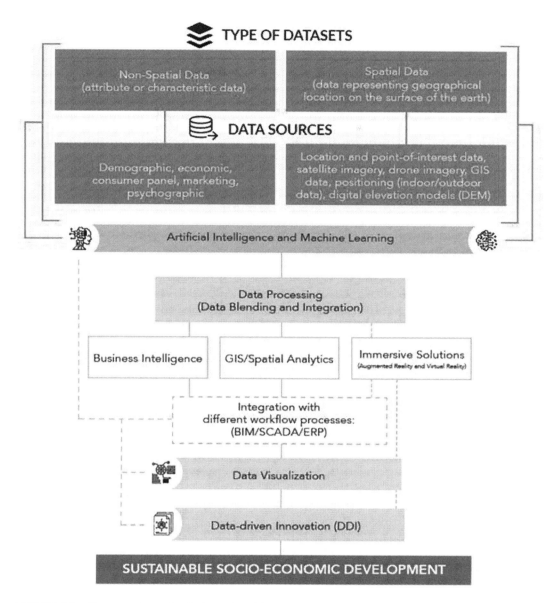

FIGURE 4.2   The emerging technologies as identified in the sustainable development goals (UN-GGIM, 2021).

4.2.3   OPEN DATA

Open data is considered to be an important component of a transparent, innovative and effective governance that can be used to provide various services for citizens. It is essential that the open data is accessible, interoperable and reusable. There are several concerns about the funds requirements for maintaining and updating the past time-series open data, due to cost involved in continuously publishing the high-value open data. Ownership of data is also a key issue. With ever increasing sensors to collect data, defining the ownership is more complex, particularly if the data is integrated from various sources to generate the new products, or solutions.

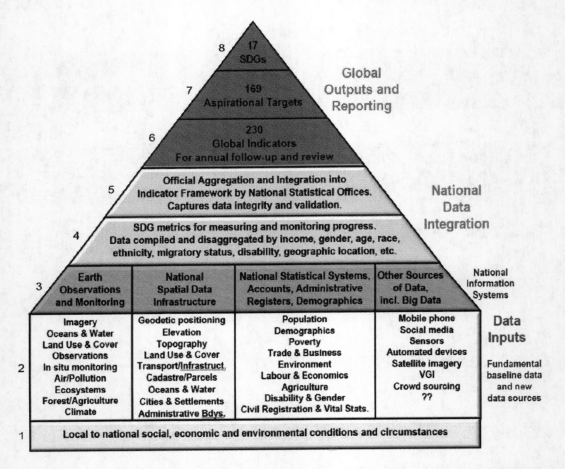

FIGURE 4.3   Data-driven innovation for sustainable socio-economic development (Scott and Rajabifard, 2017).

The examples of satellite data on open platforms include the US Geological Survey (USGS), Landsat images and the European Space Agency's Copernicus programme, Sentinel images. The Landsat offers the largest records of temporal images at moderate resolution, and the Sentinel provides high-resolution imagery, globally. The emergence of Google Earth in June 2005, which combined the geospatial data with the contents, made a great impact on the increased use of free geospatial data and information. These data and contents could be accessed free of charge from a web browser, offering visualisation of data in 2D or 3D. The use of Google Earth images and Google maps has also provided geospatial literacy to the global community. Similarly, a variety of firms and organisations are now offering free access to geospatial data, images and analytical tools to respond to humanitarian causes. These data have been used in various applications, such as forestry, water resources, natural hazards, urban and environmental mapping and monitoring. The development in 5G will further provide products and solutions required by the individual stakeholders.

4.2.4   Data Privacy, Data Ethics and Cyber Security

In 1930, Edmond Locard – the French pioneer in forensic science – identified 12 points of a fingerprint that can be successfully used to determine the identity of an individual. In a modern world, transparency, security and privacy are the major concerns about the data ownership, access and usage. Therefore, it is necessary to understand the processes of securing the digital data infrastructure.

For example, the General Data Protection Regulation (GDPR) of the European Union is the most restrictive law on data protection and privacy. Governments, businesses and individuals; all can be affected by cyber-attacks, leading to intrusion of privacy, halt of services and security risks (Garg et al., 2022). The autonomous vehicles may be a potential source for cyber threats as the moving vehicles will always be connected to networks and communication devices. Manufacturing industry is the second most industry likely to be affected by cyber-attack. These industries are subject to the vulnerability exploitation, malware, denial of service, device hacking, and so on.

4.3 ENABLING TECHNOLOGIES

The technology brings innovations and causes positive changes in the society. In digital age, innovation is very important for the socio-economic growth of a country. Innovation can solve the critical problems and help bringing out the upward changes in the society. Latest technologies allow collecting accurate and real-time data from physical world and cyber space. It is now possible to represent the activities of both real-world and cyber space in the form of digital data. Digital data transformation can take place for everything, everyone and every activity (Narvaez Rojas et al., 2021).

The great reform age, where IoT, AI, robots and life science will drastically change the industrial and social structures, has arrived (Sharma and Garg, 2021). The 4th Industrial Revolution (IR 4.0) is characterised by, among other things, Big data, AI, advanced robotics, automation, the web, smart technologies and digital disruption. Several elements of the human, physical and digital environments have merged in the IR 4.0, leading to unprecedented societal changes. These changes include all walks of life & living, policies & services, and industry & its products. According to the World Economic Forum (WEF), IR 4.0 is *more than just technology-driven change; it is an opportunity for everyone to harness converging technologies to create an inclusive human-centred future.* Geospatial infrastructure plays an important role for this revolution.

Geospatial technologies can create GIS-based intelligent maps taking inputs from satellite and aerial images which could be used for providing better services and effective decision making activities. These technologies will also be greatly benefitted from faster speed and greater connectivity of 5G networks for various applications, such as smart cities, utilities and transportation, water, forest, etc. For example, the telecommunications industry will be one of the beneficiaries from geospatial technology. The global telecom market, which was USD 1,657.7 billion in 2020, is expected to grow at a compound annual growth rate (CAGR) of 5.4% from 2021 to 2028 to reach USD 2,467.01 billion by 2028 (Market Analysis Report, 2019). This growth will be driven mainly by wireless and digital technology, IoT, high-speed internet, AR and 5G services.

The use of IoT, AI, sensors, GNSS, robotics and blockchain and geospatial data will transform the society through digital data revolution (Garg et al., 2022). Abilities of individual people can be learnt by the use of AI. The AI, the cloud, Big data, blockchain and IoT are the important technologies of Society 5.0, as shown in Figure 4.4. The analysis of Big data through AI increases the efficiency, estimates more accurate demand and creates more accurate business plans. The Big data can be stored in the cloud system and used for analysis. The advantage of using the cloud system is that it can be used by various firms through the internet and IoT. Interlinking physical systems and cyber systems, the CPS provides linkage between humans and machine and among the machines through IoT sensors, smart phones and other devices.

Worldwide, people are beginning to use geospatial data and location-based services derived through internet, cloud computing, mobile devices, unmanned aerial vehicles (UAVs), GNSS, remote sensing image, LiDAR, etc. (UN-GGIM, 2015). Automation and machine learning (ML) make the tasks easier and faster that lead to higher productivity. Big data is an essential component of using ML and deep learning (DL) methods in geospatial-based productivity. Today, the data can be created at a much faster rate the human abilities to analyse the data for various applications.

The use of wireless sensors, robotics, cameras, images, cloud computing and associated software are providing new ways to businesses to capture the reality. Satellite images, low altitude

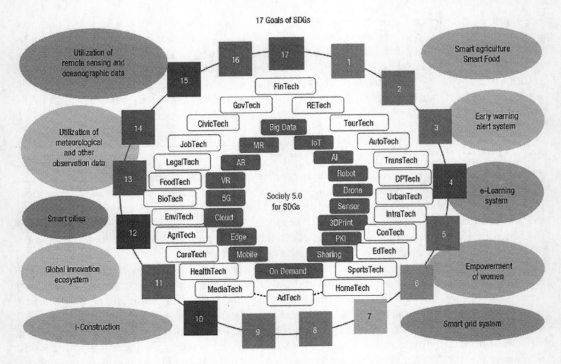

FIGURE 4.4   Various technologies, industries with Society 5.0 (Keidanren, 2017).

or vehicle-based cameras/sensors are available to us at higher resolution offering voluminous data about the Earth to monitor the area at frequent interval and at lower costs. The web service makes it further simple to develop the new products and the commercialisation of emerging technologies.

4.3.1   GLOBAL POSITIONING SYSTEM

The geospatial data technologies, such as Global Positioning System (GPS) and the GNSS, are currently being used in diverse sectors, such as transport, autonomous machines, robots, farming, construction and surveying & mapping (Garg, 2020). For example, farmers can use GNSS in precision agriculture to find best location for growing a specific crop and optimise the route planning for tractors as well as monitoring the locations of their animals. Construction industry can use it to operate heavy machinery on the basis of locational data. The removal of selective availability (SA) for precise positioning of GPS signals by the US Department of Defense in 2000 changed the concept of taking long-time observations, and given a new dimension to take "dynamic" observations, such as in-car navigation systems and other location-based services *via* mobile devices.

4.3.2   IoT

The IoT refers to a wireless network service between various objects/sensors; usually wireless network. From any time, we will now have connectivity for anyone and anything. Wireless sensors and devices can be connected through IoT and data shared at a central place. Big data collected by IoT devices and supported by AI can have access to everyone in the society (Garg et al., 2022). In Society 5.0, lives of citizens are expected to be more comfortable and easy as they are connected with the products and services at any time.

4.3.3 AI

The AI is a bigger term used to encompass the complementary techniques, originally developed from statistics, computer science and cognitive psychology (Sharma and Garg, 2021). It is the ability of a machine to perform cognitive functions as human-beings do, such as perceiving, learning, reasoning and solving problems. Using AI, one can (i) develop software or devices to solve real-world problems with accuracy, such as health issues, marketing, traffic issues, etc., (ii) create personal virtual assistant, such as, Google Assistant, Siri, etc., (iii) build robots to work in an environment where survival of human-beings is at risk and (iv) develop new technologies, devices, and opportunities.

In Society 5.0, the vast data collected in physical space from sensors and devices is stored in cyber space. In cyber space, this Big data is analysed by AI, and the results are fed back to the physical space (Narvaez Rojas et al., 2021). By doing so, it brings out new values to the industry and society. The capabilities of AI have enhanced in recent past by several technologies, particularly in ML/DL involving large volume of data. Many manual tasks can be automised by AI, for example, driving vehicle. The AI has the additional advantages that it can be used for solving complex problems, pattern recognition, prediction and decision-making. The AI-based geospatial analytics has offered a large number of business opportunities.

The AI, particularly, image analysis and information extraction, will be in great demand in next 10 years or so. It uses large volume of spatial data, collected from various IoT-based sensors, and ML to extract knowledge through automation process to get analysis in real-time. The ML is an essential component to deal with the growing data, and automation is needed to implement the AI-based solutions. The use of data-intensive ML methods has shown more evidences for decision-making for many applications, such as health care, utilities, manufacturing, insurance, finance and public services (Garg et al., 2022). Thus, AI and ML are expected to speed up the productivity and decision-making processes.

Many international companies, such as, Google, Facebook and Microsoft, are using AI in a big way, and spending funds for its further applications and growth. The most popular fields where AI is being used include reasoning, knowledge, representation, perception, natural language processing, robotics and ML. In immediate past, several developments in the ML have taken place which led to creation of new algorithms, also known as deep learning (DL). The DL will train the machine itself to do the tasks accurately and efficiently. The ML is an assistive technology that would enhance the speed of manual tasks with the automation. Increasing availability of various types of data and high-performance computing are not only used to train the ML algorithms faster, but also to make the predictions faster. The properly trained algorithms can provide scalability, speed and increased accuracy, and thus reduce the requirement of manpower workforce, as machines can search the patterns faster from large datasets with more variables than the humans. It is expected that government agencies and commercial businesses in near future will adopt automation and reduce the workforce. Therefore, the advances in AI can offer low-cost cloud computing, low-cost sensor technology and increased use of geospatial data/information.

In future, the investments in AI are likely to be on automated vehicles, face recognition and health. The AI- and ML-based applications and modeling will provide "knowledge-on-demand" that is increasingly expected by the society for faster decision-making. The technological advances would allow companies to offer solutions to individual customer needs (Garg et al., 2022). However, there are many issues and challenges remain when AI is applied. The AI is still at a developmental stage, and the predication made by the ML algorithms remains a fuzzy area. There are challenges about the availability of labelled training datasets to be used in algorithms with greater confidence. The geospatial community still has to gain confidence from the results derived from the ML; the reasons could be complexity of the algorithms used and the data integrity.

4.3.4   COMPUTER VISION

Computer vision deals with the automatic extraction, analysis, interpretation and representation of graphics, images or videos. The algorithm can be used to draw the inferences, make predictions and even generate new images based on input images and videos. With social media platforms and digital and mobile cameras, publicly available images are found in large number which is beneficial to train the computer vision algorithms. The algorithms, such as ML, DL, CNN (convolution neural network), can significantly reduce the memory and computational time for such tasks. With the availability of distributed architectures (e.g., Spark) and cost-effective cloud computing resources, such algorithms provide faster results.

4.3.5   ROBOTICS

Robotics involve designing, constructing, operating and applying robots to solve human problems. A robot can be used to move material, parts, tools or perform a variety of tasks. Robots are being deployed in large number manufacturing industry and service sectors. The AI can be used to its full capabilities in real-world through robots (Sharma and Garg, 2021). The AI and robots are being used to replace or support humans in performing the routine tasks. For example, autonomous vehicle is considered as one form of robot. In future, robots will play important roles everywhere, including homes, offices and urban areas.

4.3.6   BLOCKCHAINS

Blockchains or distributed ledger technologies are used to improve the transaction efficiency and traceability (Garg, 2020). These technologies are currently being used in cryptocurrencies, but are expected to be used in various application areas as they maintain a high level of transparency, reliability and safety in sharing the transaction data *via* internet. Blockchain technology is expected to bring radical change in the new form of credit.

4.3.7   DRONE/UAV

Developments in drone/UAV technology have made significant contributions to collect spatial data in the form of images and point cloud. The advantages of using drone/UAV include high resolution mapping of geographic areas quickly, easy monitoring of the area, collecting the data for dangerous & difficult terrain and saving in both money & time. Drone/UAV technology has been used for large scale mapping the resources, buildings, agriculture lands, disaster affected areas, forest fire, etc. (Garg, 2019). It can carry RGB cameras, multispectral sensor, thermal sensor, hyperspectral senor and LiDAR sensors for various purposes. Drones can also be used to monitor an area or surveillance purpose. A large number of companies are using UAV/drones for making delivery of goods and essential items or life-saving drugs. These characteristics of drones have opened avenues for various applications useful to a common person. For more details of drone/UAV technology, readers can refer to Garg (2019).

4.4   CONCLUSION

Society 5.0 will address the challenges and needs of the society to provide solution to them, using digital data and technologies. Society 5.0 proposed by Japan is to develop a new societal phase where digital technologies will bring a sea change. Digital data and technologies will help create a society where people can lead a better life. On the other hand, technologies may also have negative effects, such as lowering the job employment and growing disparity of wealth and information. It is therefore important to take proper care to create a balanced society. The merging of digital transformation with the creativity may lead to problem solving and value creation for a brighter future of people. It is expected that the use of spatial data along with AI, ML and predictive analytics will be common in future.

The applications of ML using geospatial data mainly include object extraction, Digital Twins, autonomous mobility, sustainable smart city, energy management, etc. In addition, the digital systems, such as smart city, e-commerce and e-health initiatives, have shown a steep progress, helping to evolve a new society (Garg et al., 2022). The technology and digital transformation continue to evolve more applications using IoT, AI, robotics and blockchains and bring positive changes in society.

Many countries are already using these digital technologies to create innovations and expand businesses. Conventional industry is shifting from "product–driven" to "service–driven," or from "mass production-driven" to "custom-made-driven". For example, vehicles have become "connected" or "autonomous driving", whereas health care data is being collected by wearable devices for better management of health. Society 5.0 can be a boon for India, as it can address various problems in various ways. Agriculture problem can be solved with mixed agriculture, mechanisation and automation. Senior citizens can access services at affordable rates using technology and innovations. Blockchain technology can ensure good governance and maximum governance. Illiteracy can be eradicated using digitisation and cloud computing. Digital technologies, such as Big data, robotics and AI can solve several problems of a modern society, such as the traffic, health care, productivity in industry and service sector.

REFERENCES

Garg, P. K., (2019), *Introduction to Unmanned Aerial Vehicles*, New Age International Pvt Ltd, Delhi.

Garg, P. K., (2020), *Digital Land Surveying and Mapping*, New Age International Pvt Ltd, Delhi.

Garg, P. K., Tripathi, Nitin, Kappas, Martin, and Gaur, Loveleen (Eds), (2022), *Geospatial Data Science in Healthcare for Society 5.0*, Springer Nature, Singapore.

Hayashi, H., Sasajima, H., Takayanagi, Y., and Kanamaru, H., (2017), International standardization for smarter society in the field of measurement, control and automation. *Proceedings of the 56th Annual Conference of the Society of Instrument and Control Engineers of Japan (SICE)*, Institute of Electrical and Electronics Engineers (IEEE), Kanazawa, Japan, https://doi.org/10.23919/sice.2017.8105723.

Keidanren, (2017), *Revitalizing Japan by Realizing Society 5.0: Action Plan for Creating the Society of the Future ~Overview*, February 14, 2017, Japan Business Federation (Keidanren), Japan.

Market Analysis Report, (2019), Telecom services market size, share & trends analysis report by service type (Mobile data services, machine-to-machine services), by transmission (Wireline, wireless), by end-use, by region, and segment forecasts, 2021–2028, Market Analysis Report.

Narvaez Rojas, C., Alomia Peñafiel, G. A., Loaiza Buitrago, D. F., and Tavera Romero, C.A., (2021), Society 5.0: A Japanese concept for a superintelligent society. *Sustainability*, 13, 6567, https://doi.org/10.3390/su13126567.

Scott, Greg and Rajabifard, Abbas, (2017), Sustainable development and geospatial information: A strategic framework for integrating a global policy agenda into national geospatial capabilities, *Geo-Spatial Information Science*, 20(2), 59–76. https://doi.org/10.1080/10095020.2017.1325594.

Sharma, Lavanya and Garg, P.K. (Eds), (2021), *Artificial Intelligence: Technologies, Applications, and Challenges*, Taylor & Francis (CRC Press), London.

Sułkowski, Ł., Kolasinska-Morawska, K., Seliga, R., and Morawski, P., (2021), Smart learning technologization in the economy 5.0-the Polish perspective. *Applied Sciences*, 11, 5261. https://doi.org/10.3390/app11115261.

UN-GGIM, (2015), *Future Trends in Geospatial Information Management: The Five to Ten Year Vision*, United Nations Committee of Experts on Global Geospatial Information Management, Great Britain.

UN-GGIM, (2021), Geospatial industry advancing sustainable development goals, Report 2021, Prepared by UN-GGIM, Great Britain and Geospatial World.

Zengin, Yunus, Naktiyok, Serkan, Kaygin, Erdogan, Kavak, Onur and Topeuoglu, Ethem, (2013), An investigation upon industry 4.0 and society 5.0 within the context of sustainable development goals, *Sustainability*, 13, 2682. https://doi.org/10.3390/su13052682.

5 The Wondrous Challenges of the Exotic Bio-Inspired Worlds of Nanomachines and Artificial Intelligence

V. Jokanović

Institute of Nuclear Science "Vinča"

ALBOS doo

CONTENTS

DOI: 10.1201/9781003324720-7

5.1 INTRODUCTION

The world of nanomachines consists, above all, of molecular nanosystems or nanosystems of some other types, which are capable of performing various sophisticated and extremely useful tasks, on nanoscale dimensions, which are of the order of 0.01–0.1 μm. Thanks to modern advances in nanosciences and nanoengineering, these exotic nanomachines are now being designed and manufactured with unprecedented sophistication and complexity, in the form of molecular self-assemblers, self-propelled nanocarriers, and "in vivo" molecular nanocomputers, using the laws of quantum mechanics, which is why they usually show an extremely wide range of very unusual physical and chemical properties [1–3].

Since such machines require very sophisticated nanomechanics, they have become an extremely attractive field of research in various branches of technology and medicine, especially in the field of nanomedicine. Thanks to that, in the last few years, machines capable of performing very specific tasks have been developed, on ever smaller scales of length. This trend is further fueled by research by Jean-Pierre Sovage, Fraser Stoddart and Bernard Lucas Fering, who won the Nobel Prize in Chemistry in 2016, as pioneers in the development of molecular machines capable of functioning as rotors, carriers, and pumps [4–6].

This gave tremendous impetus to the development of this area, so that even larger and more complex nanomachines were soon constructed, including DNA nanorobots that could serve as switches, rotors, hinges, or carriers with a logical input. Today, it is obvious that with each new step in the development of such machines, their already huge possibilities in performing the most incredible tasks on a molecular length scale are increasing [2,3,7].

This brief insight, given in this article, is based primarily on the very inspiring parts of the book: *Nanomedicine, the Greatest Challenge of the 21st Century*, the author of this text, published by Data Status, 2012, (a book that is the same was declared the book of challenges of the year by the Student Cultural Center, as the only book in the field of science, and the only book published in Serbian because all other books were books by foreign authors translated into Serbian). Like the book itself, this short review of the world of nanomachines is primarily aimed not only at bringing this topic much closer to the readers of the Galaxy but also at (what is even more important) inspiring some of them, to be concrete actors in creating such a fascinating future, which is obviously already within the reach of those in their best years [2].

5.2 SIGNIFICANCE OF NANOTECHNOLOGIES IN NANOMEDICINE

"There is a growing sense of admiration from the scientific and technical community for entering a golden new era," said Richard E.Smalley, founder of the Center for Nanoscale Science and Technology at Rice University in Texas, in his inauguration speech. The Nobel Prize in Chemistry in 1996, in order to continue in his further speech, "Throughout the last century, we have learned how biological nanomachines work, down to an incredible level in detail, and the benefits of that knowledge are already beginning to be felt in medicine." In the coming decades, we will learn how to modify and adapt these machines to extend the quality and length of life. Twenty years from now, nanotechnology will provide specially engineered drugs that are nanoscale ("cancer-targeting missiles"), using molecular technology that specifically targets mutant cancer cells in the human body, leaving everything else "blissfully lonely." To do all this, drug molecules will be large enough to possess thousands of atoms, within which we will be able to encode information, where it should go and what it should do. To humans in the future, they will be examples of the excellence of realized nanotechnologies [2,8].

Following this testimony, the President of the United States, in his speech from January 2000, announced that 475 million dollars would be invested in the development of nanotechnologies and effectively doubled the fund for research in the field of nanotechnologies for the fiscal year 2001. Annual investments in nanotechnology in 2004 already amounted to US $ 849 million and about EUR 1 billion from the European Union budget. In the private sector, since then, investments in nanomedicine have been growing at a rate of 28% above the level for each previous year. From 2003 to 2006, the amount had already reached 3 billion dollars. In medical research on nanotechnologies, this increase exceeds as much as 35% [9–11].

It is predicted that first, in a relatively short time, over the next 5 years, nanomedicine will be able to solve many significant medical problems using nanoscale structured materials and simple nanodevices that are already being made or will be made in the very near future. This includes the interactions of nanostructured materials with biological systems. Second, in the next 5–10 years, biotechnology will achieve incredible successes in molecular medicine and biorobotics (microbiological robots or engineered organisms), some of which are already on the list of realized products. Third, after a long time, perhaps 10–20 years from today, the earliest molecular machines and nanorobots will be able to connect different medical knowledge, giving physicists a very powerful tool to fight human diseases and old age [12].

5.2.1 Nanocomputers

Truly efficient medical nanorobots require computers that allow clear display and control of their work. Molecular computing has become one of the most important areas of research in the field of nanotechnology. In 2000, thanks to collaboration between the University of California, Los Angeles and Hewllet-Packard, the first laboratory demonstration of complete reversible molecular switches at room temperature, which can be used in nanoscale memory, using mechanically interconnected rings of molecules, the so-called. catenane (catenane). In recent times, the progress of molecular electronics based on nanotubes and nanowires has been particularly intense.

At least two independent companies: the Molecular Electronics Corporation in Texas and the California Molecular Electronics Corporation in California already have the explicit goal of making, in the next few years, the first commercial molecular electronic device to possess memory and other nanocomputer components for computing, using self-organization techniques. There is also the possibility of making a low-speed digital nanocomputer based on biology [13,14].

5.2.2 Self-Organization and Directed Organization of Components

There is a wide range of different molecular systems that can self-organize. Perhaps the best-known self-assembled molecular systems include those that form ordered macromolecular structures by coordinating their molecules on the surface, called self-assembled monolayers (SAMs), self-assembled thin films or Langmir Blagdet films, self-assembled lipid micelles and droplets, and self-assembled. In many such systems, the vertical axis is set at 0.1 nm by controlling the structure of the molecules that make up the monolayer, although dimensional control (in-plane dimensional control) of less than 100 nm is very difficult. It is known that self-organized molecular systems can self-replicate if their components are complex enough [2,3].

Examples offered by biology are bacteriophages and viruses that infect and take over the replication mechanisms of bacterial cells to synthesize their own molecular components such as nucleic acids and proteins [15]. The self-organization of the components of viral proteins occurs spontaneously, and it produces hundreds of viral progeny in the host cell. Although viruses, while forming, are formed through the self-organization of spontaneously distributed, randomly directed moving components of protein molecules, viral molecular components do not bind randomly (during the process of their assembly), but form their final sequences in an orderly manner.

Biologists believe that conformational incorporation into protein molecules facilitates the random assembly of bacteriophages. In a protein molecule with several binding sites, conformational inclusion causes the formation of a bond at one site to alter the conformation of another binding site. As a result, the conformational change that occurs in one assembly step predetermines the essential substrate for assembly in the next step. Several attempts have been made to achieve self-organization of small mechanical parts to avoid direct "catching" of parts. Saitou gives an example of "sequential random picking of beans" in which the process of sequentially comparing random pairs (parts) extracted from a piece of beans that initially had a random assortment of parts can produce an overlap (similar to similar) of the desired pair of parts [16].

Griffith introduced a simple "mechanical enzyme" analogous to the two-bit mechanical state of a machine that programmatically self-assembles as it floats on the interface between water and poly-fluorodecalin. The mechanical automaton has a mechanical curve that acts as a "switch" of the automaton, which produces mechanical allosteric enzymes [17]. The problem in the design of self-assembling components is the necessity to avoid unwanted metastable states by design and to create the desired geometry by the assembly process, which corresponds to the lowest energy of the system conformation. In such assemblages, for example, the right edges of the components are avoided to minimize the energy of local collisions. The programming of the engineered sequences of such conformational switches allows the self-assembly of very complicated mechanical structures.

Saitou presented a model of a self-organizing system in which instructions for self-organization are inscribed as conformational switches. The model of automated self-organization inspired Penrose on self-replication blocks. Classes of self-organized automata are defined based on the assembly of subsequences in which the components are self-organized [18]. For each class of subassembled sequences, the minimum number of conformations necessary to encode the subassembly of sequences in the class is provided. Finally, it has been shown that the three conformations of each component are sufficient to encode any subassembly sequence of a one-dimensional assembly of different components, of arbitrary length [19].

5.2.3 DNA TARGETED ASSEMBLY

Smith and Krummenacker investigated the method of targeted DNA assembly. They devised a possible way of assembling and covalently binding proteins and their parts into specific geometric orientations and arrangements determined by protein-bound hybridization of the protein. This process is known as DNA-guided Assembly of Proteins (DGAP). In this method, multiple DNA sequences bind to a specific position on the surface of each protein, while complementary sequences link together into specifically designed combinations and configurations, directing protein building blocks (which include biomolecular motors, structural protein fibers, antibodies, enzymes, or other existing functional proteins), to be stabilized by covalent interprotein bonds. These techniques can also be applied to non-protein components (which can be functionalized at a number of sites), with site-specific DNA sequences. For such types of functionalization, proteins are the most acceptable building blocks due to their size, surface chemistry, wide variety of functions and mechanical properties, which are of great importance for the process of final assembly by DNA [2,20]

DNA-directed assembly involves the nanoassembly of macromolecules (nucleoproteins), enzymes on a specific region on the surface of a target protein, which lie on nanowires of silver, gold, or some other type of nanowire. DNA is used as a molecular scaffold or a possible model for circuit construction, as a decorative DNA with fullerenes and dendrimers, DNA for assembly with nanometer gold, magnetic and other larger clusters into spontaneous lattices or magnetic chains, DNA for aggregation on silicon components, DNA directed in the two-dimensional realm, etc. Early mechanical nanorobots were made in part from DNA [2,20].

The idea to use DNA in the construction of nanoscale objects came from N. Seeman [21,22]. He showed that DNA as a building material has numerous advantages. First, it is a relatively rigid polymer. Its intermolecular interactions with other helices can be predicted and programmed as base-pairs of complementary nucleotides, as fundamental building blocks of genetic material. DNA tends to self-organize. An arbitrary sequence is often made using conventional biotechnological techniques that easily manipulate DNA, and it is easily modified by a large number of proteins. In 1980, it was developed DNA that could be "zipped" into more and more complex shapes: first, small squares [21,22],

He then concluded that the construction of a DNA-based mechanical device for nanoscale robotic actuators was possible. The mechanism consists of two rigid, several nanometer-long "arms" of double DNA helix that can cause rotation between fixed positions by introducing a positively charged cobalt compound into a solution around the molecule, causing normal DNA to be converted into unusually zipped Z-DNA. The free ends of the "arms" move to the position 2–6 nm from the starting position during the full reversible structural conversion, similar to the opening and closing of the "door hinges." It is a very simple nanomachine but also very efficient because it rotates about four times faster than a typical molecular device. The version of the large device functions as an elbow, while the small devices function as finger joints [21,22].

Simen demonstrated the operation of a DNA-based rotary motor and explained its construction and the construction of two-dimensional arrays that can serve as a model for nanomechanical assembly. He is now experimenting with genetic engineers and computer chemists to "design and manufacture practical nanoscale devices" and "make great strides in demonstrating DNA-based nanodevices, including sequence-dependent devices" that provide the variety of structures needed for nanorobots [21,22].

Some other ideas and research are related to activating the system with DNA. One such example is the hybridization of a specific DNA sequence for binding to silicone microchannels. Alberti and Mergny synthesized a sequence-dependent DNA clip composed of a 21-base oligonucleotide. Shu (Shu) and Guo (Guo) synthesized a 30 nm long chimeric pRNA (DNA-packing) engine composed of 6 strands of RNA around a central DNA helix, in the presence of ATPase. When the engine is turned on, the RNA coil pushes the DNA axis causing it to rotate or some other type of movement producing a force of about 50–60 pN. Reif designed "the first autonomous DNA nanomechanical devices that make cycles of movement without external changes in the environment." These DNA so-called. "Walking DNA" can produce arbitrary two-way movements around a circular ssDNA helix using DNA slip and two restrictive enzymes that consume ATP as an energy source. His other device is the so-called "Rolling DNA" [23,24].

5.2.4 PROTEIN-DIRECTED ASSEMBLY

Some researchers used artificial enzymes to assemble nanoscale devices. According to them, artificial multifunctional proteins called "robosomes" have the following essential properties: (i) they are untwisted, suitable for molecular building blocks, but they should be carefully kept separate from each other to avoid non-specific reactions; (ii) using specific enzyme catalytic sites near bound building blocks, they activate molecules (possibly free radicals formed), (iii) they condition the assembly of blocks that brings them into relatively precise alignment, allowing chemical reactions or reactions of another type and (iv) thanks to the ability by unwinding the proteins they allow the release of the final product [25].

In protein wrapping, the enzyme can provide a force of 10–100 pico Newtons (pN) by winding one molecule through another, mechanically producing interconnected structures of rotaxane and catenate, by adding a hydrophobic ring structure to the molecular moiety, which allows rotaxane and catenate structures to be attracted to each other, in a polar solvent such as water) without using self-organization, but only positional assembly of very small (below 1 kDa) molecular nanoscale parts. There are several groups of enzymes involved in the production of complex covalent-bound molecules, such as vitamins, enzymes, cofactors, antibiotics, and toxins with a mass below 3 kDa. Molecules larger than these are used in the manipulation of tRNA synthetases, such as spliceosomes, ribosomes, proteosomes, and DNA replication complexes [26].

By designing synthetic enzymes consisting of synthetic amino acids, the process of taking ("grabbing") molecular parts in solution can begin, and then when the enzyme "gathers," the process of bridging and aligning it continues. Such an enzymatic process is known as "nanoparticle synthesis" or "protein-directed nanoparticle assembly." Of course, RNA-based ribosomes are usually better tuned for these reactions than proteins, so that the possible applications of enzymes to form the required covalent bonds with nanoparticles have virtually no limitations.

Self-assembled proteins show structural motifs such as particles, fibers, bands, and plates. Their functions include selective transport, structural scaffolding, mineral modeling, and propagation or protection against pathogens. Improper nanoscale organization and uncontrolled protein aggregation are the source of pathogens. Such types of assembly lead to a number of neurodegenerative diseases, such as Parkinson's and Alzheimer's disease. The assembly process itself combines "in situ" AFM and Monte Carlo simulations to find the optimal pathways by which a protein is transformed from a monomeric form into an expanded ordered or amorphous structure. Pathogenesis includes the aggregation of prion cell proteins and self-organization of amelogenin.

The principle of blocking protein-based molecular motors is well known in biology. The conformational cascades of specific genetic variants of prion yeast cells have already been used as self-assemblers in rings or spirals, wrapped around the neck of ruptured vesicles, and their squeezing and compression during endocytosis are well known. Smith and his co-workers used targeted methyltransferase addressing to fuse proteins to the DNA scaffold in the construction of the molecular camshaft. This is a typical example of a specific protein/nucleic acid biostructure. Baschand and Montemagno made a biomolecular engine from ATPase protein attached to a Si3N4 propeller arm with reversible on and off.

There are numerous examples of designs and other genetic molecular engines that have been synthesized by various researchers. The specificity of the protein–protein bond was also used for binding to silicone microcantilevers. The genetically engineered chaperone protein molecule was used as a model for the targeted assembly of gold (1.4, 5 or 10 nm) and CdSe semiconductor quantum dots (4.5 nm) in the nanoscale region. Immunoglobulin (Ig) or antibody molecules were used in such constructions first to recognize and bind to specific surfaces of crystalline nanoparticles and then as handles that allow parts to be hung in known positions, even in complex assemblages [27]. Kessler and his associates grew monoclonal antibodies (Mabs) specific for 1,4-dinitrobenzene crystals, which had a well-defined structure at the molecular level. These antibodies were so specific that they did not bind to the same molecules when conjugated to a protein carrier [27].

IgG antibodies isolated from rabbit serum were injected with crystalline monosodium urate monohydrate or magnesium urea octahydrate, bearing on their binding sites the imprint of the crystal surface structure, which is why they can serve as nucleation models for crystal formation "in vitro" with extremely low efficient cross-section of activity. similar molecular and structural characteristics of these two crystals. Binding of antibodies to mono sodium urea crystals has been known for decades and viruses have been engineered with the ability to specifically recognize the environment, for ZnS nanocrystals as quantum dots. Similar to antennas with ordered multiple epitopes, crystals express chemically and geometrically different surfaces so that different antibodies can be recognized by different crystal planes (probably including diamond crystal surfaces) [2,27,28].

In doing so, interactions similar to antibody interactions on repetitive epitopes present on protein surfaces occur. For example, a single Mab on 1,4-dinitrobenzene crystals shows a specific interaction with the molecular plane, aromatic, and polar (101) planes of a given crystal, but not with other planes of the same crystal. Mabs also have a pronounced reaction to cholesterol monohydrate crystals because it recognizes their stepped surface. On the one hand, the hydrogen base of hydrophobic cholesterol in the form of "steps" is emphasized, while on the other hand, hydroxyl residues and water molecules are emphasized [28]. Crystal-specific IgM idiotype antibodies were used for recognition in both cases. Consistent with the assumption that (as opposed to many antigens used) crystals cannot be processed by antigen-presenting cells, these antibodies must be induced through independent T-cell steps [2,28].

By binding semiconductors and calcite-binding proteins, it is known that the growth of different crystal planes of a suitable material can be potentiated, as a result of which it is possible to change the characteristic patterns of its crystal growth. Sulfur-free proteins, as "free" proteins when bound to gold, recognize and covalently bind preferentially to the Au (111) crystal surface. Au-binding proteins are used in multiple repeats of 14–30 sequences of protein residues, which bind to these surfaces) [29]. Soluble (derivatized) C60 and C70 fullerenes can induce antibody production, by interactions with IgG. It is also contemplated that highly hydrophobic pure fullerene may be recognized by antibodies with hydrophobic amino acids at their binding sites or interact with a donor-NH2 or -SH group. Computer simulations show that it is possible to selectively bind antibodies to nanotubes with a specific diameter and chirality [30].

5.2.5 MICROBIAL AND VIRAL DIRECTED ASSEMBLY

Artificial microbes are also the subject of research for their application in molecular constructions. It is known that the diversity of biological molecular machines can be expressed already in linear movements, movements related to opening and closing and translational functions, as well as in rotational movements and in movements in "up and down" threads. G. J. Sussman believes that when computer parts are reduced to the size of a single molecule, engineered microbes can direct the way a complex electronic circuit is laid and connected. According to him, "bacteria are similar to a small working" nanotechnology, because they are excellent for manipulating things in the chemical and ultramicroscopic world. They can be trained to become electricians or plumbers, hiding sugar and harnessing to build in advance desirable structures.

One type of bacterium (Pseudomonas stutzeri AG259) is known to make pure silver single crystals in specific geometric shapes, such as equilateral triangles and hexagons above 200 nm in size. Also, microorganisms can accumulate material and synthesize inorganic structures composed of bismuth, CdS, Au, magnetite, silica and silver [31,32]. For targeted microbial assembly of the given parts, Kondo (Kondo) used film grooves (hollow grooves obtained by chemical precipitation of cellulose strips below 1 nm based on Cu) and thus "trained" the bacteria Acetobacter xylinum to secrete beautiful strips of cellulose at a speed of preparation. μm / minute. The Kond group also tried to genetically modify the organism to secrete altered sugar molecules that are more resistant to natural degradation. Natural fibroblasts in human tissue construct complex three-dimensional networks of extracellular matrix collagen fibers (ECM) during wound healing, fibrillogenesis, and fibroplasia [31,32].

Although the ECM coil is positioned stochastically in natural fibroblasts, the cellular functionality and characteristics of the ECM network can be altered by chemotactic factors, contact guidance and orientation, hypoxia, and local mechanical stresses. Genetically engineered fibroblasts to be capable of cross-linking collagen fibers (by covalent bonding of parts) show the ability to withstand forces of about 100 pN when introduced into a three-dimensional collagen matrix. To establish digital control of their properties through microorganisms, genetic circuits need to function as switches or computer logic elements such as AND, NAND and NOR thresholds [2,3].

In 2000, Gardner added E. coli bacteria to a memory device using two inverters for which the output protein of each was the input protein of the second inventor, while Elowitz and Leibler made an oscillator with three inverters connected in a loop. In 2002, Weiss created a fifth-gene circuit based on E. coli that can detect chemical reactions in its environment and turn on a fluorescent protein when the chemical concentration is within pre-selected limits [33,34]. A synthetic laboratory at MTI is investigating "engineered genetic blinkers" that use light to show cell input and output faster than chemically guided signals. Sets of components have also been created that are designed to be used as logical functions within a cell. Members of this family are designed to be compatible,

compatible, variable within themselves, and independent so that logic circuits can be constructed with little knowledge or concern for the origin, construction, or biological activity of the components [35].

T. Gardner says that the goal is to produce a genetic "applet, " a small program that can be "downloaded" into a cell simply by initiating DNA within it, just as a Java applet is "dawnloaded" from the Internet [36]. Bacterial memory is shown on a 150-base message, encoded with artificial DNA that is stored within the genomes of multiplied E. coli and Deinococcus radiodurans bacteria and then accurately retrieved. Jacobson's team demonstrated remote control of electronic control through the hybridization behavior of DNA molecules, by inductive coupling of a radiofrequency magnetic field with gold nanocrystals covalently bound to DNA, showing the perspective of enzymatic remote control and "radio-controlled bacteria."

Bacteria can also be used as a physical system of components. Kim tried to install live bacteria in the MEMS (microelectromechanical system) to make a cellular motor for the pump and valves. The bacterium should be completely attached (glued) inside the bioMEMS device [36]. When their whip is attached to the surface, the bacterium moves in a circle and always in the same direction. One bacterium becomes a flagellar motor or pump, but when many bacteria rotate in the same direction, it becomes a transport belt. It is similar to the bacteria Serratia marcescens, inside small pearls that allow the microbe to rotate carrying the pearl with it. Inside the fine tubes, bacteria can increase the diffusion by two times. C. Montemagro used bacteria to make a mechanical motor based on cell power. In 2003, he lithographically produced a U-shaped structure 230 nm wide and attached it to heart muscle cells, similar to a small prosthesis. When found in glucose solution, muscle cells contracted following repeat cycles, causing the mechanical structure to move at a speed of 46 nm/min with a repeat cycle controlled by the elasticity constant of the MEMS structure [37].

Sequeira and Copik used bacteria as power generators (units of power) for microscale mechanical systems. The viral membrane also provides useful models for nanoscale assembly [38]. Belcher used the capsid virus membrane as a scaffold to target nanoparticles such as quantum dots in a process described as "biomimetic synthesis of nanobiological inorganic phases with new electronic and magnetic properties of targeted proteins and their synthetic analogs." In one of the experiments, genetically engineered M13 bacteriophages with specific recognition of ZnS nanocrystals were used in the assembly of ZnS film with nanoscale arrangement of domains of the order of 72 nm [39].

5.2.6 POSITIONAL ASSEMBLY AND MOLECULAR DESIGN

The more complex the machine structure, the more difficult it is to achieve spontaneous self-assembly of parts of the system. To create complex structures, more sense is needed for the design of a mechanism that can assemble a molecular structure by positional assembly (taking and placing parts in precisely defined places). A device that is capable of positional assembly must work like the hands of a robot that makes a car on a self-assembly line and inserts electronic components in precisely defined places. Using this way of assembling, the robot manipulator takes the parts, moves them to the working part, installs, and then repeats the procedure with various other parts until it assembles the final product.

One of the main manufacturers of components for positional assembly on the molecular scale is the company Zyvex, which deals with the positional assembly of structures with atomic precision [40]. They use factory-engineered tools capable of creating molecularly precise structures at the 3D level, in a cost-effective manner. As a first step toward that goal, in 1998 Zyvex demonstrated the ability to use three independent robotic arms an inch long, to manipulate fine carbon nanotubes in three dimensions under the control of a scanning microscope whose monitor shows the movement of objects smaller than 6 nm, at speeds close to video speed scanner. Zyvex has already demonstrated the ability to positionally assemble a large number of MEMS microscale parts. And besides, it is only a part of the path that needs to be traversed to assemble nanoscale parts with the same success using adequate machines. Therefore, although research in the field of nanoscale robots is going in the right direction, their continuity is needed for such research to give real results after a long enough time.

Microscale devices can be used to pick up and place nanoscale parts in the appropriate place. Agilent Laboratory has created an ultra-precise platform for micron displacements, capable of enabling linear two-dimensional motions in 1.5 nm increments, representing a width of about 9 bound C atoms. The core of a micrometer is a stepped actuator or line motor that does not rotate but moves right or left and back and forth. The platform can travel a total of 30 μm in each direction in 2.5 ms since each micrometer consists of 1,000 nm, so for 30 μm (which is the distance of the hair's hair width), 20,000 steps are required [41].

A similar nanoposition device has been made in a number of other places. P. Kim and C. Leiber created the first nanotwister for general use [42]. They used the ends of a pair of electrically controlled carbon nanotubes made from a bundle of multilayer carbon nanotubes. In order for the twister to work, voltage is applied to the electrodes, causing one arm of the nanotube to develop a positive electrostatic charge and the other a negative one. The attractive force can increase or decrease with voltage variation: 8.5 V is the voltage at which the arm closes completely, while lower voltages give different degrees of grip (different angles between the arms). Using the tool, clusters of polystyrene spheres of size 500 nm or clusters of similar size of cell substructure were successfully captured. The device was able to move a 20 nm wide semiconductor wire from a bundle of twisted wire, using twister arms that were about 50 nm wide and 4 μm long.

Current expectations are that it will be possible to produce nanotwisters based on single-layer nanotubes that will be able to capture individual macromolecules. Kim-Lieber's nanotwister is very suitable for taking and releasing objects. It is to be expected that by the technique of creating large electric fields on the tips (dowels) of the twister, at such high voltages, the twister will be able to change the properties of the objects being manipulated. In this way, a once-constructed twister will be able to manipulate a large number of nanoobjects in a long and arduous process [43]. To improve the operation of the twister, P. Boggild used a standard micromachine process to carve out a small weak silicon cantilever microswitch to open and close electrically [43].

Hla and Reder have shown current advances in the manipulation and synthesis of individual molecules using scanning tunneling microscopy (STM). The main goal of molecular nanotechnology is the development of production technologies, capable (in a not-so-expensive process) of enabling precise distribution of atoms down to molecular details, including complex distributions (arrangements) involving millions or billions of atoms per unit of product, which is a hypothetical medical nanorobot. Such technology should be precise, flexible and inexpensive. Two control mechanisms have been proposed to achieve this goal on a molecular scale: programmable positional assembly involving the production of diamond structures using molecular raw materials and the massive parallelism of all production and assembly processes [44].

5.2.7 NANOPOROUS DEVICES

Perhaps the simplest medical nanodevice is a surface perforated with cavities or nanopores. It may be considered as one of the first nanomedical devices. During their collaboration, Desai and Ferrari used classical machining to obtain thin chambers containing cells inside a silicone carrier single crystal. The surface of the chambers with a polycrystalline silicone filter membrane, which was micro-machined, was a high-density uniform nanoporous membrane, with nanopores smaller than 20 nm in diameter [2,3].

These pores were large enough to allow small molecules of oxygen, sugar, and insulin to pass through them but also small enough to stop the passage of larger molecules of the immune system, such as immune-globulins and graft coils of viral particles. It has been experimentally shown that safely trapped between artificial barriers, immune-isolates of encapsulated rat pancreatic cells can receive nutrients and remain healthy for weeks, successfully secreting insulin through the pores, while the immune system remains "blissfully unaware" of foreign cells that would normally be attacked and rejected. Microcapsules containing replaced Langerhans cells (similar to isolated Langerhans islets of pigs) may be implanted under the skin of some diabetics. This can temporarily restore the body's delicate glucose control as a feedback loop, without the need for strong immune-suppressants that expose the patient to the risks of infection [45].

The body's supply of encapsulated new cells, in methodological terms, can be used as one way to supply the body with various enzymes or deficient hormones whose deficiency in the body causes disease, including even encapsulation of neurons, which can thus be implanted in the brain and then electrically stimulated to release neurotransmitters, which is probably the future treatment of Alzheimer's and Parkinson's disease. With the support of the biomedical company MEDD, Desai and his associates actively worked on immunoisolation and drug delivery, as well as on cell encap-sulation technologies and similar techniques. The flow of material through the nanopores obviously needs to be extremely well regulated [46,47].

The first artificial molecular sieve (with a voltage threshold) was made by C.R. Martin and his associates in 1995. Martin membranes contained cylindrical gold nanotubes with an inner diameter of 1.6 nm. When the tubes were positively charged, the positive ions were turned off and only the negative ions were transported across the membrane. When the membrane was at a negative voltage, only positive ions passed through it. Future similar nanodevices can combine the voltage threshold with the shape, size, and limitations associated with charging to achieve precise control of transport ions with significant molecular specificity. Martin's current efforts are focused on immobilization-biochemical molecular recognition agents such as enzymes, antibodies, other proteins and DNA within nanotubes as active biological nanosensors, to achieve drug separation and allow selective biocatalysis [48,49].

One highly sensitive ion channel switch (sensor) biosensor was developed by an Australian group of researchers. Such sensors, commercialized by Ambri Biosensor, can detect a change in chemical concentration equivalent to one sugar cube immersed in Sydney Harbor, which is roughly one part in a billion (10–18). Others have investigated nanoporous ion pumps and nanopores with a voltage threshold immersed in artificial membranes, dealing with studies of the molecular dynamic theory of viscosity and diffusion, etc. D. Brenton and his team conducted a series of experiments using an electric field to move various RNA and DNA polymers through the central nanopores of the α-hemolysin protein channel embedded in a lipid bilayer similar to the outer membrane of living cells. In early 1996, researchers showed that individual nucleotides making polynucleotides must pass through 2.6 nm wide pores, with a change in ion current being a measure of their length. In 1998, Brenton showed that nanopores can rapidly separate pyrimidine and purine segments (two types of nucleotide bases) along a single RNA molecule [50,51], and in 2000 some scientists suc-ceeded in perfecting a method of highly selective differentiation between DNA strands of similar lengths and composition, to levels of only one nucleotide sequence.

Current research is focused on the production of pores of specific diameters and repeatable geom-etry with high precision, as well as understanding the separation of ungrounded double-stranded DNA within the nanopore into single-stranded DNA separated through the pore, recognizing folded DNA molecules passing through the pores. Such experiments were performed at nanopores of 3–10 nm on the Si3N4 system, where the effect of adding electrically conductive electrodes to improve longitudinal resolution in nanopores "up to the level of one DNA base" was specifically investigated. Given that nanopores can rapidly separate and characterize DNA polymers with a small number of copies, it is obvious that future finer tuning of experiments will probably make it possible to provide very low-cost methods for rapid genomic sequencing [52,53].

5.2.8 BINDING SITES AND MOLECULAR IMPRINTING

Another early goal of nanomedicine is to investigate the answer to the question of how biological molecular receptors work, in order to solve the problem of designing optimal artificial binding sites according to the principle of "study and make" in order to give a specific medical result.

Molecular imprinting is a technique in which a cocktail of functional monomers interacts reversibly with a target molecule using noncovalent forces. The complex is then crosslinked and polymerized in a casting procedure, leaving behind a polymer with recognition sites that is complementary to the target molecule in both form and functionality. Each such site consists of an induced molecular "memory" capable of selectively binding to selected target sites.

In one of the experiments performed on amino acid derivatives as targets, specific artificial binding sites corresponding to a volume of (3.8 nm) 3 were created using the appropriate block polymer. Chiral separations, enzyme transient activity, and high receptor affinity of such systems have been shown in some studies [54,55]. B.D. Ratner investigated polymer surfaces containing artificial receptor regions, which were obtained using radiofrequency smoldering discharge imprints on nanometer-sized polysaccharide films in a form suitable for binding protein molecules such as albumin (the most common blood protein), fibrinogen (blood clotting protein), lysosomes and ribonucleases (two important enzymes) and immunoglobulin (antibody protein). Each protein type is glued to a pit with the shape of that protein.

Thus engineered surfaces can be used for fast biochemical separation and tests and as recognition elements in biosensors and chemosensors because such surfaces are faithful to the imprint, which is located only in specific places of the surface where the shape is imprinted [54,55]. Molecularly "imprinted" polymers have limitations, such as incomplete removal of the model material, broad affinity for "guests, "selectivity, and slow mass transfer. On the other hand, imprinting within the dendrimer may allow quantitative removal of the model, a high degree of homogeneity of the binding site, solubility in common organic solvents, and availability for inclusion of other functional groups. Such polymers can be used in clinical applications such as controlled drug release, drug monitoring devices, drug monitoring devices, biological and receptors that mimic the involved antibodies (plast-bodies) or bio-mimic enzymes (plastisim) [56].

5.2.9 QUANTUM DOTS AND NANOCRYSTALS

Fluorescent markers are widely used in medicine and biology. They are used in all types of biological tests, from the human immunodeficiency virus (HIV) test to experiments that "picture" the internal function of cells, using different dyes for different molecules, which are excited by appropriate lasers that cause their fluorescence. When organic dye molecules are applied, different dyes tend to spill together and fade quickly after application. Such disadvantages are avoided when using nanocrystals and quantum dots [2,57].

Quantum dots are very fine particles of mostly semiconductor materials, only a few nanometers in diameter, which corresponds to the dimensions of protein molecules or shorter DNA sequences. They have an unlimited palette of strictly defined colors, which result from changes in particle size and composition. Particles can excite fluorescence with white light or bind to biomolecules by acting as long-lived sensors, adapted to identify specific compounds, that give signals that are a thousand times stronger (brighter) than conventional dyes used in biological tests, and that can show the development of biological events through the simultaneous labeling of each biological component (various proteins and DNA sequences) with nanoparticles of a specific color [2,57].

Quantum Dot Corporation, a manufacturer of quantum particles, suggests that the kind of flexibility inherent in the application of quantum dots can offer an inexpensive way to check blood samples for the presence of a number of different viruses simultaneously [57]. It can give physicists a quick diagnostic tool to detect the presence of special sets of proteins that strongly indicate that a person has had a heart attack or to detect cancer as a marker of cellular cancer [58].

One of the research challenges is the ability to simultaneously label multiple biomolecules on the surface and inside the cell that allow scientists to observe complex cellular changes and disease-related events, providing valuable clues for the development of future pharmaceuticals and therapeutics. Quantum particles are useful for studying genes, proteins and drug targeting even within a single cell, as well as human and animal tissue samples. This led to a revolution in biological detection according to T. Kanamura. Quantitative dots have been invested in this project since 2003, with $ 100 million each year [59]. The subject of this project is the research of quantum dots for application in chemical sensors and for the detection of cancer cells, gene expression studies, gene mapping and DNA micro test analysis,

Researchers from Northwestern University and Argonne National Laboratory have created a hybrid "nanodevice" composed of nanocrystals of 4.5 nm biocompatible semiconductor TiO_2 to which a segment of DNA oligonucleotide is covalently bound. Experiments have shown that these nanoparticles retain not only the intrinsic photocatalytic capacity of TiO_2 and the bioactivity of DNA oligonucleotides, but more importantly, they also possess unique irradiation (light) properties. Excited nucleic acids of endonucleases are separated when exposed to light or X-rays. For example, in some studies, a strand of DNA, which matches a defective gene inside a cell, is bound to a semi-conductor scaffold (nanoparticle) and then introduced into the cell nucleus, where it binds to a defective complementary DNA helix. It has been shown that when such a structure is exposed to light or X-rays, then a defective gene is "cut off" on a given nanoparticle [59].

The popular name for this method is "Swiss Army knife" because, unlike today's drugs, this method can inject ten types of good genes into one target in an extremely specific and extremely reliable way [60]. Molecules other than nucleotides can be attached to a TiO_2 scaffold such as navigation peptides or proteins, or a viral vector, which can help a nanoparticle to invade a cell nucleus. It is assumed that simple nanocrystalline nanodevices will 1 day be used as targets for defective genes that play an important role in the treatment of cancer, neurological diseases, etc. [60].

5.2.10   FULLERENES AND NANOTUBES

Soluble fullerene derivatives such as C60 (a soccer ball shape) containing 60 carbon atoms per molecule have exceptional applicability as pharmaceutical agents. These derivatives (many of them already in clinical use) have good biocompatibility and low toxicity at relatively high doses of C60 as a therapeutic [61–63]. Fullerene compounds can also serve as antiviral agents (most often against HIV), as antibacterial agents (Escherichia coli, Streptococcus, Mycobacterium tuberculosis), for photodynamic antitumor and anticancer therapy, as antioxidants and antiapoptotic agents may be included in the treatment of lateral agents. (ALS or Lou Geiring's disease) and Parkinson's disease as well as in a number of other medical applications.

C. Sixty is a leading company for these types of materials and their medical applications. Research on nanopills (for drug delivery), which consists of two close single-layer carbon nanotubes, placed in relation to each other as "mouth to mouth," forming a capsule of the drug container, is also relevant in this company. Both types of carbon nanotubes, single-layer and multilayer, have also been investigated as biosensors, for the detection of glucose, ethanol, H_2O_2 and selected proteins such as immunoglobulins, as well as electrochemically hybridized DNA biosensors. NASA and the National Cancer Institute have developed a biosensor catheter that detects specific oligonucleotide sequences that serve as molecular "signatures" of cancer cells, with preliminary "in vitro" testing used for tissue samples of patients with chronic myeloid and acute promyelocytic leukemia [61–63].

5.2.11   NANOWRAPPERS AND MAGNETIC NANOPROBES

Researchers N. Halas and J. West have developed a platform for nanoscale drug delivery using the nanomail method on a given core material. Unlike fullerenes, slightly larger dimensions are nanowheels that make up dielectric-metal nanospheres with a silicon core and a gold sheath, whose optical resonance is a function of the relative size of the constituent layers.

Nano-wrappers are components of a nanocomposite consisting of a drug and a polymer that is aligned with the tumor target, as part of a complete system along with a composite core, which is injected into the body. Nano-wrappers circulate inside the body until they completely accumulate near the tumor cells. When illuminated with an infrared laser, nanowires (each thinner than a polio virus) selectively absorb infrared frequencies, melt the polymer, and release its drug, filling a specific site of disease. Nano-wrappers show a number of advantages over traditional cancer treatment, such as its earlier detection, much more detailed image, rapid non-invasive "imaging" and integrated detection and treatment. Techniques based on the use of nanowires can also be useful in the treatment of diabetes. In such use, instead of injecting insulin, the patient uses an infrared laser-sized ballpoint pen to heat the skin, where the polymer in the form of a nano-wheel is injected. The heat from the nano-wrap makes the polymer release the insulin pulse [64,65]. Unlike an injection that is given several times a day, the nano-wrapper-polymer system stays in the body for months.

In 2002, nano-wrap technology for commercial applications was patented at Rice University. Such a method would be used to treat cancers that are so small that they are not suitable for surgical experiments, and for insulin treatment. In mid-2003, Rice researchers announced the development of whole blood spot immunoassays using a gold nano-wrap conjugate for the antibody-nanoparticle system. By varying the thickness of the metal sheath, the Halas group showed that it is possible to precisely adjust the color of the light to match the nano-wheel, thus optimizing the wavelength for the immunotest of the blood as a whole. Successful detection of extremely low concentrations (sub-nanogram per milliliter of immunoglobulin) was achieved in salt, serum and complete blood in 10–30 minutes [53–67].

There are numerous research groups in the world that research the biological application of gold. An alternative approach to the application of gold opens up research on bound iron nanoparticles and monoclonal antibodies in nanobiosondes about 40 nm in size [67]. Chemically inert probes are injected and circulated in the body, while antibodies selectively bind to tumor cell membranes. Once the tumor is covered with bioprobes after a few hours, a magnetic field generated by a portable alternating magnetic field machine (similar to a miniaturized magnetic resonance imaging machine that heats iron particles to more than 76 0 by killing tumor cells in seconds). Once the cells are destroyed, the body expels them and removes cell debris and nanoparticles [67].

Unlike chemotherapy, which Samuel Straface, CEO of Triton BioSystems, describes as napalm that kills in large swaths, nanobiosons function much more closely like a "carefully placed explosive detonated with a remote igniter." Chemotherapy is a nasty thing. In this method, "there is no collateral damage" [68]. Mirkin's (Chad A. Mirkin) group at Northwestern University used antibody-coated magnetic nanoparticles as antibody-bound nanoparticles (13 nm probes) with similar coatings including uniquely hybridized "bar code" DNA sequences as an ultrasensitive method for detecting protein analytes (such a "bar code" for prostate is a specific antigen (PSA)) [69].

5.2.12 TARGETING NANOPARTICLES AND SMART DRUGS

Targeted drugs for specific organs or tissues, such as a cancerous tumor, allow the specific activity of the drug to be optimally regulated at the site for which it is intended antibodies [70]. Toxin proteins are normally produced by infectious bacteria. Proteins bind to the surface of host cells, penetrate inside those cells and kill them. The toxin molecule is also capable of killing cells. Antibodies are proteins produced by the immune system with the function of recognizing and binding specific foreign materials. Immunotoxin molecules are made by fusing a portion of a toxin-encoded gene with an antibody-encoded gene that recognizes the surface specificities of cancer cells.

This creates a new gene that can be used to express a new synthetic protein molecule. This new molecule binds only to cancer cells (via the antibody protein module), then penetrates and kills them (via the toxin molecule module).

The first experiments on mice showed that such engineered proteins successfully eliminated some tumors. In early 2000, the National Cancer Institute in the United States confirmed that an immunotoxin made from truncated forms of Pseudomonas exotoxin was cytotoxic to malignant B cells in patients with hair cell leukemia [71]. Another set of clinical experiments at the University of Cologne showed that ricin-based immunotoxins have moderate efficacy against Hodgkin's lymphoma in some patients [72]. Multi-segment gold/nickel nanorods were investigated, as tissue-targeted carriers for gene delivery to cells that can simultaneously bind compact DNA plasmids and target ligands into a spatially defined form and allow precise control of the composition, size and multifunctionality of the gene delivery system.

The nanowires were electrodeposited into cylindrical pores with a diameter of 100 nm on an aluminum membrane, connecting 100 nm long segments of gold and 100 nm long segments of nickel. When the aluminum model is etched, the nanowires are functionalized by attaching a transferron (cell-targeting protein) to the gold segment and binding the plasmid DNA to nickel segments, through selective molecular bonding (with each of the two metals), which allows the nanorods to be bifunctional in space sense. Leong showed that extra segments can be added to nanowires, e.g. to bind additional bifunctional elements, such as endosomolytic agents or magnetic segments that can be added to allow manipulation of nanobars in an external magnetic field [73].

Targeted radioimmunotherapeutic agents include advanced FDA- "cancer smart bombs" that kill cancer with radioactive yttrium (zevalin) or iodine (bexxar) attached to an antibody to target lymphoma (anti-CD20). Other agents, such as α-emitting actinium, bind to antibodies, forming so-called structures. "Nanogenerators" that use adopted monoclonal antibodies, for more selective killing of cells affected by leukemia because they penetrate more easily into cells, lymphomas and neuroblasts of breast, ovarian and prostate cancers, showing already with a dose of radiation at the level of becquerel (picocyria) high cancer destruction efficiency. With such systems, promising results have been obtained in mice and in the treatment of ovarian cancer [74].

Enzyme-activated drugs, discovered in 1980, are still very actively investigated today, with the functions set in relation to such drugs being divided into targeting functions and activation functions [74]. For example, an antibody-directed enzyme-targeted prodrug for cancer therapy was developed in Göttingen [75]. These target drug molecules are lethal when they reach cancer cells, while they are not harmful to healthy cells. In tests on mice, a human tumor was previously implanted in the body of a healthy mouse, after which they were given a certain dose of activated target protein that attacks only tumor cells, mostly ignoring healthy cells [75,76].

When an antitumor molecule is injected in its activated state, an antibiotic molecule of fungal origin composed of a very rigid ring of three carbon atoms opens and bursts becoming highly reactive, creating a "real havoc" among the nucleic acid molecules essential for cellular functions. However, when this molecule is injected as a prodrug, when sugar is previously bound to the ring, the disadvantage caused by the action of the antibiotic molecule of the drug, related to the stress inside the ring of the drug, no longer appears [75–77].

When the sugar is turned off, by pre-positioning the target enzyme, then the drug rearranges itself into a three-atom ring, which becomes lethally active. Other widely researched stimulants that stimulate cell response are "smart" hydrogels, including membranes made of hydrogel composites filled with insulin and the enzyme glucose oxidase, which allow the rate of insulin release to double when dipped in glucose solution, thus showing "Chemically stimulated accelerated insulin release" and "the potential of such systems to function as chemically synthesized pancreas." Nanoparticles with an even greater degree of activity were developed by R. Kopelman. The first effort is related to the production of PEBBLE (probes encapsulated with biologically localized implantation), wherein the color-coded nanoparticles are made of a polyacrylamide matrix by a conventional method; such particles are incorporated into living cells as biosensors to indicate intercellular oxygen, calcium, zinc and pH levels, metabolism or disease state [75–77].

The next goal of research in this area is the development of new molecular devices for early detection and therapy of brain cancer, using silica coated with iron oxide nanoparticles and a biocompatible polyethylene glycol coating. The miniature particle size of 20–200 nm will allow them to penetrate the area of the brain so that invasive surgery will not be necessary. Antibodies of cancer cells or other types of "tracer" molecules that adhere to cancer cells bind to iron oxide nanoparticles and, since they are attached to the nanopackage of a contrast agent, such particles become clearly visible during magnetic resonance imaging (MRI). The particles improve the killing effect of laser radiation on brain tissue. Nanoparticles allow a very small brain cell tumor, less than 50 μm, to be seen on MRI, depending on the type of cancer, where tumor cells of size 5–50 μm grow in locations outside the tumor site, and are most often invisible to the surgeon. Traditional chemotherapy and radiation kill cancer cells but also destroy healthy cells, while in nanoparticle treatment, the killing effect is directly directed at diseased cells [76].

5.2.13 DENDRIMERS AND DENDRIMER-BASED DEVICES

Dendrimers are another nanostructured material that is expected to be used rapidly as a medical therapist. These are three-dimensional polymer structures composed of different types of block copolymers, which show a pronounced branching directed from the center to their outer part. Dendrimers are formed nanometer by nanometer by a number of successive stages of synthesis of particles of well-defined size. Each molecule is several nanometers wide, but some are up to 30 nm in size, made up of more than 100,000 atoms. The peripheral layer of the dendrimer particle is made up of a dense field in which numerous molecular groups are concentrated that a loop for binding useful molecules, such as DNA, which binds to the outer branches of the dendrimer [77].

James R. Baker from the Center for Biological Nanotechnology believes that the use of dendrimers is very effective and safe in gene therapy. For Becker, these types of nanostructures are especially attractive because they make it easier for DNA to be drawn inside the cell, avoiding the immune response, unlike the viral vector that is usually used for transfection. The dendrimer is decorated with specific pieces of DNA, which are injected into biological tissue. When they come across living cells, dendrimers of a certain size cause the process of endocytosis, in which the outer cell membrane deforms into a fine bladder or vesicle. The vesicle closes the dendrimer which is then transferred to the inside of the cell. When it enters the cell, the DNA is released and migrates to the nucleus, where it becomes part of the cell's genome [77].

The group of so-called glycodendrimers having sialic acid on the surface have been presented as a glucodendrimer nanomait that serves as a trap for inactivating some influenza virus particles [77,78]. In Baker's Laboratory, the synthesis of multicomponent nanodevices called tectodendrimers, which are built of a large number of simple nuclei of dendrimer components, is in progress. Tectodendrimers consist of a single dendrimer molecule that may or may not contain a therapeutic agent surrounded by surrounding dendrim modules. Additional dendrimer modules consist of several types of modules, each type of module being designed to provide the necessary function to a smart device. Baker's group created a library of dendrimer components, which in their combinations give a large number of nanodevices [78].

Using a modular architecture, the field of smart therapeutic nanodevices can be created with little effort. For example, in apoptosis reporting modules, dendrimer contrast enhancement modules and chemotherapeutically releasing dendrimer modules (all together) attach to the dendrimer core, making a large number of such tecto dendrimers as starting material. This network structure can be adapted to fight cancer by simply replacing one of the many possible special dendrimers for cancer detection with a target dendrimer, creating a nanodevice that is adapted to destroy specific cancer cells while being harmless to normal cells [79].

Three nanodevices, synthesized using a fifth-generation ethylenediamine core of polyamido-amine dendrites with folic acid, fluorescein, and methotrexate (covalently bound to the surface) to provide targeting, imaging, and intercellular drug delivery, have been shown to deliver drugs. cytotoxic response of cells to methotrexate 100-fold relative to the free drug. At least half a dozen types of cancer cells possess at least one unique protein to which they are selectively bound. Such a protein on the surface of the dendrimer enables precise identification of the cancer. Accordingly, the genomic revolution that is evidently unfolding before us aims to identify that protein for each type of cancer [79].

The platform of tecto-dendrimer nanodevices can also be used to treat many other diseases besides cancer. Thanks to that, in the treatment of viral infections, the body can kill virus-infected cells because infected cells are easily recognized because they show inhumane viral proteins on their surface. Becker envisions the ability to deploy viruses to a virus-recognizing dendrimer depot, making it possible to create a separate antiviral dendrimer by binding a target dendrimer and a storage dendrimer to a standard tecto dendrimer. The same strategy can be applied against parasites, which also have unique inhumane surface proteins, even when it comes to parasites hidden in human cells, as in malaria [79].

Molecular modeling makes it possible to determine the optimal dendrimer surface modification for a given dendrimer function as a nanodevice and suggests suitable ways of surface dendrimer modification to improve target cell targeting. NASA and the National Cancer Institute, founded by Baker's lab, produce dendrimer-based nanodevices that have the ability to detect and report defects in cells during radiation exposure to astronauts (during their long-term space missions) [78,79].

In 2002, a device was built that detected the presence of caspase-3, one of the enzymes released during apoptosis, which is a sign of serious damage to cells by radiation. Becker's caspase dendrimer consists of two components. The first component with white blood cells resembles blood sugar so that the dendrimer is easily adsorbed on the cell surface. The second component uses fluorescence resonance energy transfer (FRET) to employ two close molecules [80]. Before the cell enters apoptosis, the FRET system remains connected together, leaving the interior of the white blood cells dark when illuminated [78,79].

Apoptosis begins when caspase-3 is released, with the bond breaking rapidly and white blood cells "bathing" in fluorescent light. The retinal diagnostic device measures the amount of fluorescence inside the astronaut's body. If the level is above the baseline, then contraindications to the effect of the drug must be taken into account [80].

5.2.14 Radio Controlled Biomolecules

Among the many already known examples of nanocrystals related to biological systems for use as biosensors, some types of nanoparticles have been investigated for potential direct control of biological processes. Josef Jacobson and a group of researchers linked fine radio frequency antennas (1.4 nm gold nanocrystals, consisting of less than 100 atoms) to DNA [81]. When a frequency of 1 GHz is passed through a fine antenna, the nanoparticles begin to rotate rapidly, due to the alternating eddy currents induced in the nanocrystals, creating heat. The biological molecules to which the crystals are attached "feel" highly localized heating, which causes the double helices of DNA to split (second) into two helices in a reversible hybridization process that leaves neighboring molecules intact. When the magnetic field is removed [81].

According to Zhang, the regulation of biomolecules by electronic radio frequency control represents a new dimension in biology. It is an exceptional tool, with which it is possible to "control one individual molecule in a cluster of molecules, which in itself is extremely valuable" [81]. The long-term goal is to use such antennas for living DNA control systems gene exclusion) through remote electronic activation. To do this, researchers at MIT (Massachusetts Institute of Technology) hooked a gold nanoparticle to specific oligonucleotides, which when added to simple DNA, bind to the complementary gene sequence, blocking the activity of these genes and effectively shutting them down. Such a tool will give pharmaceutical researchers (according to these scientists) a way to simulate the effects of a potential drug when the system is electronically turned on or off remotely [81].

G. Joice thinks that is wise to find a bridge between two different worlds: the biochemical world of nucleic acids and the physical world of electromagnetic waves. According to him, it is possible to even start thinking about different receivers, radio receivers that respond differently at different frequencies. By working at the right frequency, it will be possible to include one part of the DNA but not the other. DNA manipulation is interesting because it shows the potential of actuators and "hard driver" components and can serve as a basis for computer calculations.

Gold nanocrystals can also bind to proteins, opening up opportunities for future radio frequency biology, for electronic control of very complex biological processes such as enzymatic activity, protein folding and biomolecular assembly [82]. In late 2002, Jakobson announced that he had achieved electronic control over proteins. The researchers separated the hydrolyzing enzyme RNA, called ribonuclease S, into two parts: a large protein segment of 104 amino acids and a small one with 18 amino acid coils called S-peptide. The ribonuclease enzyme is inactive as long as a small coil is located on the "mouth" of the protein [83].

Jakobson bound the gold nanoparticle to the end of the S peptide coil and using the particles turned enzymes on and off: in the absence of a radiofrequency field, the S-peptides adapted their useful information and the ribonuclease remained active, but when the radiofrequency external field was on, the nanoparticles rotated rapidly, which prevented the S peptide from assembling into large proteins, inactivating enzymes. Jakobson expects that electronic control of proteins and nucleotides will enable molecular biologists to cut and paste genetic information electronically, and that a new organism will be able to be engineered through a computer program [83,84].

Gregory Timp and his team from the University of Illinois experimented with seven silicon-based microchips embedded in a living cell and tested its viability. Microchips had the properties of precursors for testing frequencies of the order of GHz (radio frequency microtransmitters), using carbon nanotubes as antennas within the cell [84]. Optical control (as with TV remote control) for biomolecule control has been specifically investigated.

Researchers at the University of Washington have added a reversible endoglucanase switch (an enzyme that facilitates cellulose cleavage) by attaching two light-sensitive polymer chains to the active sites of the cellulose chains. When exposed to visible light, one chain becomes hydrophilic by attracting water molecules and expanding, but when exposed to UV light, the chain becomes hydrophobic by displacing water molecules and shrinking into a coil. The second chain does the opposite, expands under UV light, and shrinks when visible. Depending on the type of light applied, the enzyme site is active for enzyme activity or blocked. The same group also reported temperature-induced enzyme activity in the form of a switch [85].

5.2.15 Microscale Biological Robots

The application of biological systems and organisms in technical and industrial processes is very challenging. In recent years, their application has been extended to genetic engineering, entering the field of genomics, proteomics, transcriptomics, genetic chips, artificial chromosomes, tissue engineering and biobotics (biorobotics). Biotechnology is no longer the primary goal of engineering in biological systems, as it now seeks to even design organic living systems, using instrumental or "wet" nanotechnologies [86,87].

5.2.16 Engineered Viruses

Bacteriophage viruses were first used for therapeutic use against bacteria by Herela (d'Herelle) in 1922, while other types of viruses are still used today as pharmaceutical agents and self-replicants. Over the past 10–15 years, bioengineered self-replicating viruses of various types and other vectors have been routinely used in experimental gene therapy as "devices" to first target and then penetrate an in vivo cell population, with objects embedded in therapeutic DNA sequences. reaching the nucleus of the human target cell. The incorporation of a new sequence into the viral genome, or a combination of components of two different viruses to create a new hybrid or chimeric virus, is a new skill, called virotherapy (9.12).

Virotherapy using oncolytic viruses whose replication is competitive in the tumor but not in normal cells provides a new approach to the treatment of malignant diseases [88,89]. Efforts are underway to design a purely rational virus, but they are still not yielding the right result. For example. Endy and co-workers computer-simulated the growth rate of the T7 mutant bacteriophage with an alternating set of genetic elements and found that, according to his prediction, a completely new genome permutation would be required for macrophage growth to be 31% faster than Of the "wild" type of bacteriophage.

Unfortunately, the experiments did not confirm this result, which indicates that it is necessary to further improve this method of computer simulation. Nevertheless, combinatorial experiments on "wild" type T7 by other researchers have produced a new immunologically unrecognizable T7 variant in which 12% of its genome has been deleted and which replicates twice as fast as the "wild" type. The synthetic biological laboratory at MIT is researching how to make a new generation of T7, a bacteriophage with a genome size of about 40 Kbp and 56 genes. With DNA synthesis, this procedure becomes cheaper and closer to the principle that "we want to redesign and rebuild the genome, creating new, better versions of T7" [90].

The approach to the redesign process includes "adding and removing restriction sites to allow for easier manipulation of different types of return codon uses and to eliminate parts of the genome that do not have a noticeable function. The synthesis of phage from sugar, according to these predictions, will enable a better understanding of how nature designs the existing organism. In 2002, a polio virus composed of 7,500 bases was successfully laboratory-produced from sugar by synthesizing the viral genetic sequence into DNA, enzymatically creating an RNA copy and sending it to the complete synthesis (and full infection) of polio viral particles [91]. Rational design and synthesis of chimeric viral replicators are possible today, but rational design and synthesis of complete artificial viral sequences leading to the production of a complete synthetic viral replicator may still be possible [91].

Mark Young and Trevor Douglas at Montana State University chemically modified the surface cage of the virus (protein chlorotic mottle virus (CCMV)), which enabled the engineering of functional groups exposed on the surface. This includes the addition of laminin peptide 11 (at the binding site of the laminin-binding protein, which is generally expressed in many types of breast cancer) to the viral coating and the incorporation of 180 Gd atoms at every 28 nm capsid, allowing these tumor-targeting particles to serves as a tumor-selective MRI contrast agent [91].

Researchers are now trying to reengineer the artificial virus to make a complete tumor-killing nanodevice, exploiting a threshold action mechanism that results from a reversible structural change in the virus [92]. Therapeutic anticancer compounds can be placed in a virus capsule or even made "in situ" using a capsid as a fine reaction vessel. The natural threshold of the chlorotic mottle virus CCMV is reengineered to allow control by redox potential (oxidative state of the local environment, which affects the tendency of molecules to lose or gain an electron). Although the CCMV virus plant does not enter human cells, the terminal delivery device should be a reconfigured human virus that also does not enter human cells [2,91].

The cell interior has a higher redox potential than blood, so that the viral capsid can be tightly closed in transit, but can also be opened when its redox-controlled threshold is exceeded, so that after entering the target cancer cell it realizes its useful carrying capacity agents, by timely dismissal. An alternative radiation-trigger/switch threshold has also been developed. The team that investigated how the modified viral capsule works on the mouse model was encouraged by the initial results [2,92].

In principle, there are five options for capsid engineering: (i) highly sensitive imaging, (ii) cell targeting, (iii) drug transport, and (iv) controlled delivery, all of which together represent a potentially powerful, minimally toxic way to fight metastatic cancer. Scientists at Osaka University used a hepatitis virus protein to synthesize a similar structure to an 80-nm cage, the surface of which was modified to include a peptide that binds to the human liver cell receptor. In one experiment, fluorescent dye was inserted into cages that reached cancerous human liver cells (both species were cultured in laboratory vessels and transplanted into mice) without affecting other cells. Alternatively, surface peptides are thought to have the potential to allow virus cages (capsules) to be used as devices to deliver drugs or genes to other tissues [93,94].

Engineered bacteria such as Salmonella typhimurium (food poison) are killed by the removal of purine-producing genes, which are of particular importance for their growth. The tamed strain cannot survive long in a healthy body, but it multiplies rapidly (1,000 times faster than in normal cells) within a tumor that is rich in pyrine. The engineered bacterium, as an available multiple serotype, was used in 2,000 clinical doses in the first phase of clinical experiments, with the aim of avoiding a potential host immune response. The next step will be to add genes to the bacteria to produce anti-cancer proteins that collect the tumor, or to modify the bacteria to deliver various enzymes, genes, or prodrugs to regulate the growth of tumor cells.

In 1998, G. Evans described possible constructions of synthetic genomes and artificial organisms. He proposed a strategy that involves determining or designing a genome DNA sequence, synthesizing and assembling the genome, then introducing synthetic DNA into a nucleated host pluripotent cell to create an artificial organism [95,96]. It is difficult to assess whether it is possible to modify existing microbes by genomic engineering by adding biochemical steps borrowed from other organisms (through their remains) because the creation of the existing system should match the unique requirements arising from very detailed knowledge of signaling pathways of such microbes.

A.P. Arkin therefore thinks that we must learn the program of cells in the same way as a computer program." Some genetic engineers have begun making the biological equivalent of most basic circuit breakers on a computer, the so-called digital flip-flop. Cells are turned on and off by genes all the time, "noted Thomas Knight, a pioneer in such research. A cell switch made of DNA and some well-characterized regulatory proteins has the ability to engage with a specific gene that is exposed to a particular chemical. This can be used in gene therapy: implanted genes can be controlled with one dose of a specially selected drug, one to turn on the gene and the other to turn it off [95,96].

A. Mushegian concluded that at least 300 genes of all genes are necessary for life, so that at least as many genes constitute the smallest possible genome corresponding to a functional microbe [97]. An organism that contains this minimal gene set would have to have a number of functions necessary for life, such as the production of cellular biomolecules, energy production, damage repair, transport of salts and other molecules responsible for chemical environmental signals and replication. The minimal microbe, the basic "cell chassis," can be specified by a genome length of only 150,000 nucleotide bases.

In 2001, G. Evans produced a DNA helix of 10,000 nucleotide bases, striving to increase this length by at least ten times. The engineered full DNA genome, once synthesized, can be located inside the cell membrane void, similar to living cells from which nuclear material has been removed [98]. Used in medicine, these artificial biorobots can be designed to produce vitamins, hormones, enzymes, or cytokines that are deficient in the patient's body, to select and metabolize into harmless end products, hazardous substances such as toxins, toxins, or indigestible intercellular waste strategies of a very challenging program venture.

A private company constructing such biological devices (its business plan is called "complete genome engineering") has already begun to fertilize capital. In November 2002, J. Craig Venter, famous for human genome sequencing, and Nobel laureate Hamilton O. Smith founded a company called the Institute for Biological Energy Alternatives (IBEA). This company, which received $ 3 million from the Energy Department to create a minimal organism, has already started with the M. genitalium microorganism [98]. Working with 25 people, the scientists first removed all the genetic material from the body and then synthesized an artificial thread of genetic material similar to what happens in a chromosome that they hoped would contain a minimum number of M. genitalium genes needed to sustain life. The artificial chromosome will be implanted in the emptied cell where the ability to survive and reproduce will be tested. To ensure safety, the cell will be intentionally mutilated to be unable to carry a human infection, it will be strictly confined and designed to die if it manages to escape into the environment.

In 2003, Glen Evans' new company, Egea Bioscineces, produced the first patent that included broad references to chemical syntheses within genes and gene networks that encompass the genome, the "operating system" of all living organisms. Their conceptual study produced a library of more than 1,000,000 programmed proteins, over 200 synthetic genes and proteins, produced the largest genes ever chemically synthesized from over 16,000 bases, as well as engineered proteins for new functions, enhanced protein expression through codon optimization, and developed adaptation of genes for protein production in specific host cells.

Ege's software allows researchers to authorize a new DNA sequence that the company's hardware can produce with a base position error specification of just 10–4, which Evans calls "global DNA processing." The end result of such research would be a DNA helix with 100,000 base pairs in length, large enough to make up a simple bacterial genome. Evans 'prototype machine can synthesize 10,000 bases in 2 days, while 100,000 bases are expected to take even weeks with some new generation of machines. Soon, as T. Knight expects we will not store DNA in large refrigerators. We will print them when we need them [98,99].

5.2.17   Medical Nanorobots

The third important direction in the development of nanomedicine, molecular nanotechnologies (MNT) or nanorobotics is within the scope of engineering of all complex mechanical medical systems, constructed at the molecular level. Biotechnology expands the range and efficiency options available thanks to nanomaterials, while the advent of molecular nanotechnologies enables enormous efficiency, comfort and speed of future medical treatments, with reduced risk, cost and invasiveness. Molecular nanotechnologies (MNTs) will enable doctors in the future to perform direct "in vivo" surgery even on a single individual human cell. New possibilities for the design, construction and development of a large number of microscopic medical nanorobots will make this possible [100].

5.2.17.1   History

The first and most famous scientist in the field of nanotechnology and their application was Nobel laureate R. P. Feynman. In his extremely inspiring 1959 speech known as "There is plenty of room at the bottom," Feynman gave a vision of machine tools making smaller and smaller machines all the way to the atomic level. According to him, such nanomachines, nanorobots and nanodevices will be used for the development of a wide range of atomically precise microscopic instruments and production tools, which belong to the domain of nanotechnologies. In this way, Feynaman clearly emphasized the medical applications of new technologies [2,100].

B. Hobbes estimated that although Feynman's idea of such a small machine is almost crazy, it can still be interesting for surgery. It sounds almost unbelievable that it is technically feasible to "put a small mechanical surgeon inside the blood vessels, who can enter the heart and look around, and then register which flap is not good and take a small knife, which precisely removes thin layers of damaged tissue, bringing them back in a normal state. Other small machines could be constantly present inside the body, to help properly regulate some inadequate function of an organ [100,101].

In his aforementioned 1959 speech, Feynman insisted on considering the possibility of linking nanotechnology to cell biology, so that they could make objects suitable for maneuvering at the same level. Two decades later, K. E. Drexler published as a student his technical work suggesting that it is possible to construct nanodevices from biological parts that can enter a human cell and make repairs inside the cell. That, a decade after Drexler's seminar paper, became the foundation for molecular machines and nanorobots. [101,102].

5.2.18   Nanorobotic Parts and Components

The extension of nanomedicine to molecular machine systems probably requires (among many other requirements) primarily the ability to make precise structures, actuators-actuators and molecular-level motors, with the possibility of manipulation and locomotion. In 1992, K. Eric Drexler theoretically concluded that an efficient nanomechanical bearing must be connected to two graphite plates in a cylinder of different diameters, so that one smaller plate is installed inside the other larger one. In 2000, J. Cumings and A. Zettl demonstrated experimentally that two carbon nanotubes, inserted into each other, allow this type of nanotube to show truly extremely low friction at the interface between such nanotubes.

5.2.19 NANO BEARINGS AND NANOGEARS

To lay the right foundation for the molecular design of nano-bearings and nano-gears, it is necessary to first create and analyze possible designs for nanoscale mechanical parts that could be manufactured. Designers aim to incorporate molecular dynamics simulations into their studies instead of relying on "ab initio" structural analysis and computer research. According to Drexler, our ability to model molecular machines (systems and devices) of specific types, designed in part to be easier to model, is far from our ability to actually make them. Yet budget design and computer experiments allow theoretical studies of these devices, regardless of whether technology is able to implement them [101,102].

In nanoscale design, the building materials do not change continuously as in cutting and shaping, but above all they must be treated as if they were made of individual atoms. Nanoscale components are supermolecules. Any stray atom or molecule within such a structure can act as an impurity that can block and disable the device because scale vibrations, electric forces, thermal expansion, magnetic interactions and surface tension are of such dimensions that they can cause dramatic changes in various phenomena in the system, when the system moves from microscale to nanoscale. Molecular bearings are perhaps the most favorable class of components to design because of their structure and function (operation) which is quite simple [103,104].

One of the simplest examples is Drexler's bearing design, which consists of a ball, rod, and infill and is based on the "overlap overlap" principle [103,104]. This bearing has exactly 206 atoms including C, Si, O and H atoms and it has small shafts that rotate within a sleeve ring of 2.2 nm in diameter. The shaft atoms are arranged in sixfold symmetry, and the rings in 14 fold symmetry, the combination of which provides a low energy barrier for shaft rotation. On the atomic scale, two opposite surfaces have periodic "growths" and cavities, where the periodicity of these "growths" is different for two surfaces, which are disproportionate. Two disproportionate surfaces cannot be locked to each other in either position because the barriers to their free rotation are very small, of the order of only 0. 001 kT (this is the value corresponding to the value of thermal noise at room temperature). Components of highly rotational symmetry must have internal curves, tensioned membranes (shells) or some other special type of structure.

Molecular gear is another suitable component for molecular design in a given product. Drexler and Merkle designed a planetary gear with 3,557 atoms. The internal assembler has 12 moving parts; has a diameter of 4.3 nm, a length of 4.4 nm, a molecular weight of 51,009,844 Da and a molecular volume of 33,458 nm³. The computer simulation animation shows a central axis that rotates fast and a peripheral output axis that rotates slowly. The small planetary gear rotates around a central axis and is surrounded by an annular gear that holds the planetary part in place and allows the other components to rotate properly [103,104]. The gear ring is a stressed silicone shell with terminated sulfur atoms [101–104].

Under normal operating conditions, there is no gear overheating for the speeds for which the given components are designed (frequency slightly less than 1GHz and linear interfacial speed slightly less than 10 m/s). It rotates steadily from room temperature to approximately 400 K. At a frequency of about 100 GHz, instabilities occur although the device is not destroyed. Drexler and Merkle proposed a second generation of planetary gears designed with 4,235 atoms and a molecular mass of 72,491,947 Da [105]. This new vision is more stable, but it also shows significant slippage at the highest frequencies

That is why Goddard proposed a design that bears no resemblance to a macroscopic system because the teeth of the gears in the xy plane cannot be atomically smooth in the z-direction. Therefore, he proposes to develop a V design so that the V shape of the gear teeth in the direction is placed inside the V notch in the strip, for stability in the z-direction when the gear teeth are in contact with the xy plane.

5.2.20 NANOMOTORS AND ENERGY SOURCES

The second class of theoretical nanodevices that have been designed so far include the molecular gas engine or the molecular gas pump [106]. The pump and the walls of the chamber are segments containing 6,165 atoms, whose molecular mass is 88,190,813 Yes, and whose molecular volume is 63,984 nm³. Such a device can serve either as a pump for neon gas atoms (or if it works in the opposite direction) as an engine that converts gas pressure into rotational power. The helical motor has a beveled cylindrical bearing at one end, which is supported by a screw with a threaded cylindrical segment in the middle. During rotation, the shaft drives a helical ring on the longitudinal grooves inside the pump housing. Such a chamber is optimal for small gas molecules. Where the edges of the grooves intersect, there is a movement of the points of intersection and their movement from one side to the other, when the shaft rotates,

Goddard presented a preliminary molecular dynamic simulation of this device, really showing its pump function, although "structural deformations" in the rotor can cause instabilities at low and high rotational frequencies. Forced translations show that even at very low normal forces during pump activity, the total energy increases significantly and the structure deforms again [107]. Merkle's conclusion is that the pump moves neon atoms with an energy of 1,850 Kcal/mol/nm, which is not efficient enough for future fine-tuning of this rough design.

This design proposed by researchers in the field of molecular nanotechnology is limited by the possibilities of theory and computer simulation of machines themselves, based on theoretical foundations valid for design and testing of large structures or complete nanomachines and compilation of a growing library of numerous examples of molecular design of such machines. Working on these types of machines is relatively cheap and does not require the support of a large team. Of course, the calculations on many systems are very complicated and difficult. Therefore, every computer calculation requires a number of simplifying assumptions for faster computation (nuclei as point masses, electrons that are treated as a continuous distribution of charge, a three-dimensional energy potential function that has a semi-empirical character for given experimental data and treats the field of action of nanoelements on each other as a classical field of action, although it is quantum of mechanical character).

Goddard noted that future nanosystem simulations may require 1–100 million atoms to be considered explicitly, requiring future improvements in molecular dynamics methodology when it comes to the multimillion number of atoms [108]. Other researchers have given an experimental approach to the development of an organic nanomotor for future nanorobots. Carlo Montemagno modified the natural biomotor by inserting non-biological parts into it, thus creating the so-called artificial hybrid nanomotor [109,110]. Montemago began its research with natural ATPase (an enzyme found in living organisms that helps convert food into the useful energy of living cells). The moving part of the ATPase molecule is the central protein shaft (or rotor, in the term of the electric motor) that rotates, where this rotation is a specific type of response to electrochemical reactions with each of the three proton molecular channels (comparable to the electromagnets in the stator coil of an electric motor). ATP (adenosine triphosphate) is a fuel that drives a molecular engine with its power.

Using genetic engineering tools, Montemagno added ATPase amino acid residues that bind to the metal. This allowed each motor molecule to bind strongly to the stand, which was prepared by electron beam lithography. Properly oriented motor molecules have a diameter of 12 nm when attached to a stand with an accuracy of about 15 nm. A 100 nm Si3N4 band binds to the rotor subunit of each self-assembling molecule. On a microscopic video presentation, you can see dozens of strips turning as if they were in a field of small propellers. The group of the first integrated engines worked for 40 minutes with 3–4 revolutions per second. The following engines ran continuously for hours when charged with ATPase [109,110].

Montemagno measured sizes, such as horsepower, by a conventional test, close to any mechanical engineer who tests cars. Montemagno also tried to make a solar-powered biomolecular engine, as an autonomous nanodevice, in which light energy is converted into ATP, which serves as the engine's fuel source. "We think," says Montemagno, "that it is possible to make an autonomous device that will work with the help of light energy on a scale of 1μm and smaller, smaller even than the size of a bacterium."

Montemagno has developed a chemical way to turn this hybrid engine on and off. By engineering the design of secondary binding sites, according to Montemagne, it will be possible to influence the cascades of cellular signals, on the basis of which it will be possible to use the sensor system of living cells to control non-devices implanted in the cell. His vision is to build a small chemical factory inside the cells. He speculates that these nanofactories will be able to target specific cells, such as tumor cells, where they will be able to synthesize and deliver chemotherapeutic agents. In a few years, he expects to have an engine assembled inside a living cell, with cellular physiology that will provide energy for its movement.

His 10-year goal is to make a device that will harvest individual molecules inside a living cell, which will metaphorically represent a new type of cell pharmacy that produces a drug, stores it inside the cell and then releases it after receiving the signal. In terms of technology, the production of such useful devices before 2050 is not predictable. He thinks we have a pretty good start. But there is a long way to go before it is certain that we will be able to manage these machines in the right way and that they will not be lost in the human body.

Research on the experimental nanomotor is on the rise in other laboratories as well. T. R. Kelly researched a chemical-powered DNA engine, while Wong and Leigh designed a 58-atom solar-powered molecular engine. consists of catenate large rings that rotate under the action of a UV laser and that can rotate the rings at millions and billions of revolutions per minute if needed. The white light of the bromine solution resets the engine, returning the ring to its original position [111].

Motors are being developed that use trapped bacteria or immobilized enzymes, which are filled with organic materials such as sugar and convert chemical energy into electricity, which is used to start electric motors. Also, motors running on micron batteries, motors with multilayer nanotubes on a SiO2 flat surface or on a silicon carrier, nanomotors with gold rotors of 110–300 nm, motors with nanotube anchors and oppositely placed stators around the nanotubes are being developed (nanotubes were previously corroded to would be sufficiently cleaned for use in a nanomotor, while nanomotors are controlled acoustically and/or ultrasonically) [111].

5.2.21 MECHANOSYNTHESIS OF DIAMONDS

Programmable positioning on the molecular scale is the central mechanism for achieving good flexibility and perfect precision in production. In contrast to positioning on the centimeter or meter scale, positional assembly on the molecular scale is still at a "rudimentary" level, but expectations in the future are enormous. A comprehensive analysis of how to use positional assembly to design different atomic distributions is now extremely complex. More than 100 elements of the periodic table, each with its own unique chemical properties, with their various variations and permutations create a real "explosion" of possible combinations whose complete analysis preoccupies researchers around the world [112].

It is much easier to implement a management project with small sets of position-controlled nanoneeds (tools) that can be used in the mechanosynthesis of solid hydrocarbons and analysis of hydrocarbon classes (especially diamonds) that can be synthesized using nanoneeds as a tool. Why a diamond? There are four important reasons for this: first because it has been experimentally and theoretically well researched, so that many practical issues related to the molecular structure of diamond have been resolved; second, the development of admentin chemistry has shown that conventional bulk material and small molecules of pure diamond crystal in specific isomeric forms contain more than 50 atoms (including more than 22 carbon atoms), and in some cases allow rational regionally selective functionalization of these molecules; third, the field of synthesis with chemical deposition from the gas phase (CVD) of microscale thin films of diamond and similar hydrocarbon structures is very developed, and techniques for the growth of diamond crystals are also known; fourth, the diamond possesses a number of outstanding properties, such as extreme hardness, high thermal conductivity, low coefficient of friction, chemical inertness, and wide gap energy. Under normal pressure, it is the strongest known solid material. It is used in MEMS devices, optics, radiology, biochemical analysis, medicine, and electronic devices. The method of precise design of microscopic and nanoscale diamond structures is of great importance for science and industry, both in the present and in the future [112].

In contrast to high-pressure diamond synthesis and low-pressure diamond syntheses, gas phase reactions that take place by CVD processes, positional mechanosynthesis is a completely new method, first proposed by Drexler's design for precision structures. Mechanosynthesis is a specific chemical synthesis based on the introduction of chemical transformations controlled by a positional operating system with precision on the atomic scale (using SPM (scanning probe microscopy)), which allows direct positional selection of reaction sites on the workpiece. In addition, STM shows a high ability to manipulate surface structures at the atomic level [113].

5.2.22 SIGNIFICANCE OF DIAMOND SYNTHESIS METHODS FOR NANOMEDICINE AND MEDICAL NANOROBOTICS

Many researchers suggest a method involving STM to direct chemical reactions on a surface by releasing a strong electric field on a subnano region of a given surface to activate chemical reactions, manipulating chemistry with a tip that has the function of a catalyst that can be precisely introduced into the region. desired reactions or that surface reactions are activated by the process of releasing the mechanical energy of the tip itself. The reaction selectivity of these methods is in line with the exponential dependence of the reaction rates on the activation barriers, which show reduced values for reactions on a precisely defined area of the surface during mechanosynthesis.

Mechanosynthesis should be distinguished from simple piezochemistry, the term which describes chemical processes in solutions under the action of homogeneous, isotropic, slightly varying pressure (0.1–2 GPa in commercial laboratory devices), as a result of which the chemical reactivity of the surface material is modified. At a pressure of 2 GPa at room temperature, the graphite surface is transformed into a diamond. Unlike the mechanical forces of hydrostatic pressure, mechanochemical tool types are highly anisotropic and inhomogeneous on a molecular scale [114]. High loads (including compression, stress, shear, and torsion) can be applied to specific atoms and bonds in a controlled manner.

Stress is a scale-independent parameter, so that tool types for mechanosynthesis in diamond making can achieve pressures equal to those on the macroscale required for diamond synthesis, within the pressing cell (pressures greater than 550 GPa). The non-doped diamond consists of a rigid C atom cell passivated with H atoms, so that a necessary aspect of diamond mechanosynthesis involves position-controlled subtraction and addition of H atoms on the diamond surface.

Selective removal of H atoms from the crystal surface of a given material was performed for the first time experimentally by Musgrave and Lyding. They showed how it is possible to subtract individual H atoms from a specific atomic position in a covalently bonded H monolayer on the surface of Si (100), using electrical pulses of STM nanoigles in vacuum. The addition of H atoms has also been described theoretically, but has not yet been studied in more detail. Although this was a demonstration of the highly localized STM-catalyzed rehydrogenation of dehydrogenated hydrocarbon clusters adsorbed on the Pt (111) surface, and the addition of hydrogen to the prepared azide-coated surface, it is assumed that a similar specific hydrogen removal and addition reaction tool is possibly performed on a diamond surface as well.

The main challenge in diamond mechanosynthesis is the controlled addition of C atoms to the growing surface of the lattice of diamond crystals. Theoretical analysis of C atom incorporation and placement of C dimers on a diamond surface is one of the topics in which many authors have been involved [115,116]. The possibility of precise incorporation of individual C atoms, small hydrocarbon molecules or small clusters of C atoms on the C (111) or C (100) diamond surface in specific places is supported by computer calculations by Walch and Merkle. They analyzed several mechanosynthetic reactions including the placement of a C dimer on a C (111) surface, the incorporation of a position-controlled carbene into that dimer, and the incorporation of a position-controlled carbene on the surface of a dimer on a C (100) surface using a nine-atom cluster to model a diamond surface.

As a reminder, carbene is a molecule containing a carbon atom with six valence electrons, with the general formula: RR'C. We distinguish two types of carbene: singlet with paired spins and triplet, with unpaired spins. Singlet carbines with unfilled p-orbitals are electrophilic or nucleophilic and participate in stereospecific helleotropic reactions, while triplet carbines are diradicals that participate in stepped stereoselective radical reactions.

Subsequent studies have shown that the installation can be performed without a barrier, according to computer calculations "ab initio" using Gaussian with a 6–31 G base set and B3LYP density function, if the appropriate trajectory is followed. By moving the mechanosynthetic tool type with such a defined trajectory, the movement of the C atom into the bridge structure of the dimer is ensured. These theoretical and experimental results confirm the general possibility of molecular positioning operations which can be used to modify the surface of a diamond workpiece, adding or removing small hydrocarbon clusters or individual atoms and dimers under appropriate conditions [117]. By simply repeating such basic operations, it is expected that it will be possible to build complex and atomically precise molecular structures.

The mechanosynthetic strategy is based on three basic assumptions: (i) highly reactive tools (it is generally assumed that reactions take place through CVD diamond synthesis involving highly reactive species; a molecular tool such as tips is highly reactive, and the synthesis of diamond structures with it is facilitated); (ii) inert environment (because molecular tools are highly reactive an inert environment must be used; mechanosynthetic tools should be used in vacuum so as to avoid contact with solvents or gas molecules (contaminants such as oxygen, nitrogen, hydrogen or water and unwanted by-products of internal chemical reactions) with the molecular tool and the surface to be treated because due to the mutual reaction, mechanochemical operations could be disrupted, which are performed at pressures of about 10–12 atm (which can be achieved with UHV systems); (iii) the working volume in which the process is performed optimized to a value less than 4,000 μm^3 can be increased if the concentration of free gas molecules decreases to negligible values); (iv) controlled paths (molecular tools are positionally controlled at all times; they are not free to move arbitrarily; their controlled trajectories are such as to completely avoid unwanted eccentrics of the outer surfaces of the tool carrier tips or its housing; adverse reactions between radicals and surfaces, also, they should be avoided either by suitable positioning of the tips or by specific pre-design of the surface to be inert and resistant to attack by such radicals) [114].

The assumption of such an efficient positional control of a highly reactive tool within an inert working atmosphere should enable the design of relatively simple reaction paths. Simply put, the primary goal of this method is to achieve a stable vacuum environment, with a relatively simple set of reactions and molecular tools to produce a wide range of nanoscale diamond structures with atomic precision [117,118].

5.2.23 Mass Parallel Production of Nanomachines

Complex objects assembled from simple components can be produced either in series or in parallel. In serial assembly, objects are produced at a given time in a gradual production process. Examples include e.g. antique pocket watches, classic industrial "mass production" such as cars coming out of the lane one at a time at the end of the assembly line, or traditional serial production of digital computers with one-by-one instructions in a linear sequence.

In parallel assemblage, objects are produced along many pathways simultaneously or in many different places, such as polysomes in living cells (translation of multiple currants into a single mRNA coil simultaneously), or by masking lithography of multiple circuits simultaneously on a single semiconductor carrier, or by similar to modern parallel computers, which at any time implement various instructions with a thousand or even tens of thousands of independent processors in a highly parallel way. Parallel designed systems can have many possible approaches to control/architectural configuration of analogs with SIMD (Single instruction multiple data), as well as approaches characteristic of convergent and fractal assemblages, agoric algorithms, and various other design analogues taken from high-performance parallel computing [119,120].

Biology, perhaps, provides the best examples of massive parallelism in assembly. A single ribosome, which is capable of making a protein that is directed by a single molecule of information RNA, is a great design system. However, this has little economic effect for now. However, the billions of ribosomes that work together in every living cell can make all the proteins on a tree, with all the proteins in it growing "as fast as seagrass growing 15 cm a day." The difference between serial and parallel processing is especially important in molecular design, when the basic part is very small. If it is a simple component, its volume is of the order of $1 \, nm^3$, so that if viewed from that angle, only $1 \, cm^3$ of assembled volume in the design process requires the assembly of 1,000 billion (1,021) simple molecular components. For series production, it would take thousands of years for one component to be installed on time, even at 1 GHz, which is economically pointless

With parallel design, a huge number of components can be produced simultaneously, reducing that time to days, hours or even less. Massive parallel assembly is obviously the key to the economic acceptability of molecular design. Two important ways to achieve mass molecularly precise parallel assembly of well-defined physical structures are: self-organization and positional assembly [121,122]. In commercial chemical synthesis, self-organization is present in the fluid phase between moles (1,023 molecules of reactants interact to produce a mole of molecular product). In Seeman's experiments, including supermolecular or biochemical assembly, the number of products of objects produced per batch is much smaller than the amount of moles, but is very large by conventional standards in macroscale manufacturing.

The inherent parallelism of self-organization is the main advantage of these steps in positional production assembly. To maximize this advantage and reap the full benefits from the standpoint of flexibility, precision and quality, in the 21st century molecular design will use positional assembly, also known as the mechanical phase of nanotechnology, which is a new technique of mass parallel positional assembly that must be further developed. At least two such techniques with such a high application potential have so far been identified: (i) a massive parallel array manipulator and (ii) replicating systems only. The mass parallel array manipulator uses very large arrays of independent manipulation devices (scanning probes, nanoneeds, robot arm, etc.) to process a very large number of molecularly precise components, simultaneously building large product facilities. To produce a large number of nanoparticles and nanoassemblies, mass parallel scanning microscope probe (SPM) arrays and microscale SPMs are most suitable.

Force-sensitive devices such as piezoelectrics, piezoresistive systems, and capacitive microcantilevers make it possible to construct microscale AFMs without an external deviation sensor. An interesting alternative, patented by Zyvex, called Rotapod, is an exponential design concept in which one robot arm on a Si carrier makes the other robot arm on the surface by taking a micronsized lithographically produced piece, carefully placing it in a pre-selected correct location so is a small hand robot can find and assemble. The two robot hands then make twice as many robot hands, one on each of the two surfaces of the face. These four robotic arms, two on each side, make four new robotic arms. This process with the number of robotic arms continues in ascending order in the sequence 1, 2, 4, 8, 16, 32, 64 and so on until the manufacturing limit is reached, when both surfaces are completely covered with small robotic arms [123].

Therefore, a single manipulator is used to provide the parts to make a large array manipulator which then undertakes the desired massive parallel design and production operations. Rotapod design is still in development and requires more precision to achieve flexible and molecularly precise production of a given product.

Self-replication systems achieve massive parallel assembly first by fabricating copies of themselves and then allowing those copies to fabricate new copies resulting in a very rapid increase in the number of copies of the system. When the system population replication manipulator is large enough, the population manipulator can be redirected to produce other useful objects, instead of its own copy. Only replicating systems are widespread in biology, but are not explicitly feasible in macroscale design for at least two reasons: (i) they are widespread (ii) misperceptions of great technical difficulties are wrong despite the correct perceptions of such massive parallelism necessary for macroscale production.

NASA has done engineering studies of self-replicating factories on the moon, with the necessary automation of production, which is slowly advancing towards the set goal of building fully self-replicating factories. There is nothing disputable that self-replicating systems could be remotely controlled, fully automated, and that different combinations between them are possible. Parallel row manipulators and individual replicators are processes with high production potential of complex nanomachines and their products, with each of these two approaches having some advantages and some disadvantages. Ordinary systems must be efficient from the point of view of positional specialization of the process, while individual replicators must be tolerant of errors in components [123].

In the last 5 years, research interest related to mechanical replication systems alone has been renewed, for the reason that it is assumed that replication from a fundamental point of view is probably a simple process. Joseph Jacobson from MTI suggested that many applications of engineered systems would be useful, it is necessary that such systems must be able to produce multiple copies. According to Jakobson, self-replicating systems represent a new discipline in engineering. Today, there are several university research programs on theoretical and experimental grounds related to mechanical (non-biological) self-replicating machines. Biotechnology and molecular engineering are the subject of serious studies related to the operation of mechanical self-replicators at the nanosilk level.

Current methods of self-assembly, although allowing massive parallel assembly, lack the flexibility, precision, and quality required for 21st century molecular production. In addition, positional assembly methods, which include massive parallel row manipulators and replication systems only and which should allow molecularly precise mass parallel assembly, are still insufficiently studied, so further theoretical and experimental work is necessary for the full realization of such ideas. The foreseeable future as well as the storage of a large amount of information does not require nanomechanical replicators. The physical replicator becomes a remotely controlled manipulator for receiving instructions from the outside, which step by step, lead the process of assembling the manipulator first, and then the desired nanosystems to the end. After a number of repeated cycles, in the first phase of assembly of the manipulator, a large number of remotely controlled manipulators is obtained. These manipulators can be used to assemble a large number of useful products by changing the instructions sent to the devices of replicated manipulators, during the second phase of the process [124].

5.3 POSSIBLE RANGE OF NANOROBOT APPLICATIONS AND SCALING STUDIES

The idea of an autonomous nanorobot, which works using its own power as an analogue of similar structures present in the human body, has been present for a long time. More than 40 trillion single-celled microbes swim through our colon, exceeding our cell count by almost 10 times. Many bacteria move at breakneck speed around small tails, or flagella, which are driven by a 30-nm biological ion engine, whose power is conditioned by the pH difference between the inside and outside of the bacterial cell. Our body maintains a population of more than a trillion mobile biological nanodevices, about 10 µm in size. These natural nanorobots are constantly swimming inside us, repairing damaged cells, attacking microbes intruders, merging with foreign bodies and transporting them to various organs for disposition in the body.

There have been many attempts to build on MEMS-based microrobots with the intention of using "in vivo" [125]. The sub-project of the NanoRobotics Laboratory of the Ecole Polytechnique in Montreal is one such example. In this approach, a variable MRI (magnetic resonance imaging) magnetic field generates a magnetic force of a robot consisting of ferromagnetic particles, which allows the miniaturization of the propulsion system, capable of developing a force directed at a small device within the human body. First-generation prototype applications include targeted drug delivery, reopening of blocked arteries, and biopsy. The project provides the necessary information based on which to define the rules for designing microrobots with the long-term goal of miniaturizing the system and creating a robot made of nanometer parts, which will be suitable for medical applications in blood vessels that are inaccessible.

Other approaches to MEMS-based microrobots are intended to use magnetically controlled "cibote" and "caribot" robots designed to perform wireless intercellular surgery. There are a number of preliminary proposals for hybrid bionanorobots that could be constructed according to some future, in principle already conceived technologies. In line with this idea, Carlo Montemagno plans to use modified ATPase motors to create nanorobots that will act as "pharmacy in the cell" entering the cell, "grabbing" proteins produced by unused cells and storing them until they are not needed by the patient. The device would consist of a small nickel drum, attached to an ATPase biological engine, which is coated with antibodies that adsorb to the target molecules, after which the electric field pulls such molecules into the storage chamber and holds them in place.

It is predicted that the greatest success of nanomedicine will follow in 10–20 years, when we will learn to design and construct artificial nanorobots using diamond-shaped parts of nanometer dimensions and subsystems such as sensors, motors, manipulators, power sources, and molecular computers. If this assumption is reasonable, one day we will be able to make these diamond-shaped medical nanorobots and make them cheap enough and in large enough numbers to be therapeutically useful. What medical implications could follow from this? There are many possibilities, but the development of a signal path that mimics the signal path of cells will be long and difficult.

The first theoretical scaling studies were used as an approach to the basic concept of nanorobot feasibility. These baseline studies rely on computer simulations of specific nanorobotic components and ensembles, and finally system simulations, which are fully integrated with additional simulations of mass parallel production processes, consistent with the design of the assembly engineering philosophy. Once we master the possibilities of such production, experimental efforts will be able to include first the production of components and testing of component ensembles, and final prototypes, and then mass production of complete nanorobots, eventually leading to clinical trials. To date, advances in medical nanorobot research have remained largely at the level of the feasibility stage concept [126,127].

5.3.1 BIO-INSPIRED NETWORKING

The dynamics of biological systems are the basis of inspiration for many researchers, who are trying to understand their basics in order to devise new methodologies and tools for the design and management of communication systems and information networks. Such networks are inherently adaptable to a dynamic environment, heterogeneous, scalable, self-organizing, and evolutionary. Accordingly, probably the most promising communication mechanism between nano-machines that form nanoscale networks would involve the application of molecular communication, ie coding and transmission of information using molecules. This mechanism is essentially to mimic the cellular signaling network in living organisms [128].

Unlike early communication systems composed of transmitter/receiver and communication channel pairs, which are static, such networks would be very dynamic in terms of the behavior of communication nodes, the mode of traffic within them, network bandwidth and channels that make up that network. Obviously, many biological entities in organisms have similar structures to nano-machines. For example, all living cells have the ability to detect the environment, receive external signals and perform certain tasks on a nano scale. In addition, thanks to the existence of transfer and receiving molecules, cells in a biological organism establish cellular signaling networks [129], through which they communicate to perform complex vital tasks, such as immune system tasks and reactions. Bio-inspired algorithms, show the possibility of efficient customization, so they are suitable for optimization, research and mapping processes, as well as for pattern recognition [130,131].

In the development of bio-inspired methods that have an outstanding impact in the researched domain, the following steps are important: (i) Identification of analogies, which allow to determine methods that lead to defining similar structures, (ii) Understanding, which involves detailed modeling of real biological behavior, (iii) Engineering, which allows model simplification and tuning for technical applications Biology - inspired computing involves a class of algorithms aimed at efficient computing, e.g. for optimization processes and pattern recognition The difference between wireless and insect population networks and projected wireless sensor networks consist of insects encoding messages with semiochemicals (also known as infochemicals) rather than radio frequencies [130,131].

Ant colony optimization (ACO) is probably the most deeply analyzed branch of algorithms based on swarm intelligence. Swarm intelligence is known to be based on observing the collective behavior of decentralized and self-organized systems, such as ant colonies, schools of fish, or swarms of bees or birds. Thanks to their pheromone communication, ants are able to solve complex tasks by simple local means. There is only indirect interaction between individuals through modifications of the environment, such as pheromone traces, which are used to efficiently search for algorithms based on artificial intelligence that should mimic the functions of the immune system, which shows perfect learning and memory abilities [132].

5.3.2 CELLULAR SIGNALING NETWORKS

The term signaling describes interactions between individual signaling molecules [133]. This type of communication is also known as signaling pathways [133,134]. It represents a very efficient and specific communication within the cells. In such communication, the signal from the extracellular source is transmitted through the cell membrane. Within the target cell, as a consequence of the received signal, complex signaling cascades occur through which information is further transmitted (signal transduction), which ultimately leads to the expression of certain genes or a change in the activity of the corresponding enzymes. This is how the cellular response is defined, which then follows. In addition to intracellular communication, there is also intercellular communication, in which cells can communicate through molecules of the cell surface, which can be defined as a set of nanomachines, which communicate with each other and share information to achieve a common goal. Nano-networks allow nanomachines to communicate harmoniously and share any type of information, such as smell, taste, light, or any chemical state to accomplish specific tasks. According to such settings, nanomachines can be categorized into two types: one that mimics existing electro-mechanical machines, and the other that mimics natural nano-machines, such as molecular motors and receptors [133,134].

Due to the nanoscale size of nano-machines, traditional wireless communication with radio waves cannot be used to communicate with each other, since some nano-machines may consist of only a few moles of atoms or molecules and are only a few nanometers in size. That is why their possible architectural elements and the mechanisms of their communication, which take place at the molecular level, are extremely interesting. It is clear that many biological entities in organisms have similar structures with nano-machines, or cells, and similar mechanisms of interaction and vital processes, such as cell signaling [129], with nano-networks. In the cells of living organisms, nano-machines are present that function as molecular motors, such as dynein, myosin [135], whereby they achieve intracellular communication through chemical energy transformation. It is known that the basic communication mechanism of cellular signaling is based on the transmission or reception of a certain type of molecule, ie on molecular communication, which is the most promising communication mechanism in the application of nanonetworks. Such communication between biological entities takes place through the ligand receptor binding mechanism, so that, for example, in the biological endocrine system, glandular cells emit hormones into the intercellular environment; after which the hormone molecules diffuse into the appropriate cells. This type of interaction is converted by the corresponding cells into biologically important information [125].

5.3.3 MOLECULAR CELLULAR NETWORKS IN MEDICINE

Great attention has been paid to molecular communication because they represent an alternative approach to electromagnetic communications due to their unique characteristics of biocompatibility and minimal invasiveness, which are extremely important for application in medicine. Such communication involves the use of relatively small molecules, which in addition to hormones, include other small proteins (eg cytokines), peptides, carbohydrates, lipids and combinations thereof, which can be used to transmit information. Today, by imitating such structures, chemists have succeeded in artificially realizing some of the cellular components, such as artificial ribosomes, which can be used for artificial protein synthesis [7,8].

5.3.4 BIOCYBER INTERFACE AND INTERNET OF BIO-NANO THINGS

The concept of the Internet of Bio-Nano Things (IoBNT) aims to establish a link between biological nanomachines and cyber Internet to exchange information. Numerous studies have focused on the efficiency of communication between nano-devices in a given network, as well as the issues of IoBNT security of interface connections between the nanonetwork and the Internet. Particularly challenging are biocyber interfaces, in IoBNT. The proposed chaotic system is based on a command signal coming from medical personnel to a biocyber device embedded in the human body. IoBNT is a special version of the Internet Nanothings (IoNT) that involves the use of embedded computer nano-devices inside the body [136]. In addition, the new concept of IoNT and IoBNT includes communication between nano devices, which are interconnected via the Internet [137]. Molecular communication (MC), is a promising new mechanism because it involves the use of biochemical signals to exchange information between natural and artificial machines with bio-nanoscales over short distances. Therefore, MC is increasingly used in the field of nanomedicine, bioengineering and environmental safety [138,139].

Such a design can allow drug particles to be delivered, as drug molecules are information carriers, to a communication channel formed by a network of blood vessels, while the receiver is represented by target tissue nanodevices, which can be used as analytical and imaging tools, biochemical sensors and tissue engineering for tissue repair and reengineering in vivo; Thus, it is possible to improve the diagnosis, monitoring and treatment of the disease [138,139]. In nano-networks inside the body, the number of such biological nano-devices is measured in millions. The concept of IoBNT is based on the need to improve a given nanonetwork and to ensure smooth coordination communication between it and nano devices connected to other networks, or macroscopic networks such as the Internet.

Through the IoBNT system, such nano devices would be suitable for performing some simple tasks, such as the detection, storage and release of synthesized molecules [138–140]. It is clear that there are a number of challenges facing the engineering and implementation of practical IoBNT. These challenges include the design and development of nanodevices, the coordination of molecular communication within the nano-network, and the connection of the interface between the nano-network and the Internet. The model of such a system consists of the following seven units: Internet, access point, wireless channel, device with encrypted biocyber interface, blood vessel channel, extracellular channel and target cells.

To ensure that the binary code that the medical staff sends to the biocyber interface, it is necessary to use the encryption technique. This procedure involves modeling from a wireless channel to a blood vessel channel via an encrypted biocyber interface device, as well as modeling from blood vessels to a target cell via an extracellular channel [138–140].

5.3.5 CENTRIC MATRIX NANO-NETWORKING

The combination of nano communication within the body with the Internet of Things (IoT) as the Internet of Nano Things (IoNT), enables a wide range of new applications, especially in the biomedical domain. One of the most complex research challenges in the functional sense of designing such networks is addressing and naming nodes in a nano network.

Since the location is key information for medical application, the focus of the disease needs to be reported as precisely as possible, and treatment must also be carried out at a specific location. Therefore, it is necessary that nano machines in the network have location awareness to act accordingly. Communication must be reliable enough to ensure successful message transmission. It must take place in real time. For surgical procedures in the body, biocompatible communication is necessary because the communication itself must not harm or disturb the biological balance in the human body [141].

Given that traditional electromagnetic communication suffers from additional attenuation compared to airborne transmission, such communication would direct orders to the nano network within the body, and sensor data from the nano network, which would be received by the body would be directed outwards to the analysis and control of the cells. For molecular communication, the device needs to have a direct connection to the same medium that nano machines use (such as the bloodstream) to send and receive messages. Such a device would be an implant or at least have a connection port, such as a receiver [142,143].

To be distributed throughout the body or the desired area, such devices need to use one type of signaling molecules. In addition to addressing nano machines to fulfill the task, we can reprogram cells in the target area to suit our purpose by changing cell behavior. This may be possible by gene delivery [142]. Message information is encoded in DNA and a micro or macro device, which directs it to the target area by active or passive transport. To prevent degradation of the DNA content, the message should be in the medium, which provides the complex protection [38] that is an integral part of the network layer packet. Upon reaching the desired cell or any other cell that can bind the packet to the appropriate receptor, the given cell takes over the contents of the packet. At the target site, DNA changes the cell nucleus, and thus the behavior of the cell itself, changing the lines of protein production until the cell is reset through mitosis [141–143].

5.3.6 NANONETWORKS INSIDE HUMAN BODY

The human body is a massive molecular communication network consisting of billions of interactive nanomachines, or cells. Biological systems within the body are closely interconnected and communicate primarily through molecular information packets, so that vital activities within the human body are regulated by the communication performance and operations of molecular nano-networks within the body [144,145].

A special challenge in the design of nanomachines is their physical characteristics, such as the dimensions of nanomachines, scarce memory, efficiency of information processing and their working environment. Several communication assumptions are at play when considering the use of nanonets, among which the most promising is molecular communication, in which molecules are used to encode, transmit, and receive information. The human body is a large heterogeneous communication network consisting of billions of interactive nanomachines, ie cells, whose functionalities primarily depend on nanoscale molecular communications. Thus, the vitality of the human body directly depends on the performance, reliability and continuous functioning of molecular nano-networks within the body [144,145].

It is known that human biological systems are interconnected and that they communicate primarily through molecular transactions. For example, the nervous system is an extremely large communication network of nerve cells (neurons), transmits an external stimulus to the brain, and enables communication between different systems by transmitting information using a molecular impulse signal, known as a spike. The heart is a nano-network of muscle cells (cardiomyocytes), in which information is transmitted through cardiac electrical impulses, or action potentials, through molecular communication channels. The endocrine system is a network of glands that provides communication between cells through specific molecular information carriers (hormones).), and regulates the concentration of molecules within the body [144,146,147].

The network of molecular nano-networks within the body functions to maintain equilibrium, ie. homeostasis, within the human body. Any failure in communication and damage that cannot be repaired in time leads to disease. Thus, damage to the communication abilities of neurons leads to multiple sclerosis (MS), excessive production and transfer of action potentials lead to tachycardia, or excessive heart rhythm, while insufficient secretion and transfer of insulin, or inability of cells to respond to endocrine molecular information (insulin) leads to diabetes.

The identification of existing mechanisms of molecular communication within the body, as well as the establishment of information-theoretical bases related to it, will be a significant step towards the development of real applicable architectures and communication techniques for new applications of nano-networks. Therefore, the introduction of molecular communication models leads to an understanding of their communication, network and information capabilities and contributes to the development of ICT-inspired solutions for certain diseases., as well as some other communication processes, such as cellular signaling pathways [146] of protein interaction networks [147], gene regulatory networks [148] and approaches to DNA processing [149], especially from the point of view of medical and computer biology.

The channels of molecular communication within the body work together to accomplish complex vital activities. In addition to the coexistence of these systems, each of them consists of a communication network of molecular cell structures that aim to perform certain biological tasks. This is achieved through the molecular transmission of information through molecular ion channels or by transduction of the action potential in the process of signaling to target cells. The molecular nanonetwork consists of three main functional blocks, which consist of a transmitter, an information transmission channel and a receiver, which should have a satisfactory efficiency of emission, propagation and signal reception.

Molecular information coding mechanism, e.g. the molecular concentration and type of molecules responsible for the action potential of the membrane of a given cell depend on the patency of the molecular communication channel, the amplitude and velocity of electrochemical impulses (spikes) in the neuro-spikes communication channel. A typical mechanism for receiving information between living cells is based on the process of ligand-receptor binding [140], in which molecules arriving in the nanomachine of the receiver collide and bind to a specific receptor of the receiver

There are three main nano-dimensional molecular communication channels in the body: (i) the neuro-spike communication channel, (ii) the action potential-based molecular communication cardiomyocyte channel, and (iii) the hormonal molecular communication channel. As it is already known, the neural nano-network is composed of ganglia, ie nerve cells as network nodes. This network is responsible for gathering information from different parts of the body, processing it and generating the necessary body response. This network is distributed throughout the body and extends to the extremities [150].

Neurons are nerve cells that can be excited by electricity and are able to store, process and transmit information through chemical and electrical signaling mechanisms. They are nano transceivers of the neural network. They work by receive signals from other neurons or sensory cells, causing a change in the electrical polarization of the membrane. The electric potential spreads along the cell body and combines at the base of the axon, causing the creation of action potentials, which is then transmitted through the axon and reaches its branches, where the neuron interfaces with other neurons, i.e., between postsynaptic and presynaptic cells [150], where cellular signals are generated [141]. Action potentials, ie spikes or impulses, are used to transfer information from one neuron to another.

There are mainly two different types of synapses, the electrical and the chemical synapse [151]. An electrical synapse is a mechanical and electrically conductive connection that aw makes in a narrow gap between two neurons, a presynaptic and a postsynaptic neuron. Despite the loss of amplitude in the transmitted signal, it conducts nerve impulses faster compared to the chemical synapse. Generally, electrical impulses can be transmitted in both directions [151]. Unlike electrical synapses, chemical synapses are specialized connections through which signals are transmitted from neurons to other neurons and non-neuronal cells. Chemical synapses allow neurons to form communication pathways within CNN, thus allowing the neural network to communicate and control other networks in the body, which are crucial for biological calculations. The nerve impulse causes the release of neurotransmitters, that is, a change in the action potential, resulting in an unusually rapid process of cell secretion. Neuro-spike communication between one presynaptic neuron and one postsynaptic neuron includes the axonal and synaptic phases, and finally the spike generation phase [151].

There are two main sources of shima in neurospic communication, axonal and synaptic noise. The heart, which serves both as a source, ie a transmitter, and as a destination, ie a receiver, for the cardiovascular network, can be modeled as a transceiver of the communication system of the whole body. On the other hand, hormones can be viewed as modulated carriers of information about the molecular endocrine network. In doing so, the endocrine glands are controlled by a neural network. When this is signaled by cellular receptors, the glands secrete certain hormones (chemical transporters) directly into the blood vessels, since the endocrine glands do not have their own channels. The secreted hormone targets a specific tissue and directs it to produce a specific substance [152]. According to the ability to diffuse through the cell membrane of the receiver, hormones can be divided into two groups: hormones that are soluble in lipids, such as steroids and can diffuse across the membrane and which can directly transmit a message, ie stimulate or inhibit certain regions of DNA. In contrast, lipid-insoluble hormones cannot penetrate the cell membrane on their own, and they need additional messengers to transmit the message to the cytoplasm of the target cell [143,152].

The neural nano network is essentially a large network of nano-transceivers, ie neurons, which cover the whole body. It is divided into two main subnets: the central neural network (CNN) and the peripheral neural network (PNN). CNN integrates sensory input information and provides motor output to effector cells, i.e., muscle cells and glandular cells. It is the main processor of the body. PNN is grouped into two parts: the somatic neural subnet (SoNS) and the autonomic neural subnet (ANS). ANS transmits the motor outputs generated by CNN to muscles and glands via motor neurons, to smooth muscle, heart muscle, and gland [150]. Therefore PNN represents a kind of Internet in the human body. ANS consists of two subnets: the sympathetic neural subnet (SNS) and the parasympathetic neural subnet (PSNS). The SNS controls most internal organs, nervous and hormonal stress and communicates directly with the cardiovascular and endocrine networks. PSNS is a center for preserving and recovering the body's energy, unlike the SNS network, which uses that energy through its constant activity [150–153].

The sympathetic subnet requires quick responses, while the parasympathetic subgroup has activities that do not require an immediate response. Finally, the brain, which is made up of complex synaptic connections of interconnected neurons to CNN, also possesses the neural communication network itself as the main processor and memory for information coming from all other networks within the human body and controlling their activity. It acts as a large-scale intra-network switch that mediates between different networks within us and collects sensor inputs for further processing in CNN, Delivering motor outputs through the spinal cord, it communicates with the rest of the internal Internet different forest sources. These are sensations at the sensory level and at the cellular level, in addition to the axonal and synaptic noises that are characteristic of a channel with nano-scale dimensions of neuro-spikes. Sensory noise is noise in sensory signals and sensory receptors. It limits the amount of information available to other areas of CNN. Cellular noise (C) is conditioned by the variability of the neurons themselves. Finally, synaptic noise (V) is the result of biochemical processes that underlie synaptic information transfer [150–153].

5.3.7   MOLECULAR COMMUNICATIONS AMONG BIOLOGICAL NANOMACHINES

It is important to note that bio-nanomachines consist of biological materials (proteins, nucleic acids, lipids, biological cells) with or without the addition of non-biological materials (magnetic particles). In addition, the size of bio-nanomachines varies from the size of macromolecules to the size of a bio-logical cell, although cells have a size that is significantly larger than nano-dimensions (1–100 nm). Complementary DNA sequence in the environment and cuts and releases a segment of the DNA sequence by enzymes, a protein motor capable of binding to a particular type of molecule [154], a liposome capable of taking over and/or releasing certain types of molecules, genetically modified cells capable of detecting whether a particular type of molecule in its environment is within a given concentration range, as well as biological cells functionalized with non-biological materials such as photosensitive polymers and magnetic particles [155–159].

The layered architecture of molecular communication implies the decomposition of large-scale systems into a set of smaller units (layers) functionally independent of each other, with a specific interaction between the layers. This enables better functionality of the communication system within a given communication range, while the molecular network layer enables communication over longer distances. The molecular transport layer enables end-to-end communication functionality, while the application layer provides functionality for a given type of application, etc. [160,161].

Nanomechanical memory is a physical component that is realized in the form of biochemical conditions (Ca ion concentration or pH value) in its internal environment or within its own three-dimensional structure. For example, a bio-nanomachine may be either in a state in which its Ca ion concentration increases or decreases, or its pH level is high or low, or its three-dimensional structure is functional or non-functional, thus expressing its 1-bit memory. After that, the biological cell can start the exocytosis of connexin (a protein that is present in the ion channels), which will cause the closure of the corresponding channel in case of detection of increased Ca levels. Many proteins must be assembled into the most energetically favorable conformation of proteins, in order to perform various biochemical functions, while DNA must change its shape from zipped (compacted form) to non-zipped form to begin DNA replication or transcription [159–161].

The storage of molecules is usually provided through vesicles or liposomes, which are built into the construction of a bio-nanomachine for storing molecules. Bio-nanomachines process given molecules through biochemical reactions and/or through changes in the conformation of the molecule it stores or the molecules that are in its environment. An actuator is a physical component that a bio-nanomachine uses for its spontaneous and active movement, consuming energy, in the form of a protein flagellin and a rotary motor to move the flagellum, similar to bacteria, while an identifier allows identifying bio-nanomachines or groups of bio-nanomachines, most often shit heir location [159–161].

5.3.8   CELL MATRIX DESIGN AND NANOCOMPUTING

Great effort has been invested in the development of atomic scale switches and the construction of computers from atomic scale components. They have been proposed as optimal constructions of physically homogeneous, undifferentiated hardware that later, after production, differentiates into different digital circuits. This enables the realization of a specific central process unit and memory architecture using atomic scale switches, and the construction of a corresponding digital circuit, using the same production process. The cell matrix is based on one atomic unit, the so-called cell, which is constantly repeated thus forming a multidimensional matrix of cells. In this way, it is possible to build systems that use many more rows of components than in the past. Such a remarkable expansion of physical hardware enables numerous innovations in computer architecture. In particular, control structures and processes must be developed so that an extremely large amount of components can operate in a synchronized and productive manner [162].

The architecture of such a cell matrix uses extremely fine-grained reconfigurable process elements called cells, in a simple interconnection topology. The design of the cell is simple and uniform throughout the matrix. Computational complexity is related to the need for subsequent programming of cells, not because of their hardware definition. The word "cell" refers to the units from which the Cell Matrix hardware is made. Nodes in the network correspond to individual cells, and the network-to-cell interconnections. Each cell has the ability to perform simple logic functions on its inputs and create outputs. The set of possible logic functions includes typical integration logic functions of small scale, NAND, KSOR, etc. For example, a four-sided cell is capable of implementing over 1,019 different functions with its four inputs, and hexagonal and over 10,115 functions [162,163].

The small memory contained in a cell is used to specify a logical function. This memory block functions as a machine code of the central processing unit, which dictates the full range of the cell's response at the input. In this way, the region of the cell matrix is "configured" to behave as a specific circuit because the memory block of each cell is configured to perform some of the operations from the total set of operations of the larger circuit [162,163].

The answer to the question of how in a cell matrix each cell becomes a certain part of the circuit is very important, that is, how the memory blocks of cells are set up or configured. Cells are twofold in interpreting incoming information. When a cell responds to inputs based on its cell configuration, it operates in combinatorial mode, or data processing mode, as a combinatorial logic block. An additional mode, called modification mode, allows a cell to interpret incoming information/bits as new code for its memory block. If all C inputs are 0, the cell is in combinatorial mode but if any of its C inputs are 1, the cell is in modification mode [162,163].

The investigations which joined artificial intelligence with smart health care, brain function through brain-computer interface with external artificial intelligence and influence of the development of synthetic biology joined with artificial intelligence and brain-computer interface on the future evolution and healing of various diseases, are described in our previous references [164–169]. Particularly, the energetic approach dedicated to the future development of artificial intelligence to the cells physical functions is described in the reference [169], and briefly discussed in the reference [164].

5.4   CONCLUSION

Molecular communication has been a promising field for nanoscale communication applications, and state-of the-art technology enables the production of nanomachines, i.e., simple nano devices capable of a wide range of tasks, especially for ICT and nanomedicine applications. Human body itself has never been predicated on a resource for ICT field although it houses different kinds of communication channels, and nanonetworks of sensory, signaling and molecular pathways. Besides, the overall internal network, which we term as human internal Internet in this article, supports the integrity of all biological systems by various controlling mechanisms through communication of molecules and signals, as information carriers. In brief, investigation of the fundamental intra-body communication paths, and their role in providing the integrity of all biological systems through nanonetwork relations broadens the contributions and promotes the development of ICT field.

REFERENCES

1. Bayda S., Adeel M., Tuccinardi T, Cordani M., Rizzolio F, (2020) The history of nanoscience and nanotechnology: From chemical–physical applications to nanomedicine, *Molecules* 25, (112), 1–15.

2. Jokanović V, (2012) *Nanomedicine, the Greatest Challenge of 21th century, Monograph*, (830 pages), Data Status, Beograd.

3. Jokanović V, (2013) *How Died and Lives Our Cells, Monograph*, (p. 530), Institute of Nuclear Science Vinča, Beograd.

4. Sauvage JP, (2016) *From Chemical Topology to Molecular Machines*, Nobel Lecture.

5. Balzani V, Credi A, Raymo FM, Stoddart JF, (2000) Artificial molecular machines, *Angew. Chem. Int. Ed.* 39, (19), 3348–3301.

6. Pease AR, Jeppesen JO, Stoddart JF, Luo Y, Collier CP, (2001) Heath switching devices based on interlocked molecules, *Acc. Chem. Res.* 34, (6), 433–444.

7. Li J, Ávila BEF, Gao W, Zhang L, Wan J, (2017) Micro/nanorobots for biomedicine: Delivery, surgery, sensing, and detoxification, *Sci. Rob.* 2, (4), 1–15.

8. Roco MC, (2007) *National Nanotechnology Initiative - Past, Present, Future, Handbook on Nanoscience, Engineering and Technology*, 2nd ed., Taylor and Francis.

9. U.S. House Testimony of Richard E. Smalley, (1999) http://www.house.gov/science/smalley_062299.html.

10. Roco MC, (2004) *National Nanotechnology Investment in the FY, 2004 Budget Request*, AAAS Report XXVIII: Research & Development FY.

11. (2003) *RB-162 Biomedical Applications of Nanoscale Devices*, Business Communications Company, Inc., Norwalk, CT.

12. Simpson RL, Wiria FE, Amis AA, Chua CK, Leong KF, Hansen UN, (2008) Development of a 95/5 poly(L-lactide-co-glycolide)/hydroxylapatite and beta-tricalcium phosphate scaffold as bone replacement material via selective laser sintering, *J. Biomed. Mater. Res. B* 84B, 17–25.

13. Collins PG., Arnold MS., Avouris P, (2001) Engineering carbon nanotubes and nanotube circuits using electrical breakdown, *Science* 292, 706–709.

14. Tour JM, (2003) *Molecular Electronics: Commercial Insights, Chemistry, Devices, Architecture and Programming*, World Scientific, Singapore.

15. Stupp SI, Le Bonheur V, Walker K, Li LS, Huggins KE, Keser M, Amstutz A, (1997) Supramolecular materials: Self-organized nanostructures, *Science* 276, 384–389.

16. Saitou K, Jakiela M, (1996) On classes of one-dimensional self-assembling automata, *Complex Syst.* 10, 391–416.

17. Griffith SC., Owens I.PF, Thuman KA, (2002) Extra pair paternity in birds: A review of interspecific variation and adaptive function, *Mol. Ecol.* 11, 2195–2212.

18. Penrose LS, (1959) Sekf-reproducing machines, *Sci. Amer.* 200, 105–114.

19. Brittain ST, Schueller OJA., Wu H, Whitesides S, Whitesides GM, (2001) Microorigami: Fabrication of small, three-dimensional, metallic structures, *J. Phys. Chem. B* 105, 347–350.

20. Wendel JA, Smith SS, (1998) Uracil as an alternative to 5-fluorocytosine in addressable protein targeting, *Nanotechnology* 9, 297–304.

21. Drexler KE, (1994) Molecular nanomachines: Physical principles and implementation strategies, *Annu. Rev. Biophys. Biomol. Struct.* 23, 377–405.

22. Seeman NC, (1999) DNA engineering and its application to nanotechnology, *Trends Biotechnol.* 17, 437–443.

23. Alberti P, Mergny JL, (2003) DNA duplex–Quadruplex exchange as the basis for a nanomolecular machine. *Proc. Natl. Acad. Sci.* 100, 1569–1573.

24. von Kiedrowski G, Eckardt LH, Naumann K, Pankau WM, Reimold M, Rein M, (2003) Toward replicatable, multifunctional, nanoscaffolded machines. A chemical manifesto, *Pure Appl. Chem.* 75, (5), 609–619.

25. Seeman NC, (1999) Synthetic DNA topology, in Jean-Pierre Sauvage, C. Dietrich-Buchecker, eds., *Molecular Catenanes, Rotaxanes and Knots*, Wiley-VCH Verlagsgesellschaft Mbh, Weinheim, 323–356.

26. Cramer P, Bushnell DA, Kornberg RD, (2001) Structural basis of transcription: RNA polymerase II at 2.8 Ångstrom resolution, *Science* 292, 1863–1876.

27. Freitas RA Jr. NIH Roadmap (2003) *Nanomedicine*. Bethesda: National Institutes of Health.

28. Kessler N, Perl-Treves D, Addadi L, (1996) Monoclonal antibodies that specifically recognize crystals of dinitrobenzene, *FASEB J.* 10, 1435–1442.

29. Ozgur U, Seker S, Demir HV, (2011) Material binding peptides for nanotechnology, *Molecules* 16, (2), 1426–1451.

30. Dagani R, (2000) Molecular magic with microwaves, *Chem. Eng. News* 78, (6), 25–33.

31. Kowshik M, Deshmukh N, Vogel W, Urban J, Kulkarni SK, Paknikar KM, (2002) Microbial synthesis of semiconductor CdS nanoparticles, their characterization, and their use in the fabrication of an ideal diode. *Biotechnol. Bioeng.* 78, 583–588.

32. Naik RR, Stringer SJ, Agarwal G, Jones SE, Stone MO, (2002) Biomimetic synthesis and patterning of silver nanoparticles, *Nat. Mater.* 1, 169–172.

33. Elowitz MB, Leibler S, (2000) A synthetic oscillatory network of transcriptional regulators, *Nature* 403, 335–338.

34. Gardner TS, Cantor CR, Collins JJ, (2000) Construction of a genetic toggle switch in Escherichia coli, *Nature* 403, 339–342.

35. Klarreich E, (2003) Digital cells, computer circuits made of genes may soon program bacteria *Sci. News* 163 10, 267–268.

36. Hamad-Schifferli K, Schwartz JJ, Santos AT, Zhang S, Jacobson JM, (2002) Remote electronic control of DNA hybridization through inductive coupling to an attached metal nanocrystal antenna, *Nature* 415, 152–155.

37. Kim TH, Cho KS, Lee EK, Lee SJ, Chae J, Kim JW, Kim DH, Kwon JY, Amaratunga G, Lee SY, Choi BL, Kuk Y, Kim JM. Kim K, (2011) Full-colour quantum dot displays fabricated by transfer printing, *Nature Photon.* 5, 176–182.

38. Soong RK, Bachand GD, Neves HP, Olkhovets AG, Craighead HG, Montemagno CD, (2000) Powering an inorganic nanodevice with a biomolecular motor, *Science* 290, 1555–1558.

39. Lee SW., Mao C., Flynn CE, Belcher AM, (2002) Ordering of quantum dots using genetically engineered viruses, *Science* 296, 892–895.

40. Zyvex Corp., http://www.zyvex.com.

41. Martel S, (2000) *Introduction to the NanoWalker: A Miniature Autonomous Robot Capable of Various Tasks at the Molecular and Atomic Scales.* MIT Bioinstrumentation Laboratory.

42. Kim P, Lieber CM, (1999) Nanotube nanotweezers, *Science* 286, 2148–2150.

43. Boggild P, Hansen TM, Tanasa C, Grey F, (2001) Fabrication and actuation of customized nanotweezers with a 25 nm gap, *Nanotechnology* 12, 331–335.

44. Hla SW, Rieder KH, (2002) Engineering of single molecules with a scanning tunneling microscope tip, *Superlattices Microstruct.* 31, 63–72.

45. Desai TA, Chu WH, Tu JK, Beattie GM, Hayek A, Ferrari M, (1998) Microfabricated immunoisolating biocapsules, *Biotechnol. Bioeng.* 57, 118.–120.

46. Leoni L, Desai TA, (2001) Nanoporous biocapsules for the encapsulation of insulinoma cells: Biotransport and biocompatibility considerations, *IEEE Trans. Biomed. Eng.* 48, 1335–1341.

47. Tao SL, Desai TA, (2003) Microfabricated drug delivery systems: From particles to pores, Adv. *Drug Deliv. Rev.* 55, 315–328.

48. Ahmed A, Bonner C, Desai TA, (2002) Bioadhesive microdevices with multiple reservoirs: A new platform for oral drug delivery, *J. Controlled Release* 81, 291–306.

49. Martin C. R., Kohli P., (2003) The emerging field of nanotube biotechnology, *Nat. Rev. Drug Discov.* 2, 29–37.

50. Lee SB, Mitchell DT, Trofin L, Nevanen TK, Soderlund H, Martin CR, (2002) Antibody-based bio-nanotube membranes for enantiomeric drug separations, *Science* 296, 2198–2200.

51. Meller A, Nivon L, Brandin E, Golovchenko J, Branton D, (2000) Rapid nanopore discrimination between single polynucleotide molecules, *Proc. Natl. Acad. Sci.* 97, 1079–1084.

52. Meller A., Nivon L., Branton D., (2001) Voltage-driven DNA translocations through a nanopore, *Phys. Rev. Lett.* 86, 3435–3438.

53. Li J., Stein D., McMullan C., Branton D., Aziz MJ, Golovchenko J.A, (2001) Nanoscale Ion beam sculpting, *Nature* 412, 166–177.

54. Deamer DW, Akeson M, (2000) Nanopores and nucleic acids: Prospects for ultrarapid sequencing, *Trends Biotechnol.* 18, 147–151.

55. Shi H., Ratner BD, (2000) Template recognition of protein-imprinted polymer surfaces, *J. Biomed. Mater. Res.* 49, 1–11.

56. Bruggeman FJ, Bakker BM, Hornberg JJ, Westerhoff HV, (2006) Introduction to computational models of biochemical reaction networks, *Comput. Syst. Biol.* 127–148.

57. Quantum Dot Corp., http://www.qdots.com/.

58. Wu X., Liu H., Liu J., Haley KN, Treadway JA, Larson JP, Ge N, Peale F, Bruchez MP, (2003) Immunofluorescent labeling of cancer marker Her2 and other cellular targets with semiconductor quantum dots, *Nat. Biotechnol.* 21, 41–46.

59. Medintz IL, Clapp AR, Mattoussi H, Goldman ER, Fisher B, Mauro JM, (2003) Self-assembled nanoscale biosensors based on quantum dot FRET donors, *Nat. Mater.* 2, 830–838.
60. Paunesku T., Rajh T., Wiederrecht G., Maser J., Vogt S., Stojicevic N., Protic M., Lai B., Oryhon J., Thurnauer M., Woloschak G., (2003) Biology of TiO2–oligonucleotide nanocomposites, *Nat. Mater.* 2, 343–346.
61. Zhu Z, Schuster DI, Tuckerman ME, (2003) Molecular dynamics study of the connection between flap closing and binding of fullerene-based inhibitors of the HIV-1 protease, *Biochemistry* 42, 1326–1333.
62. Dugan LL, Lovett E, Cuddihy S, Ma B, Lin T-S, Choi DW, (2000) *Fullerenes: Chemistry, Physics, and Technology* in K. M. Kadish, R. S. Ruoff, eds., Wiley, New York, 467.
63. Huang YY, Sharma SK, Yin R, Agrawal T, Chiang LY, Hamblin MR, (2014) Functionalized fullerenes in photodynamic therapy, *J. Biomed. Nanotechnol.* 10, (9), 1918–1936.
64. West JL, Halas NJ, (2000) Applications of nanotechnology to biotechnology: Commentary, *Curr. Opin. Biotechnol.* 11, 215–217.
65. Sershen SR, Westcott SL, Halas NJ, West JL, (2000) Temperature-sensitive polymer–nanoshell composites for photothermally modulated drug delivery, *J. Biomed. Mater. Res.* 51, 293–298.
66. Zimmerman SC, Wendland MS, Rakow NA, Zharov I., Suslick KS, (2002) Synthetic hosts by monomolecular imprinting inside dendrimers, *Nature* 418, 399–403.
67. Hirsch LR, Jackson JB, Lee A., Halas NJ, West, (2003) A whole blood immunoassay using gold nanoshells, *Anal. Chem.* 75, 2377–2382.
68. Subramani K, Hosseinkhani H, Khraisat A, Hosseinkhani M, Pathak Y, (2009) Targeting nanoparticles as drug delivery systems for cancer treatment, *Curr. Nanosci.* 5, 135–140.
69. Nam JM, Thaxton CS, Mirkin CA, (2003) Nanoparticle-based bio–bar codes for the ultrasensitive detection of proteins, *Science* 301, 1884–1886.
70. Robbins DH, Margulies I, Stetler-Stevenson M, Kreitman R, (2000) Hairy cell leukemia, a B-cell neoplasm that is particularly sensitive to the cytotoxic effect of anti-tac(Fv)-PE38 (LMB-2), *J. Clin. Cancer Res.* 6, 693–700.
71. Schnell R, Borchmann P, Staak JO, Schindler J, Ghetie V, Vitetta ES, Engert A, (2003) Clinical evaluation of ricin A-chain immunotoxins in patients with Hodgkin's lymphoma, *Ann. Oncol.* 14, 729–736.
72. Salem AK, Searson PC, Leong KW, (2003) Multifunctional nanorods for gene delivery, *Nat. Mater.* 2, 668–671.
73. McDevitt MR, Ma D, Lai LT, Simon J, Borchardt P, Frank RK, Wu K, Pellegrini V, Curcio MJ, Miederer M, Bander NH, Scheinberg DA, (2001) Tumor therapy with targeted atomic nanogenerators, *Science* 294, 1537–1540.
74. Tietze LF, Feuerstein T, Fecher A, Haunert F, Panknin O, Borchers U, Schuberth I, Alves F, (2002) Proof of principle in the selective treatment of cancer by antibody-directed enzyme prodrug therapy: The development of a highly potent prodrug, angew. *Chem. Int. Ed. Engl.* 41, 785–787.
75. Sumner JP, Aylott JW, Monson E, Kopelman R, (2002) A fluorescent PEBBLE nanosensor for intracellular free zinc, *Analyst* 127, 11–16.
76. Xu H, Yan F, Monson EE, Kopelman R, (2003) Room-temperature preparation and characterization of poly (ethylene glycol)-coated silica nanoparticles for biomedical applications, *J. Biomed. Mater. Res.* 66A, 870–879.
77. Eichman JD, Bielinska AU, Kukowska-Latallo JF, Baker, JR Jr., (2000) The use of PAMAM dendrimers in the efficient transfer of genetic material into cells, *Pharm. Sci. Technol. Today* 3, 232–245.
78. Patri AK, Majoros IJ, Baker JR Jr., (2002) Dendritic polymer macromolecular carriers for drug delivery, *Curr. Opin. Chem. Biol.* 6, 466–471.
79. Kaup R, Hove JB, Velders AH, Dendroids, (2021) Discrete covalently cross-linked dendrimer superstructures, *ACS Nano* 15, (1), 1666–1674.
80. Muthukumaran, G, Ramachandraiah, U, Samuel, DGH, (2015) Role of nanorobots and their medical applications, *Adv. Mater. Res.* 1086, 61–67.
81. Hamad-Schifferli K., Schwartz JJ, Santos AT, Zhang S, Jacobson JM, (2002) Remote electronic control of DNA hybridization through inductive coupling to an attached metal nanocrystal antennam, *Nature* 415, 152–155.
82. Zhang C, Macfarlane RJ, Young KL, Choi CHJ, Hao L, Auyeung E, Liu G, Zhou X, Mirkin CA, (2013) A general approach to DNA-programmable atom equivalents, *Nat. Mat.* 12, 741–746.
83. Service RF, (2002) Biology offers nanotechs a helping hand, *Science* 298, 2322.–2323
84. Heng JB, Ho C, Kim T, Timp R, Aksimentiev A, Grinkova YV, Sligar S, Schulten K, Timp G, (2004) Sizing DNA using a nanometer-diameter pore, *Biophys. J.* 87, 2905–291.

85. Shimoboji T, Larenas E, Fowler T, Hoffman AS, Stayton PS, (2003) Temperature-induced switching of enzyme activity with smart polymer–enzyme conjugates, *Bioconjug. Chem.* 14, 517–525.

86. Stock G, (2002) *Redesigning Humans: Our Inevitable Genetic Future*, Houghton Mifflin, Boston, MA.

87. Elcin YM, (2004) Stem cells and tissue engineering, *Biomaterials* 553, 301–316.

88. Jokanović V, Živković M, Živković S, (2021) Viruses as potential nanomachines, *Serbian Dent. J.* 68, (1), 31–38.

89. Endy D, Brent R, (2001) Modelling cellular behavior, *Nature* 409, 391–395.

90. Cello J, Paul AV, Wimmer E., (2002) Chemical synthesis of poliovirus cDNA: Generation of infectious virus in the absence of natural template, *Science* 297, 1016.–1018.

91. Klem MT, Willits D, Young M, Douglas T, (2003) 2-D array formation of genetically engineered viral cages on au surfaces and imaging by atomic force microscopy, *J. Am. Chem. Soc.* 125, 10806–10807.

92. Yamada T., Iwasaki Y., Tada H., Iwabuki H., Chuah MKL, Driessche TV, Fukuda H, Kondo A, Ueda M, Seno M, Tanizawa K, Kuroda S, (2003) Nanoparticles for the delivery of genes and drugs to human hepatocytes, *Nat. Biotechnol.* 21, 885–890.

93. Baban CK, Cronin M, O'Hanlon D, Sullivan GCO, Tangney M (2010) Bacteria as vectors for gene therapy of cancer, *Bioeng. Bugs.* 1, (6), 385–394.

94. Alberts B, Johnson A, Lewis J, Raff M, Roberts K, Walter P, (2003) Molecular biology of the cell, *Scan. J. Rhewum.* 32, (2), 125–125.

95. Mushegian AR, (1999) The minimal genome concept, *Curr. Opin. Genet. Dev.* 9, 709. 714.

96. Yue Y, Jin F, Deng R, Cai J, Dai Z, Lin CM, Kung HF, Mattebjerg MA, Andresen TL, Wu C, (2011) Revisit complexation between DNA and polyethylenimine — Effect of length of free polycationic chains on gene transfection, *J. Controlled Release* 152, 143–151.

97. Phillips JD, Gillis DJ, Hanner RH, (2019) Incomplete estimates of genetic diversity within species: Implications for DNA barcoding, *Ecol. Evol.* 9, 2996–3010.

98. Beissenhirtz, MK, Willner I, (2006) DNA-based machines, *Org. Biomol. Chem.* 4, 3392–3401.

99. Ramezani H, Dietz H, (2020) Building machines with DNA molecules, *Nat. Rev. Genet.* 21, (1), 5–26.

100. Phoenix C, Drexler E, (2004) Safe exponential manufacturing, *Nanotechnology* 15 869–872.

101. Feynman RP, 1960) There's plenty of room at the bottom, *Eng. Sci. CalTech.* 23, 22–36.

102. Drexler KE, (2001) Machine-phase nanotechnology, *Nanovisions* 74–75.

103. Cumings J, Zettl A, (2000) Low-friction nanoscale linear bearing realized from multiwall carbon nanotubes, *Science* 289, 602–604.

104. Drexler KE, (1999) Building molecular machine systems, *Nanotechnology* 17, 5–7.

105. Drexler KE, (2019) *Reframing Superintelligence Comprehensive AI Services as General Intelligence*, Technical report, Future of Humanity Institute, University of Oxford.

106. Cagin T., Jaramillo-Botero A., Gao G., Goddard III WA., (1998) Molecular mechanics and molecular dynamics analysis of Drexler–Merkle gears and neon pump, *Nanotechnology* 9, 143–152.

107. Tomalia DA, Naylor AM, Goddard WA., (1996) Starburst dendrimers: Molecular-level control of size, shape, surface chemistry, topology, and flexibility from atoms to macroscopic matte, *Angewandte. Chemie.* 29, (2), 138–175.

108. Soong RK, Bachand GD, Neves HP, Olkhovets AG, Craighead HG, Montemagno CD, (2000) Powering an inorganic nanodevice with a biomolecular moto, *Science* 290, 1555–1558.

109. Liu H, Schmidt JJ, Bachand GD, Rizk SS, Looger LL, Hellinga HW, Montemagno CD, (2002) Control of a biomolecular motorpowered nanodevice with an engineered chemical switch, *Nat. Mater.* 1, 173–177.

110. Kelly TR, De Silva H, Silva RA, (1999) Unidirectional rotary motion in a molecular system, *Nature* 401(6749), 150–152. doi: 10.1038/43639. PMID: 10490021.

111. Wang J, (2013) *Nanomachines, Fundamentals and Applications*, Willey –VCH, Werlag GmbH, Weinheim.

112. Dischler B, Wild C, eds., (1998) *Low-Pressure Synthetic Diamond: Manufacturing and Applications*. Springer, New York.

113. Jenner GJ, (1985) The pressure effect on strained transition states. Correlation between strain and volume of activation: Mechanistic and synthetic involvements, *Chem. Soc. Faraday Trans. I* 81, 2437–2460.

114. Hemley RJ, Mao HK, (1990) Critical behavior in the hydrogen insulator-metal transition, *Science* 249, 391–393.

115. Ricca A, Bauschlicher CW Jr., Kang JK, Musgrave CB, (1999) The hydrogen abstraction from a diamond (Ill) surface in a uniform electric field, *Surf. Sci.* 429, 199–209.

116. Foley ET, Kam AF, Lyding JW, Avouris PH, (1998) Cryogenic UHV-STM study of hydrogen and deuterium desorption from Si(100), *Phys. Rev. Lett.* 80, 1336–1338.

117. Walch SP, Merkle RC, (1998) Theoretical studies of diamond mechanosynthesis reactions, *Nanotechnology* 9, 285–286.

118. Sternberg MH, David A, Redfern PC, Zapol P, Curtiss LA, (2005) Theoretical studies of CN and C_2 addition to a (100)–(2×1) diamond surface: Nanocrystalline diamond growth mechanisms, *J. Comp. Theor. Nanosci.* 2, (2), 207–213.

119. Carbone A., Seeman NC, (2002) A route to fractal DNA-assembly, *Nat. Comp.* 1, 469–480.

120. Toth-Fejel T, (2000) Agents, assemblers, and ANTS: Scheduling assembly with market and biological software mechanisms, *Nanotechnology* 11, 11133–11137.

121. Lutwyche MI, Wada ., (1995) Observation of a vacuum tunnel gap in a transmission electron microscope using a micromechanical tunneling microscope, *Appl. Phys. Lett.* 66, 2807.

122. Baltes H, Brand O, Hierlemann A, Lange D, Hagleitnerm C, (2002) "CMOS MEMS – Present and future" *Technical Digest. MEMS 2002 IEEE International Conference. Fifteenth IEEE International Conference on Micro Electro Mechanical Systems (Cat. No.02CH37266)*, Las Vegas, NV, USA, 2002, pp. 459–466, doi: 10.1109/MEMSYS.2002.984302..

123. Chirikjian GS, Suthakorn J, (2002) *Proceedings of the Eighth International Symposium on Experimental Robotics (ISER '02)*, Italy.

124. Freitas RA. Jr., Merkle RC, (2004) *Kinematic Self-Replicating Machines*, Landes Bioscience, Georgetown, TX.

125. Ishiyama K, Arai KI, Sendoh M, Yamazaki A, (2000) Spiral-type micro-machine for medical applications, *MHS2000. Proceedings of 2000 International Symposium on Micromechatronics and Human Science (Cat. No.00TH8530)*, Nagoya, 65–69.

126. Requicha AAG, (2003) Nanorobots, NEMS, and nanoassembly, *Proc. IEEE* 91, (11), 1922–1923.

127. Cavalcanti A, Shirinzadeh B, Freitas RA Jr, Hogg T, (2008) Nanorobot architecture for medical target identification, *Nanotechnology* 19, 015103.

128. Dressler F, Akan OB, (2010) A survey on bio-inspired networking, *Comput. Netw.* 54, (6), 881–900.

129. Alberts B, Bray D, Lewis J, Raff M, Roberts K, Watson JD, (1994) *Molecular Biology of the Cell*, 3rd ed., Garland Publishing, Inc.

130. Welbourne W, Battle L, Cole G, Gould K, Rector K, Raymer S, Balazinska M, Borriello G, (2009) Building the internet of things using RFID, *IEEE Inter. Comput.* 33, (3), 48–55.

131. Timmis, M. Neal JH, (2000) An artificial immune system for data analysis, *Biosystems* 55 143–150.

132. Dorigo M, Maniezzo V, Colorni A, (1996) The ant system: Optimization by a colony of cooperating agents, *IEEE Trans. Syst. Man. Cybern.* 26, (1), 1–13.

133. Weng G, Bhalla US, Iyengar R, (1999) Complexity in biological signaling systems, *Science* 284, (5411), 92–96.

134. Pawson T, (1995) Protein modules and signalling networks, *Nature* 373, (6515), 573–580.

135. Bustamante C, Chelma Y, Forde N, Izhaky D, (2004) Mechanical processes in biochemistry, *Annu. Rev. Biochem.* 73, 705–748.

136. El-Fatyany A, Wang H, Abd El-atty SM, Khan M, (2020) Biocyber interface-based privacy for internet of bio-nano things, *Wirel. Pers. Commun.* 114, 1465–1483.

137. Xu X, Kim K, Li H, Fan DL, (2012) Ordered arrays of Raman nanosensors for ultrasensitive and location predictable biochemical detection, *Adv. Mater.* 24, 5457–5463.

138. Esteban-Fernández de Ávila B, Martín A, Soto F, Lopez-Ramirez MA, Campuzano S, Vásquez-Machado GM, Gao W, Zhang L, Wang J, (2015) Single cell real-time miRNAs sensing based on nano-motors, *ACS Nano* 9, 6756–6764.

139. Anker JN, Koo YE, Kopelman R, (2007) Magnetically controlled sensor swarms, *Sens. Actuators B Chem.* 121, 83–92.

140. Buck SM, Koo YE, Park L, Xu H, Philbert MA, Brasuel MA, Kopelman R, (2004) Optochemical nanosensor PEBBLEs: Photonic explorers for bioanalysis with biologically localized embedding, *Curr. Opin. Chem. Biol.* 8, 540–546.

141. Stelzner M, Dressler F, Fischer S, (2017) Function centric nano-networking: Addressing nano machines in a medical application scenario, *Nano Commun. Netw.* 14 29–39.

142. Wysocki BJ, Martin TM, Wysocki TA, Pannier AK, (2013) Modeling nonviral gene delivery as a macro-to-nano communication system, *Nano Commun. Netw.* 4, (1), 14–22.

143. Crook K, McLachlan G, Stevenson B, Porteous D, (1996) Plasmid DNA molecules complexed with cationic liposomes are protected from degradation by nucleases and shearing by aerosolisation, *Gene Ther.* 3, (9), 834–839.

144. Atakan B, Akan OB, (2010) Deterministic capacity of information flow in molecular nanonetworks, *Nano Commun. Netw. J.* 1, 31–42.

145. Malak D, Akan OB, (2012) Molecular communication nanonetworks inside human body, *Nano Commun. Netw.* 3 19–35.

146. Liu JQ, Nakano T, (2007) An information theoretic model of molecular communication based on cellular signaling, *2007 2nd Bio-Inspired Models of Network, Information and Computing Systems*, Budapest, Hungary, 316–321. doi: 10.1109/BIMNICS.2007.4610136.

147. Vázquez A, Flammini A, Maritan A, Vespignani A, (2003) Global protein function prediction in protein–protein interaction networks, *Nat. Biotechnol.* 21, 697–700.

148. Hasty J, McMillen D, Isaacs F, Collins JJ, (2001) Computational studies of gene regulatory networks: In numero molecular biology, *Nat. Rev. Gene.* 2, 268–279.

149. Fanning E, Klimovich V, Nager AR, (2006) A dynamic model for replication protein A (RPA) function in DNA processing pathways, *Nucleic Acids Res.* 34, 4126–4137.

150. Paradiso MA, Bear MF, Connors BW, (2007) *Neuroscience: Exploring the Brain*, Lippincott Williams & Wilkins.

151. Purves D, Augustine GJ, Fitzpatrick D, Hall WC, La Mantia AS, McNamara JO, (2008) *White LE, Neuroscience*, Sinauer Associates Inc.

152. Balevi E, Akan OB, (2013) A physical channel model of nanoscale neurospike communication, *IEEE Trans. Com.* 61, (3), 1178–1187.

153. Kasper DL, Braunwald E, Hauser S, Longo D, Jameson JL, Fauci AS, (2004) *Harrison's Principles of Internal Medicine*, McGraw Hill.

154. Goel A, Vogel V, (2008) Harnessing biological motors to engineer systems for nanoscale transport and assembly, *Nat. Nanotechnol.* 3, 465–475.

155. Karl H, Willig A, (2007) *Protocols and Architectures for Wireless Sensor Networks*, Wiley, Hoboken, NJ, USA.

156. Sasaki Y, Shioyama Y, Tian WJ, Kikuchi J, Hiyama S, Moritani Y, Suda T, (2010) A nanosensory device fabricated on a liposome for detection of chemical signals, *Biotechnol. Bioeng.* 105, 37–43.

157. Mukai M, Maruo K, Kikuchi J, Sasaki Y, Hiyama S, Moritani Y, Suda T, (2009) Propagation and amplification of molecular information using a photo-responsive molecular switch, *Supramol. Chem.* 21, (3–4), 284–291.

158. Basu S, Gerchman Y, Collins CH, Arnold FH, Weiss R, (2005) A synthetic multicellular system for programmed pattern formation, *Nature* 434, (2005), 1130–1134.

159. Fakhrullin RF, Zamaleeva AI, Minullina RT, Konnova SA, Paunov VN, (2012) Cyborg cells: Functionalisation of living cells with polymers and nanomaterials, *Chem. Soc. Rev.* 41, (11), 4189–4206.

160. Zimmermann H, (1980) Osi reference model—The iso model of architecture for open systems interconnection, *IEEE Trans. Commun.* 28, (4), 425–432.

161. Tanenbaum AS, (2010) *Computer Networks*, Prentice-Hall, Upper Saddle River, NJ.

162. Durbeck LJK, Macias NJ, (2001) The cell matrix: An architecture for nanocomputing, *Nanotechnology* 12, 217–230.

163. Kotb A, Zoiros KE, Guo C, (2018) All-optical XOR, NOR, and NAND logic functions with parallel semiconductor optical amplifier-based Mach-Zehnder interferometer modules, *Opt. Laser Technol.* 108, 426–433.

164. Jokanović V, (2020) Smart healthcare in smart cities, in *Towards Smart World: Homes to Cities Using Internet of Things*, 1st ed., Chap. 4. Taylor and Francis Group, 45–73.

165. Jokanović V, Jokanović B, (2021) Brain-computer interface: State of art, challenges and future, in *Artificial Intelligence Technologies, Applications, and Challenges* (paper in printing), Chap. 27, Taylor and Francis Group.

166. Jokanović V, Živković S, Živković M, (2021) State of the art of artificial intelligence in dentistry and its expected future, in *Computer Vision and Internet of Things: Technology and Applications* (paper in printing), Taylor and Francis Group,

167. Jokanović V, (2021) Synthetic biology and artificial intelligence, *Computer Vision and Internet of Things: Technology and Applications* (paper in printing), Taylor and Francis Group.

168. Jokanović V, (2016) *Bridge between Nanophysics and Alternative Medicine: A New Energetic Approach to the Human Cell Treatment and Their Healing*, LAP LAMBERT Academic Publishing.

169. Jokanović V, Živković S, Živković M, (2021) Artificial intelligence as a powerful tool in overcoming substantial health problems of the COVID-19 pandemic, *Serb. Dent.* 68, (3), 143–152.

6 A Vision-Based System in Healthcare
Use Cases and Real-Time Applications

Mukesh Carpenter
Alshifa Multispecialty Hospital

Lavanya Sharma
Amity University

Sudhriti Sengupta
Galgotias University

Abhishek Kumar
Venkateshwar Hospital

CONTENTS

DOI: 10.1201/9781003324720-8

6.1 INTRODUCTION

Over the last few years, computer vision (CV) has influenced and revolutionized most of the industries worldwide. It has tremendous real-time applications including healthcare industry. This industry is also known as one of the digital pillars of smart society, which is also known as "Society 5.0". Basically, it is a machine ability to mimic human-based vision. Techniques of CV has several applications in medical domain such as medical imaging, surgical planning and continue to acquire widespread usage [1]. In the healthcare industry, the worldwide market for CV solutions is predicted to drastically increase to $2.4 billion by 2026 from $262 million in 2019. As per Ernst & Young (EY) Limited, a Swiss company emphasizes the importance of CV and artificial intelligence (AI) technologies and considers its key role to the development of the healthcare industry [2] as shown in Figure 6.1. AI and CV technologies are accelerating the track of change in healthcare domain. Recently, visual AI strategies enabled computer systems to visualize and process the digital images and videos faster, cost effectively and accurately than any highly trained medical practitioner. CV-based systems are designed with Health Insurance Portability and Accountability Act (HIPAA) compliance in mind. This Act sets the standard for sensitive patient data protection. For security reasons, these systems can deploy on the edge. This means it runs on processor without cloud connectivity. This makes overall less vulnerable to security breaches [1,2,4–14].

In healthcare and medicine, a large amount of data are generated using sensors and digital cameras. The availability of this data from medical devices and records systems rapidly increased the potential of deep learning (DL) applications as well. This chapter provides the detailed concept of DL, AI, and CV technologies, their impact, use cases, and real-time applications in healthcare industry. This chapter also provides a brief concept of these technologies for healthcare professionals toward digital excellence [15–18].

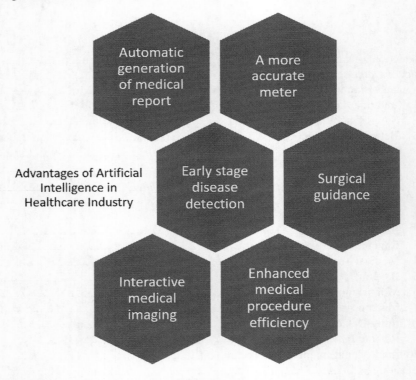

FIGURE 6.1   Advantages of artificial intelligence in healthcare industry.

6.2 IMPACT OF DEEP LEARNING AND COMPUTER VISION

DL is a sub-domain of ML and emerging as a technology over the last few years. This technology trend is driven by rapid increase in the computational powers such as GPU and parallelized computing. DL trend is also driven by the availability of a large number of new datasets. This technology brings an advancement in CV that makes systems to understand the visual data. In the case of conventional ML, expert designed feature extractors are required to develop algorithms, which can detect the data pattern. But DL is composed of various sequentially arranged layers of representations [5–10,19–28]. Machine takes input with raw data and is able to build specific representation for pattern recognition. In the case of image recognition, highly complexed functions can be learned which have very high accuracy.

6.3 COMPUTER VISION IN HEALTHCARE-USE CASES

CV mainly focuses on insight of video and images. It deals with segmentation, classifications of images, and detection of moving object. Medical Imaging (MI) is highly benefited from recent advancements of these technologies. In literature, several studies are available that show promising outcomes in case of complex medical diagnosis such as radiology, pathology, and many more. DL technology can aid clinicals by flagging the particular areas in digital images. However, convolutional neural networks (CNN) help in classifying the object present in the images. CV and AI technologies play an important and game changer role in the healthcare industry. CV technology provides several benefits to the healthcare industry [2,4,15–19,29]. Some of them are listed below:

1. Image analysis (IA)
2. Smart operation theaters (OT)
3. Better patient identification (PI)
4. Increased healthcare safety
5. Enhanced medical research (MR)
6. Tumors and cancers detection

6.3.1 IMAGING ANALYSIS (IA)

In medical Imaging (MI), CV technologies result in improvement of both accuracy and efficiency in case of recognition of hidden pattern. As per the recent studies, the visual AI systems can analyze the images more accurately as compared to the radiologist. It provides the outcomes with reducing false positive (FP) and false negative (FN) in case of breast cancer patient images, as shown in Figure 6.2. FP results are very common. While approximately 12% of 2D screening mammograms or **X-ray image of the breast** are recalled for more work-up, only 4.4% of those recalls, or 0.5% overall, conclude with a cancer diagnosis [5–12,19,21–28].

This technology can also act as another pair of "eyes" to support accurate diagnoses. This will be especially critical in the coming years as demand for medical image analysis continues to outpace the number of skilled human workers capable of providing these services. As per the recent reports, United States (U.S) Bureau of Labor Statistics estimates a 9% radiologic increasing factor and magnetic resonance imaging (MRI) technicians in the U.S by 2028. Researchers are assuming that the digital pathology market will grow by 11.8% by 2027 [15,16]. At present, their shortage of radiologic and MRI technicians, but this technology can provide benefits to the healthcare industry (i) by reducing the MI workloads, (ii) reducing labor costs, and (iii) easing the manpower shortages irrespective of high demand.

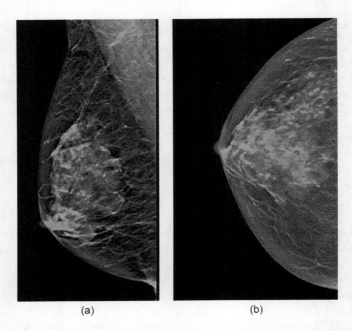

(a)   (b)

FIGURE 6.2   (a and b) Synthetic 2D images from a false positive (FP) 3D mammogram.

6.3.2 SMART OPERATION THEATRES (OT)

In electronic health record (EHR) systems, surgical nurses are required for surgical procedure documentation. CV systems can complete the task efficiently and accurately. It eliminates the requirement of manpower by observation and documentation. With this advanced technology, clinicals can provide better patient care, helps in less stress for providers, and can provide better treatment as well. In today's scenarios, all the OT are well equipped with the CV-based devices and result in prevention of any kind of error [15,16].

Smart operating rooms with this technology can also prevent errors. Zejnullahu et.al. [17] provide a detail that about 1,500 surgeries every year result in foreign object being left in patient. CV can keep track of all surgical instruments that are used in surgical procedure to avoid these situations to protect against injuries caused by so-called "retained surgical bodies" (RSBs) [10–14,30–40]. The use of CV technologies in the healthcare industry results in significantly improvement in patient care and surgical outcomes, as shown in Figure 6.3.

6.3.3 BETTER PATIENT RECOGNITION

In India, several cases are reported of mistaken patient identity in healthcare. As per the recent study by "Ponemon institute", approximately 86% cases of patient being mistaken for someone else. It is also estimated that the average hospital risks losing $17.4 million due to identification error such as personal injury or malpractice claim. If these errors not corrected at early stage, then it can be dangerous as patient can end up taking wrong medicines, treatment, and diagnosis. To overcome this issue, AI-powered facial authentication system can accurately recognize patients. AI system offers multiple-layered security and access of patient identity [1–4,15,19–24].

6.3.4 IMPROVED HEALTHCARE SECURITY

AI-empowered technology can treat related injuries and illnesses at hospital. Even they can help in patient injuries as well. In case of unavoidable conditions, AI system can send immediate alarm to

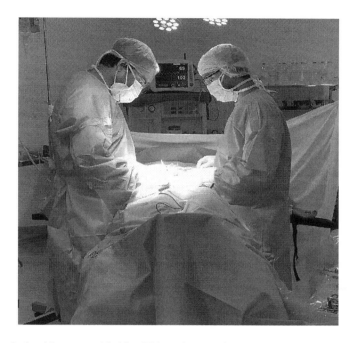

FIGURE 6.3 Surgical guidance provided by AI-based system in surgical operation theatre.

the concerned authorities. Most of the cases occur due to leniency of staff member toward safety protocols related to sterile processing [2–4,15,16,10–14,30–39]. This technology can reduce the injuries related to listed failures:

- This system accurately identifies when staff fail to use the safety equipment such as goggles, face shield, mask which can result in major issues.
- AI system accurately recognizes sterile processing malfunctioning. In case of not proper device cleaning, disinfection or sterilization, the risk of surgical site infection (SSI) increases. The SSI has 3% mortality rate and an associated annual cost of $3.3 billion. CV and AI systems can accurately detect and track whether medical staff are obeying to sterile processing protocols or not.
- At hospital, fir or smoke injuries are also of great concern. AI-based system has ability to immediately detect the subtle sign of fire or smoke. This system can also trigger an alarm to the concerned team [40–45]. Apart from this, CV and AI system can detect in case a staff member or patient falls, immediately alerting medical teams, and record the case for legal or insurance purposes, as shown in Figure 6.4.

6.3.5 ENHANCED MEDICAL RESEARCH (MR)

CV and AI-based systems for MR provide better investigation process and testing new technologies for treatment. Some of the examples are listed below:

- **Accurate Cell Counting:** According to a study on cell counting methods, 71% of 400 researchers used a hemocytometer cell counting. But this process is prone to misuse and lead to inaccurate [5,17,18,27]. CV systems can count and type cells much faster and accurately as compared to human. This technology allows medical researcher (MR) amenities to accomplish faster outcomes, as shown in Figure 6.5.

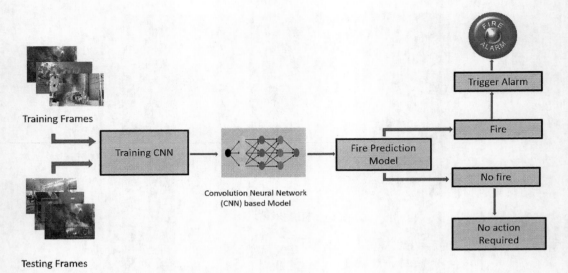

FIGURE 6.4   A convolution neural network (CNN)-based fire system for healthcare.

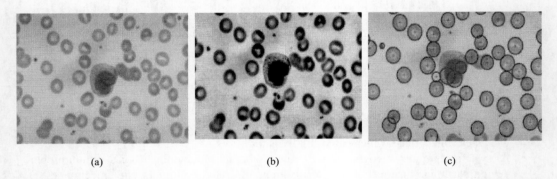

(a)   (b)   (c)

FIGURE 6.5   Detection of blood cell using Hough transformation (a) Original blood cell image (b) Contrast blood cell image (c) Detected blood cell image.

- **Accurate Cohort Detection:** MR can use visual AI systems to speeden up the visually analyzing procedure and discovering the clinical data such as in case of pediatrics asthma patients CV-based system can assist with cohort detection [2,4,8,15–18,29,39–48]. These systems provide accurate and efficient detection of cohorts as compared to traditional approaches.

6.3.6   TUMORS AND CANCERS DETECTION

CV and AI-based systems accurately and efficiently detect the brain tumors as compared to the traditional approaches or human radiologist. CV systems can also be trained with ML and DL with data of benign tumor with healthy tissues in order to detect the skin and breast cancer more accurately [16,17]. Several studies show that CV and DL-based models accurately diagnose breast cancer using ultrasonic images. Google has also created a cancer detecting app for the diagnosis of breast and skin cancer [13,29,30,36,47–58]. Accurate and location of tumor detection in MRI images plays a vital role in various diagnostic applications. Due to its high quantity data and blurred boundaries, segmentation and classification of tumor become very difficult. An MRI brain tumor image is classified and segmented using CNN network, as shown in Figure 6.6.

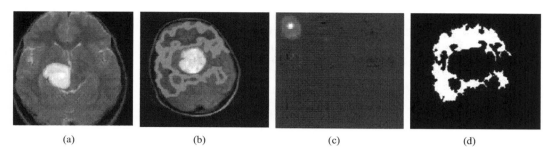

(a)   (b)   (c)   (d)

FIGURE 6.6 Classification and segmentation of MRI brain image using CNN: (a) Input image (b) Tumor area localization (c) Discrete wavelet transformation (DWT) image (d) Brain segmented image.

6.4 REAL-TIME APPLICATIONS OF AI AND CV-BASED SYSTEM

CV and AI have various innovative implications in the healthcare industry. Some of them are listed below:

6.4.1 TUMOR DETECTION

CV, AI, and DL systems have proven very beneficial in the healthcare sector, especially in brain tumors detection. If it left untreated, then it rapidly spread to other parts of the brain and spinal cord. CV and DL-based system make it possible to detect the tumor at early stage that result in patient lifesaving. Health professionals can use CV techniques such as Mask-R Convolutional Neural Networks (Mask R-CNN) to detect the tumor less time-consuming, tedious, and less chances of error.

6.4.2 MEDICAL IMAGING

CV and AI technology has been used in various healthcare sectors to assist clinicals in decision-making in the treatment of patients. Medical imaging (MI) is a technique that captures a visualization of particular body organs and tissues to enable a accurate diagnosis. With this MI analysis, it becomes convenient for clinicals and surgeons to identify the abnormalities found in the particular organ of patient image [59–63]. Some of the MI techniques used by healthcare professionals are X-ray radiography, ultrasound (USG), MRI, endoscopy, CT scan.

6.4.3 CANCER DETECTION

DL and CV model have also been used in the detection of breast cancer, lung cancer, kidney cancer, ovarian cancer, and skin cancer. For example, skin cancer can be difficult to detect at the time as the warning sign often resembles those of common skin diseases. As a remedy, researchers used CV applications to differentiate between cancerous skin lesions and non-cancerous lesions effectively. CV-based models are trained with huge datasets that consist of various benign and non-benign images of tissues; it can help in automate the detection process and reduce the chances of human error [50–56,60].

6.4.4 MEDICAL TRAINING

CV technology is also used for medical skill training purpose. Nowadays simulation-based surgical platforms have emerged as an useful medium for training and assessing the surgical skill. With this technology, surgeons are now not dependent on traditional operation theater for actual practice.

With this, surgeons get opportunity of developing their surgical skill before entering the operating room [61–66]. It allows them to have detailed feedback and assessment of their performance, and patient care before operating the patient. Surgeons can also maintain the quality of surgery using CV-based systems by calculating the activities and movement detection.

6.4.5 BATTLING COVID-19 VIRUS

This pandemic becomes a huge challenge for healthcare workers worldwide. Globally, countries are struggling with combating this virus, but in this scenario, CV plays an important role by diagnosis the lung infection at an early stage, as shown in Figure 6.7. Due to rapid advancement in CV-based technology, COVID-19 diagnosis, treatment and prevention using X-ray, USG becomes possible. The prototype application for COVID-19 diagnosis, developed by "Darwin AI" from Canada, has shown results with 92.4% accuracy. CV also used for face mask detection that helps in prevention of this disease [64–66].

6.4.6 MONITORING OF HEALTH

CV and AI technology are most widely used to monitor the health of a patient. With these analyses, clinicals can make better and accurate decision for patient in emergency cases. CV model can also measure the amount of blood loss during surgery. "Triton", developed by Gauss Surgical, is one such application that effectively monitors and calculates the amount of blood lost during surgical procedure [50–60,67]. It helps surgeons to determine the amount of blood needed by the patient during or after the surgery.

6.4.7 MACHINE-ASSISTED DIAGNOSIS

With the advancement of CV technologies in healthcare sector, it become more easier to detect ailments more accurately and efficiently. This technology has proven better than human experts in identifying pattern to spot disease with any error. It also helps clinicals to detect minor variations in tumor to identify any malignancy. By scanning medical images (MI), it provides the detection, prevention, and treatment of various diseases [56–67].

6.4.8 EARLY DETECTION OF DISEASE

In case of tumor and cancer disease, life of patient depends on the accurate and early detection and treatment. Detecting the early sign provides higher ratio of patient survival. CV systems are trained with huge amount of dataset that enables to detect even minute difference accurately.

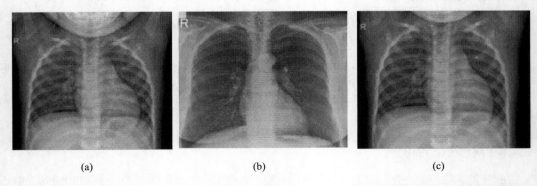

(a)   (b)   (c)

FIGURE 6.7   Radiography (x-ray) technique row-wise: (a) Normal lungs of a patient (b) Lungs of a patient infected with COVID-19 virus.

As a result, clinical professionals can identify such minute changes that can be missed with human eyes [39,49,50,62–66].

6.4.9 Remote Patient Monitoring

Several patients prefer to rehabilitate at home rather than hospital. With CV-based technologies, it becomes possible for clinicals to track their progress virtually. CV can also aid in remote monitoring of patients RPM or the elderly patient in a non-intrusive manner. Video-assisted analysis of standardized medical tests such as the TUG test (Timed Up and Go test) is another technique of patient monitoring with CV [64,66]. This system measures the time required to perform an evaluation test to measure functional mobility. The TUG test can be used to calculate the possibility of falling or the ability to keep balance while walking.

6.4.10 Lean Management in Healthcare

To minimize the chances of error, clinicals have to spend a lot of time in examining the report of a patient. But with the advancement of CV technologies, clinicals can examine the report in less time and with accurate diagnosis that overall leads to timely diagnosis and treatment of a patient. These technologies also help hospitals to have maximum value for patients by less waiting queue and disposal waste [5,38,63–66].

6.5 CONCLUSION

With the advancement of CV technologies in healthcare sector, it becomes more easier to detect ailments more accurately and efficiently. This chapter provides the detailed introduction of vision-based technologies and their impact on the healthcare industry. This chapter also provides use cases of vision-based technologies in healthcare such as image analysis, smart operation theaters, better patient identification, increased healthcare safety, enhanced medical research, and early detection and treatment of tumors and cancers. Finally, this chapter summarizes vision-based real-time applications such as disease detection, medical Imaging, medical training, battling with COVID-19, regular health monitoring, remote patient monitoring (RPM), and lean management in healthcare.

REFERENCES

1. Computer vision and AI. Available at https://viso.ai/applications/computer-vision-in-healthcare/ [accessed on 20 June 2022].
2. Computer vision and Healthcare. Available at https://www.ey.com/en_ch/ai/from-code-to-clinic-what-is-holding-healthcare-back [accessed on 20 June 2022].
3. Overview of Computer vision. Available at https://research.aimultiple.com/computer-vision-healthcare/ [accessed on 20 June 2022].
4. Computer vision and Healthcare. Available at https://www.himss.org/resources/value-computer-vision-healthcare [accessed on 20 June 2022].
5. Lavanya Sharma, Nirvikar Lohan, Performance analysis of moving object detection using BGS techniques in visual surveillance. *International Journal of Spatiotemporal Data Science, Inderscience.* 2019; 1: 22–53.
6. Akshit Anand, Vikrant Jha, Lavanya Sharma, An improved local binary patterns histograms techniques for face recognition for real time application. *International Journal of Recent Technology and Engineering.* 2019; 8(2S7): 524–529.
7. Lavanya Sharma, Dileep Kumar Yadav, Histogram based adaptive learning rate for background modelling and moving object detection in video surveillance. *International Journal of Telemedicine and Clinical Practices, Inderscience.* 2016. doi: 10.1504/IJTMCP.2017.082107.
8. Lavanya Sharma, Nirvikar Lohan, Performance analysis of moving object detection using BGS techniques. *International Journal of Spatio-Temporal Data Science, Inderscience.* 2019; 1: 22–53.

9. Lavanya Sharma, Nirvikar Lohan, Internet of things with object detection, in *Handbook of Research on Big Data and the IoT*, IGI Global, pp. 89–100, 2019. doi: 10.4018/978-1-5225–7432–3.ch006.

10. Lavanya Sharma, *Introduction: From visual surveillance to internet of things, From Visual Surveillance to Internet of Things*, Taylor & Francis, CRC Press, Vol. 1, p.14, 2019.

11. Lavanya Sharma, P.K. Garg *Block based Adaptive Learning Rate for Moving Person Detection in Video Surveillance, From Visual Surveillance to Internet of Things,* Taylor & Francis, CRC Press, Vol. 1, p. 201, 2019.

12. S. Makkar, L. Sharma. A face detection using support vector machine: challenging issues, recent trend, solutions and proposed framework. In: Singh M., Gupta P., Tyagi V., Flusser J., Ören T., Kashyap R. (eds.). *Advances in Computing and Data Sciences. ICACDS 2019. Communications in Computer and Information Science*, vol. 1046. Springer, Singapore, 2019. https://doi.org/10.1007/978-981-13-9942-8_1.

13. Lavanya Sharma, P.K. Garg *IoT and its Applications, From Visual Surveillance to Internet of Things,* Taylor & Francis, CRC Press, Vol. 1, p.29.

14. L. Sharma, D.K. Yadav, S.K. Bharti, An improved method for visual surveillance using background subtraction technique. *2015 2nd International Conference on Signal Processing and Integrated Networks (SPIN)*, pp. 421–426, 2015, doi: 10.1109/SPIN.2015.7095253.

15. Computer vision and healthcare applications. Available at Radiologic and MRI Technologists: Occupational Outlook Handbook: U.S. Bureau of Labor Statistics (bls.gov) [accessed on 20 June 2022].

16. Computer vision and AI. Available at Digital Pathology Market Size & Trends Report, 2030 (grandviewresearch.com) [accessed on 20 June 2022].

17. V.A. Zejnullahu, B.X. Bicaj, V.A. Zejnullahu, A.R. Hamza. Retained surgical foreign bodies after surgery. *Open Access Macedonian Journal of Medical Sciences.* 2017; 5(1): 97–100. doi: 10.3889/oamjms.2017.005.

18. Computer vision and IoT. Available at https://www.future-science.com/doi/pdf/10.2144/000113407 [accessed on 20 June 2022].

19. Computer vision and IoT. Available at https://health.ucdavis.edu/news/headlines/half-of-all-women-experience-false-positive-mammograms-after-10-years-of-annual-screening-/2022/03 [accessed on 20 June 2022].

20. T.M. Peters, C.A. Linte, Z. Yaniv, J. Williams. *Mixed and Augmented Reality in Medicine.* CRC Press, Boca Raton. 2018.

21. H. Luo, Q. Hu, F. Jia. Details preserved unsupervised depth estimation by fusing traditional stereo knowledge from laparoscopic images. *IET Healthcare Technology Letters.* 2019; 6(6): 154–158.

22. E. Colleoni, S. Moccia, X. Du, E. De Momi, D. Stoyanov. Deep learning based robotic tool detection and articulation estimation with spatio-temporal layers. *IEEE Robotic Automation Letters.* 2019; 4: 2714–2721.

23. B.J. Park, S.J. Hunt, C. Martin, G.J. Nadolski, B.J. Wood, T.P. Gade. Augmented and Mixed Reality: Technologies for Enhancing the Future of IR. *Journal of Vascular and Interventional Radiology.* 2020; 31(7): 1074–1082.

24. F. Chen, D. Wu, H. Liao. Registration of CT and ultrasound images of the spine with neural network and orientation code mutual information. *Medical Imaging and Augmented Reality.* 2016; 9805: 292–301

25. T.M. Ward, P. Mascagni, Y. Ban, G. Rosman, N. Padoy, O. Meireles, D.A. Hashimoto. Computer vision in surgery. *Surgery.* 2021; 169(5): 1253–1256. doi: 10.1016/j.surg.2020.10.039.

26. S. Sengupta, N. Mittal, M. Modi. Improved skin lesions detection using color space and artificial intelligence techniques. *Journal of Dermatological Treatment.* 2020; 31(5): 511–518. doi: 10.1080/09546634.2019.1708239.

27. S. Sengupta, N. Mittal M. Modi, Edge detection in dermascopic images by linear structuring element. *2018 7th International Conference on Reliability, Infocom Technologies and Optimization (Trends and Future Directions) (ICRITO)*, 2018, pp. 419–424, doi: 10.1109/ICRITO.2018.8748610.

28. L. Sharma, P. Garg (Eds.). *From Visual Surveillance to Internet of Things.* Chapman and Hall/CRC, New York, 2020, https://doi.org/10.1201/9780429297922.

29. Computer vision and AI. Available at https://www.forbes.com/sites/robertglatter/2021/05/21/google-announces-new-ai-app-to-diagnose-skin-conditions/?sh=7109c1ae4a0c [accessed on 20 June 2022].

30. D.K. Yadav, L. Sharma, S.K. Bharti, Moving object detection in real-time visual surveillance using background subtraction technique. *2014 14th International Conference on Hybrid Intelligent Systems*, pp. 79–84, 2014, doi: 10.1109/HIS.2014.7086176.

31. Lavanya Sharma, Annapurna Singh, Dileep Kumar Yadav, *Fisher's Linear Discriminant Ratio Based Threshold for Moving Human Detection in Thermal Video, Infrared Physics and Technology*, Elsevier, 2016; 78: 118–128. doi.org/10.1016/j.infrared.2016.07.012.

32. L. Sharma (Ed.). *Towards Smart World*. Chapman and Hall/CRC, New York, 2021, https://doi.org/10.1201/9781003056751.

33. L. Sharma, *Human Detection and Tracking Using Background Subtraction in Visual Surveillance", Towards Smart World*. Chapman and Hall/CRC, New York, pp. 317–328, 2020, https://doi.org/10.1201/9781003056751.

34. Lavanya Sharma, Dileep Kumar Yadav, Sunil Kumar Bharti, An improved method for visual surveillance using background subtraction technique. *IEEE, 2nd International Conference on Signal Processing and Integrated Networks (SPIN-2015)*, Amity Univ. Noida, India, February 19–20, 2015.

35. Dileep Kumar Yadav, Lavanya Sharma, Sunil Kumar Bharti, Moving object detection in real-time visual surveillance using background subtraction technique. *IEEE, 14th International Conference in Hybrid Intelligent Computing (HIS-2014)*, Gulf University for Science and Technology, Kuwait, December 14–16, 2014.

36. Lavanya Sharma, D.K. Yadav, Manoj Kumar, A morphological approach for human skin detection in color images. *2nd national conference on Emerging Trends in Intelligent Computing & Communication*, GCET, Gr., Noida, April 26–27, 2013.

37. Lavanya Sharma, Sudhriti Sengupta, Birendra Kumar, An improved technique for enhancement of satellite images, *Journal of Physics: Conference Series*. 2021; 1714: 012051.

38. Supreet Singh, Lavanya Sharma, Birendra Kumar, A machine learning based predictive model for coronavirus pandemic scenario. *Journal of Physics: Conference Series*. 2021; 1714 012023.

39. G. Jha, L. Sharma., S. Gupta, Future of augmented reality in healthcare department. In: Singh P.K., Wierzchoń S.T., Tanwar S., Ganzha M., Rodrigues J.J.P.C. (eds.). *Proceedings of Second International Conference on Computing, Communications, and Cyber-Security. Lecture Notes in Networks and Systems*, vol. 203. Springer, Singapore, 2021. https://doi.org/10.1007/978-981-16-0733-2_47.

40. G. Jha, L. Sharma, S. Gupta, E-health in internet of things (IoT) in real-time scenario. In: Singh P.K., Wierzchoń S.T., Tanwar S., Ganzha M., Rodrigues J.J.P.C. (eds.). *Proceedings of Second International Conference on Computing, Communications, and Cyber-Security. Lecture Notes in Networks and Systems*, Vol. 203. Springer, Singapore, 2021. https://doi.org/10.1007/978-981-16-0733-2_48.

41. S. Kumar, P. Gupta, S. Lakra, L. Sharma, R. Chatterjee, The zeitgeist juncture of "big data" and its future trends. *2019 International Conference on Machine Learning, Big Data, Cloud and Parallel Computing (COMITCon)*, pp. 465–469, 2019, doi: 10.1109/COMITCon.2019.8862433.

42. S. Sharma, S. Verma, M. Kumar, L. Sharma, Use of motion capture in 3D animation: Motion capture systems, challenges, and recent trends. *2019 International Conference on Machine Learning, Big Data, Cloud and Parallel Computing (COMITCon)*, pp. 289–294, 2019, doi: 10.1109/COMITCon.2019.8862448.

43. M. Carpenter, An accidentally detected diaphragmatic hernia with acute appendicitis. *Asian Journal of Case Reports in Surgery*. 2021; 9(2): 19–24. Retrieved from https://www.journalajcrs.com/index.php/AJCRS/article/view/30260.

44. Artificial Intelligence Technologies, Applications, and Challenges. Available at: https://www.routledge.com/Artificial-Intelligence-Technologies-Applications-and-Challenges/Sharma-Garg/p/book/9780367690809 [access on 20 July 2021].

45. A. Chaudhary, S.S. Singh, Lung cancer detection on ct images by using image processing. *2012 International Conference on Computing Sciences*, pp. 142–146, 2012, doi: 10.1109/ICCS.2012.43.

46. B.V. Ginneken, B.M. Romeny, M.A. Viergever, Computer-aided diagnosis in chest radiography: A survey. *IEEE, transactions on medical imaging*. 2001; 20(12), pp. 156–162.

47. S. Beucher, F. Meyer, The morphological approach of segmentation: The watershed transformation. In: Dougherty, E. (ed.). *Mathematical Morphology in Image Processing*, pp. 43–481. Marcel Dekker, New York, 1992.

48. K. Suzuki et al., False-positive reduction in computer-aided diagnostic scheme for detecting nodules in chest radiographs by means of massive training artificial neural network. *Academic Radiology*. 2005; 12(2): 191–201.

49. H.T. Nguyen et al., Watersnakes: Energy-driven watershed segmentation. *IEEE Transactions on Pattern Analysis and Machine Intelligence*. 2003; 25(3): 330–342.

50. Lavanya Sharma, Computer-aided lung cancer detection and classification of CT images using convolutional neural network. In: *Computer Vision and Internet of Things: Technologies and Applications*. Taylor & Francis, CRC Press, pp. 247–262, 2022.

51. Lavanya Sharma, Analysis of machine learning techniques for airfare prediction. In: *Computer Vision and Internet of Things: Technologies and Applications*. Taylor & Francis, CRC Press, pp. 211–231, 2022.

52. Lavanya Sharma, Innovation and emerging computer vision and artificial intelligence technologies in coronavirus control. In: *Computer Vision and Internet of Things: Technologies and Applications.* Taylor & Francis, CRC Press, pp. 177–192, 2022.

53. Lavanya Sharma, Self-driving cars: Tools and technologies. In: *Computer Vision and Internet of Things: Technologies and Applications.* Taylor & Francis, CRC Press, pp. 99–110, 2022.

54. Lavanya Sharma, Computer vision in surgical operating theatre and medical imaging. In: *Computer Vision and Internet of Things: Technologies and Applications.* Taylor & Francis, CRC Press, pp. 75–96, 2022.

55. Lavanya Sharma, Preventing security breach in social media: threats and prevention techniques. In: *Computer Vision and Internet of Things: Technologies and Applications*, Taylor & Francis, CRC Press, pp. 53–62, 2022.

56. Lavanya Sharma, Mukesh Carpenter, Use of robotics in real-time applications. In: *Computer Vision and Internet of Things: Technologies and Applications*, Taylor & Francis, CRC Press, pp. 41–50, 2022.

57. Lavanya Sharma et al., An overview of security issues of internet of things. In: *Computer Vision and Internet of Things: Technologies and Applications*, Taylor & Francis, CRC Press, pp. 29–40, 2022.

58. Lavanya Sharma, Rise of computer vision and internet of things. In: *Computer Vision and Internet of Things: Technologies and Applications*, Taylor & Francis, CRC Press, pp. 5–17, 2022.

59. G.S. Pilli, K.P. Suneeta, A.V. Dhaded, V.V. Yenni, Ovarian tumors, study of 282 cases. *Journal of the Indian Medical Association.* 2002; 100(420): 423–424.

60. N. Gupta, D. Bishit, A.K. Agarwal, V.K. Sharma. Retrospective and prospective study of ovarian tumors and tumor like lesions. *Indian Journal of Pathology & Microbiology.* 2007; 50: 525–527.

61. M.M. Bhattacharya, A clinicopathological analysis of 270 ovarian tumors. *Journal of Postgraduate Medicine.* 1980; 26: 103.

62. S.K. Mondal, Histologic pattern, bilaterality and clinical evaluation of 957 ovarian neoplasms; A 10 year study in a tertiary hospital of eastern India. *Journal of Cancer Research and Therapeutics.* 2011; 7: 433–437.

63. A. Malineh. Surgical histopathology of benign ovarian cysts. A multicentric study. *Iranian Journal of Pathology.* 2010; 5(3): 132–136.

64. S. Yasmin. Clinico histopathological pattern of ovarian tumors in peshawar region. *Journal of Ayub Medical College Abbottabad.* 2008; 4: 20.

65. M. Cohen, Sites of endometriosis. *La Revue du Praticien.* 1990; 40: 1091–1096.

66. L. Sharma, M. Carpenter (Eds.). *Computer Vision and Internet of Things: Technologies and Applications* (1st ed.). Chapman and Hall/CRC, 2022. https://doi.org/10.1201/9781003244165.

67. S. Kayastha. Study of ovarian tumors in Nepal medical college teaching hospital Nepal. *Nepal Medical College Journal.* 2009; 11: 200–202.

7 Drones for Societal Development

Mayank Sharma and Rahul Dev Garg
Indian Institute of Technology

CONTENTS

7.1 INTRODUCTION

Technology changes human lives a lot and, thus, directly impacts our society. New technology may result from an innovative idea or the advancements in the existing one. The future of any technology depends on its acceptance by the public (Comtet & Johannessen, 2022; Osakwe et al., 2022). People generally adopt new technology if it makes their lives comfortable compared to previous ones. Sometimes, people in our society are not the direct consumers of new technology; instead, the administration, government, or various service providers adopt a new technique or technology that impacts our community (Bijker & Law, 1994). There is a direct and indirect impact of technological advancements in society that also changes human behaviour and needs (Rao et al., 2016). For example, mobile phones and the internet have become a daily need of an individual nowadays. They have opened a gateway to a plethora of opportunities for every individual. Everything is just a few clicks away from accessing information about anything to booking a ticket for a journey. People even cannot avoid their mobile phones for long. These instances show how technology influences the behaviour of humans. The period of the COVID-19 pandemic has also proved how technology changed our lifestyle. Online classes for school children and work from home for office employees are possible because of technological advancements. Drones are also a result of such technological advancement or development.

Nowadays, drones or UAVs (unmanned aerial vehicles or uncrewed aerial vehicles) are trendy terms. Now, almost everyone is aware of what basically a drone is. They are lightly weighted platforms that fly without a pilot onboard. They are remotely operated aerial vehicles and thus are also known as remotely piloted aircraft (RPA) or aerial robots. Various names are given to these aerial platforms; however, drones and UAVs are more common among the public (Colomina & Molina, 2014). Drones primarily operate on batteries and thus are environmentally friendly, as they do not pollute the air (Borghetti et al., 2022). Earlier, drones were explicitly used for military applications (Watts et al., 2012), mostly during wars (McCann, 2022), but their commercialization has resulted in significant demands for civilian applications.

Light-weight aircrafts with compact sizes are available at a meagre cost, thus having numerous applications. Drones can be used in multiple applications as they can carry different payloads as per the requirements. The payload carrying capacity depends on the design specifications of drones. They are the best alternative for remotely sensed data acquisition over inaccessible areas as they acquire high-resolution data within a few minutes of flight. A wide range of UAVs are available, including semi-automated to fully automated models, at a very low cost. These are a few characteristics that promote the usage of drones in a wide range of applications. However, technology indeed has both pros and cons, and drones are not far from this. The primary concern for the broad application of drones is safety and security. It is essential to note that drones are unmanned, and thus their supervision is of utmost importance because of the unintentional risks associated with them (Oudes & Zwijnenburg, 2011). The battery backup of drones is another crucial factor that limits their applications. These are a few limitations in UAV technology that hinder the growth of drone industry. Thus, despite having numerous advantages, UAV applications are restricted under several rules of the Ministry of Civil Aviation and other regulatory authorities. This chapter briefs the evolution, development, and application of UAV technology for societal benefits. Challenges in the deployment of drones at a larger scale are also discussed.

7.1.1 HISTORY AND BACKGROUND

It is always fascinating to think of flying; however, human beings do not have wings. So, people were making serious efforts to make them fly. These efforts could not develop the wings on the human body, but the evolution of technology made it possible to fly in the air when the first airplane was demonstrated by the Wright brothers in 1903. The date goes back to the 1970s to develop the first fixed-wing motorized remotely controlled aerial vehicle (Przybilla & Wester-Ebbinghaus, 1979). Before this, many attempts were made to carry some weight into the air. The invention of the hot air balloon by the Montgolfier brothers in 1782 proved to be a milestone for further development towards making humans able to fly (Baker, 1994; Bilstein, 2001; Kirk, 1995). Thus, although drones or UAVs are unmanned aircrafts or aerial platforms that have resulted from technological advancement and are utilized in a wide range of applications; however, unmanned flying objects for various applications are still not new. Many facts prove that people have been using unmanned flying objects from more than 200 years when even piloted aircrafts were also unavailable. Hot air balloons were the first unmanned flying objects used to carry the bombs during the wars, and later on, kites were also used as unmanned aerial platforms with cameras onboard for aerial data acquisition (Bowen, 1977; Colomina & Molina, 2014; Haydon, 2000; Watts et al., 2012).

Drones carry a wide range of sensors and other types of equipment that make the flight smooth and free from the risk of failure. A few standard sensors and other essential equipment present onboard are navigational sensors such as Global Navigation Satellite System (GNSS) receiver and Inertial Measurement Unit (IMU), radio link receivers, speed controlling mechanism, and a power

FIGURE 7.1   Description of an unmanned aircraft system.

supply source. Propellors along with motors are also essential components. All these equipments, when mounted over a solid frame (made up of plastic/metal/fiber), constitute a drone (Colomina & Molina, 2014; Rao et al., 2016). So, a drone is simply an aerial platform that carries a payload, other essential sensors, and other useful accessories. Drones/UAVs are controlled from the ground through radio communication, so the controlling assembly present on the ground is known as a ground control station, and together all these constitute an unmanned aerial system or unmanned aircraft system (UAS). So, a UAS basically consists of a UAV, a ground control station, and a communication control system. Figure 7.1 provides the basic description of a UAS.

7.2   TYPES OF DRONES OR UAVs

Due to technological advancements, drones are available in multiple shapes and sizes. The classification of drones is highly complex as it is based on various parameters, and there is no globally accepted classification of drones. For example, drones can be classified based on their controlling methods (fully autonomous, semi-autonomous, and manual). They can further be classified based on size, weight, flying altitude, and manufacturing design specifications. The drones are primarily categorized into rotary-wing, fixed-wing, and hybrid VTOL (vertical take-off and landing). Further details of the characterization of drones are given in the following section.

7.2.1   Types of Drones Based on the Source of Power Supply

As per Eisenbeiss (2009), drones may be powered or unpowered. Powered drones generally consist of electronic components and circuits, thus requiring power supply source for the drone's proper functioning, whereas unpowered drones do not require any battery or power source for their operation. For example, quadcopters and hexacopters need power supply or battery to function properly, whereas balloons and kites fall under the category of unpowered drones. The powered drones are far better than the unpowered drones, as the effects of wind are more in unpowered drones. Thus, powered drones are flexible for maneuverability.

7.2.2   Design-Based Characterization of Drones

Powered drones are available in multiple designs; however, they are majorly classified into three categories which are as follows:

7.2.2.1   Rotary-Wing

As the name indicates, rotary-wing UAVs consist of rotating parts. These rotating parts are mainly the propellers driven by the motors. The number of propellers/ motors in a drone varies as per the design specifications. They are primarily divided into single rotor and multi-rotor drones. Quadcopters and hexacopters are famous examples of rotary-wing UAVs consisting of four and six propellers, respectively. The capability to take off and land vertically, and hover at a particular place make them suitable for flights at low altitudes. Thus, making them ideal for security and surveillance applications. Figure 7.2a and b show the quadcopter and hexacopter rotary-wing UAVs, respectively.

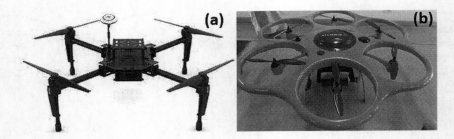

FIGURE 7.2   Examples of rotary-wing drones (a) Quadcopter and (b) Hexacopter.

7.2.2.2   Fixed-Wing

Fixed-wing drones have no rotating parts, as signified by their name. They are similar to manned aircraft but differ in size. The facility for vertical take-off and landing is not available in the case of fixed-wing drones. A clear runway is required for the launching and landing of these drones. Catapult launch is another alternative for the take-off of fixed-wing drones. Due to the proper launching requirements, flights at lower altitudes are impossible for fixed-wing drones; however, they have higher cruising speed and endurance (Gupta et al., 2013), making them suitable for long-range aerial surveys (Figure 7.3).

7.2.2.3   Hybrid Drones

These are advanced drones that have the capability of both rotary and fixed-wing drones. Their architecture is a mix of fixed-wing and rotary-wing drones, which means they have both rotating parts and fixed wings. This hybrid nature provides the feature of VTOL and higher cruising speed. They are more commonly known as VTOL drones. Thus, they are suitable for multiple applications, including security and surveillance to long-range surveys (Figure 7.4).

7.2.3   Types of Drones Based on their Weight

Drones are available in different shapes and sizes, so their weights are also different. As per the Drone Rules (2021) published by the Ministry of Civil Aviation, India, drones are classified into five categories. All the five categories are mentioned in Table 7.1, with corresponding permissible weight limits in each category. The range of weight listed in Table 7.1 includes the payload as well.

7.2.4   Types of Drones Based on the Mode of Operation or Control

Mode of operation is also a vital characteristic of drones that distinguishes them into the following three categories:

7.2.4.1   Manual

Manually operated drones are entirely operated by a remote pilot that transfers the control signals through the radio communication link. The remote pilot fully manages the take-off, landing and motion of the drone. As complete control is available to the pilot, these drones are used in the application where more significant details or continuous monitoring are required. For example, the film industry uses drones in manual mode. Maneuvering is possible in these drones.

7.2.4.2   Fully Autonomous

Fully autonomous drones do not require any manual interference for the take-off, landing, and other flight controls. They primarily need a well-defined flight plan to cover the desired area of interest. These days a wide range of flight planning software is available that provides the flexibility to control the flight plan as per their desired specifications.

FIGURE 7.3   Example of a fixed-wing drone (Source: Mulero-Pázmány et al., 2022).

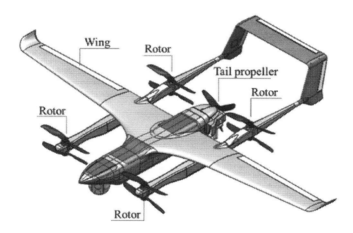

FIGURE 7.4   Hybrid VTOL drone (Source: Zong et al., 2021).

TABLE 7.1
Classification of Drones Based on Weight

Type of Drone	Range of Weight
Nano	Less than or equal to 250 g
Micro	More than 250 g and less than or equal to 2 kg
Small	Greater than 2 kg and less than or equal to 25 kg
Medium	Greater than 25 kg and less than or equal to 150 kg
Large	Greater than 150 kg

TABLE 7.2

Classification of UAS Based on Size, Mass, and Performance

Category	Range (km)	Flight Altitude (m)	Endurance (h)
Nano	<1	100	<1
Micro	<10	250	1
Mini	<10	150–300	<2
Close Range	10–30	3,000	2–4
Short Range	30–70	3,000	3–6
Medium Range	70–200	5,000	6–10
Medium Range Endurance	>500	8,000	10–18
Low Altitude Deep Penetration	>250	50–9,000	0.5–1
Low Altitude Long Endurance	>500	3,000	>24
Medium Altitude Long Endurance	>500	14,000	24–48
High Altitude Long Endurance	>2,000	20,000	24–48
Unmanned Combat Aerial Vehicle	~1,500	10,000	~2
Lethal	300	4,000	3–4
Decoy	0–500	5,000	<4
Stratospheric	>2,000	20,000–30,000	>48

Source: Van Blyenburg (2009).

7.2.4.3 Semi-Autonomous

Semi-autonomous drones support a hybrid mode of operation where they can be operated both in manual and automatic mode. In general, the remote pilot controls the take-off and landing of these drones, whereas a flight plan is required to make them fly automatically. Recent advancements have given the flexibility of automatic landing in these UAVs. These types of drones are more common in the remote sensing domain.

7.2.5 Types of Drones Based on Range, Endurance, and Flying Height

There could be various other classifications of drones based on their range (close, medium, and short), endurance (low, medium, and high), and flying height (low altitude, medium altitude, high altitude, and stratospheric) (Colomina & Molina, 2014; Eisenbeiss, 2009). All the details of the mentioned classification are given in Table 7.2.

7.3 ADVANTAGES OF DRONES

Drones have multiple advantages that make them suitable for numerous applications. A few of the significant benefits of drones are listed below:

- Low weight
- Low cost
- Compact size
- Flexibility to carry different payloads
- Reliability

- Easy to operate
- Easily transportable
- High spatial resolution
- High temporal resolution
- Flexibility to acquire data
- Stability
- Autonomous flights with flexibility for height variation
- Access to inaccessible locations
- Faster flights result in rapid data collection and fast deliveries
- Environment friendly

7.4   DISADVANTAGES OF DRONES

Drones have multiple advantages; however, a few limitations hinder their application at a larger scale and impact the drone industry's growth. The significant hurdles to the usage of drones are listed below:

- Safety and security
- Regulations for drone operation
- Higher wind speed affects proper drone operation
- Data volume is large
- High-resolution data acquired through drones requires complex processing
- Due to low altitude flying, coverage is smaller, and thus multiple flights are required
- Lower flight times with limitations in payload capacity
- Danger to air traffic
- Require properly trained pilots
- Privacy issues
- No possible flight for restricted locations

7.5   APPLICATIONS OF DRONES

Earlier, the scope of drone application was limited to military operations only (Kraus et al., 2020). However, due to changes in rules and regulations made by the governing authorities, drones are finding their applications for civilian purposes. They have both commercial and scientific applications. It is necessary to mention that drones' commercial, scientific or research applications indirectly impact society because research and commercial operations are meant to benefit society/community/humanity.

Drones can carry a payload, the weight of which depends on the strength of the drone and its design specification. They can carry the sensors or other payloads as per the requirement of the application. Remote-sensing applications of drones for earth observation mainly involve optical, and multispectral cameras, microwave, hyperspectral, LiDAR (light detection and ranging) sensors, etc. At the same time, other applications may use drones to carry some weight. Nowadays, constellations or groups of drones (swarm) are also utilized in high-security surveillance and other applications (Kumar et al., 2022). As Kolesnikov (2022) demonstrated, a swarm could be immensely useful during disasters for rapid aid delivery.

Drones are now utilized in numerous applications such as environmental monitoring, agriculture, forestry, fisheries, photogrammetry, remote sensing, firefighting, emergency response, energy sector, crop dusting, search and rescue, border security, traffic management, wildlife monitoring, archaeological site survey, entertainment, sports, surveillance and reconnaissance, etc. (Everaerts, 2009). High-resolution mapping is the primary application of drones because of their capability to acquire high-resolution data within a short time period. Cadastral mapping from drone data and property taxation has already been well demonstrated (Cunningham et al., 2012). Preliminary surveying and mapping through drones are now common for large infrastructure projects. Datasets obtained through drones provide detailed information that helps planners, designers and other professionals to execute their tasks effectively. Drone surveys reduce overall cost, workforce, and time compared to traditional surveys. High-resolution data is also crucial for land use land cover (LULC) classification (Laliberte et al., 2011). People have also presented case studies to highlight landslide mapping, monitoring, and characterisation (Carvajal et al., 2012; Niethammer et al., 2010). There are many more such applications of UAVs that prove them as the best aerial platform.

UAVs can fly over inaccessible areas, where humans usually lack due to high risk and challenges. It avoids the risk to human life and boosts the development of drones at a higher pace. This unique characteristic of drones flying over inaccessible areas opens the door to their applications for emergency response (Choi & Lee, 2011). Even the forest departments use drones for forest monitoring and fire detection. Forest fires are fatal and risk humans and wildlife both. Due to the increase in temperature and smoke, forest fire regions are inaccessible. However, drones could easily and quickly fly over those regions along with the required sensors such as thermal sensor to detect forest fires. The use of thermal sensor can delineate the areas with active fire (areas burning with flames) to those having just the smoke. This also helps the forest department to respond immediately and perform rescue operations. Various studies are available that show the potential of drones in forest-related applications. Rufino & Moccia (2005) utilized a mini UAV to develop a system of thermal and hyperspectral sensors to monitor forest fires.

The use of aerial data acquired through drones is also common for measuring the height, diameter of trees, and width of tree crowns (Wallace et al., 2012). Even wildlife monitoring is another potential application of drones. Drones equipped with high-resolution cameras can fly close to wild animals and provide inaccessible information. This helps in exploring the wildlife with finer details without interfering with the typical lifestyle of animals. The high-resolution aerial view from the drones helps to monitor the forests and to identify and curb poaching and illegal cutting activities, thus could help in saving the endangered species (Petronzio, 2017). Similarly, underwater drones or remotely piloted vehicles (RPVs) facilitate the exploration of aquatic species. RPVs can penetrate to large depths and provide adequate information to explore different underwater features.

The agricultural sector is another primary sector where drones are beneficial and prove their utility in multiple ways. Proper farm planning, pesticide spray, crop monitoring, etc., are a few applications of drones. Nowadays, commercial ventures have even demonstrated the sowing of seeds through drones. Drones in the agricultural sector are not new; people have utilized these economic aerial platforms for more than two decades. Herwitz et al. (2002) mentioned the application of UAVs for high-resolution data collection from digital cameras for the analysis of coffee plantations, weed detection, and highlighting the problematic zones of drip agriculture.

Nowadays, drones are more commonly used for reconnaissance surveys for highway planning, and other civil constructions. Proper monitoring during the construction work is also done with drones. National Highway Authority of India (NHAI) uses the periodical drone survey data to monitor the progress of their various highway projects. Several studies have also shown that drones are highly useful in detecting cracks present on the roads. The use of aerial images to generate a digital surface model (DSM) of a highway and ortho rectified image for its adequate monitoring is well demonstrated by Zhang (2008). Drones are also used a lot in the entertainment industry and sports. High-resolution cameras mounted over them are used to shoot films and television serials. Aerial coverage of the sports tournaments is also done with drones.

Mining is one of the most important sectors where drones are utilized more frequently. Mineral detection and volume estimation through drones are the most common application in the mining sector. They are even used to detect vehicles and humans buried during the mine collapse (Eck & Imbach, 2012). High-resolution cameras onboard light aerial unmanned vehicles provide images that are further processed to generate high-resolution surface models and orthorectified images of the study area. These high-resolution images acquired through drones were used by Erenoglu

(2021) for the morphological analysis of a mining area through a digital surface model (DSM) and orthoimage.

Drones are also primarily used in disasters such as flash floods, earthquakes, landslides, etc., because of their capability to fly over inaccessible areas. Pre and post-disaster drone datasets could help in the damage assessment effectively. These datasets could also effectively help in disaster mitigation and risk assessment. They also assist the response team in quick response for the rescue operations. During disasters, rescue teams find it challenging to reach the disaster victims to provide medical and food aid; thus, drones are the best alternatives for this humanitarian task. One of the critical studies highlighting the application of drones during the emergency situation of a nuclear explosion was done by Towler et al. (2012). Sensors were used in this study to acquire the aerial images and detect radiation to help the response team for a faster response with adequate safety.

The utility of drones for civilian applications has been demonstrated many times, which show how useful they are for our society. The use of drones for social applications is not so easy because of the associated privacy, safety, and security concerns. In 2021, a pilot experiment was conducted in the Vikarabad district of Telangana, where a drone carried a 12 kg box full of medicines and vaccines to a primary health center. This project was named *Medicines from the Sky* (DC Correspondent, 2021). United Nations International Children's Emergency Fund (UNICEF) has also conducted various pilot projects in remote areas to supply vaccines and medicines. These were the areas with complex terrain, and drones served the purpose effectively by covering the entire area within a few minutes of flight (Archundia, 2019). In a situation like the COVID-19 pandemic, where the health of the individuals in society was a major concern, medicine delivery through drones could be beneficial and important for both service providers and the users. Drones have been used to sanitize streets and other public places (Euchi, 2021).

Even the manufacturing industries have started using drones to transfer their goods from high-risk zones to other places within their premises. It ensures the safety of their workers and reduces risk to human life. Companies like Amazon and Walmart have already included and demonstrated package delivery operations through drones. It is estimated that the drone package delivery market will reach 8 billion USD by 2027 (Vazhavelil & Sonowal, 2022). Delivery of packages to their final destination, also referred to as last-mile delivery is the most recent application of drones (Fehling & Saraceni, 2022). Many countries have already performed trial operations on drones for last-mile delivery, but they are still not employed at a larger scale due to security and privacy concerns.

The use of drones in the energy sector is remarkable. They are used to detect the faults and damages in wind turbines and thus eliminate the risk of human life where workers used to reach the top of wind turbines using ropes and ladders. The improper functioning of solar panels can also be detected by using thermal sensors on drones (Villaflor, 2017). Similarly, monitoring dams to detect damages and cracks is another potential application of drones. Drones can be helpful in the monitoring of thermal power plants and other energy sectors involving renewable sources of energy. This also reduces the risk to human life as drones can easily capture high-risk zones inaccessible to humans.

China has used drones for air pollution control which is a severe problem for society. They have used drones to detect harmful emissions from industries during the night. Reducing air pollution using parachutes carrying chemical agents was attempted by a Chinese company (Petronzio, 2017).

In India, several drone service providers, private companies, and commercial vendors have developed case studies to demonstrate the use of drones in the social sector. Emergency response during the fire, flood inundation modelling, road network management, monitoring railway projects, biodiversity conservation, and high-resolution land mapping are a few applications of drones demonstrated by the Indian companies (Mukharya, 2017). High-resolution images from drones may help map utilities and resources that facilitate nearby population in cities and villages. This allows the administrators, policy, and decision-makers to properly plan and manage resources and effectively regulate the government schemes.

7.6   DRONES RULES AND REGULATIONS

The primary concern with the operation of drones is safety and security, keeping in mind the citizens' privacy. Safety and security not only relate to the citizens but also to drones to protect them from external threats (Rao et al., 2016). Drones themselves have threats from outside attacks. Also, they are a threat to the users on the ground as well as in the airspace (Galkin, 2021; Watts et al., 2012). Drones are unmanned and remotely operated, making themselves vulnerable and a threat to people and private/public property, resulting in liability issues. The communication of the ground control station with the drone is also vulnerable, and if by any chance the control signals are modified by hijackers, then it may result in unintended activities, which is a serious threat (Boyle, 2015). Privacy of the citizens is another major concern. Drones equipped with consumer-grade cameras may pose a serious threat to someone's privacy due to the mischievous act of others. The safety of both the drones and the public is essential. With these serious concerns, different governments have formulated certain rules and regulations for the easy operation of drones.

In India, the Directorate General of Civil Aviation (DGCA) is the regulatory body under the Ministry of Civil Aviation (MoCA) for regularizing drone operations. They also monitor the imports of UAS. Drones in India are allowed as per the regulations of the DGCA. MoCA published *"The Drone Rules, 2021"* on August 25, 2021. It is noteworthy that the drones owned by defense units (including Airforce, Navy, and Army) do not come under Drone Rules (2021). They majorly categorized the drones into three primary categories given below:

a. Aeroplane
b. Rotorcraft
c. Hybrid UAS

Further, they classified the drones according to their weight (including payload). Its details are given in Section 7.2.3. As per the Drone Rules (2021), registration is mandatory for all the categories of drones except nano. Registration provides a unique identification number to a drone, without which no flight is possible for unregistered drones except in the exempted category. The digital sky platform hosts the application form for drone registration. Registration includes the serial number of the drone, module of flight control and remote pilot station. Any change in the mentioned instruments is impossible without updating their serial number in the digital sky platform. Those who want to fly a drone also require a remote pilot certificate; however, as per the Drone (Amendment) Rules 2022, pilot certificate is not required for non-commercial purposes using drones of less than 2 kg weight (nano and micro drones). DGCA provides the remote pilot certificate based on the recommendation of the authorized training partners. This certificate is valid initially for 10 years and can be renewed further. Anyone aged between 18 and 65 years, with a qualification of at least matric level from a recognized board and passed the pilot training from DGCA approved remote pilot training centers, may apply for a remote pilot certificate. There is a provision for third-party insurance of all the drones except nano drones under Motor Vehicles Act, 1988. They have also divided the airspace into the following three zones:

a. **Red Zone:** The red zone is near the operational airports, international borders, military establishments, and other high-security places. The red zone consists of prohibited and restricted areas. No flight is permitted in prohibited areas, whereas prior approval is required for restricted zones.
b. **Yellow Zone:** It is controlled airspace, and prior permission is required for the flight.
c. **Green Zone:** No permissions are required for the green zone. Its airspace is up to 400 ft and reduced to 200 ft near airports.

7.6.1 FLIGHT RESTRICTIONS FOR DRONES IN INDIA

As per the guidelines issued by DGCA, the restrictions imposed for drone flight are as follows:

- Drones with a weight limit of up to 2 kg (micro-drones) cannot fly above 60 m from ground level and can attain a maximum speed limit of 25 m/s (Garg, 2022).
- Small drones (weight up to 25 kg) cannot fly above 120 m from ground level and can attain a maximum speed limit of 25 m/s.
- Flight of medium and large drones must be as per the conditions in the operator permit of DGCA.
- No flight is possible in the red zone, whereas proper prior approvals are required to conduct a flight in the yellow zone.
- Failure to comply with the DGCA guidelines may result in a strong penalty as per Section 10A of the Aircraft Act, 1934 and suspension of license/certificate/registration.

7.7 CONCLUSION

Drones have become an advanced aerial platform with various advantages such as low cost, lightly weighted, compact size, rapid data collection, etc. With so many benefits, they can be utilized in numerous applications. Earlier, their applications were limited to military applications only; however, recent regulations have also enabled their use in civilian applications. These small, lightly weighted aircrafts are finding their applications in various domains, including agricultural, forestry, geological, hydrology, glaciology, surveying, entertainment, wildlife, urban modeling, smart city planning, highway planning, security and surveillance, gaming industry, road traffic monitoring and routing and package delivery, etc. Their numerous applications have helped in identifying the true potential of drones. The commercialization of drones is revolutionary and can bring out effective development of society. They are utilized in both research and commercial applications and thus boost the development of our community directly and indirectly.

Drones can fly over inaccessible areas, reducing human life risk. This characteristic makes them more demanding. Also, in severe conditions such as the COVID-19 pandemic, package delivery through drones could be the best solution to reduce human contact. Ultimately all these applications are enhancing the development of our society. However, drones' safety, security, and privacy concerns have forced the government to formulate strict laws and guidelines. The monitored use of drones and appropriate policy planning can change the future of drones and society too. Technology is growing rapidly, and it is the responsibility of the users to use it and not misuse it. The government is responsible for defining the guidelines, but ultimately the users must act responsibly to handle drones and utilize these platforms appropriately to maintain privacy, safety, security, and integrity.

REFERENCES

Archundia, J. (2019). Drones for social good | UNICEF office of innovation. https://www.unicef.org/innovation/stories/drones-social-good.

Baker, D. (1994). *Flight and Flying: A Chronology*. Facts on File. New York: Facts on File

Bijker, W. E., & Law, J. (1994). *Shaping Technology/Building Society: Studies in Sociotechnical Change*. MIT Press.

Bilstein, R. E. (2001). *Flight in America- From the Wrights to the Astronauts(Book)*. Baltimore, MD: Johns Hopkins University Press.

Borghetti, F., Caballini, C., Carboni, A., Grossato, G., Maja, R., & Barabino, B. (2022). The use of drones for last-mile delivery: A numerical case study in Milan, Italy. *Sustainability (Switzerland)*, 14(3), 1–19. https://doi.org/10.3390/su14031766.

Bowen, D. (1977). Encyclopedia of War Machines: An Historical Survey of the World's Great Weapons. London: Peerage Books.

Boyle, M. J. (2015). The race for drones. *Orbis*, 59(1), 76–94. https://doi.org/10.1016/j.orbis.2014.11.007.

Carvajal, F., Agüera, F., & Pérez, M. (2012). Surveying a landslide in a road embankment using unmanned aerial vehicle photogrammetry. *The International Archives of the Photogrammetry, Remote Sensing and Spatial Information Sciences*, XXXVIII-1, 201–206. https://doi.org/10.5194/isprsarchives-xxxviii-1-c22-201-2011.

Choi, K., & Lee, I. (2011). A uav based close-range rapid aerial monitoring system for emergency responses. *The International Archives of the Photogrammetry, Remote Sensing and Spatial Information Sciences*, XXXVIII-1, 247–252. https://doi.org/10.5194/isprsarchives-XXXVIII-1-C22-247-2011.

Colomina, I., & Molina, P. (2014). Unmanned aerial systems for photogrammetry and remote sensing: A review. *ISPRS Journal of Photogrammetry and Remote Sensing*, 92, 79–97. https://doi.org/10.1016/j.isprsjprs.2014.02.013.

Comtet, H. E., & Johannessen, K. A. (2022). A socio-analytical approach to the integration of drones into health care systems. *Information*, 13(2), 1–22. https://doi.org/10.3390/info13020062.

Cunningham, K., Walker, G., Stahlke, E., & Wilson, R. (2012). Cadastral audit and assessments using unmanned aerial systems. *ISPRS - International Archives of the Photogrammetry, Remote Sensing and Spatial Information Sciences*, XXXVIII-1, 213–216. https://doi.org/10.5194/isprsarchives-XXXVIII-1-C22-213-2011.

DC Correspondent. (2021). First time in India, drone delivers medicines; Scindia calls it revolutionary. Deccan Chronicle. https://www.deccanchronicle.com/opinion/columnists/110921/in-a-first-drone-flies-5-km-delivers-12-kg-medicines.html.

Eck, C., & Imbach, B. (2012). Aerial magnetic sensing with an uav helicopter. *The International Archives of the Photogrammetry, Remote Sensing and Spatial Information Sciences*, XXXVIII-1, 81–85. https://doi.org/10.5194/isprsarchives-xxxviii-1-c22-81-2011.

Eisenbeiss, H. (2009). UAV photogrammetry. Ph.D. Thesis. Zurich: Institut für Geodesie und Photogrammetrie, ETH Zurich. https://doi.org/https://doi.org/10.3929/ethz-a-005939264.

Erenoglu, O. (2021). Uav for 3d morphological mapping applications: A case study of koru mining site, canakkale, NW Turkey. *Technical Gazette*, 28(3), 1044–1050. https://doi.org/10.17559/TV-20190701203009.

Euchi, J. (2021). Do drones have a realistic place in a pandemic fight for delivering medical supplies in healthcare systems problems? *Chinese Journal of Aeronautics*, 34(2), 182–190. https://doi.org/10.1016/j.cja.2020.06.006.

Everaerts, J., 2009. NEWPLATFORMS – Unconventional platforms (Unmanned Aircraft Systems) for remote sensing. Technical Report 56. European Spatial Data Research (EuroSDR).

Fehling, C., & Saraceni, A. (2022). Feasibility of drones & agvs in the last mile delivery: Lessons from Germany. *SSRN Electronic Journal*. https://doi.org/10.2139/ssrn.4065011.

Galkin, B. (2021). L&rs spotlight: Consumer and commercial drones-how a technological revolution is impacting irish society. *Oireachtas Library & Research Service 2021, Dublin*.

Garg, R. (2022). Drone laws in India – iPleaders. https://blog.ipleaders.in/drone-laws-in-india/.

Gu, H., Lyu, X., Li, Z., Shen, S., & Zhang, F. (2017). Development and experimental verification of a hybrid vertical take-off and landing (VTOL) unmanned aerial vehicle(UAV). *2017 International Conference on Unmanned Aircraft Systems, ICUAS 2017*, November, 160–169. https://doi.org/10.1109/ICUAS.2017.7991420.

Gupta, S. G., Ghonge, M., & Jawandhiya, P. M. (2013). Review of unmanned aircraft system (UAS). *International Journal of Advanced Research in Computer Engineering & Technology*, 2(4), 1646–1658. https://doi.org/10.2139/ssrn.3451039.

Haydon, F. S. (2000). *Aeronautics in the Union and Confederate armies: With a Survey of Military Aeronautics Prior to 1861* (In Militar, Vol. 1). Baltimore, MD: Johns Hopkins University Press.

Herwitz, S. R., Johnson, L. F., Arvesen, J. C., Higgins, R. G., Leung, J. G., & Dunagan, S. E. (2002). Precision agriculture as a commercial application for solar-powered unmanned aerial vehicles. *1st UAV Conference*. https://doi.org/10.2514/6.2002-3404.

Kirk, S. (1995). *First in Flight: The Wright Brothers in North Carolina*. Winston-Salem, NC: John F. Blair Publisher

Kolesnikov, V. (2022). Modelling a swarm of delivery drones for disaster relief utilizing an organization approach. *Journal of Physics: Conference Series*, 2224(1). https://doi.org/10.1088/1742-6596/2224/1/012115.

Kraus, J., Kleczatský, A., & Hulínská, Š. (2020). Social, technological, and systemic issues of spreading the use of drones. *Transportation Research Procedia*, 51(2019), 3–10. https://doi.org/10.1016/j.trpro.2020.11.002.

Kumar, A., Augusto de Jesus Pacheco, D., Kaushik, K., & Rodrigues, J. J. P. C. (2022). Futuristic view of the internet of quantum drones: Review, challenges and research agenda. *Vehicular Communications*, 36, 100487. https://doi.org/10.1016/j.vehcom.2022.100487.

Laliberte, A. S., Goforth, M. A., Steele, C. M., & Rango, A. (2011). Multispectral remote sensing from unmanned aircraft: Image processing workflows and applications for rangeland environments. *Remote Sensing*, 3(11), 2529–2551. https://doi.org/10.3390/rs3112529.

McCann, S. R. (2022). Drones in wine and medicine. *Bone Marrow Transplantation*, 57(2), 154–155. https://doi.org/10.1038/s41409-021-01511-7.

Mukharya, P. (2017). Using drones for social sector research. Ideas for India. https://www.ideasforindia.in/topics/miscellany/using-drones-for-social-sector-research.html.

Mulero-Pázmány, M., Martínez-de Dios, J. R., Popa-Lisseanu, A. G., Gray, R. J., Alarcón, F., Sánchez-Bedoya, C. A., Viguria, A., Ibáñez, C., Negro, J. J., Ollero, A., & Marrón, P. J. (2022). Development of a fixed-wing drone system for aerial insect sampling. *Drones*, 6(8), 189. https://doi.org/10.3390/DRONES6080189/S1

Niethammer, U., Rothmund, S., James, M. R., Travelletti, J., & Joswig, M. (2010). UAV - based remote sensing of landslides. *International Archives of Photogrammetry, Remote Sensing and Spatial Information Sciences, Part 5. Commission V Symposium*, XXXVIII(2005), 496–501.

Osakwe, C. N., Hudik, M., Říha, D., Stros, M., & Ramayah, T. (2022). Critical factors characterizing consumers' intentions to use drones for last-mile delivery: Does delivery risk matter? *Journal of Retailing and Consumer Services*, 65(2021). https://doi.org/10.1016/j.jretconser.2021.102865.

Oudes, C., & Zwijnenburg, W. (2011). Does unmanned make unacceptable ? Exploring the debate on using drones and robots in warfare. Utrecht: IKV Pax Christi.

Petronzio, M. (2017). 9 incredible ways we're using drones for social good I Mashable. https://mashable.com/article/drones-social-good-humanitarian-aid.

Przybilla, H.-J., & Wester-Ebbinghaus, W. (1979). Bildflug mit ferngelenktem Kleinflugzeug. *Bildmessungund Luftbildwesen, Zeitschriftfuer Photogramme Trieund Fernerkundung*, 47(5), 137–142.

Rao, B., Gopi, A. G., & Maione, R. (2016). The societal impact of commercial drones. *Technology in Society*, 45, 83–90. https://doi.org/10.1016/j.techsoc.2016.02.009.

Rufino, G., & Moccia, A. (2005). Integrated VIS-NIR hyperspectral / thermal-IR electro-optical payload system for a mini-UAV. *Collection of Technical Papers - InfoTech at Aerospace: Advancing Contemporary Aerospace Technologies and Their Integration*, 2(September 2005), 915–923. https://doi.org/10.2514/6.2005-7009.

Rules, D. (2021). Drone rules 2021 India. https://egazette.nic.in/WriteReadData/2021/229221.pdf.

Towler, J., Krawiec, B., & Kochersberger, K. (2012). Radiation mapping in post-disaster environments using an autonomous helicopter. *Remote Sensing*, 4(7), 1995–2015. https://doi.org/10.3390/rs4071995.

Van Blyenburg (2009). *Unmanned Aircraft Systems, the Global Perspective 2009/2010*. UAS Yearbook (7th ed., Vol. 2009, p. 224 p.). Blyenburgh & Co. Retrieved from http://www.uvs-international.org/uvs-info/Yearbook2009/005_Preface_The-Global-Perspective_Peter-van-Blyenburgh_UVS-International.pdf

Vazhavelil, T., & Sonowal, A. (2022). The future of delivery with drones: Contactless, accurate, and high-speed - Wipro. https://www.wipro.com/business-process/the-future-of-delivery-with-drones-contactless-accurate-and-high-speed/.

Villaflor, M. V. (2017). How to use drones in development projects I Development Asia. https://development.asia/explainer/how-use-drones-development-projects.

Wallace, L., Lucieer, A., Watson, C., & Turner, D. (2012). Development of a UAV-LiDAR system with application to forest inventory. *Remote Sensing*, 4(6), 1519–1543.

Watts, A. C., Ambrosia, V. G., & Hinkley, E. A. (2012). Unmanned aircraft systems in remote sensing and scientific research: Classification and considerations of use. *Remote Sensing*, 4(6), 1671–1692. https://doi.org/10.3390/rs4061671.

Zhang, C. (2008). An UAV-based photogrammetric mapping system for road condition assessment. *The International Archives of the Photogrammetry, Remote Sensing and Spatial Information Sciences*, 627–632. http://citeseerx.ist.psu.edu/viewdoc/download?doi=10.1.1.150.8490&rep=rep1&type=pdf.

Zong, J., Zhu, B., Hou, Z., Yang, X., & Zhai, J. (2021). Evaluation and comparison of hybrid wing VTOL UAV with four different electric propulsion systems. *Aerospace*, 8(9), 256. https://doi.org/10.3390/AEROSPACE8090256.

Part III

Smart Society-based Applications

8 Traffic Management and Intelligent Transportation Systems

Anuj Kumar Atrish
Manav Rachna International Institute of Research and Studies

CONTENTS

DOI: 10.1201/9781003324720-11

8.1 HISTORY OF TRAFFIC MANAGEMENT

Traffic management is the arrangement, organization, direction and control of both stationary and moving traffic, including pedestrians, cyclists and all types of vehicles for ensuring the safe, orderly and efficient transport of people, goods and to enhance the quality of the local environment to ensure safe movement. A traffic jam can be a transportation condition in which there is massive congestion that slows vehicles and increases the number of vehicles on the road. By 1950, traffic congestion on city avenue networks has extended hastily. When traffic demand is high, vehicle-to-vehicle interaction slows traffic and ultimately leads to traffic jams. With our country's rapid population growth, an intelligent traffic management system provides people to have smooth transportation network, find ways to quickly reach their destinations, and improve journeys forever. An intelligent traffic management system can be initiated to overcome such situations in the current scenario. This system monitors the flow of traffic lights and vehicles by means of image processing using a CCTV camera. CCTV cameras process images and help identify the number of vehicles passing on the road. They help reduce road traffic congestion and fuel consumption of the automobiles. Sensors are used to record the number and speed of vehicles. CCTV cameras and sensors can work together to send the collected information to a variable message sign (VMS) panel. This panel displays traffic information to road users. It helps in diverting and changing the roads at the earliest to reduce wait times. Although the waiting time is reduced, fuel is consumed automatically. It protects transportation facilities and improves where possible. Therefore, reduction in fuel consumption helps reduce air pollution. By building control systems and understanding the problems happening on the road, we can reduce congestion and provide a traffic-free environment [1–12].

8.2 BACKGROUND OF INTELLIGENT TRANSPORTATION SYSTEM

ITS is an integrated application of advanced technology using electronics, computers, communications, and advanced sensors. The intelligent transportation system provides critical information to travelers while improving the safety and efficiency of transportation systems (Figure 8.1).

Short answer=**"technology in transportation"**

- USDOT Definition=" ITS means any communication, electronic device, or any information's processing used to improve the safety or efficiency of surface transport systems."

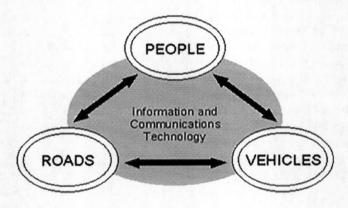

FIGURE 8.1 Information and communications technology in ITS.

- The term Intelligent Transport Systems (ITS) refers to communication and information technologies enforced to transportation framework and vehicles to better transportation result such as:
  - Network Operation Resilience
  - Social Equity
  - Travel Reliability
  - Transport Productivity
  - Transportation freedom
  - Ecological Achievement

ITS capabilities have matured significantly in the 25 years since the ITS Joint Program Office was established. This document celebrates progress in this field and explores its exciting future while serving as a guide for his future ITS research programs. ITS is an advanced application, without embodying intelligence itself, which aims to provide innovative services related to various modes of transport and traffic management and to serve a wider range of users that enable informed, safer, more coordinated and "smarter" usage transport network.

8.3 NEED OF INTELLIGENT TRANSPORTATION SYSTEM

- In addition, ITS can play a position in speedy mass evacuation of humans in city facilities after excessive injuries inclusive of the ones as a result of herbal failures or threats.
- Interest in ITS stems from synergies between the problems posed by traffic congestion and new information technologies for simulation, real-time control, and communication networks.
- With the progress of motorization, urbanization, population growth, and changes in population density, traffic congestion has become a serious problem worldwide.
- Congestion reduces the efficiency of transport infrastructure, increasing travel times, air pollution and fuel consumption.
- Congestion reduces the performance of transportation infrastructure, growing tour times, air pollutants, and gasoline consumption.

8.4 IMPORTANT OF INTELLIGENT TRANSPORTATION SYSTEM

The ITS aims to minimize traffic problems and achieve traffic efficiency. We will enhance advance traffic information, real-time on-site driving information, free seat information, etc., shorten commuting time, and improve safety and convenience.

Importance based on the several parameters is as given below.

- **Travel:**
  a. Save time
  b. Few accidents and fatalities
  c. Enhanced security and protection
  d. Cost avoidance
  e. Improved reliability
  f. Improved travel planning
  g. Improving emergency response
- **Economic:**
  a. Improve customer satisfaction
  b. Improved productivity
  c. Delivery date
- **Environment:**
  a. Fuel savings
  b. Reduction of air pollution

8.5   OBJECTIVE ITS

ITS uses advanced communication technologies to improve road safety and mobility, and increase productivity. ITS covers a wide range of wireless and traditional communication-based information and electronic technologies.

Objectives of ITS are as given below.

1. Congestion management on highways and highways
2. Increase coordination
3. Increase efficiency
4. Improving mobility and improving quality
5. Increased economic productivity
6. Improved security
7. Reduce energy consumption and negative environmental impact
8. Improving public-private partnerships

8.6   TECHNOLOGIES OF INTELLIGENT TRANSPORTATION SYSTEM

Various kinds of technologies are given below (Figure 8.2)

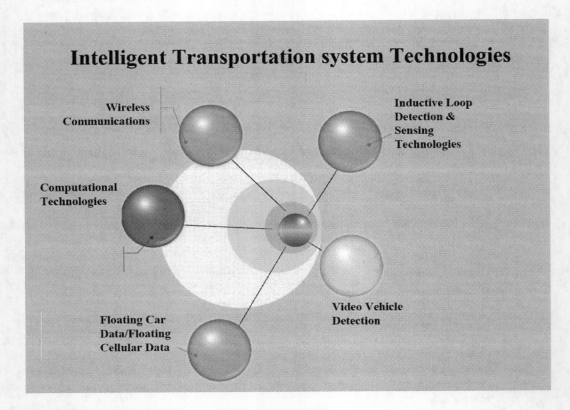

FIGURE 8.2   Technologies of intelligent transportation system.

1. Wireless communication
2. Computer technology
3. Floating car data/floating cellular data
4. Inductive loop detection/sensing technology
5. video vehicle detection

8.6.1 WIRELESS COMMUNICATION

Radio modem communications on UHF and VHF frequencies are widely used for short-range and long-range communications within ITS. Communication over short distances (less than 450 m) can be done using the IEEE 802.11 protocol. Theoretically, the reach of these protocols can be extended through mobile ad-hoc or mesh networks. Long-distance communication has been proposed using infrastructure networks such as WiMAX (IEEE 802.16), Global System for Mobile Communications (GSM), or 3G.

8.6.2 COMPUTER TECHNOLOGY

A typical vehicle in the early 2000s contained 20–100 individual networked microcontroller/programmable logic controller modules running non-real-time operating systems. The current trend is towards fewer and more expensive microprocessor modules with hardware memory management and real-time operating systems. New embedded systems platforms enable the implementation of more sophisticated software applications such as model-based process control, artificial intelligence, and perhaps ubiquitous computing. The most important of these for intelligent transportation systems is artificial intelligence.

8.6.3 FLOATING CAR DATA/FLOATING CELLULAR DATA

"Floating car" or "probe" data collection is a relatively inexpensive set of methods for obtaining travel time and speed data for vehicles traveling on roads, highways, highways, and other transportation routes.

Floating car data/floating cellular data have several benefits over other traffic measurement methods.

1. Low cost than cameras and sensors
2. Possibly including all locations and streets- More coverage
3. Faster setup
4. Less maintenance
5. Works in all weather conditions including heavy rain.

Broadly speaking, three methods were used to obtain the raw data.

a. Triangulation Procedures
b. Vehicle re-identification;
c. GPS-based method.

8.6.3.1 Triangulation Procedures

In the mid-2000s, attempts were made to use mobile phones as anonymous traffic probes. Just like a car, the signal from your mobile phone inside the car also travels. Data were transformed into traffic flow information by measuring and analyzing network data using triangulation, pattern matching, or cell-sector statistics (anonymous format). More traffic means more cars, more phones, and therefore more probes. In urban areas, the distance between antennas is reduced, theoretically increasing accuracy. The advantage of this method is that no infrastructure needs to be built along the road. Only mobile networks are used. In the early 2010s, triangulation declined in popularity.

8.6.3.2   Vehicle Re-Identification

This method requires a series of detectors placed along the road. With this technique, the unique serial numbers of the devices in the vehicle are obtained in one place and reacquired (re-identified) later. Travel time and speed are calculated by comparing the time a particular device is detected by a pair of sensors. This can be performed using the Bluetooth device's MAC address (Machine Access Control) or his RFID serial number on an electronic toll collection (ETC) transponder.

8.6.3.3   GPS-Based Method

An increasing number of vehicles are equipped with in-vehicle GPS (satellite navigation) systems and have two-way communication with traffic data providers. Position readings from these vehicles are used to calculate vehicle speed.

8.6.4   Inductive Loop Detection

An inductive loop can be placed on the roadbed to detect vehicles as they pass through the loop's magnetic field. The simplest detector simply counts the number of vehicles that pass through the loop in a unit of time (usually 60 seconds in the US).

More advanced sensors estimate vehicle speed, length, weight, and distance between vehicles. Loops can be placed in a single lane or multiple lanes and work with very slow or stationary vehicles as well as fast moving vehicles speed. This is often used in traffic lights to coordinate vehicle dwell times in relation to vehicle numbers.

Sensor technology

Technological advances in telecommunications and information technology, coupled with cutting-edge microchips, radio frequency identification (RFID), and low-cost intelligent beacon detection technology, enable driver safety benefits for intelligent transportation. Strengthened our technical ability to systems around the world. ITS sensor systems are vehicle and infrastructure based network systems. Infrastructure sensors are indestructible devices that are installed or embedded in or around roadways as needed and can be deployed manually during preventive maintenance of roadways or by sensor injection machines for rapid deployment. They can also be expanded.

8.6.5   Video Vehicle Detection

Another form of vehicle detection is traffic flow measurement and automatic event recognition using video cameras. Video detection systems, such as those used for automatic license plate recognition, do not embed components directly into the pavement or bed, so this type of system is known as a "non-intrusive" traffic detection method. Video from a black-and-white or color camera is sent to a processor that analyzes the changing characteristics of the video image as vehicles pass by. Cameras are usually mounted on poles or structures above or beside the road. Most video detection systems require an initial configuration to "teach" the processor a baseline background image. Known measurements are typically entered, such as the distance between lanes or the height of the camera above the lane (Figure 8.3).

8.7   APPLICATIONS OF INTELLIGENT TRANSPORTATION SYSTEM

1. Emergency vehicle notification system
2. Automatic road monitoring
3. Variable speed limit
4. Collision avoidance system
5. Dynamic traffic light sequence

8.7.1   EMERGENCY VEHICLE NOTIFICATION SYSTEMS

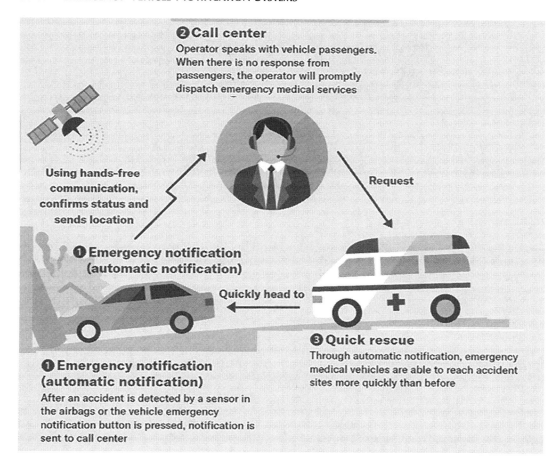

FIGURE 8.3   Emergency Vehicle Notification Systems.

8.7.2   AUTOMATIC ROAD ENFORCEMENT

a. Speed cameras to identify vehicles exceeding legal speed limits. Many of these devices use radar to detect vehicle speed and hidden electromagnetic loops in each lane of the road.
b. A red light camera that detects vehicles crossing the stop line or designated stop area while the light is on.
c. Bus lane cameras that identify vehicles traveling in dedicated bus lanes. In some jurisdictions, bus lanes are also used by taxis and vehicles participating in carpools.

FIGURE 8.4   Variable speed limit.

   d. Level crossing cameras to identify vehicles illegally crossing the tracks.
   e. Dual white line cameras to identify vehicles crossing these lines.
   f. High occupancy lane cameras to identify vehicles violating HOV requirements.

8.7.3 VARIABLE SPEED LIMITS

Deploying variable speed limits requires standard traffic information to assess need and implement strategies. Data on traffic volumes, travel speeds, local climate, and weather conditions, and the presence and location of incidents are essential to determining the need for intervention (Figure 8.4).

8.7.4 COLLISION AVOIDANCE SYSTEMS

Collision avoidance is one of the most important elements of safe driving. Collision avoidance system "CAS", also known as pre-crash system, forward collision warning system, collision mitigation system. However, currently all collision avoidance techniques are mechanical and fragile. It doesn't take into account how humans drive or handle dangerous situations (Figure 8.5).

8.7.5 DYNAMIC TRAFFIC LIGHT SEQUENCE

Developed since 1912, traffic signals are signaling devices made to regulate the flow of traffic at intersections, pedestrian crossings, railroad tracks, etc. A traffic light can accommodate three different colored lights.

A green signal allows traffic to proceed in the specified direction, a yellow signal warns vehicles to prepare to slow down, and a red signal stops all vehicle progress. Current dynamic systems used in developed countries are too expensive to install in the real world. Based on current traffic conditions, dynamic time-based adjustments can be suggested wherever traffic light green times are allocated. It helps to automatically search for emergency vehicles around you and warn normal traffic through special traffic lights on traffic lights whenever traffic light conditions change as needed. The system also includes an emergency vehicle subsystem that uses transmitters and receivers to clear the road for emergency vehicles by prioritizing the road, turning the light green until the vehicle crosses the intersection (Figure 8.6).

Collision Avoidance Systems

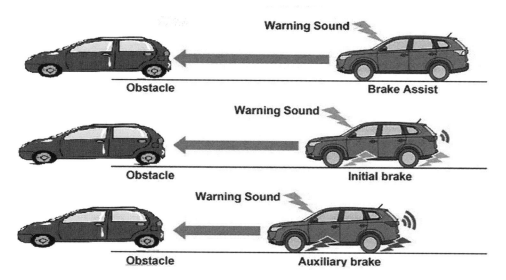

FIGURE 8.5 Collision avoidance system.

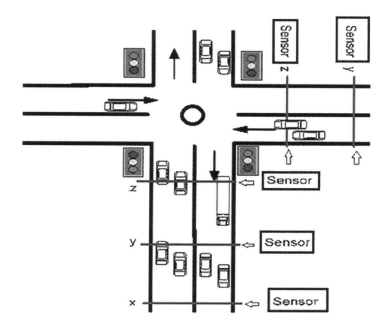

FIGURE 8.6 Dynamic traffic light sequence.

8.8 BENEFITS OF INTELLIGENT TRANSPORTATION SYSTEM

1. Time savings
2. Fewer accidents and fatalities
3. Energy and environmental benefits

4. Reduce the possibility of overload
5. Improve customer satisfaction
6. Improving emergency response times and services
7. Cost avoidance

8.9   SERVICES OF INTELLIGENT TRANSPORTATION SYSTEM

1. Vehicle services
2. Traveler information
3. Vehicle services
4. Traffic management and operations
5. Public transport
6. Transport-related electronic payment
7. Freight transport

8.10   SUBSYSTEMS OF INTELLIGENT TRANSPORTATION SYSTEM

Major areas of ITS (Figure 8.7):

1. Advanced traffic management system "ATMS"
2. Advanced Travel Information System (ATIS)
3. Advanced Local Transport System (ARTS)

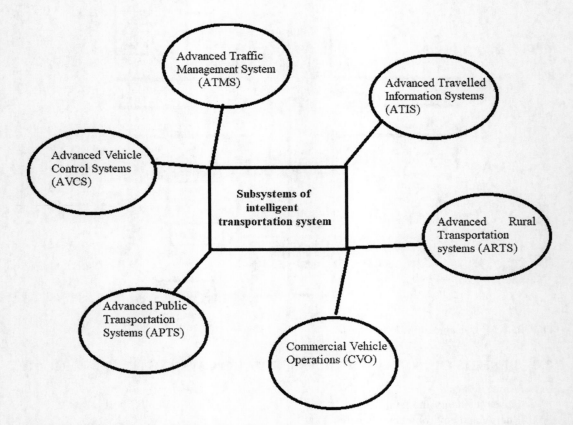

FIGURE 8.7   Subsystems of intelligent transportation system.

4. Commercial Vehicle Operation (CVO)
5. Advanced Public Transport System (APTS)
6. Advanced Vehicle Control System (AVCS)

8.10.1 Advanced Traffic Management System

The Advanced Traffic Management Systems (ATMS) field is a major sub-field within ITS. Domain. The ATMS view is primarily a top-down management perspective that integrates technology to improve vehicle traffic flow and safety. Real-time traffic data from cameras, speed sensors, etc. flows into the Traffic Management Center (TMC) where it can be consolidated and processed (e.g. incident detection) and lead to actions (e.g. traffic routing, DMS, messages). The purpose is to improve the flow of traffic. The National ITS Architecture defines the following key goals and indicators for ITS:

It increases the efficiency of transport systems, improves mobility, improves safety, reduces fuel consumption and environmental costs, increases economic productivity and creates an environment for the ITS market. The primary goal of our advanced traffic management system is to enable private concessionaires, highway operators, or government agencies to ultimately improve road user safety, improve traffic flow, and improve the efficiency of transportation systems. Providing traffic management solutions enables you to take actions that increase efficiency, increase economic productivity, and improve mobility.

8.10.2 Advanced Traveller Information Systems

Advanced information system (ATIS) is used for travelers. A system that collects, analyzes, and presents information to assist land travelers in navigating from their point of origin (origin) to their intended destination. ATIS can operate entirely on information provided within the vehicle (autonomous system) or use data provided by a traffic control center. Relevant information includes the location of the accident, weather and road conditions, best routes, recommended speeds, and lane restrictions. All of these are part of the ITS.

Travel information systems utilize various communication technologies to deliver information. The most common are wireless broadcasts, electronic data lines to remote terminals, and telephone advisory messages. Traveler information is presented as map database icons, alphanumeric text messages, and recorded messages accessible by phone.

8.10.3 Advanced Rural Transportation systems

Advanced Rural Transport System (ARTS) is a program to meet the needs of travelers to and through rural areas and the authorities responsible for the operation and maintenance of rural transport systems. "Rural" is defined as areas that do not have the same access to resources and infrastructure elements as metropolitan areas. Rural areas include farmlands/ranches, national parks, isolated small communities, and suburbs where some city services are inaccessible.

8.10.4 Commercial Vehicle Operations

Commercial vehicle operations (CVOs) are the application of Intelligent Transportation systems to trucks, typically purchased by trucking company managers. Each truck was equipped with a satellite navigation system, a small computer and a digital radio. Every 15 minutes the computer will send where the truck has been. The digital radio service forwards the data to the headquarters of the forwarding company. A computer system at headquarters manages the fleet in real time under the control of a dispatcher team. CVO technologies that improve commercial fleet productivity, including weigh-in-transit (WIM), pre-approval processes, and interstate coordination.

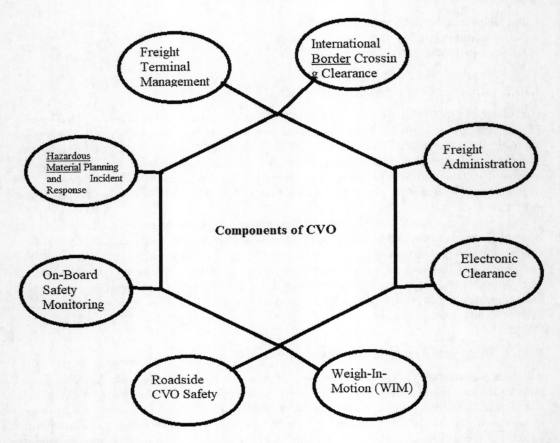

FIGURE 8.8 Components of CVO.

Controlled routes allow trucks to avoid congestion due to rush hour, accidents or road works. Governments are now providing digital notifications when road capacity is known to be decreasing. A good system allows computers. Dispatchers and drivers work together to find the appropriate route or method to move your parcel. A particular advantage is that the computer can automatically eliminate routes through roads that cannot support the weight of the truck or roads with obstacles. Drivers typically register with the system. This system prompts the driver to take a break. A well-rested driver operates a forklift more skillfully and safely (Figure 8.8).

Components of CVO include:

8.10.5 Advanced Public Transportation Systems

Advanced public transport system (APTS) makes transport safer, more reliable, more efficient and reduce costs. It also enables safe, reliable, and fastest transportation, reduces commute time between shipments, and reduces transit fees. It's user-friendly, so new innovations are coming out every day to improve transportation.

8.10.5.1 Objective of APTS

1. Improving communication with transport operators towards better response and improved disposal
2. have the ability to track the location of real-time transportation vehicles to improve dispatch and customer service;

3. Meet growing demand for services through efficiency without adding staff or equipment. Improve service quality.
4. Improve convenience for transit customers and improve visibility of transit services by introducing a real-time passenger information system.
5. Has the ability to track the real-time location of transport vehicles for better planning.
6. Improved safety, emergency response, and incident management;
7. Increased passenger numbers to support the division's long-distance transportation plans.
8. Improve the handling of complaints and disputes between the public, businesses, and management;
9. Use technology to realize the cost and quality benefits associated with maintenance of transportation vehicles.
10. Provide a more accessible, responsive, and efficient transportation system by using capital resources to reduce long-term operating costs.
11. Ensure more effective management and accountability.

8.10.5.2 Components of APTS
1. Automatic vehicle tracking
2. Operating software
3. Mobile data terminal
4. Silent alarm/hidden microphone/surveillance camera
5. automatic passenger counter
6. Automatic Passenger Information
7. Vehicle diagnosis
8. Signal Priority
9. Electronic Fare Payment
10. Initiatives for Intelligent Vehicles

8.10.6 Advanced Vehicle Control Systems

Autonomous driving has long been a dream of mankind. The past decade has seen pioneering developments in the field of automation, and it won't be long before the streets are filled with self-driving cars. A self-driving car is basically defined as a passenger car that drives itself. Most of the prototypes that have been produced so far have performed automatic steering by sensing paint lines on the road and magnetic monorails embedded in the road. Researchers today use sensors and advanced software along with other custom-made hardware to build self-driving cars. Although the prototype looks very successful, no fully self-driving car reliable enough to drive on the road is yet commercially available. This is mainly due to the difficulty of controlling the vehicle in unpredictable urban traffic conditions.

8.10.6.1 Need of AVCS

Accidents occur at a constant pace and people are injured all over the world due to several stressed factors such as glare at night when oncoming traffic cannot be seen. The goal of the AVCS is to contribute to large-scale projects aimed at fully automating vehicles and preventing collisions. We are talking about intelligent driver support using digital interfaces. We aim for a symbiotic relationship between cars and drivers. This control system equips the vehicle with various intelligent systems to improve the driver's skill and enable more efficient interaction with the vehicle.

Transportation systems are an integral part of human activity. On average, it is estimated that 40% of the population spends at least 1 hour on the road each day (Junping et al. 2011). In recent years, people have become more dependent on transportation. The transportation system itself faces not only multiple opportunities but also multiple challenges. First, as the number of vehicles on the road increases, congestion becomes an increasingly important problem globally.

8.10.6.2 Benefits of AVCS

Accidents occur at a constant pace and people are injured all over the world due to several stressed factors such as glare at night when oncoming traffic cannot be seen. The goal of the AVCS is to contribute to large-scale projects aimed at fully automating vehicles and preventing collisions. We are talking about intelligent driver support using digital interfaces. We aim for a symbiotic relationship between cars and drivers. This control system equips the vehicle with various intelligent systems to improve the driver's skill and enable more efficient interaction with the vehicle. Transportation systems are an integral part of human activity. On average, it is estimated that 40% of the population spends at least 1 hour on the road each day (Junping et al. 2011). In recent years, people have become more dependent on transportation. The transportation system itself faces not only multiple opportunities, but also multiple challenges. First, as the number of vehicles on the road increases, congestion becomes an increasingly important problem globally.

8.10.6.3 AVCS Safety Advantage

Auto accidents are now the leading cause of death in certain population groups. In 2010, at least 1.3 million people died worldwide and 50 million were injured in road accidents (Fred 2012). Finally, to the extent that technology can replace safety-related driver functions, automated systems can be much safer than existing systems. This is because the technology can be applied directly to issues that are now almost entirely under driver control. Automotive automation may therefore be the greatest public health advancement of the 21st century.

A central theme of AVCS is to improve the throughput and safety of highway traffic by replacing human drivers with precise and rapid responses of automated controls. Driving in traffic jams is one of the most difficult problems in metropolitan traffic management. According to data from Madrid, Spain, about 1 million workers waste 30 minutes or more in rush hour traffic jams every day. Estimated annual costs he is more than 800 million euros. This issue is being addressed by both the automotive industry and transportation research groups with the goal of reducing these numbers. Regarding the automotive division, we have put particular effort into the development of vehicle speed control. The main purpose of these controls is to improve vehicle occupant safety by relieving the human driver of tedious tasks in order to make driving easier and traffic flow more efficient (Milanes et al. 2012). An efficient solution to all these problems is to use AVCS.

8.11   FUTURE SCOPE

Improved data collection – Vehicles are constantly on the move and the data collected is often not accurate, complete or reliable. Research on techniques that provide better data quality is important. In the age of the Internet of Things, many new sensor techniques could help improve data collection and quality. In addition, research on the adoption of automated data collection techniques that reduce manual data entry could help improve data quality.

Managing massive amounts of data – With the growth of the Internet of Things, data is a huge percentage. Seamless integration and processing of data is also a major challenge, and much research is required to manage data. Technologies such as cloud computing and edge computing can be used. Collecting city-wide traffic data using big data technology provides practical data for traffic control and urban planning, and solves problems related to traffic congestion analysis, traffic flow prediction, and traffic rational planning can be resolved.

8.12   CONCLUSION

This chapter describes the interaction of two new technologies: Traffic management and ITS. ITS alleviates traffic congestion. The options of ITS options are broad; ITS spans multiple technologies and has the potential to alleviate most traffic problems. However, the application should depend on the nature of the site for which traffic needs to be managed. Using the right ITS for the type of location reduces travel times and queues as well as improves safety and productivity.

REFERENCES

1. Kaur, A., Kaur, M.G.H. (2017). *Review of Traffic Management Control Techniques.* IJARCSSE, ISSN: 2277 128X.
2. Sen, R., Raman, B. *Intelligent Transport Systems for Indian Cities.* https://www.umtc.co.in/intelligent-transportation-systems-umtc-249
3. Koonce, P. (2005). *Benefits of Intelligent Transportation Systems Technologies in Urban Areas: A literature Review.* Portland State University, Portland.
4. Hatcher, G. (2014). *Intelligent Transportation Systems Benefits, Costs, and Lessons.* U.S. Department of Transportation, Washington, DC.
5. Randolph, L. (2015). Texas variable speed limit pilot project. In: *National Rural Intelligent Transportation Systems Conference*, San Antonio, TX.
6. Scriba, T. (2004). *Intelligent Transportation Systems in Work Zones: A Case Study - Real Time Work Zone Traffic Control System.* Federal Highway Administration, U.S. DOT, Springfield, IL.
7. Jenelius, E., Koutsopoulos, H.N. (2017). Urban network travel time prediction based on a probabilistic principal component analysis model of probe data. *IEEE Transactions on Intelligent Transportation Systems*, 19(2), 436–445.
8. Avatefipour, O., Sadry, F. (2018). Traffic management system using IoT technology-A comparativereview. In: *2018 IEEE International Conference on Electro/Information Technology (EIT)*, Rochester, MI, USA, 1041–1047.
9. Barros, J., Araujo, M., Rossetti, R.J. (2015). Short-term real-time traffic prediction methods: A survey. In: *2015 International Conference on Models and Technologies for Intelligent Transportation Systems (MT-ITS)*, USA, 132–139.
10. Chhatpar, P., Doolani, N., Shahani, S., Priya, R.L. (2018). Machine learning solutions to vehiculartraffic congestion. In: *2018 International Conference on Smart City and Emerging Technology(ICSCET)*, Budapest, Hungary, 1–4. IEEE.
11. Chung, J., Sohn, K. (2018). Image-based learning to measure traffic density using a deepconvolutional neural network. *IEEE Transactions on Intelligent Transportation* Systems, 19(5), 1670–1675.
12. Guo, F., Polak, J.W., Krishnan, R. (2010). Comparison of modelling approaches for short term trafficprediction under normal and abnormal conditions. In: *13th International IEEE Conference onIntelligent Transportation Systems*, Funchal, Portugal,1209–1214. IEEE.

9 Moving Objects Detection for Video Surveillance Applications in Society 5.0

*Wieke Prummel, Anastasia Zakharova,
and Thierry Bouwmans*
La Rochelle University

CONTENTS

9.1   INTRODUCTION

Video surveillance applications in Society 5.0 are required to detect and recognize moving objects such as humans, animals and vehicles in order to optimize home and traffic monitoring. These tasks involve computer vision algorithms, which rely on mathematical concepts, machine learning or signal-processing models. The most efficient methods depend on background subtraction and have been used more and more in various video surveillance applications. To model the background, the methods use either mathematical concepts, machine learning or signal-processing models to tackle the challenges encountered in videos.

The rest of this chapter is organized as follows: In Section 9.2, we first present a short preliminary overview about moving objects detection with background subtraction. Section 9.3 reviews methods based on mathematical concepts. Section 9.4 provides an overview of unsupervised and supervised machine learning methods. In Section 9.5, signal-processing models are surveyed. Finally, a conclusion and perspectives are provided.

DOI: 10.1201/9781003324720-12

9.2   MOVING OBJECTS DETECTION: A PRELIMINARY OVERVIEW

Background subtraction is the most common method for detecting moving objects and provides the best compromise between robustness and real-time requirements. From a static standpoint, only moving objects are in motion. Based on this statement, background subtraction methods follow the general process illustrated in Figure 9.1. Background initialization is a process of determining the first image. Background modeling describes the model used to outline the background. Background maintenance is the mechanism for updating the model to adapt to changes as they occur over time. Foreground detection involves classifying pixels into the "background" class or the "moving objects" class.

The background model is a description of the model used for background representation. Many unsupervised, supervised and semi-supervised methods exist in the literature. Readers may refer to valuable books [1,2] and extensive surveys which cover this issue for further details [3–7]. Multiple models emanating from mathematical theories, machine learning and signal processing have been used for background modeling. This includes (i) unsupervised models such as crisp models [8–10], statistical models [11–14], fuzzy models [15–17], Dempster–Schafer models [18], subspace learning models [19–23], and robust learning models [24–27], (ii) supervised models such as neural networks models [28–30] and (iii) semi-supervised models including graph signal processing based models [31–34]. For the most part, researchers develop and test these models on PCs and then supply CPU implementations. Nevertheless, their objective resides mostly in focusing on the robustness against challenges encountered in the videos paying less attention to the real-time and memory requirements and the portability of these algorithms to global video systems, embedded systems and Society 5.0 applications. In the following, we survey different ways to model the background in order to detect moving objects.

9.3   MATHEMATICAL CONCEPTS

Methods based on mathematical tools utilize either crisp theory [8–10], statistics [11–14], fuzzy concepts [15–17] or Dempster-Schafer concepts [18]. The main purpose of these techniques is to tackle imprecision, uncertainty and incompleteness in the data images due to noise, illumination changes, dynamic backgrounds, etc.

9.3.1   CRISP THEORY

The most straightforward manner to model a background is to compute the temporal average [8], the temporal median [9], or the histogram over time [10]. In the 1990s, owing to their simplicity, these methods were commonly used in traffic surveillance, but are not robust to the challenges faced in video surveillance, such as camera jitter, illumination variations and dynamic backgrounds.

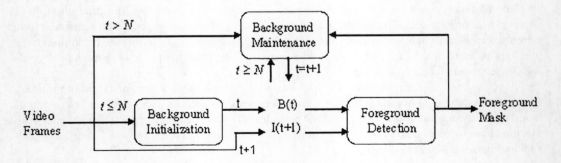

FIGURE 9.1   Background subtraction with a static camera, general scheme.

9.3.2 STATISTICS

Initially, Stauffer and Grimson proposed in 1999 a Gaussian Mixture Model (GMM) [13], also called Mixture of Gaussian (MoG) model [12] to detect foregrounds from a video scene. This pixel-based parametric procedure considers that the pixel intensity values come from a mixture of probability density functions (pdf's). Thenceforth, numerous researchers implemented and ameliorated the GMM model for better accuracy. Kernel Density Estimation (KDE) [11,35] is a pixel-based non-parametric model, which calculates the underline distribution by estimating the pdf from the available pixel information.

9.3.3 FUZZY CONCEPTS

A further theory that permits the tackling of imprecision, uncertainty and incompleteness is based on the fuzzy concept. In 2006–2008, many authors handled concepts such as Type-2 fuzzy sets [16,36,37], Sugeno integral [38,39] and Choquet integral [15,40,41]. These fuzzy models demonstrate robustness in dynamic backgrounds [36] scenarios.

9.3.4 DEMPSTER–SCHAFER CONCEPTS

Dempster–Schafer theory (also known under the name of evidence theory) [18] is a mathematical scheme enabling one to merge evidence from distinct sources and to provide a degree of belief obtained via belief functions and plausible reasoning that take into account all the available evidence. Dempster–Shafer theory have been employed in the foreground detection step [18].

9.4 MACHINE LEANING CONCEPTS

Machine learning-based approaches are categorized into representation learning, neural networks and deep learning methods. Representation learning techniques attempt to be robust to perturbations causing outliers in the low-rank structure. Neural networks and deep learning methods seek to learn as many scenes as possible to robustly detect in different environments. In deep learning algorithms, massive hardware architecture is trained with a large volume of original training images and ground-truth images.

9.4.1 REPRESENTATION LEARNING

- **Subspace Learning:** To learn the background in an unsupervised way, reconstructive subspace learning models [42], such as Principal Component Analysis (PCA) [19], have been developed in 1999. Subspace learning models handle illumination changes more robustly than statistical models [43]. In further methods, discriminative [20–22] and mixed [23] subspace learning models have been used to boost the performance for foreground detection. Nevertheless, each of these regular subspace methods presents a high sensitivity to outliers, noise and missing data.
- **Robust subspace Learning:** To address these limitations, since 2009, a robust PCA through decomposition into low-rank plus sparse matrices [24–27] has been commonly implemented in the field. The previous listed techniques are not only robust to variations in illumination but also to dynamic backgrounds [44–47]. However, these methods require batch algorithms, making them inoperable for real-time applications. To tackle this limitation, dynamic robust PCA and robust subspace tracking [48–50] have been designed to reach a real-time performance of RPCA-based methods. In this subspace learning category, the most accomplished techniques are GRASTA [51], incPCP [52], ReProCS [53], and MEROP [54]. Nevertheless, tensor RPCA-based methods [55–58] permit to consider temporal and spatial constraints leading them to be more robust to noise.

9.4.2   NEURAL NETWORKS MODELING

– **Neural Networks**: In 1996, Schofield et al. [30] initiated the use of neural networks for background modeling and foreground detection by means of a Random Access Memory (RAM) neural network. Although a RAM-NN requires the images to outline the background of the scene correctly without going through a background maintenance stage, because once a RAM-NN is trained with a single pass of background images, it is impossible to modify this information. In 2005, Tavakkoli [59] came up with a neural network approach within the new detector concept. In the course of the training phase, the background is split into blocks. Each block is associated to a Radial Basis Function Neural Network (RBF-NN). As a result, each RBF-NN is trained with samples of the background matching its related block. The decision to use RBF-NN is because it operates as a detector and not a discriminant, resulting in a closer boundary for the known class. RBF-NN methods are capable of treating dynamic object detection as a single class problem and learning the dynamic background. However, it takes an enormous amount of samples to represent the general background scenarios. In 2008, Maddalena and Petrosino [60,61] introduced a method called Self Organizing Background Subtraction (SOBS) based on a 2D self-organizing neural network architecture that preserves pixels' spatial relationships. The method is regarded as non-parametric, multi-modal, recursive and pixel-based. Through the neurons' weights of the network, the background is automatically modeled. Every single pixel is represented by a neural map with $n \times n$ weight vectors. The neural weight vectors are initialized with the respective color pixel values using the HSV color space. After the model initialization, each novel pixel information from a new video frame compares to its up-to-date model to determine if the pixel belongs to the background or to the foreground. In further works, SOBS was improved in several variants such as Multivalued SOBS [62], SOBS-CF [63], SC-SOBS [64], 3dSOBS+ [65], Simplified SOM [66], Neural-Fuzzy SOM [67] and MILSOBS [68] which allow this technique to be in the leading methods on the CDnet 2012 dataset [69] for a long time. SOBS also demonstrates good performance for stopped object detection [70–72]. However, one of the main drawbacks of SOBS-based methods is the need to manually adjust four or more parameters.

– **Support Vector Modeling:** SVM models are supervised learning models with related learning algorithms which analyze the data used for classification and regression analysis. There are three main categories of support vector formulations:

1. **Support Vector Machines:** VM was introduced in 1999 by Vapnik [73]. In the classification task, the SVM models determine a hyperplane within a large dimensional feature space to divide the training data into two classes. The best hyperplane is derived by minimizing a margin, which represents the smallest distance between the hyperplane and the data. Several authors used SVM for background modeling [74–85]. The original method has been introduced in 2002 by Lin et al. [82] and utilizes a probabilistic setup to map the output of a trained SVM onto a probability value representative of the probability of a pixel belonging to the background model. The main advantage of this method resides in its ability to learn an estimated model for every single background pixel. Thus, making this technique a suitable tool for initializing background models for indoor and outdoor scenes. Nevertheless, this technique suffers from a disadvantage that affects most two-class classification models used for background subtraction. This means that this formulation of the SVM classifier requires a balanced training set for both background and non-background pixel values. After this first work, several authors proposed incremental algorithms [75,76], real-time GPU implementations [74,75,78], a competing algorithm with a foreground model [79], an algorithm with mapping convergence [80,81], and block-based algorithms [77,85].

2. **Support Vector Regression:** SVR enables the estimation of a function from a set of training data. In effect, it estimates as not only a function that does well on the training data but also takes account of the possible deviation of the test data from the estimated function. While considering a new input, SVR provides a tolerance that characterizes the regression estimate being away from the true estimate by a certain distance, and thus allowing foreground detection. Furthermore, online SVR learning algorithms may be used to update the background model. In the literature, Wang et al. [86,87] are the only authors to have used this method for background modeling. Background subtraction for foreground target detection is then carried out by subtracting the pixel values that match the background model. If the difference between the observed value and the SVR model is greater than a given threshold, the pixel is part of the background, else it is classified as a foreground pixel. However, choosing a proper threshold is essential to maintain the accuracy of this approach by properly classifying pixels as background or foreground. To tackle this issue, an iterative approach can be employed by combining foreground detection and tracking steps of the algorithm to adaptively adjust the threshold values for each pixel of the SVR model [86,87]. Experimental results [86,87] demonstrate that SVR is adapted to slow illumination changes. Hsu and Chang [88] also used SVR for background modeling in video surveillance applications.

3. **Support Vector Data Description:** SVDD models have been proposed by Tax and Duin [89] in 2004 and are based on the Support Vector Classifier. SVDD models make it possible to obtain a spherical boundary around a given dataset, and it can also be made flexible by using other kernel functions. The method is made robust against outliers within the training set and is able to tighten the description with negative examples. In the literature, Tavakkoli et al. [90–92] used with success SVDD for background modeling by also providing a fast and efficient training algorithm based on genetic approach [93], and incremental SVDD algorithms [94,95] for background maintenance. Experiments [90–92] demonstrate that SVDD is suited for dynamic background environments.

– **Deep Neural Networks Modeling:** Since 2016, DNNs have also been successfully applied to the generation of background [96–99], background subtraction [100–107], enhanced foreground detection[108], generation of ground-truth [109], and deep spatial features learning [110–114]. More practically, Restricted Boltzman Machines (RBMs) were first used by Guo and Qi [96] and Xu et al. [98] for background generation to further achieve moving object detection through background subtraction. Similarly, Xu et al. [99,115] employed deep auto-encoder networks to accomplish the same task, while Qu et al. [97] used context-encoder to initialize the background. Another approach is that Convolutional Neural Networks (CNNs) have also been used for background subtraction by Braham and Droogenbroeck [102], Bautista et al. [101], and Cinelli [103]. Other authors have used improved CNNs such as cascaded CNNs [109], deep CNNs [100], structured CNNs [104] and two stage CNNs [116]. Through another approach, Zhang et al. [114] employed a Stacked Denoising Auto-Encoder (SDAE) for robust spatial features learning and modeled the background with density analysis, whereas Shafiee et al. [112] used Neural Response Mixture (NeREM) for deep features learning, which is used in the Mixture of Gaussians (MOG) model [13]. In 2019, Chan [117] introduced a deep learning-based scene-awareness approach to detect changes in video sequences, and thus applying the appropriate background subtraction algorithm for the corresponding type of challenge.

9.5 SIGNAL-PROCESSING CONCEPT

Based on signal processing, these models considered the pixels' temporal history as a 1-D dimensional signal. In this way, several signal-processing methods can be used: (i) signal estimation models (i.e. filters), (ii) transform domain functions, and (iii) sparse signal recovery models (i.e. compressive sensing).

9.5.1   FILTER BASED MODELS

In 1990, Karmann et al. [118] suggested a background estimation algorithm based on the Kalman filter. Pixels that deviate significantly from their predicted value are stated as foreground. Many variants have been proposed to improve this approach when there are changes in illumination and dynamic backgrounds [119–121]. In 1999, Toyama et al. [122] introduced their algorithm called Wallflower a pixel-level algorithm that permits probabilistic predictions of which background pixel values are to be expected in the next live image using a one-step Wiener prediction filter. Chang et al. [123,124] employed a Chebychev filter for background modeling. All these filter approaches show good performance in the presence of slow lighting changes, but less when scenes have complex dynamic backgrounds.

9.5.2   TRANSFORM DOMAIN MODELS

In 2005, Wren and Porikli [125] estimated the background model that captures spectral signatures of multi-modal backgrounds using the features of the Fast Fourier Transform (FFT) through a method known as Waviz. In this case, FFT features are then used to detect changes in the scene which are variable over time. An algorithm called Wave-Back has been developed in 2005 by Porikli and Wren [126], which generated a representation of the background using the frequency decomposition of pixel history. The Discrete Cosine Transform (DCT) coefficients are used since the features are calculated for the background and the current images. Next, the coefficients from the current image are compared with the background coefficients to generate a distance map for the image. Then, the distance maps are merged within the same temporal window of the DCT to improve the noise robustness. Finally, the distance maps are thresholded in such a way that foreground detection is achieved. This algorithm works effectively in the presence of undulating trees.

9.5.3   SPARSE SIGNAL RECOVERY MODELS

In 2008, Cevher et al. [127] pioneered the use of a compressive sensing approach for background subtraction. Rather than learning the entire background, Cevher et al. [127] learned and adapted a low-dimensional compressed representation of it which is sufficient to capture the different changes. Following this, moving objects are estimated directly by means of compressive samples with no auxiliary image reconstruction. However, to get simultaneous appearance recovery of the objects using compressive measurements, it needs to reconstruct an auxiliary image. To mitigate this constraint, many improvements have been proposed in the literature [128–132] and Bayesian compressive sensing approaches [133–136] are yielding good results in performance.

9.5.4   GRAPH SIGNAL PROCESSING

The first GSP-MOS algorithm has been proposed in [137] and named Graph BackGround Subtraction with Total Variation minimization (GraphBGS-TV), this method employes a Mask Region CNN (Mask R-CNN) [138] with a set of handcrafted features. GraphBGS-TV solves the problem of semi-supervised learning by means of Total Variation (TV) of graph signals [139]. The GraphBGS method was proposed by Giraldo and Bouwmans [140], where the segmentation step utilizes a Cascade Mask R-CNN [141], and where the problem of semi-supervised learning is solved with the Sobolev norm of graph signals [142]. Finally, Giraldo et al. [143] proposed the Graph Moving Object Segmentation (GraphMOS) algorithm. This method employs superpixel segmentation with deep and handcrafted features. With the Sobolev norm or TV of graph signals, GraphMOS is capable of solving the semi-supervised learning problem. Furthermore, Giraldo et al. [143] extended the GSP-MOS ideas to Video Object Segmentation (VOS), and they invented their algorithm under the name of GraphVOS.

9.6 CONCLUSION

In this chapter, we reviewed and classified different strategies developed over time to reach an efficient algorithm that can be implemented in Society 5.0. First, methods based on mathematical concepts show a great potential with a low computational cost of background subtraction methods although the resolution of the videos increases over time. Second, unsupervised or supervised machine learning models demonstrate better ability in more challenging situations. Third, graph signal-processing models can also be applied in a context with less labeled data.

REFERENCES

1. T. Bouwmans, F. Porikli, B. Horferlin, A. Vacavant, *Handbook on Background Modeling and Foreground Detection for Video Surveillance*, CRC Press, Taylor and Francis Group, NY, USA (2014).
2. T. Bouwmans, N. Aybat, E. Zahzah, *Handbook on Robust Low-Rank and Sparse Matrix Decomposition: Applications in Image and Video Processing*, Taylor and Francis Group, NY, USA (2016)
3. T. Bouwmans, B. Hofer-lin, F. Porikli, A. Vacavant, Traditional approaches in background modeling for video surveillance, *Handbook Background Modeling and Foreground Detection for Video Surveillance*, Taylor and Francis Group (2014).
4. T. Bouwmans, B. Hoferlin, F. Porikli, A. Vacavant, Recent approaches in background modeling for video surveillance, *Handbook Background Modeling and Foreground Detection for Video Surveillance*, Taylor and Francis Group, (2014).
5. T. Bouwmans, Traditional and recent approaches in background modeling for foreground detection: An overview, *Computer Science Review* 11 (2014) 31—66.
6. T. Bouwmans, C. Silva, C. Marghes, et al., On the role and the importance of features for background modeling and foreground detection, *Computer Science Review* 28 (2018) 26—91.
7. L. Maddalena, A. Petrosino, Background subtraction for moving object detection in RGB-D data: A survey, *MDPI Journal of Imaging* 4(5) (2018) 71.
8. B. Lee, M. Hedley, Background estimation for video surveillance, *Image & Vision Computing New Zealand (IVCNZ '02)*, Auckland, NZ, 315—320 (2002).
9. P. Graszka, Median mixture model for background-foreground segmentation in video sequences, *22nd International Conference in Central Europe on Computer Graphics, Visualization and Computer Vision*, 7 (2014) 103—110.
10. S. Roy, A. Ghosh, Real-time adaptive histogram min-max bucket (HMMB) model for background subtraction, *IEEE Transactions on Circuits and Systems for Video Technology* 28 (2017) 1513—1525.
11. A. Elgammal, L. Davis, Non-parametric model for background subtraction, *ECCV* 1843 (2000) 751—767.
12. R. Caseiro, P. Martins, J. Batista, Background modelling on tensor field for foreground segmentation, *BMVC* 2010 (2010) 1—12.
13. C. Stauffer, E. Grimson, Adaptive background mixture models for real-time tracking, *IEEE Conference on Computer Vision and Pattern Recognition, CVPR*, Fort Collins, CO, 246—252 (1999).
14. S. Varadarajan, P. Miller, H. Zhou, Spatial mixture of Gaussians fordynamic background modelling, *2013 10th IEEE International Conference on Advanced Video and Signal Based Surveillance*, Krakow, 63—68 (2013).
15. F. E. Baf, T. Bouwmans, B. Vachon, Fuzzy integral for moving object detection, *2008 IEEE International Conference on Fuzzy Systems (IEEE World Congress on Computational Intelligence)*, Hong Kong, 1729—1736 (2008).
16. F. E. Baf, T. Bouwmans, B. Vachon, Type-2 fuzzy mixture of Gaussians model: Application to background modeling, *ISVC*, Las Vegas 772—781 (2008).
17. F. E. Baf, T. Bouwmans, B. Vachon, Fuzzy statistical modeling of dynamic backgrounds for moving object detection in infrared videos, *IEEE-Workshop OTCBVS* 2009 (2009) 60—65.
18. O. Munteanu, T. Bouwmans, E. Zahzah, R. Vasiu, The detection of moving objects in video by background subtraction using Dempster-Shafer theory, *Transactions on Electronics and Communications* 60 (1) (2015) 1—11.
19. N. Oliver, B. Rosario, A. Pentland, A Bayesian computer vision system for modeling human interactions, *IEEE Transactions on Pattern Analysis and Machine Intelligence* 22 (8) (1999) 831—843.
20. D. Farcas, T. Bouwmans, Background modeling via a supervised subspace learning, *International Conference on Image, Video Processing and Computer Vision*, Orlando (2010) 1—7.

21. D. Farcas, C. Marghes, T. Bouwmans, Background subtraction via incremental maximum margin criterion: A discriminative approach, *Machine Vision and Applications* 23 (6) (2012) 1083–1101.
22. C. Marghes, T. Bouwmans, Background modeling via incremental maximum margin criterion, *ACCV 2010 Workshop Subspace*, New Zealand, volume 6469, 394–403 (2010).
23. C. Marghes, T. Bouwmans, R. Vasiu, Background modeling and foreground detection via a reconstructive and discriminative subspace learning approach, *Proceedings of the International Conference on Image Processing, Computer Vision, and Pattern Recognition (IPCV)*, 1–7 (2012).
24. E. Candes, X. Li, Y. Ma, J. Wright, Robust principal component analysis? *International Journal of ACM* 58 (3) (2011) 1–37.
25. A. Sobral, T. Bouwmans, E. Zahzah, Double-constrained RPCA based on saliency maps for foreground detection in automated maritime surveillance, *2015 12th IEEE International Conference on Advanced Video and Signal Based Surveillance (AVSS)*, Karlsruhe, 1–6 (2015).
26. S. Javed, A. Mahmood, T. Bouwmans, S. Jung, Motion-aware graph regularized RPCA for background modeling of complex scenes, scene background modeling contest, *2016 23rd International Conference on Pattern Recognition (ICPR)*, Cancun, Mexico, 120–125 (2016).
27. S. Javed, A. Mahmood, T. Bouwmans, S. Jung, Spatiotemporal low-rank modeling for complex scene background initialization, *IEEE Transactions on Circuits and Systems for Video Technology* 28 (6) (2016) 1315–1329.
28. G. Ramirez-Alonso, M. Chacon-Murguia, Self-adaptive SOM-CNN neural system for dynamic object detection in normal and complex scenarios, *Pattern Recognition* 48 (4) (2015) 1137–1149.
29. J. Ramirez-Quintana, M. Chacon-Murguia, Self-organizing retinotopic maps applied to background modeling for dynamic object segmentationin video sequences, *The 2013 International Joint Conference on Neural Networks (IJCNN)*, Dallas, TX, 1–8 (2013).
30. A. Schofield, P. Mehta, T. Stonham, A system for counting people in video images using neural networks to identify the background scene, *Pattern Recognition* 29 (1996) 1421–1428.
31. J. Giraldo, S. Javed, T. Bouwmans, Graph moving object segmentation, *IEEE Transactions on Pattern Analysis and Machine Intelligence* 44(5) (2022) 2485–2503.
32. J. Giraldo, S. Javed, M. Sultana, S. Jung, T. Bouwmans, The emerging field of graph signal processing for moving object segmentation, *International Workshop on Frontiers of Computer Vision, IW-FCV*, Daegu (2021).
33. J. Giraldo, T. Bouwmans, GraphBGS: Background subtraction via recovery of graph signals, *International Conference on Pattern Recognition, ICPR*, Milan (2020).
34. J. Giraldo, T. Bouwmans, Semi-supervised background subtraction of unseen videos: minimization of the total variation of graph signals, *IEEE International Conference on Image Processing, ICIP*, Abu Dhabi (2020).
35. Z. Zivkovic, F. Heijden, Recursive unsupervised learning of finite mixture models, *IEEE Transaction on Pattern Analysis and Machine Intelligence* 5 (26) (2004) 651–656.
36. T. Bouwmans, F.E. Baf, Modeling of dynamic backgrounds by type-2 fuzzy Gaussians mixture models, *MASAUM Journal of Basic and Applied Science* 1 (2) (2009) 265–277.
37. Z. Zhao, T. Bouwmans, X. Zhang, Y. Fang, A fuzzy background modeling approach for motion detection in dynamic backgrounds, *International Conference on Multimedia and Signal Processing*, Springer, Berlin, Heidelberg (2012).
38. H. Zhang, D. Xu, Fusing color and gradient features for background model, *2006 8th international Conference on Signal Processing*, Guilin (2006).
39. H. Zhang, D. Xu, Fusing color and texture features for background model, *International Conference on Fuzzy Systems and Knowledge Discovery, FSKD*, Springer, Berlin, Heidelberg, 887–893 (2006).
40. F.E. Baf, T. Bouwmans, B. Vachon, Foreground detection using the Choquet integral, *International Workshop on Image Analysis for Multimedia Interactive Integral, WIAMIS*, Klagenfurt, Austria, 187–190 (2008).
41. P. Chiranjeevi, S. Sengupta, Interval-valued model level fuzzy aggregation-based background subtraction, *IEEE Transactions on Cybernetics* 47 (9) (2017) 2544–2555.
42. T. Bouwmans, Subspace learning for background modeling: A survey, *Recent Patents on Computer Science* 2 (3) (2009) 223–234.
43. T. Bouwmans, E. Zahzah, Robust PCA via principal component pursuit: A review for a comparative evaluation in video surveillance, *Computer Vision and Image Understanding* 122 (2014) 22–34.
44. S. Javed, S. Oh, A. Sobral, T. Bouwmans, S. Jung, Background subtraction via superpixel-based online matrix decomposition with structured foreground constraints, *Workshop on Robust Subspace Learning and Computer Vision, ICCV*, Santiago, Chile (2015).

45. S. Javed, A. Mahmood, T. Bouwmans, S. Jung, Background-foreground modeling based on spatiotemporal sparse subspace clustering, *IEEE Transactions on Image Processing* 26(12) (2017) 5840–5854.
46. B. Rezaei, S. Ostadabbas, Background subtraction via fast robust matrix completion, *International Workshop on RSL-CV in conjunction with ICCV* (2017).
47. B. Rezaei, S. Ostadabbas, Moving object detection through robust matrix completion augmented with objectness, *IEEE Journal of Selected Topics in Signal Processing* 12(6) (2018) 1313–1323.
48. N. Vaswani, T. Bouwmans, S. Javed, P. Narayanamurthy, Robust subspace learning: Robust PCA, robust subspace tracking and robust subspace recovery, *IEEE Signal Processing Magazine* 35 (4) (2018) 32–55.
49. N. Vaswani, T. Bouwmans, S. Javed, P. Narayanamurthy, Robust PCA and robust subspace tracking: A comparative evaluation, *Statistical Signal Processing Workshop, SSP*, Freiburg im Breisgau, Germany (2018).
50. S. Prativadibhayankaram, H. Luong, T. Le, A. Kaup, Compressive online video background–foreground separation using multiple prior information and optical flow, *Journal of Imaging* 4(7) (2018).
51. J. He, L. Balzano, A. Szlam, Incremental gradient on the grassmannian for online foreground and background separation in subsampled video, *International on Conference on Computer Vision and Pattern Recognition, CVPR* (2012).
52. P. Rodriguez, B. Wohlberg, Incremental principal component pursuit for video background modeling, *Journal of Mathematical Imaging and Vision* 55 (1) (2016) 1–18.
53. H. Guo, C. Qiu, N. Vaswani, Practical ReProCS for separating sparse and low-dimensional signal sequences from their sum, *2014 IEEE International Conference on Acoustics, Speech and Signal Processing (ICASSP)*, Florence, 4161–4165 (2014).
54. P. Narayanamurthy, N. Vaswani, A fast and memory-efficient algorithm for robust PCA (MEROP), *IEEE International Conference on Acoustics, Speech, and Signal, ICASSP*, Calgary, AB, Canada (2018).
55. S. Javed, T. Bouwmans, S. Jung, Stochastic decomposition into low rank and sparse tensor for robust background subtraction, *ICDP*, London (2015).
56. A. Sobral, S. Javed, S. Jung, T. Bouwmans, E. Zahzah, Online stochastic tensor decomposition for background subtraction in multispectral video sequences, *Workshop on Robust Subspace Learning and Computer Vision, ICCV* (2015).
57. C. Lu, J. Feng, Y. Chen, W. Liu, Z. Lin, S. Yan, Tensor robust principal component analysis with a new tensor nuclear norm, *IEEE Transactions on Pattern Analysis and Machine Intelligence* 42 (4) (2020) 925–938.
58. D. Driggs, S. Becker, J. Boyd-Graberz, Tensor robust principal component analysis: Better recovery with atomic norm regularization, Preprint.
59. A. Tavakkoli, Foreground-background segmentation in video sequences using neural networks, *Intelligence Systems Neural Network Applications*.
60. L. Maddalena, A. Petrosino, A self-organizing approach to detection of moving patterns for real-time applications, *Advances in Brain, Vision, and Artificial Intelligence* 4729 (2007) 181–190.
61. L. Maddalena, A. Petrosino, A self organizing approach to background subtraction for visual surveillance applications, *IEEE Transactions on Image Processing* 17 (7) (2008) 1168–1177.
62. L. Maddalena, A. Petrosino, Multivalued background/foreground separation for moving object detection, *International Workshop on Fuzzy Logic and Applications, WILF*, 263–270 (2009).
63. L. Maddalena, A. Petrosino, A fuzzy spatial coherence-based approach to background/foreground separation for moving object detection, *Neural Computing and Applications* 2010 (2010) 1–8.
64. L. Maddalena, A. Petrosino, The SOBS algorithm: What are the limits? *IEEE Workshop on Change Detection, CVPR*, (2012).
65. L. Maddalena, A. Petrosino, The 3dSOBS+ algorithm for moving object detection, *Computer Vision and Image Understanding* 122 (2014) 65–73.
66. M. Chacon-Muguia, S. Gonzalez-Duarte, P. Vega, Simplified SOM-neural model for video segmentation of moving objects, *International Joint Conference on Neural Networks, IJCNN*, Atlanta, GA, USA, 474–480 (2009).
67. M. Chacon-Murguia, G. Ramirez-Alonso, S. Gonzalez-Duarte, Improvement of a neural-fuzzy motion detection vision model for complex scenario conditions, *International Joint Conference on Neural Networks, IJCNN*, (2013).
68. G. Gemignani, A. Rozza, A novel background subtraction approach based on multi-layered self organizing maps, *IEEE International Conference on Image Processing (ICIP)*, Quebec City 462–466 (2015).
69. N. Goyette, P. Jodoin, F. Porikli, J. Konrad, P. Ishwar, Changedetection.net: A new change detection benchmark dataset, *IEEE Workshop on Change Detection, CDW 2012 in Conjunction with CVPR* (2012).

70. L. Maddalena, A. Petrosino, 3D neural model-based stopped object detection, *International Conference on Image Analysis and Processing, ICIAP 2009*, 585–593 (2009).
71. L. Maddalena, A. Petrosino, Self organizing and fuzzy modelling for parked vehicles detection, *Advanced Concepts for Intelligent Vision Systems, ACVIS 2009*, 422–433 (2009).
72. L. Maddalena, A. Petrosino, Stopped object detection by learning foreground model in videos, *EEE Transactions on Neural Networks and Learning Systems* 24 (5) (2013) 723–735.
73. V. Vapnik. An overview of statistical learning theory. *IEEE Transactions on Neural Networks*, 10(5) (1999) 988–999.
74. L. Cheng, M. Gong. Real time background subtraction from dynamics scenes. *International Conference on Computer Vision, ICCV 2009*, Kyoto, Japan (2009).
75. L. Cheng, M. Gong, D. Schuurmans, T. Caelli. Real-time discriminative background subtraction. *IEEE Transaction on Image Processing* 20 (5)(2011) 1401–1414.
76. L. Cheng, S. Wang, D. Schuurmans, T. Caelli, S. Vishwanathan. An online discriminative approach to background subtraction. *IEEE International Conference on Advanced Video and Signal Based Surveillance, AVSS 2006*, (2006).
77. A. Glazer, M. Lindenbaum, S. Markovitch. One-class background model. *International Workshop on Background Models Challenge, ACCV 2012* (2012).
78. M. Gong, L. Cheng. Real time foreground segmentation on GPUs using local online learning and global graph cut optimization. *International Conference on Pattern Recognition, ICPR 2008*, Tampa, FL, USA (2008).
79. M. Gong, L. Cheng. Foreground segmentation of live videos using locally competing 1SVMs. *International Conference on Computer Vision and Pattern Recognition, CVPR 2011*, (2011).
80. I. Junejo, A. Bhutta, H. Foroosh. Dynamic scene modeling for object detection using single-class SVM. *International Conference on Image Processing, ICIP 2010*, 1541–1544 (2010).
81. I. Junejo, A. Bhutta, H. Foroosh. Single class support vector machine (SVM) for scene modeling. *Journal of Signal, Image and Video Processing* 42 (7) (2011).
82. H. Lin, T. Liu, J. Chuang. A probabilistic SVM approach for background scene initialization. *International Conference on Image Processing, ICIP 2002*, Rochester, NY, USA, 893–896 (2002).
83. H. Lin, T. Liu, J. Chuang. Learning a scene background model via classification. *IEEE Transactions on Signal Processing*, 57(5) (2009) 1641–1654.
84. S. Liu, J. Dong, S. Wang, G. Chen. Road junction background reconstruction based on median estimation and support vector machines. *International Conference on Machine Learning and Cybernetics, ICMLC 2006*, Dalian, China, 4200–4205, (2006).
85. X. Zhang, C. Blanco, C. Cuevas, F. Jaureguizar, N. Garcia. High-quality regionbased foreground segmentation using a spatial grid of SVM classifiers. *IEEE International Conference on Consumer Electronics, ICCE 2014*, Las Vegas, NV, USA, 488–499, (2014).
86. J. Wang, G. Bebis, R. Miller. Robust video-based surveillance by integrating target detection with tracking. *IEEE Workshop on Object Tracking and Classification Beyond the Visible Spectrum in conjunction with CVPR 2006*, New York, NY, USA (2006).
87. J. Wang, G. Bebis, M. Nicolescu, M. Nicolescu, R. Miller. Improving target detection by coupling it with tracking. *Machine Vision and Application* 12 (2008) 1–19.
88. C. Hsu C. Chang. Video surveillance mining on object detection and tracking. *Video Signal Processing Final Project Report* (2007).
89. D. Tax R. Duin. Support vector data description. *Machine Learning*, 54 (2004) 45–66.
90. A. Tavakkoli. Novelty detection: An approach to foreground detection in videos. *Pattern Recognition*, INTECH (2010).
91. A. Tavakkoli, M. Nicolescu, G. Bebis. Novelty detection approach for foreground region detection in videos with quasi-stationary backgrounds. *International Symposium on Visual Computing, ISVC 2006*, 40–49, (2006).
92. A. Tavakkoli, M. Nicolescu, G. Bebis, M. Nicolescu. A support vector data description approach for background modeling in videos with quasi-stationary backgrounds. *International Journal of Artificial Intelligence Tools*, 17 (4) (2008) 635–658.
93. A. Tavakkoli, A. Ambardekar, M. Nicolescu, S. Louis. A genetic approach to training support vector data descriptors for background modeling in video data. *International Symposium on Visual Computing, ISVC 2007* (2007).
94. A. Tavakkoli, M. Nicolescu, M. Nicolescu, G. Bebis. Efficient background modeling through incremental support vector data description. *International Conference on Pattern Recognition, ICPR 2008*, Tampa, FL, USA (2008).

95. A. Tavakkoli, M. Nicolescu, M. Nicolescu, G. Bebis. Incremental SVDD training: Improving efficiency of background modeling in videos. *International Conference on Signal and Image Processing, ICSIP 2008* (2008).

96. R. Guo, H. Qi, Partially-sparse restricted Boltzmann machine for background modeling and subtraction, *International Conference on Machine Learning and Applications, ICMLA 2013*, Miami, FL, USA, 209–214 (2013).

97. Z. Qu, S. Yu, M. Fu, Motion background modeling based on contextencoder, *IEEE International Conference on Artificial Intelligence and Pattern Recognition, ICAIPR 2016*, Lecce, Italy (2016).

98. L. Xu, Y. Li, Y. Wang, E. Chen, Temporally adaptive restricted Boltzmann machine for background modeling, *American Association for Artificial Intelligence, AAAI 2015* (2015).

99. P. Xu, M. Ye, Q. Liu, X. Li, L. Pei, J. Ding, Motion detection via a couple of auto-encoder networks, *International Conference on Multimedia and Expo, ICME 2014* (2014).

100. M. Babaee, D. Dinh, G. Rigoll, A deep convolutional neural network for background subtraction, Preprint (2017). https://doi.org/10.48550/arXiv.1702.01731

101. C. Bautista, C. Dy, M. Manalac, R.O. Orbe, M. Cordel, Convolutional neural network for vehicle detection in low resolution traffic videos, *2016 IEEE Region 10 Symposium (TENSYMP)*, Bali, Indonesia, 277–281 (2016).

102. M. Braham, M.V. Droogenbroeck, Deep background subtraction with scene-specific convolutional neural networks, *International Conference on Systems, Signals and Image Processing, IWSSIP 2016*, 1–4 (2016).

103. L.P. Cinelli, *Anomaly Detection in Surveillance Videos Using Deep Residual Networks*, Master Thesis, Universidade de Rio de Janeiro (2017).

104. K. Lim, W. Jang, C. Kim, Background subtraction using encoder-decoder structured convolutional neural network, *IEEE International Conference on Advanced Video and Signal based Surveillance, AVSS 2017*, Lecce, Italy (2017).

105. S. Choo, W. Seo, D. Jeong, N. Cho, Multi-scale recurrent encoder-decoder network for dense temporal classification, *IAPR International Conference on Pattern Recognition, ICPR 2018*, Beijing, China, 103–108 (2018).

106. S. Choo, W. Seo, D. Jeong, N. Cho, Learning background subtraction by video synthesis and multi-scale recurrent networks, Asian Conference on Computer Vision, ACCV 2018 (2018).

107. A. Farnoosh, B. Rezaei, S. Ostadabbas, DeepPBM: deep probabilistic background model estimation from video sequences, Preprint (2019). https://doi.org/10.48550/arXiv.1902.00820

108. D. Zeng, M. Zhu, Combining background subtraction algorithms with convolutional neural network 28 (1) (2018) 1.

109. Y. Wang, Z. Luo, P. Jodoin, Interactive deep learning method for segmenting moving objects, *Pattern Recognition Letters* 96 (2017) 66–75.

110. S. Lee, D. Kim, Background subtraction using the factored 3-way restricted boltzmann machines, Preprint (2018).

111. T. Nguyen, C. Pham, S. Ha, J. Jeon, Change detection by training a triplet network for motion feature extraction, *IEEE Transactions on Circuits and Systems for Video Technology* 29 (2) (2019) 433–446.

112. M. Shafiee, P. Siva, P. Fieguth, A. Wong, Embedded motion detection via neural response mixture background modeling, *International Conference on Computer Vision and Pattern Recognition, CVPR 2016*, Las Vegas, NV, USA (2016).

113. M. Shafiee, P. Siva, P. Fieguth, A. Wong, Real-time embedded motion detection via neural response mixture modeling, *Journal of Signal Processing Systems* 90 (2018) 931–946.

114. Y. Zhang, X. Li, Z. Zhang, F. Wu, L. Zhao, Deep learning driven blockwise moving object detection with binary scene modeling, *Neurocomputing* 168 (2015) 454–463.

115. P. Xu, M. Ye, X. Li, Q. Liu, Y. Yang, J. Ding, Dynamic background learning through deep auto-encoder networks, *ACM International Conference on Multimedia* (2014).

116. X. Zhao, Y. Chen, M. Tang, J. Wang, Joint background reconstruction and foreground segmentation via a two-stage convolutional neural network, Preprint (2017).

117. Y. Chan, Deep learning-based scene-awareness approach for intelligent change detection in videos, *Journal of Electronic Imaging* 28 (1) (2019) 013038.

118. K. Karmann, A. V. Brand, Moving object recognition using an adaptive background memory, *Time-Varying Image Processing and Moving Object Recognition*, Elsevier (1990).

119. M. Boninsegna, A. Bozzoli, A tunable algorithm to update a reference image, *Signal Processing: Image Communication* 16 (4) (2000) 1353–365.

120. S. Messelodi, C. Modena, N. Segata, M. Zanin, A Kalman filter based background updating algorithm robust to sharp illumination changes, *International Conference on Image Analysis and Processing, ICIAP 2005*, 163–170 (2005).

121. D. Fan, M. Cao, C. Lv, An updating method of self-adaptive background for moving objects detection in video, *International Conference on Audio, Language and Image Processing, ICALIP 2008*, Shanghai, China, 1497–1501 (2008).

122. C. Wren, A. Azarbayejani, Pfinder: Real-time tracking of the human body, *IEEE Transactions on Pattern Analysis and Machine Intelligence* 19 (7) (1997) 780–785.

123. T. Chang, T. Ghandi, M. Trivedi, Vision modules for a multi sensory bridge monitoring approach, *International Conference on Intelligent Transportation Systems, ITSC 2004*, Washington, WA, USA, 971–976 (2004).

124. T. Chang, T. Ghandi, M. Trivedi, Computer vision for multi-sensory structural health monitoring system, *International Conference on Intelligent Transportation Systems, ITSC 2004* (2004).

125. C. Wren, F. Porikli, Waviz: Spectral similarity for object detection, *IEEE International Workshop on Performance Evaluation of Tracking and Surveillance, PETS 2005* (2005).

126. F. Porikli, C. Wren, Change detection by frequency decomposition: Waveback, *International Workshop on Image Analysis for Multimedia Interactive Services, WIAMIS 2005* (2005).

127. V. Cevher, D. Reddy, M. Duarte, A. Sankaranarayanan, R. Chellappa, R. Baraniuk, Compressive sensing for background subtraction, *European Conference on Computer Vision, ECCV 2008* (2008).

128. J. Mota, L. Weizman, N. Deligiannis, Y. Eldar, M. Rodrigues, Reference based compressed sensing: A sample complexity approach, *IEEE International Conference on Acoustics, Speech and Signal Processing, ICASSP 2016,* Shanghai, China (2016).

129. G. Warnell, D. Reddy, R. Chellappa, Adaptive rate compressive sensing for background subtraction, *IEEE International Conference on Acoustics, Speech, and Signal Processing,* Kyoto, Japan (2012).

130. G. Warnell, S. Bhattacharya, R. Chellappa, T. Basar, Adaptive-rate compressive sensing via side information, *IEEE Transactions on Image Processing* 24 (11) (2015) 3846–3857.

131. R. Davies, L. Mihaylova, N. Pavlidis, I. Eckley, The effect of recovery algorithms on compressive sensing background subtraction, *Workshop Sensor Data Fusion: Trends, Solutions, and Applications* (2013) 1–6.

132. H. Xiao, Y. Liu, M. Zhang, Fast l1-minimization algorithm for robust background subtraction, *EURASIP Journal on Image and Video Processing* 45 (2016) (2016). https://doi.org/10.1186/s13640-016-0150-5

133. D. Kuzin, O. Isupova, L. Mihaylova, Compressive sensing approaches for autonomous object detection in video sequences, *Sensor Data Fusion: Trends, Solutions, Applications* 2015 (2015) 1–6.

134. D. Kuzin, O. Isupova, L. Mihaylova, Compressive sensing approaches for autonomous object detection in video sequences, *2015 Sensor Data Fusion: Trends, Solutions, Applications (SDF)*, Bonn, Germany, 2015, pp. 1–6, doi: 10.1109/SDF.2015.7347706

135. D. Kuzin, O. Isupova, L. Mihaylova, Spatio-temporal structured sparse regression with hierarchical Gaussian process priors, *IEEE Transactions on Signal Processing* 66 (17) (2018) 4598–4611.

136. D. Kuzin, *Sparse Machine Learning Methods for Autonomous Decision Making*, PhD Thesis, University of Sheffield (2018).

137. J.H Giraldo, T. Bouwmans, Semi-supervised background subtraction of unseenvideos: Minimization of the total variation of graph signals. *IEEE ICIP,* Abu Dhabi, United Arab Emirates (2020).

138. K. He, G. Gkioxari, P. Dollár and R. Girshick, Mask R-CNN. *2017 IEEE International Conference on Computer Vision (ICCV)*, Venice, Italy, 2980–2988 (2017), doi: 10.1109/ICCV.2017.322.

139. A. Jung et al., Semi-supervised learning in network-structured data via total variation minimization. *IEEE T-SP* 67 (24) (2019) 6256–6269.

140. J.H. Giraldo, T. Bouwmans, GraphBGS: Background subtraction via recovery of graph signals, *2020 25th International Conference on Pattern Recognition (ICPR)*, Milan, Italy, 6881–6888 (2021), doi: 10.1109/ICPR48806.2021.9412999.

141. Z. Cai, N. Vasconcelos, Cascade R-CNN: High quality object detection and in-stance segmentation. *IEEE Transactions on Pattern Analysis and Machine Intelligence*, 43 (5) (2021) 1483–1498, doi: 10.1109/TPAMI.2019.2956516.

142. J.H. Giraldo, T. Bouwmans, On the minimization of Sobolev norms of time-varying graph signals: Estimation of new coronavirus disease 2019 cases. *020 IEEE 30th International Workshop on Machine Learning for Signal Processing (MLSP)* (2020).

143. J.H. Giraldo, S. Javed, T. Bouwmans, Graph moving object segmentation. *IEEE Transactions on Pattern Analysis and Machine Intelligence*, 44 (5) (2022) 2485–2503, doi: 10.1109/TPAMI.2020.3042093.

10 A New Era in Forensic Investigation-Virtual Autopsy

Vedant Kulshrestha
Uttar Pradesh University of Medical Sciences

CONTENTS

10.1 INTRODUCTION

The word autopsy is derived from the Greek word 'autopsia' means 'to see for oneself'. Autopsy is the examination of bodies after death, where whole surface of the body as well as all the body cavities are explored to record the findings. While doing so, we have to collect all the possible findings, which will help in establishing the circumstances leading to the death like cause of death, mode and manner of death etc. and also help the law enforcing agencies. It is also known as 'Necropsy' or 'Postmortem examination' or 'Thanatopsy'. The classical or conventional autopsy technique involves the traditional means of external examination and involves 'invasive body opening' procedure to examine all internal organs. Now with the advancement of technology, the combination of new technologies such as artificial intelligence (AI), big data, cloud computing, Internet of Things (IoT), Machine learning (ML) and other technologies developed various solutions to effectively influence digital pillar of society by completely transforming the means of living. Healthcare is one of the digital pillars of Society 5.0. Virtual autopsy is a new medical technology that plays an important role in hospital conducting medicolegal autopsies. Now new radiological imaging methods, such as multi detector computed tomography (MDCT) and magnetic resonance imaging (MRI) have become a recent addition to autopsy workflow and can even modify the classical 'body opening' autopsy to a new field of 'non invasive' or 'minimally invasive' autopsy procedure. This high-tech

DOI: 10.1201/9781003324720-13

method of postmortem examination which becomes popular in some countries is known as 'virtual autopsy' or 'virtopsy' or 'digital autopsy'. [1]. Dead body is first scanned with MDCT and MRI then Radiologists generate a single 3D vision of the decedent's body, that can allow pathologists, coroners, and medical examiners to investigate the condition of body tissues, organs, bones and blood vessels to trace the exact cause and manner of death. A full body scan takes approximately 20 seconds and on the other hand, graphics workstation compiles the complete data into a 3-D images within 1 minute [2]. Systemic research studies of virtual autopsy were started in Switzerland in late 1990s and later spread to the other European Countries, Australia, Japan, Malaysia and many other countries [3–5]. In a developing country like India, virtual autopsy projects have been started at few places, but it is still a new concept, and the application of virtual autopsy will become increasingly prominent and recognized as the time progresses [6–8]

10.2   TECHNIQUES OF VIRTOPSY

Virtopsy does not destroy some of the key forensic evidences, which may be destroyed in conventional autopsy. The following techniques [2,9,10], as shown in Figures 10.1 and 10.2, are used in Virtopsy:

1. **Photogrammetry:** Photogrammetry is the practice of determining the geometric properties of objects from photographic images. A more sophisticated technique called stereo-photogrammetry, involves estimating the three-dimensional coordinates of points on an object. It is done using 3D optical surface scanner.
2. **Radiography:** Conventional radiography is the mainstay of postmortem imaging.
3. **Ultrasonography:** The use of US in postmortem imaging has been limited, but it can be used to guide biopsy procedures in cases of a minimal invasive autopsy.

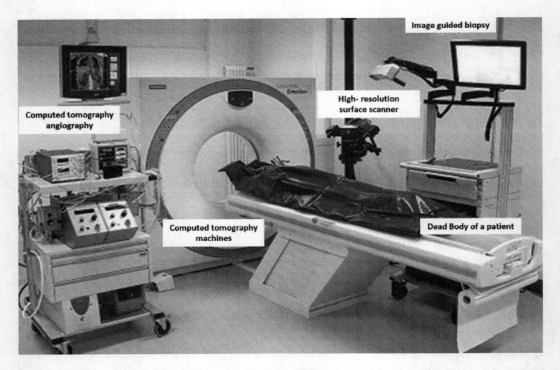

FIGURE 10.1   A virtual autopsy setup with 3D surface scanner, imaging of dead body with CT scan machine, CT angiography and image-guided biopsy.

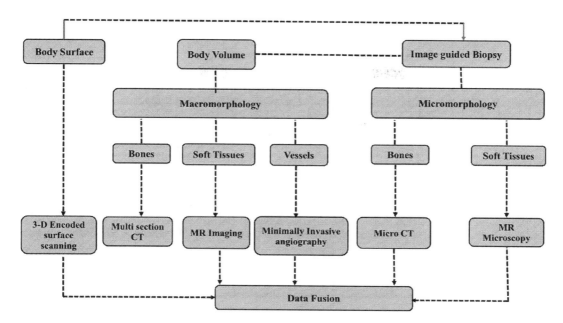

FIGURE 10.2 Showing flow chart of different techniques used in virtual autopsy and final data fusion and data analysis done by software.

4. **Multi Slice/Multi Detector Computed Tomography:** Postmortem CT is a fast technique that allows imaging of the whole body inside a body or coffin. 2D and 3D images are possible with MSCT/MDCT.
5. **Magnetic Resonance Imaging and Magnetic Resonance Spectroscopy:** MRI scanners provides multi planar, multidirectional sectional images and good anatomical details, superior contrast and resolution compared to CT.
6. **Micro Imaging:** Micro CT and magnetic resonance microscopy provide finer anatomic details of small specimens.
7. **Post-Mortem Angiography:** For postmortem cardiac diagnostics, minimal invasive coronary angiography with MSCT can be used. Perfusions studies of the myocardium can be made with both MRI and MSCT.

Nowadays, many companies are available in the market who have developed their software related to virtual autopsy and 3D virtual autopsy dissection table on which we can do virtual dissection of dead body without making an incision and note the internal findings [11], as shown in Figure 10.3.

10.3 MEDICO LEGAL IMPORTANCE OF VIRTUAL AUTOPSY

Virtual autopsy will be helpful to the forensic expert to solve the following medico legal aspects.

10.3.1 CAUSE OF DEATH

• MDCT finding of frothy airway fluid or high attenuation of airway sediment is suggestive of drowning.
• Demonstration of injuries to deeper structures and visceral organs become easy using virtopsy technique. There are two images as shown in Figure 10.4. (i) 3D reconstruction of the skull of a person who fell from height and results in extensive fractures and

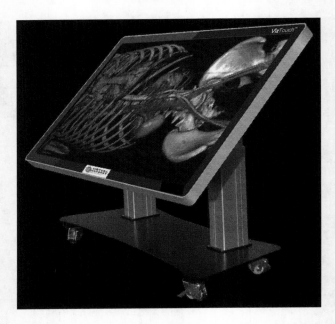

FIGURE 10.3 Advanced 3D virtual autopsy dissection table viztouch. (Courtesy: Virtual autopsy solutions, UK & virtual autopsy India.)

(ii) a patient was assaulted and sustained fractures of the facial bones (left maxilla, zygomatic arch and orbital bones).
- Laryngeal foreign bodies can be identified which help to find out the cause of death.
- Electric injuries are studied by micro MR. In gunshot injuries it is possible to determine the entrance and exit wounds from the fracture pattern and beveling of bone and it is excellent to view the track of projectile.
- Air embolism, pneumothorax, emphysema and hyperbaric trauma can be better appreciated with MSCT.

10.3.2 Identification of the Deceased

MSCT has a potential value for anthropological study in order to estimate age or to visualize features to enable identification of corpse with cranial CT data obtained in a dead body; it is possible to reconstruct any ante mortem radiographic picture for comparison. Postmortem CT data can be correlated with ante mortem dental records of suspected missing persons.

10.3.3 Identification of Accused

Color-coded three D surface images of bite mark on the victim's skin can be correlated with the dentition of possible offenders.

10.3.4 Identification of Weapon

Micro CT has been used to demonstrate a knife blade to determine the injury pattern and weapon used.

10.3.5 Postmortem Interval

MR spectroscopy measures the metabolites formed due to decomposition.

10.3.6 RECONSTRUCTION OF THE ACCIDENT

With the CT data concerning the skeletal joints and fractures in the deceased person, it is possible to reconstructs the position of the body at the time of accident. It can be correlated with the 3D image of the vehicle and allow forensic reconstruction of the accident.

10.3.7 MECHANISM OF DEATH: HAEMORRHAGE, PULMONARY EDEMA ETC. CAN BE IDENTIFIED BY THE MRI AND CT SCANNING

10.4 ADVANTAGES OF VIRTOPSY

This is a recent advancement in the field of investigation of the cause of death, which has many advantages and disadvantages. Some of the major advantages are listed below:

- Less time-consuming and body can be released immediately after the scanning.
- Complete, non-destructive gathering of findings from head to toe.
- Non-invasive.
- Images can be digitized and can be used easily as evidence in court of law. In virtual autopsy, there is more precise and three-dimensional portrayal of injuries such as stab wounds and firearm wounds, which is easy to understand even for a non-medical person, e.g. lawyers and judges.
- Easy and more accurate detection of air and fluid inside the body cavities, fractures, foreign bodies, soft tissue trauma and injury to blood vessels is done in virtual autopsy.
- Documentation of postmortem findings is done in a completely objective manner, free of subjective bias which may occur in a written postmortem report of conventional autopsy.
- As all the data obtained are in a digital format, so these can be stored for several years even after the cremation or burial of the body.
- Certain religious committee rejecting traditional autopsy may accept this method because it is noninvasive.
- Storage of data become easy. The complete saved data-set can be re-examined at any time if a second expert opinion is required. Also data can be transmitted over internet to any part of the world for subsequent/expert/re-opinion.

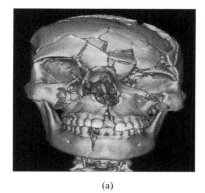
(a)

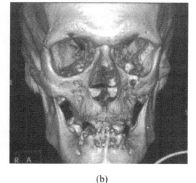
(b)

FIGURE 10.4 CT, 3D reconstruction of the skull: (a) Extensive fractures of skull bones after falling from a height and (b) Facial bone fractures in a case of physical assault.

- There is less risk of infection due to less manual handling, so it is particularly suitable for dead bodies having infectious diseases such as swine flu, HIV, tuberculosis, COVID-19, etc. and for decomposed bodies.
- Facilities for MRI & CT scan are already present in some centers. If the facilities are available at distant centers, the bodies may be transported by ambulance to these centers for virtopsy.
- The biopsies obtained can be reported by Forensic pathologists using the Telepathology system, which is coming up rapidly all over the country.

10.5   DISADVANTAGES OF VIRTOPSY

This is an advanced imaging technique which takes less times as compared to the physical autopsy, but this has several disadvantages also that are listed below:

- Highly expensive due to high cost of equipment needed for the technique and expertise is needed for taking and understanding CT and MRI.
- Postmortem gas formation may be difficult to distinguish with other gases.
- Due to stoppage of circulation contrasts CT and postmortem angiography may not be feasible.
- Parenchymal and vascular injuries are difficult to differentiate.
- MRI is time-consuming procedure.
- No color documentation is possible which gives important information about status of inflammation and age of injuries etc. It can neither differentiate between antemortem and postmortem injuries nor it can detect postmortem artifacts.
- Rigor Mortis and Livor mortis which are helpful in determining time since death cannot be appreciated.
- Smell of the tissues cannot be appreciated.
- Collection of evidence in case of firearm injuries is not possible.
- Collection of samples for histopathological examination of organs to diagnose exact pathology in different organs and chemical analysis of viscera to detect poisons is not possible until unless we make it as minimally invasive procedure from completely noninvasive one.
- The biggest question mark regarding this technology is its acceptability in the court of law in some countries [8–12].

10.6   VIRTUAL AUTOPSY IN INDIA

This is a new emerging technology that allows medical practitioners to perform a postmortem of a dead body to find out the death cause without any incisions on body using advanced technologies such as MRI or CT scans. These advancements provide a detailed overview about several body organs from different angles that help doctors to analyse issues and diseases without any incision or cut on corpses. In India and South East Asia, All India Institute of Medical Sciences (AIIMS), New Delhi becomes the first institute to start the virtual autopsy in the year 2021. This facility was inaugurated by Indian Council of Medical Research (ICMR) director general Balram Bhargava in the same year. This novel technique is a step toward noble management of body. There is no need to any incision on the dead body and for other research purposes also the forensic team can get various important information related to position of organs, cause of death using this facility [13,14].

As this autopsy is conducted with advanced imaging technology and involves analysis of body tissues and organs using CT scan imaging it can it generates approximately 25,000 images of a body within few seconds, which can be later analysed by specialists. This makes is better than physical autopsy that will take about 6 hours to complete a process. In India, others institutes have also started this facility such as North Eastern Indira Gandhi Regional Institute of Health and Medical Sciences (NEIGRIHMS), Meghalaya and **St. John's Medical College & Hospital**, Bangalore. As per the report, AIIMs conduct 3,000 postmortem examinations in a year, and 30%–50% of cases does not require the any dissection or incision. These cases mainly include suicidal, hanging, or accidental deaths. As per the police investigation, autopsy plays an important role in case of unnatural death. On the basis of complexity of case, it will take several days for autopsy, but using virtual autopsy, it can be done in less time. This will also result in less human error and in evidence collection as all the data is available in digital format [13–18].

10.7 CASE STUDIES

A comparative analysis of the findings of postmortem computed tomography scan and traditional autopsy in traumatic deaths by Mishra B et al. in AIIMS, New Delhi from 2010 to 2015 on 77 patients of trauma who were declared brought dead at arrival to the emergency department to know whether this technology mutually complementing or exclusive. They found that CT was superior in picking up most of the bony injuries, air-containing lesions, hemothorax, and hemoperitoneum. However, traditional autopsy was found more sensitive for soft-tissue and solid visceral injuries. Both modalities were equally helpful in identifying extremity fractures. Statistically significant agreement (>95%) on cause of death by both modalities was not achieved in any patient of trauma. They concluded that postmortem CT scan is promising in reporting injuries in traumatic deaths and can significantly complement the conventional autopsy. However, at present, it cannot be considered as a replacement for TA [19]. Norzailin et al. in Malaysia conducted a similar study in 2016 on 61 road traffic accidental death cases who underwent both PMCT and conventional autopsy. The imaging findings were compared to the conventional autopsy findings. They concluded that PMCT has high specificity and negative predictive value for liver and splenic injuries; however, the sensitivity and positive predictive value are low. The overall accuracy is not high enough to enable PMCT to be used as a replacement for conventional autopsy; however, it is a useful complementary examination and has potential to be used as decision making tool for selective internal autopsy [20]. However, with the advancement of technology and usage of other techniques like MRI, these shortcomings can be reduced to some extent.

10.8 FUTURE OF VIRTOPSY

Virtopsy can be effectively used in various aspects of postmortem examination. Its drawbacks can be minimized by imaging with MDCT and 3D methods and body surface scanning and making it as minimally invasive autopsy. This method of documenting the findings is investigator independent, objective and noninvasive and will lead to qualitative improvements in forensic pathologic investigation, since the digitally stored data may be recalled at any time to provide fresh, intact topographic and anatomic clinical information.

10.9 CONCLUSION

The traditional autopsy, though it is an old procedure, may remain as a gold standard. The virtual autopsy is a newly developed procedure and will enhance the traditional autopsy. In some cases, the virtopsy could also replace the normal autopsy. In some developing countries, the cost of the virtual autopsy setup would not have been affordable. In present scenario, invasive traditional autopsies have to be the norm for at least a next few years. But ideal approach would be combining both traditional and virtual autopsy, i.e., external examination of dead body to note the external findings like color and nature of injuries, etc. as in traditional autopsy and use imaging techniques of virtual autopsy for internal findings.

ACKNOWLEDGMENT

I am thankful to Dr. Hemanth Naik, COO & CMO, Virtual Autopsy Solutions (UK) & Virtual Autopsy India for his help in understanding technical aspects of virtual autopsy and providing the image of 3D virtual autopsy dissection table of his company.

REFERENCES

1. Aggrawal A. *Essentials of Forensic Medicine and Toxicology.* 1st ed. Avichal Publishing Company; 2014, pp. 85–99.
2. Dirnhofer R, Jackowski C, Vock P, Potter K, Thali MJ. Virtopsy: Minimally invasive, imaging-guided virtual autopsy. *Radiographics* 2006;26:1305–1333.
3. Buck U, Naether S, Braun M, Bolliger S, Friederich H, Jackowski C, Aghayev E, Christe A, Vock P, Dirnhofer R, Thali MJ. Application of 3D documentation and geometric reconstruction methods in traffic accident analysis: With high resolution surface scanning, radiological MSCT/MRI scanning and real data based animation. *Forensic Sci Int* 2007;170(1):20–28.
4. Thali MJ, Yen K, Vock P, Ozdoba C, Kneubuehl BP, Sonnenschein M, Dirnhofer R. Image-guided virtual autopsy findings of gunshot victims performed with multi-slice computed tomography and magnetic resonance imaging and subsequent correlation between radiology and autopsy findings. *Forensic Sci Int* 2003;138(1–3):8–16.
5. Wichmann D, Heinemann A, Weinberg C, Vogel H, Hoepker WW, Grabherr S, Pueschel K, Kluge S. Virtual autopsy with multiphase postmortem computed tomographic angiography versus traditional medical autopsy to investigate unexpected deaths of hospitalized patients: A cohort study. *Ann Intern Med* 2014;160(8):534–541.
6. Patowary AJ. Virtopsy: One step forward in the field of Forensic Medicine-A review. *J Indian Acad Forensic Med* 2008;30(1):32–36.
7. Jain A, Adarsh K, Bhardwaj DN, Sinha US. Future trends in medicolegal documentation – Pros and cons of virtopsy. *JFMT* 2010;27(1):7–10.
8. Kumar A. Digital autopsy (Virtopsy) in India: Steps taken and journey ahead. *J Indian Acad Forensic Med* 2022;44(Suppl):S43–S46.
9. Sharija S. Virtopsy - The most modern technique for post-mortem examination. *Indian J Forensic Med Tox* 2013;7(1):183–186.
10. Chandru K. Virtopsy: The emerging trend in forensic medicine. *Indian J Forensic Med and Tox* 2019;13(3):16–18.
11. Virtual autopsy - Evolving to a new era in post mortem examinations through visualisation [Online]. 2022 [cited 2022 Sept 30]; Available from: https://virtualautopsyuk.com/.
12. Bollinger SA, Thali MJ. Imaging and virtual autopsy: looking back and forward. *Phil Trans R Soc B* 2015;370:20140253.
13. Virtual Autopsy. https://www.news18.com/news/buzz/aiims-becomes-first-in-south-se-asia-to-start-virtual-autopsy-with-no-cuts-what-is-it-3558146.html [accessed on 20 August 2022].
14. Virtual Autopsy. Available at: https://timesofindia.indiatimes.com/city/delhi/aiims-set-to-start-virtual-autopsy-no-cuts-needed/articleshow/81595090.cms [accessed on 20 August 2022].
15. Council of Medical Research. Available at: https://main.icmr.nic.in/ [accessed on 20 August 2022].
16. All India Institute of Medical Sciences. Available at: https://www.aiims.edu/en.html [accessed on 20 August 2022].
17. North Eastern Indira Gandhi Regional Institute of Health and Medical Sciences. Available at: http://www.neigrihms.gov.in/ [accessed on 20 August 2022].
18. St. John's National Academy of Health Sciences. Available at: https://stjohns.in/ [accessed on 20 August 2022].
19. Mishra B, Joshi MK, Lalwani S, Atin K, Adarsh K, Subodh K, et al. A comparative analysis of the findings of postmortem computed tomography scan & traditional autopsy in traumatic deaths: Is technology mutually complementing or exclusive? *Arch Trauma Res* 2018;7:24–29.
20. Norzailin AB, Noor Azman S, Mohd Helmee MN, Khairul Anuar Z. The sensitivity, specificity and predictive values of post mortem computed tomography in detecting liver and splenic injury due to road traffic accident. *Med J Malaysia* 2016;71:1–7.

11 An Advanced Laparoscopic and Diagnostics Imaging in Surgical Operating Theatre
Case study

Mukesh Carpenter
Alshifa Multispecialty Hospital

Abhishek Kumar
Venkateshwar Hospital

Dharmendra Carpenter
Narayana Multispecialty Hospital

Vinod Kumar Jangid
Medical College Kota

CONTENTS

11.1 INTRODUCTION

Modern healthcare is one of the important digital pillars of Society 5.0 and is advanced, machine learning and artificial intelligence (AI)-based that provides a wide range of services and specialties for early diagnosis of disease. Advanced diagnostic imaging (ADI) means better diagnostic drive and better treatment. In today's scenario, healthcare facilities are growing day by day from early

DOI: 10.1201/9781003324720-14

diagnosis to treatment of patient. But still there are open challenges, such as diagnostic errors, present from administration management to therapeutics in the healthcare system, which may be due to misdiagnosis of patient's health, poor timely and efficient resources, lack of knowledge of technology, low published evidence to support diagnostic progress, etc. According to the patient-safety coordinator of World Health Organization (WHO), there can be three main reasons why patients get harmed are listed below:

- Misdiagnosis and screening errors
- Medical prescription and treatment errors
- Inappropriate usage and dosage of prescribed drugs by clinicals

The best medicine begins with the most accurate screening and diagnosis of disease. Advanced diagnosis imaging (ADI) provides clinicals with reliable diagnostic data so that they can treat their patients accurately and successfully. ADI mainly includes technologies such as 3D digital mammogram, pinpoint precision of magnetic resonance imaging (MRI), X-ray, computed tomography (CT), electroencephalogram (EEG), electrocardiogram (ECG), positron emission tomography (PET), and ventilator machines [1–4]. With these advanced technologies, clinicals will provide accurate and effective means of treatment. ADI systems offer advanced surgery, cardiology, accurate diagnosis of disease, and other healthcare services, as shown in Figure 11.1.

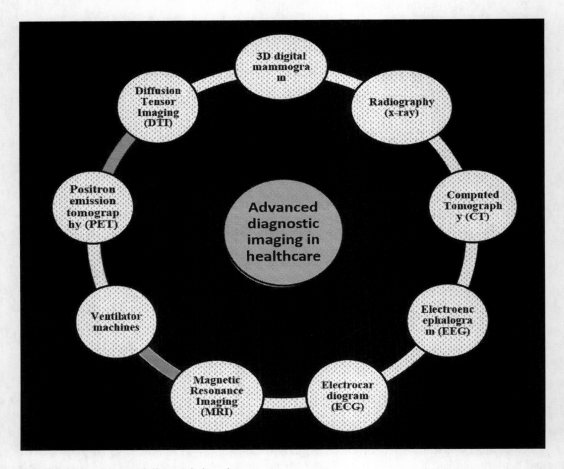

FIGURE 11.1   Advanced diagnostic imaging.

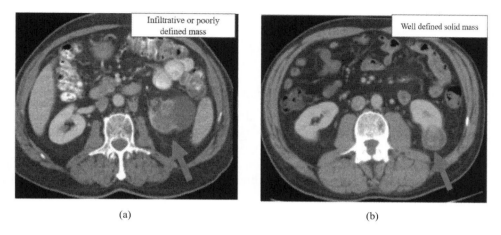

(a) (b)

FIGURE 11.2 Kidney tumor detection in CT images (a) Infiltrative or poorly defined mass (b) Well-defined solid mass.

ADI can benefit patients when used appropriately. It detects diseases and conditions early. It allows medical practitioners to guide patients to the medical services they require as per the diagnosis of disease. But, if it is used inappropriately, ADI provides clinicals or practitioners and patients with less medical benefits, wastes limited healthcare resources, and can even threaten the safety of patient. As a profitable service with growing demand and low barricades to entry, in the past few years, diagnostic MRI, CT, and nuclear medicine imaging, such as PET, have attracted various new providers. There has been a remarkable proliferation in the level of diagnostic medical imaging (MI) services prescribed by clinicals, including non-radiologists, raising concerns about the safety of patient, expenses, and consequences for the healthcare industry [1–13].

In case of small kidney tumor, treatment option can be active surveillance, partial or total nephrectomy. In most of the cases, treatment should result in saving the kidney. In Figure 11.2, there are two images of patient one with poorly defined mass also termed as infiltrative by the radiologist. The tumor in Figure 11.2a was biopsied and detected to be lymphoma. In this case, patient can be treated with chemotherapy without any surgery. On the other hand, patient had a robotic-assisted "partial nephrectomy" and was detected to have a well-defined tumor or solid mass. It can also term as clear cell kidney cancer as shown in Figure 11.2b.

11.2 ADI TECHNIQUES

Medical or diagnostic imaging (DI) is a noninvasive technique inside the body of a patient for diagnostic and treatment purpose. It is also known as radiology. In this process, medical practitioners recreate several images of body parts of patient diagnostic or treatment perspectives. These procedures allow clinicals or medical practitioners to examine injuries and anomalies for bones and tissues without being intrusive [13–43]. A radiologist can analyze the images. Advanced diagnostic techniques are as follows:

- Radiography (x-ray)
- 128-slice CT scanner
- Magnetic resonance imaging
- 3D Digital mammography
- 3.0T MRI with Diffusion Tensor Imaging (DTI)
- DEXA (bone density)
- Ultrasound/doppler

- Diffusion Tensor Imaging
- positron emission tomography
- Diagnostic medical sonography

11.2.1 Radiography (X-ray)

These are a kind of radiation known as "electromagnetic waves". Radiography imaging creates images of the inside of patient body. The captured images display the parts of patient body in black and white format. The shades are in the form of black and white because different body tissues absorb various amounts of radiation. In this technique, ionized radiations are used, which penetrate the body parts to produce digital images of bones and tissues for examination of abnormality or illness [15–32]. Recently, this advanced diagnostic technique is most widely used for COVID-19 (deadly virus) detection in the lungs of a patient as shown in Figure 11.3. Early warning signs of this COVID-19 can be fever, breathing problem, sore throat, headache, and dropped saturation level that can be easily detected using this technique [33,44–48].

11.2.2 CT Scanner

CT scanner is a DI technique that generates a detailed view of patient body organs, bones, blood vessels and soft tissues. It is the most commonly used diagnostic tool for anomalies detection or in case of internal injuries. In this technique, a series of X-Ray taken from different angles around the body to produce 3D images of bones and soft tissues. CT scans allow clinicals to examine cross-sectional images (slices) of patient body. This slice shows heart and lung tissue [49–62]. The term slice is the number of rows of detectors in the z-axis of a CT scanner. The first scanner has only single slice CT (SSCT) images, but nowadays, there are multiple slice CT (MSCT) scanners such as 16 slices, 128 slices, 256 slices,and 640 slices. CT angiography coronary 256 slice is used for the diagnosis of coronary artery disease, mainly for patient with chest pain and low to medium risk profiles and for patients with inconclusive outcomes from a stress test, as shown in Figure 11.4.

The 640-slice 4D CT scanner provides better images as compared to the previous slice scanner. It is a noninvasive test and has various advanced features such as minimal radiation, safer technique

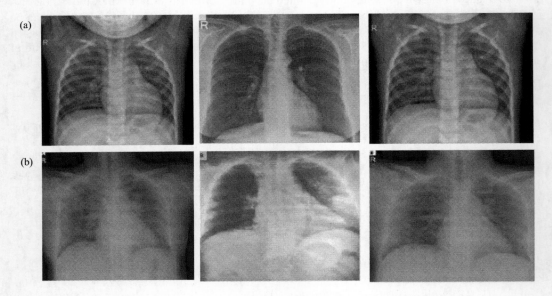

FIGURE 11.3 Radiography (X-ray) technique row-wise: (a) Normal lungs of a patient (b) Lungs of a patient infected with COVID-19 virus.

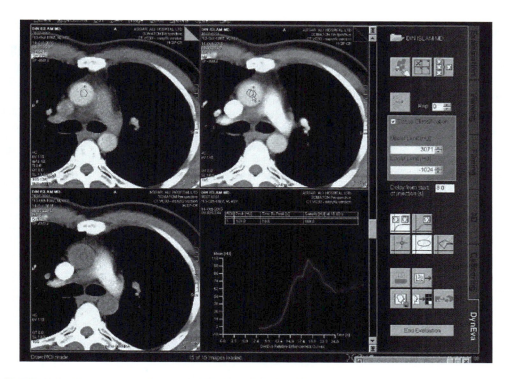

FIGURE 11.4   T coronary angiogram -128 slice: 128 slice CT has more detectors and has large volume coverage and shorter scan time as compared to others.

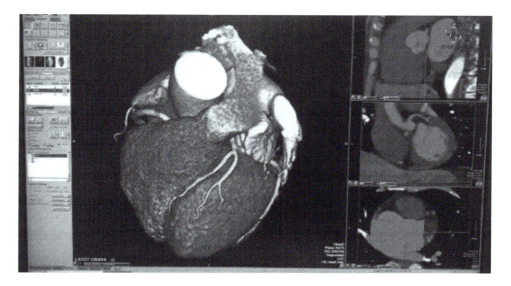

FIGURE 11.5   The 640-slice 4D CT scanner: shows the entire heart scan in one single heartbeat.

and less time-consuming [34–42,62–70]. It scans in entire heart in one single heartbeat as shown in Figure 11.5. It is mainly recommended for patient with above 55 years of age and those having health issues such as hypertension, diabetes, and high cholesterol. In India, Apollo hospital is the first one having this type of scanner.

11.2.3 Magnetic Resonance Imaging

It is also a non-invasive and advanced DI technique that produces 3D anatomical images of a patient. It is most commonly used for the disease detection, diagnosis, and treatment monitoring of a patient. It consists of magnetic field, its gradients and a system-generated radio waves to scan the internal body organs [1–28,71–77]. This technology excites and detects the variations in the direction of rotational axis of protons found in water, which makes up the living tissue. This technique detects the condition that affects the body organs such as:

- Being and non-being tumor
- Spinal or joint injury
- Soft tissue injury such as damaged ligaments
- Internal body organ injury such as brain, heart, digestive organ, and kidney.

Figure 11.6 shows an MRI of a patient where the right occipital scalp lesion shows DWI restriction. No significant interval changes. There is possibility of Epidermoid cyst.

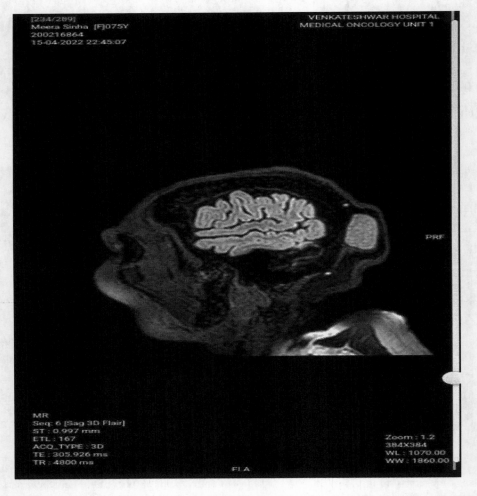

FIGURE 11.6   MRI of a patient: A 2.5 × 2.6 × 4.8 cm (AP × ML × CC) sized altered signal intensity is seen in the scalp over the right occipital region. This shows hypointense signal on T1, hyperintense signal on T2/FLAIR with true restriction of diffusion on DWI with reversal on the ADC. Few T2 hypointense incomplete septation within. Underlying scalloping swelling seen subjacent to the lesion.

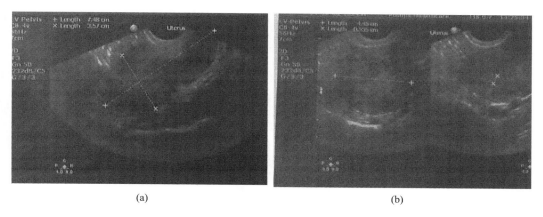

(a)   (b)

FIGURE 11.7   Medical sonography of uterus of a female patient: (a) Endometrium thickness (b) Both right and left ovaries of female patient that seems to be normal.

11.2.4   MEDICAL SONOGRAPHY

Medical Sonography is a diagnostic medical process that uses high-frequency sound waves or ultrasound to generate dynamic graphical images of body organs, tissues, and blood flow inside the body of a patient. This type of technique is often known as a sonogram or ultrasound. This technique is considered to be the safest examination during pregnancy because it uses sound waves or echo waves to generate internal body organ images [36–42,78–82]. Figure 11.7 shows sonography of a female patient with normal uterus. Some important features of this technique are listed below:

- Safe scanning process and most common technique used for diagnosis.
- Most commonly used to check pregnancy progress.
- No prior preparation is required for sonography

11.2.5   POSITRON EMISSION TOMOGRAPHY CT

It uses small amounts of radioactive materials known as "radiotracers" or "radiopharmaceuticals", a special camera, and a system to examine organ and tissue of patient's body. By detecting the changes at the cellular level, PET CT can detect the early outbreak of disease as compared to other imagings. It is an effective means to detect several conditions such as cancer, brain disorder and heart disease. This scan can help in the diagnoses of new or recurrent cancer [1,22,26,34–36,68–70,62,82,83]. The clinical or medical practitioner can use this information for diagnosis, monitoring, and treatment of patient. In Figure 11.8, PET CT scan findings of a patient show the 50×30 mm space-occupying lesion with hypermetabolic activity.

11.2.6   DEXA (BONE DENSITY)

Bone density (strength) scan uses low-beam X-rays to examine how dense (or strong) patient bones are. This test is also known as DEXA scan. This is an enhanced form of X-ray technology [33,40–54,44–56,83,84]. This scan is most commonly used for diagnosis or assessment of the risk of osteoporosis (bone loss) and fracture (bone break). This test can also evaluate the body composition such as body fat and muscle mass. Figure 11.9 shows the DEXA scan finding where Figure 11.9a shows full body scan, (b) with normal bone and (c) with osteoporotic bone. Studies using DEXA scan have shown that person with osteoporosis (bone loss) have considerably lower bone density as compared to the normal age-matched persons.

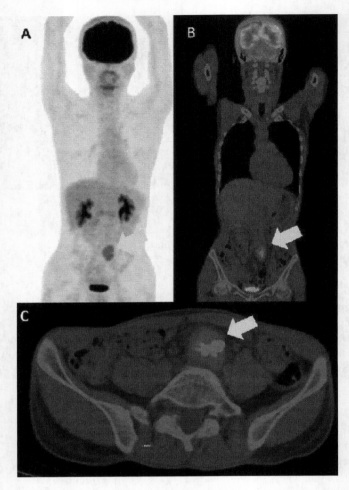

FIGURE 11.8   PET CT scan findings. (a and b) PET CT scan sagittal. (c) PET CT scan axial; the arrow shows the 50 × 30 mm space-occupying lesion with hypermetabolic activity (SUVmax at 4.1) in the pelvic retroperitoneal. PET CT, position emission tomography CT.

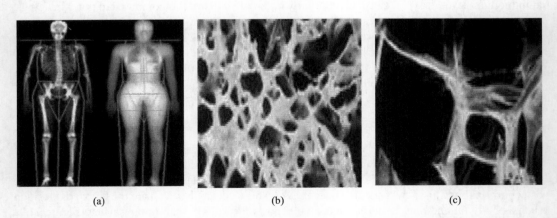

(a)   (b)   (c)

FIGURE 11.9   DEXA Scan. (a) Shows full body scan of a patient. (b) Normal bone (no abnormality found during the test (c) Osteoporosis (bone loss).

11.2.7 Diffusion Tensor Imaging

It is an MRIbased neuroimaging technique which detects how water travel along with the white matter tracts in the human brain or we can say it is a technique that uses anisotropic diffusion to calculate the axonal (white matter) structure of the human brain. Using this technique, it becomes possible to assess the position, orientation, and anisotropy of the axonal tracts of the human brain. Compared to other neuroimaging techniques, it helps clinicals to understand the structure of the brain after stroke [34–42,58–70,78–83,85–87]. Figure 11.10 shows the DTI findings with Colormap where the color system provides the clinicals to visualize the directional orientation of primary eigenvector in L-R (left to right), anterior-posterior, superior-inferior co-ordinate system. Fibre tractography of a white matter is performed using DTIstudio (Figure 11.11).

11.2.8 Surgery

In today's scenario, surgical cameras are used for a powerful visual information in surgical practices. This information helps surgeons in decision-making by providing the clinical site. This signal can be used by computer vision (CV), machine learning (ML), and AI models, which help in instruments detection, or any activities related to surgical room and post-operatively for evaluation and surgical insight [31,53,58,62,65,72,77,83].

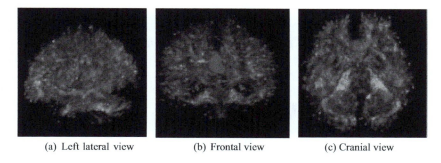

| (a) Left lateral view | (b) Frontal view | (c) Cranial view |

FIGURE 11.10 DTI colormap findings shows (a) Left lateral view of brain (b) Frontal view of brain (c) Cranial view of brain. Lateral view shows white matter structures passing through the corpus callosum (represented as RED), rising pyramidal pathways with Blue and fronto-temporo-occipital pathway with green.

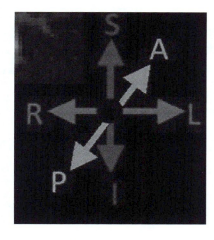

FIGURE 11.11 ColorMap (CM) of the DTI findings. In this figure, arrows represent the fibre tractography of a white matter of the brain.

11.3   OVARIAN CYSTECTOMY USING ADVANCED LAPAROSCOPIC TECHNIQUE-CASE STUDY

Due to the availability of surgical visual sources and emerging technologies around the storage devices, existing solutions, and product support vision becomes a vital part of advanced surgical competencies as shown in Figure 11.12. In today's world, most of the surgical operation theatres (OT) are well equipped with AI/ML/CV such as digital cameras for visualizing the surgical site. With these emerging technologies, surgery also moved towards the laparoscopic or minimally invasive surgery (MIS). During the surgical procedure, the video generated using the digital camera contains several valuable information such as shape, function or size of object or body organ and instrumentation within it [18,22,27,28,62,64,65,67–70,35–42,78–83,85–87]. In this section, a case study of ovarian cystectomy is presented.

A 24-year-old married female belongs to middle class came to hospital with complaints of progressive enlargement of the lower abdomen, dragging sensation, and increased frequency of micturition. Her cycles are 28 days with 3–4 days of heavy bleeding. On investigation, her CA 125 level is 70 U/mL on imaging (USG whole abdomen) and CT whole abdomen suggestive of 18 × 12 × 10 cm large left multilocular cyst with solid areas. Rest routine investigations are normal. Patient underwent laparoscopic ovarian cystectomy. Histopathology suggestive of begin tumor of left ovary -teratoma of left ovary representing two embryonic layers with no malignant potential as shown in Figure 11.13. Patient has been discharged the next day morning. Sutures have been removed after 7 days of surgery as shown in Figure 11.14. In MIS surgery, a patient can be discharged within 2–3 days after surgery, less no of scars and get back to work soon as compared to open surgery.

At the time of the surgical procedure, video is recorded that can contain data about surgical process, instruments used, complications, risks and steps taken for surgery. Later, the recorded videos can be used in future for educational or research purpose, medical meetings [31,32,64,65,83]. In the literature, various surgical dataset is available for training and validation of new algorithm that results in one step ahead towards the advancement of technologies in the medical domain.

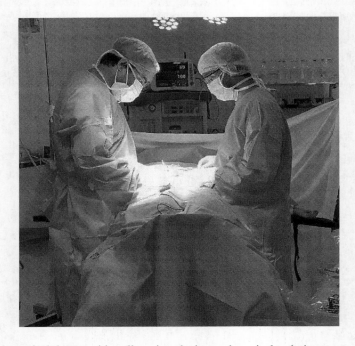

FIGURE 11.12   A surgical theatre with well-equipped advanced surgical techniques.

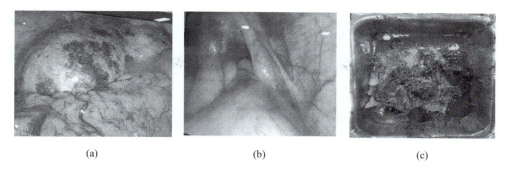

(a)   (b)   (c)

FIGURE 11.13   Minimal access surgery (a) Ovarian cyst (b) Ovarian cystectomy (c) Ovarian cyst after removal.

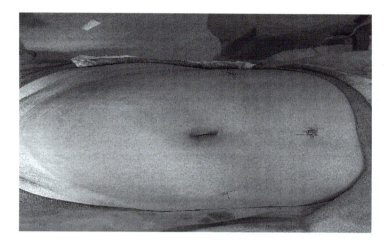

FIGURE 11.14   A patient underwent laparoscopic ovarian cystectomy.

The use of ML/CV/AI technologies to process the data from various intra-operative imaging of digital cameras can be divided into three distinct applications:

11.3.1   INSIGHT SURGICAL PROCEDURE

Surgical procedure can be classified as dissection, anastomosis, suturing, etc. Furthermore, detection and localization of these assignments allow for modelling and workflow assessment of surgery. This enables the MIS practice towards the formation of guidelines and protocols for job execution, optimal positioning of tool with respect to anatomy, few complications, and cost-effective surgical procedures. This MIS surgery results in high-level security, lessen stress level, less amount of blood loss, and less pain [65–68,80–83,85–87]. CV/AI technology-based digital cameras and sensors make surgical operations more effective. Intraoperative videos provide a lot of important information related to quality and workflow.

11.3.2   DETECTION OF OBJECT

Detection of object in digital images is the main vital component of AI/CV. Surgical videos help in envisioning clinical goals and sensitive areas to optimise and increase the procedure safety such as surgical instrument detection (automatic detection and localization that help in positioning

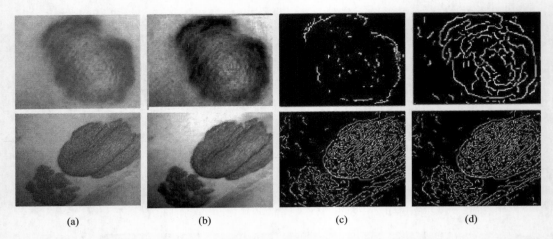

(a)   (b)   (c)   (d)

FIGURE 11.15 Detection of skin lesion using AI technique (a) Original image 1 (b) Grey scale image (c) Prewitt operator (d) Canny operator.

of instrument accurately and ensure that the critical structures are not injured), lesion detection (AI-based system helps in highlighting the lesions or anomalies which couldn't be possible without these systems) as shown in Figure 11.15, anatomy detections that provide guidance and avoid accidental damage of nerves and vessels) [14–17,29–31,53,62,65–70,34–42,78–83,85–87].

11.3.3 COMPUTER-ASSISTED NAVIGATION

In the last few decades, CV/AI becomes emerging technology and is widely used for mapping of environment and localization using surgical cameras. These technologies provide detailed anatomy and accurate diagnosis that help in decision-making. In MIS, AI-based system aids in locating the position of endoscopy within the body organ, and at the same time, it detects the silhouette of explored body organ [34–42,78–83,85–87].

11.4 CONCLUSION

AI and CV means processing of digital frames sequence from video data for object detection and tracking. ADI can be used in medical field to enhance the efficiency of medical professionals. These algorithms provide early-stage diagnosis such as ovarian cyst or lesion or cancer or tumor and effective means of treatment. In this chapter, basic concepts of AI/CV and ADI techniques are discussed. Furthermore, this chapter presents a case study of female patient diagnosed with ovarian cyst and operated on using the advanced laparoscopic technique. In further sections, the importance of AI-based technique in surgical OT such as understanding of procedure, detection of particular object or object of interest and computer-aided navigations are discussed.

REFERENCES

1. https://www.adhealthcare.com/services-specialties/services/diffusion-tensor-imaging/.
2. https://www.cronj.com/blog/how-advanced-technologies-evolve-healthcare-screening-diagnostics/.
3. https://www.bu.edu/aphasiaresearch/research/neural-markers/white-matter-connectivity/.
4. Computer Vision Applications. Available at: https://tel.archives-ouvertes.fr/tel-01557522/document [accessed on 10 June 2021].
5. https://www.hopkinsmedicine.org/health/conditions-and-diseases/kidney-cancer/kidney-cancer-diagnosis.

6. Computer Vision and Artificial Intelligence in Healthcare. Available at: https://bdtechtalks.com/2020/04/29/ai-computer-vision-health-care/ [accessed on 10 June 2021].

7. Transformation of Healthcare using Computer Vision. Available at: https://www.allerin.com/blog/how-computer-vision-can-transform-healthcare [accessed on 10 June 2021].

8. Computer Vision. Available at: https://arxiv.org/abs/2004.05436v1 [accessed on 10 June 2021].

9. Computer Vision in Diagnosis and Treatment. Available at: https://www.itnonline.com/content/ct-provides-best-diagnosis-novel-coronavirus-covid-19 [accessed on 10 June 2021].

10. Schultheiss M, Schober SA, Lodde M et al. A robust convolutional neural network for lung nodule detection in the presence of foreign bodies. *Sci Rep* 10, 12987 (2020). https://doi.org/10.1038/s41598-020-69789-z.

11. Chen YB, Chen OTC. Image segmentation method using thresholds automatically determined from picture contents *EURASIP J Image Video Process* 1–15 (2009).

12. Real-Time Applications of Computer Vision. Available at: https://www.quantib.com/blog/artificial-intelligence-neurology-promising-research-and-proven-application [accessed on 10 June 2021].

13. Real-Time Applications of Computer Vision. Available at: https://www.appliedradiology.com/communities/Artificial-Intelligence/fda-clears-siemens-ai-based-mri-interpretation-assistants#:~:text=Based%20on%20AI%20algorithms%2C%20the,Disease%20Neuroimaging%20Initiative%20(ADNI) [accessed on 10 June 2021].

14. D'Ettorre C, Dwyer G, Du X, Chadebecq F, Vasconcelos F, De Momi E et al. Automated pick-up of suturing needles for robotic surgical assistance. *IEEE Int Conf Robot Autom* 6, 1370–1377 (2018).

15. Du X, Kurmann T, Chang PL, Allan M, Ourselin S, Sznitman R et al. Articulated multi-instrument 2-D pose estimation using fully convolutional networks. *IEEE Trans Med Imaging* 37(5), 1276–1287 (2018).

16. Colleoni E, Edwards P, Stoyanov D. Synthetic and real inputs for tool segmentation in robotic surgery. *Conf Med Image Comput Comput Assist Interv* 12263, 700–710 (2020).

17. Bouget D, Allan M, Stoyanov D, Jannin P. Vision-based and marker-less surgical tool detection and tracking: A review of the literature. *Med Image Anal* 35, 633–654 (2017).

18. Maier-Hein L, Mountney P, Bartoli A, Elhawary H, Elson D, Groch A et al. Optical techniques for 3-D surface reconstruction in computer assisted laparoscopic surgery. *Med Image Anal* 17, 974–996 (2013).

19. Liu X, Zheng Y, Killeen B, Ishii M, Hager GD, Taylor RH, Unberath M. Extremely dense point correspondences using a learned feature descriptor. 2020. https://arxiv.org/abs/2003.00619.

20. Bano S, Vasconcelos F, Tella Amo M, Dwyer G, Gruijthuijsen C, Deprest J et al. Deep sequential mosaicking of fetoscopic videos. *Conf Med Image Comput Comput Assist Interv* 11764, 311–319 (2019).

21. Rau A, Edwards PJE, Ahmad OF, Riordan P, Janatka M, Lovat LB et al. Implicit domain adaptation with conditional generative adversarial networks for depth prediction in endoscopy. *Int J Comput Assist Radiol Surg* 14, 1167–1176 (2019).

22. Ma R, Wang R, Pizer S, Rosenman J, McGill SK, Frahm J-M. Real-time 3d reconstruction of colonoscopic surfaces for determining missing regions. *Conf Med Image Comput Comput Assist Interv* 11768, 573–582 (2019).

23. Peters TM, Linte CA, Yaniv Z, Williams J. *Mixed and Augmented Reality in Medicine*. CRC Press, Boca Raton (2018).

24. Luo H, Hu Q, Jia F. Details preserved unsupervised depth estimation by fusing traditional stereo knowledge from laparoscopic images. *IET Healthc Technol Lett* 6(6), 154–158 (2019).

25. Colleoni E, Moccia S, Du X, De Momi E, Stoyanov D. Deep learning based robotic tool detection and articulation estimation with spatio-temporal layers. *IEEE Robot Autom Lett* 4, 2714–2721 (2019).

26. Park BJ, Hunt SJ, Martin C, Nadolski GJ, Wood BJ, Gade TP. Augmented and mixed reality: Technologies for enhancing the future of IR. *J Vascular Interv Radiol* 31(7), 1074–1082 (2020).

27. Chen F, Wu D, Liao H. Registration of CT and ultrasound images of the spine with neural network and orientation code mutual information. *Med Imaging Augmented Reality* 9805, 292–301 (2016).

28. Ward TM, Mascagni P, Ban Y, Rosman G, Padoy N, Meireles O, Hashimoto DA. Computer vision in surgery. *Surgery* 169(5), 1253–1256 (2021). https://doi.org/10.1016/j.surg.2020.10.039.

29. Sengupta S, Mittal N, Modi M. Improved skin lesions detection using color space and artificial intelligence techniques. *J Dermatolog Treat* 31(5), 511–518 (2020). https://doi.org/10.1080/09546634.2019.1708239.

30. Sengupta S, Mittal N, Modi M. Edge detection in dermascopic images by linear structuring element. *2018 7th International Conference on Reliability, Infocom Technologies and Optimization (Trends and Future Directions) (ICRITO)*, pp. 419–424 (2018), https://doi.org/10.1109/ICRITO.2018.8748610.

31. Sharma L, Garg P. (Eds.). *From Visual Surveillance to Internet of Things*. New York: Chapman and Hall/CRC (2020), https://doi.org/10.1201/9780429297922.

32. Sharma L, Lohan N. Performance analysis of moving object detection using BGS techniques in visual surveillance, *IJSTDS* 1, 22–53, (2019).

33. Anand A, Jha V, Sharma L, An improved local binary patterns histograms techniques for face recognition for real time application, *Int J Recent Technol Eng* 8(2S7), 524–529 (2019).

34. Sharma L, Computer-aided lung cancer detection and classification of CT images using convolutional neural network, In: *Computer Vision and Internet of Things: Technologies and Applications*, Taylor & Francis, CRC Press, pp. 247–262 (2022).

35. Sharma L. Analysis of machine learning techniques for airfare prediction, In: *Computer Vision and Internet of Things: Technologies and Applications*, Taylor & Francis, CRC Press, pp. 211–231 (2022).

36. Sharma L. Innovation and emerging computer vision and artificial intelligence technologies in coronavirus control, In: *Computer Vision and Internet of Things: Technologies and Applications*, Taylor & Francis, CRC Press, pp. 177–192 (2022).

37. Sharma L. Self-driving cars: Tools and technologies, In: *Computer Vision and Internet of Things: Technologies and Applications*, Taylor & Francis, CRC Press, pp. 99–110 (2022).

38. Sharma L. Computer vision in surgical operating theatre and medical imaging, In: *Computer Vision and Internet of Things: Technologies and Applications*, Taylor & Francis, CRC Press, pp. 75–96 (2022).

39. Sharma L. Preventing security breach in social media: Threats and prevention techniques, *Computer Vision and Internet of Things: Technologies and Applications*, Taylor & Francis, CRC Press, pp. 53–62 (2022).

40. Sharma L, Carpenter M. Use of robotics in real-time applications, *Computer Vision and Internet of Things: Technologies and Applications*, Taylor & Francis, CRC Press, pp. 41–50 (2022).

41. Sharma L et al. An overview of security issues of internet of things, *Computer Vision and Internet of Things: Technologies and Applications*, Taylor & Francis, CRC Press, pp. 29–40 (2022).

42. Sharma L. Rise of computer vision and internet of things, *Computer Vision and Internet of Things: Technologies and Applications*, Taylor & Francis, CRC Press, pp. 5–17 (2022).

43. DeKroon CD, Sandy V, Houwe H, Lingen JC, Jansen FW. Sono graphic assessment of nonmalignant ovarian cysts. Does sonohistology exists? *Hum Reprod* 19, 2138–2143 (2004).

44. Sharma L, Yadav DK, Histogram based adaptive learning rate for background modelling and moving object detection in video surveillance, *IJTMCP* (2016), https://doi.org/10.1504/IJTMCP.2017.082107.

45. Sharma L, Lohan N, Performance analysis of moving object detection using BGS techniques, *IJSTDS, Inderscience* 1, 22–53 (2019).

46. Sharma L, Lohan N, Internet of things with object detection, in *Handbook of Research on Big Data and the IoT*, IGI Global, pp. 89–100 (2019). ISBN: 9781522574323, https://doi.org/0.4018/978-1-5225–7432–3.ch006.

47. Sharma L, *Introduction: From Visual Surveillance to Internet of Things, From Visual Surveillance to Internet of Things*, Taylor & Francis, CRC Press, Vol. 1, p.14 (2019).

48. Sharma L, Garg PK *Block based Adaptive Learning Rate for Moving Person Detection in Video Surveillance, From Visual Surveillance to Internet of Things*, Taylor & Francis, CRC Press, Vol. 1, p.201 (2019).

49. Makkar S, Sharma L. A face detection using support vector machine: Challenging issues, recent trend, solutions and proposed framework. In: Singh M, Gupta P, Tyagi V, Flusser J, Ören T, Kashyap R (eds.), *Advances in Computing and Data Sciences. ICACDS 2019. Communications in Computer and Information Science*, Vol. 1046. Springer, Singapore (2019). https://doi.org/10.1007/978-981-13-9942-8_1.

50. Sharma L, Yadav DK, Bharti SK. An improved method for visual surveillance using background subtraction technique, *2015 2nd International Conference on Signal Processing and Integrated Networks (SPIN)*, pp. 421–426 (2015), https://doi.org/10.1109/SPIN.2015.7095253.

51. Yadav DK, Sharma L, Bharti SK. Moving object detection in real-time visual surveillance using background subtraction technique, *2014 14th International Conference on Hybrid Intelligent Systems*, pp. 79–84 (2014), https://doi.org/10.1109/HIS.2014.7086176.

52. Sharma L, Singh A, Yadav DK. Fisher's linear discriminant ratio based threshold for moving human detection in thermal video, *Infrared Phys Technol* 78, 118–128 (2016).

53. Sharma, L (Ed.). *Towards Smart World*, Chapman and Hall/CRC, New York (2021), https://doi.org/10.1201/9781003056751.

54. Sharma, L. *Human Detection and Tracking Using Background Subtraction in Visual Surveillance, Towards Smart World*, Chapman and Hall/CRC, New York, pp. 317–328 (2020), https://doi.org/10.1201/9781003056751.

55. Sharma L, Yadav DK, Bharti SK. An improved method for visual surveillance using background subtraction technique, *IEEE, 2nd International Conference on Signal Processing and Integrated Networks (SPIN-2015)*, Amity Univ., Noida, February 19–20 (2015).

56. Yadav DK, Sharma L, Bharti SK. Moving object detection in real-time visual surveillance using background subtraction technique, *IEEE, 14th International Conference in Hybrid Intelligent Computing (HIS-2014)*, Gulf University for Science and Technology, Kuwait, December 14–16 (2014).

57. Sharma L, Yadav DK, Kumar M. A morphological approach for human skin detection in color images, *2nd National Conference on Emerging Trends in Intelligent Computing & Communication*, GCET, Gr., Noida, April 26–27 (2013).

58. Sharma L, Sengupta S, Kumar B. An improved technique for enhancement of satellite images, *J Phys: Conf Ser* 1714, 012051 (2021).

59. Singh S, Sharma L, Kumar B. A machine learning based predictive model for coronavirus pandemic scenario, *J Phys: Conf Ser* 1714, 012023 (2021).

60. Jha G., Sharma L.., Gupta S. Future of augmented reality in healthcare department. In: Singh PK, Wierzchoń ST, Tanwar S, Ganzha M, Rodrigues JJPC (eds.), *Proceedings of Second International Conference on Computing, Communications, and Cyber-Security. Lecture Notes in Networks and Systems*, Vol. 203, Springer, Singapore (2021). https://doi.org/10.1007/978-981-16-0733-2_47.

61. Jha G., Sharma L., Gupta S. E-health in internet of things (IoT) in real-time scenario. In: Singh PK, Wierzchoń ST, Tanwar S, Ganzha M, Rodrigues JJPC (eds.), *Proceedings of Second International Conference on Computing, Communications, and Cyber-Security. Lecture Notes in Networks and Systems*, Vol. 203, Springer, Singapore (2021). https://doi.org/10.1007/978-981-16-0733-2_48.

62. Nguyen HT et al. Watersnakes: Energy-driven watershed segmentation, *IEEE Trans on Pattern Anal Mach Intelli* 25(3), 330–342 (2003).

63. Kumar S, Gupta P, Lakra S, Sharma L, Chatterjee R. The zeitgeist juncture of "big data" and its future trends, *2019 International Conference on Machine Learning, Big Data, Cloud and Parallel Computing (COMITCon)*, pp. 465–469 (2019), https://doi.org/10.1109/COMITCon.2019.8862433.

64. Sharma S, Verma S, Kumar M, Sharma L. Use of motion capture in 3D animation: Motion capture systems, challenges, and recent trends, *2019 International Conference on Machine Learning, Big Data, Cloud and Parallel Computing (COMITCon)*, pp. 289–294 (2019), https://doi.org/10.1109/COMITCon.2019.8862448.

65. Carpenter M. An accidentally detected diaphragmatic hernia with acute appendicitis. *Asian J Case Rep Surg* 9(2), 19–24 (2021). Retrieved from https://www.journalajcrs.com/index.php/AJCRS/article/view/30260.

66. Artificial Intelligence Technologies, Applications, and Challenges. Available at: https://www.routledge.com/Artificial-Intelligence-Technologies-Applications-and-Challenges/Sharma-Garg/p/book/9780367690809 [access on 20 July 2021].

67. Chaudhary A, Singh SS. Lung cancer detection on CT images by using image processing, *2012 International Conference on Computing Sciences*, pp. 142–146 (2012), https://doi.org/10.1109/ICCS.2012.43.

68. Ginneken BV, Romeny BM, Viergever MA. Computer-aided diagnosis in chest radiography: A survey, *IEEE, Transa Med Imaging* 20(12), 1228–1241 (2001).

69. Beucher S, Meyer F. The morphological approach of segmentation: The watershed transformation, In: Dougherty E (ed.), *Mathematical Morphology in Image Processing*, Marcel Dekker, New York, pp. 43–481 (1992).

70. Suzuki K et al, False-positive reduction in computer-aided diagnostic scheme for detecting nodules in chest radiographs by means of massive training artificial neural network, *Acad Radiol* 12(2), 191–201 (2005).

71. Hamberlin, J, Kocher, MR, Waltz, J et al. Automated detection of lung nodules and coronary artery calcium using artificial intelligence on low-dose CT scans for lung cancer screening: accuracy and prognostic value. *BMC Med* 19, 55 (2021). https://doi.org/10.1186/s12916-021-01928-3.

72. Yoo H, Kim KH, Singh R, Digumarthy SR, Kalra MK. Validation of a deep learning algorithm for the detection of malignant pulmonary nodules in chest radiographs. *JAMA Netw Open* 3(9), e2017135 (2020). https://doi.org/10.1001/jamanetworkopen.2020.17135.

73. Chan BK, Wiseberg-Firtell JA, Jois RH, Jensen K, Audisio RA. Localization techniques for guided surgical excision of non-palpable breast lesions. *Cochrane Database Syst Rev* 31(12), CD009206 (2015). https://doi.org/10.1002/14651858.CD009206.pub2.

74. Tardioli S, Ballesio L, Gigli S, DI Pastena F, D'Orazi V, Giraldi G, Monti M, Amabile MI, Pasta V. Wire-guided localization in non-palpable breast cancer: Results from monocentric experience. *Anticancer Res* 36(5), 2423–2427 (2016).

75. Unnikrishnan R, Pantofaru C, Hebert M, Towards objectiveevaluation of image segmentation algorithms, *IEEE Trans Pattern Anal Mach Intell* 29, 929–944 (2007).

76. Tripathi P, Tyagi S, Nath MA. Comparative analysis of segmentation techniques for lung cancer detection. *Pattern Recognit Image Anal* 29, 167–173 (2019). https://doi.org/10.1134/S105466181901019X.

78. Kayastha S. Study of ovarian tumors in Nepal medical college teaching hospital Nepal. *Medcoll J* 11, 200–202 (2009).

79. Pilli GS, Suneeta KP, Dhaded AV, Yenni VV. Ovarian tumors, study of 282 cases. *J Indian M Ass* 100(420), 423–424 (2002).

80. Gupta N, Bishit D, Agarwal AK, Sharma VK. Retrospective and prospective study of ovarian tumors and tumor like lesions. *Indian J Pathol Microbiol* 50, 525–527 (2007).

81. Bhattacharya MM. A clinicopathological analysis of 270 ovarian tumors. *J Post grad Med* 26, 103 (1980).

82. Mondal SK. Histologic pattern, bilaterality and clinical evaluation of 957 ovarian neoplasms; A 10 year study in a tertiary hospital of eastern India. *J Can Res Ther* 7, 433–437 (2011).

83. Sharma L, Carpenter M (Eds.). *Computer Vision and Internet of Things: Technologies and Applications* (1st ed.). Chapman and Hall/CRC (2022). https://doi.org/10.1201/9781003244165.

84. Sharma L, Garg PK. *IoT and its Applications, From Visual Surveillance to Internet of Things,* Taylor & Francis, CRC Press, Vol. 1, p.29 (2019).

85. Malineh A. Surgical histopathology of benign ovarian cysts. A multicentric study. *Iran J Pathol* 5(3), 132–136 (2010).

86. Yasmin S. Clinico histopathological pattern of ovarian tumors in Peshawar region. *J Ayub Med Coll Abbottabad* 4, 20 (2008).

87. Cohen M. Sites of endometriosis. *Rev Prat* 40, 1091–1096 (1990).

12 Smart Agriculture Platforms
Case Studies

Tushar Bharadwaj, Akash Kumar, and Siddhartha Khare
Indian Institute of Technology

CONTENTS

12.1 INTRODUCTION

Embedding different technological innovations such as multispectral satellite images, drones and UAVs, IoT, ground-based sensors, artificial intelligence, robots, etc., to conventional farming systems for better production in terms of both quality and quantity need of the day all over the globe. Using these techniques to improve agriculture's overall structure and production is much required. Smart agriculture is a way forward in food production and security worldwide (Goel et al. 2021).

Indian agriculture and allied sectors employ 54.2% of the total human capital of India (Ministry of Agriculture and Farmers' Welfare 1990). Still, the percentage share of GVA of agriculture and allied sector to the economy is around 20% (National Statistical Office (NSO), M/o Statistics & PI). This disguised human resource can be used in other sectors to improve the overall development of India.

Satellite-based smart agriculture platforms are helpful in the mapping and resource management of large farms. Mapping accurate agriculture areas is valuable for production control and support actions, especially in paddy fields (Nguyen et al. 2020). Satellite image-processing tools, such as Mapping Evapotranspiration at high Resolution with Internalized Calibration (METRIC™), are used to assess the evapotranspiration (Allen et al. 2011). Satellite images are helpful in managing different sections of farms to evaluate water and fertilizer requirements (Cancela et al. 2019; Ray et al. 2022).

Satellite-based Information communication technology (ICT) in the agriculture domain helps to maintain the output yield due to changes in weather patterns, soil conditions, and epidemic of pests and diseases (Patil and Kale 2016). Unmanned aerial vehicles (UAVs) are one of the smart agriculture platforms to map and survey an agriculture field (Christiansen et al. 2017). Data-intensive studies on big data using machine learning and data-based analysis are helpful for precision agriculture decision-making (Tantalaki et al. 2019).

DOI: 10.1201/9781003324720-15

12.2   NEED OF THE STUDY

Global trends show that the cropland per capita is reducing every year. A report by Food and Agriculture Statistics, United States, 38% of the total land on earth is an agricultural area, and only one-third is used for crop production; the rest is for meadows and pastures for grazing livestock. The cropland per capita is reduced from 0.45 to 0.21 hectares (Figure 12.1). As the world's population is increasing, it is a serious concern for food security worldwide.

In India, major economic activities are driven by agriculture and allied sectors. India, being second largest agriculture producer and seventh largest exporter of agricultural goods, must embrace newer technologies and be proactive on food vs feed challenges around the globe. Different smart agriculture platforms have emerged using technologies which are able to increase the productivity of farms. Land distribution by the Indian population in agricultural and non-agricultural households is shown in Figure 12.2. It is seen that most agricultural households have less than 2 hectares of land. Upliftment of small and marginal farmers is necessary. Smart agriculture platforms are the key to the betterment of this marginalized section of society.

Rainfall patterns in India have changed, which affects the crop yield negatively. According to Indian Metrological Department (IMD), till August, the total rainfall has declined in the last eight decades (Figure 12.3).

Rainfall not only declined but also skewed. In the last decade, 50% of total rainfall was seen over an average of 40.4 days minimum in the last ten decades. These fast rainfall patterns have an adverse effect on crop production. On the other hand, groundwater depletion and exponential increment in energy usage have worsened resource management. Smart agriculture platforms can handle these problems.

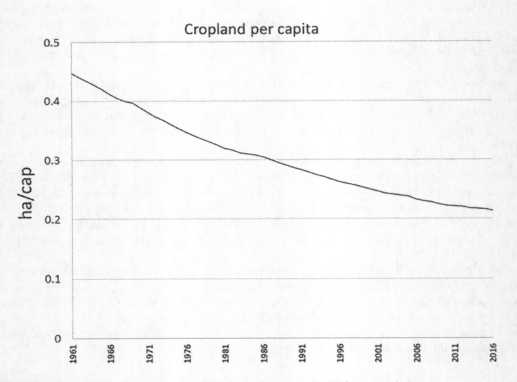

FIGURE 12.1   Global cropland per capita (World Agriculture: - An FAO perspective).

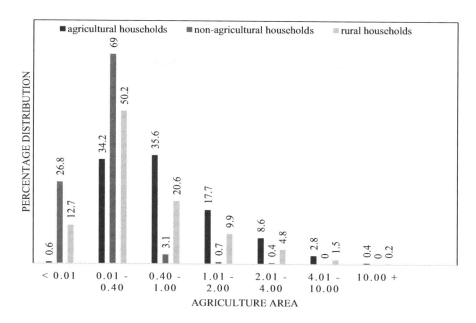

FIGURE 12.2 Percentage distribution of agricultural and non-agricultural households by size class of land possessed (ha.) for the agricultural year July 2018 – June 2019 (NSSO-77th round of survey).

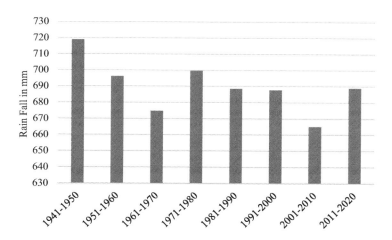

FIGURE 12.3 Average total monsoon rainfall in India up to August (IMD).

12.3   RECENT STUDIES ON SMART AGRICULTURE

With the advancement in science and innovation, the agriculture sector has developed several tech-nologies to improve the quality and quantity of agriculture. Different techniques of smart agricul-ture are shown in Figure 12.4.

Satellite images, being freely available and covering a large area, are generally used for com-parative study on large fields. Satellite images are not able to provide fine details on the ground and have a specific revisit time. On the other hand, near-surface remote sensing can provide finer details along with critical time series data. Land-based techniques are connected with the cloud generally and provide data at specified time intervals. Being in contact with soil and ground directly provides

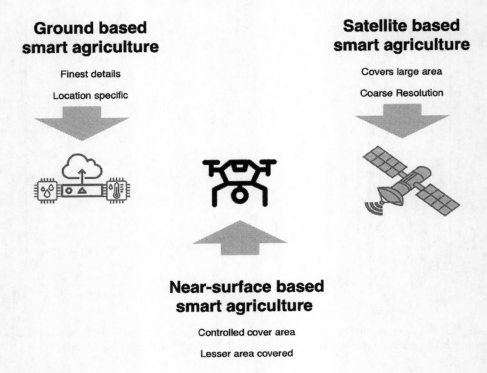

FIGURE 12.4 Different smart agriculture platforms.

the most accurate results but the sensors used must be operated carefully. In subsequent sections, different smart agriculture platforms are discussed separately.

12.3.1 Satellite Based Smart Agriculture

Satellites have always been helpful for agriculture and related fields. Several weather monitoring satellites predict the monsoon and help the farmers to take measures accordingly. Satellite images were used for drought monitoring by yield anomalies and precipitation patterns (Kogan 1995). But in recent times, some multispectral satellite images are available for free all over the world. Nowadays, due to the wide availability of satellite images dataset, they can be used to estimate crop yield using machine learning and artificial intelligence (Arumugam et al. 2021; Kamir, Waldner, and Hochman 2020; Zhang et al. 2020). Satellite-based assessments play a crucial role in transformation of rural livelihood (Burke and Lobell 2017). Vegetation indices (VI) are formed using multispectral bands to provide information about different aspects of vegetation. The most frequently used vegetation index is normalized difference vegetation index (NDVI) (Giovos et al. 2021). Other VI such as enhanced vegetation index (EVI), soil adjusted vegetation index (SAVI), etc., are used for biomass estimation and vegetation density (Giovos et al. 2021).

Different VI are used for different categories of classification. These categories and the number of VI are mentioned in Table 12.1 below.

Time series analysis to analyse satellite data for estimating the production using various data analysis tools give satisfactory results for a large area (Aghighi et al. 2018). Multispectral images are used for agricultural boundary delineation, Habitat and agriculture land cover mapping, and crop classification (Lucas et al. 2007; North, Pairman, and Belliss 2019; Wardlow, Egbert, and Kastens 2007). Too large intervals or missing images are significant challenges for rule-based maps using multispectral satellite images (Lilburne and North 2010). Satellites being far away from the Earth's

TABLE 12.1

Vegetation Indices Count for different Categories of Vegetation Classification (Giovos et al. 2021)

Vegetation Indices	Count
Chlorophyll	97
Pigment	101
Biophysical parameter	150
Biomass density	216
Water content	9

surface gives the advantage of looking at the fields in a respective manner, but at the same time, it is not able to provide finer details than UAVs and drones.

12.3.2 AERIAL-BASED SMART AGRICULTURE

There is no denial that satellites-based remote sensing technology is a popular and helpful platform for collecting aerial photographs. However, this system has many drawbacks for agricultural applications, including poor spatial and temporal resolutions, long revisit intervals, susceptibility to weather, and high cost (Xiang and Tian 2006). A new approach to agricultural monitoring and management has emerged in the last 10 years with the emergence of platforms for UAVs. UAVs are a relatively new technology that could fill the void between manned aerial surveys and satellite remote sensing (Klemas 2015). Because they are inexpensive, portable, and have low speed and altitude with adjustable flight paths that enable them to gather information and secure more than manned aircrafts, UAVs have proven a potential ability for agricultural remote-sensing data collection (Lelong et al. 2008).

Xiang and Tian (2011) developed an unmanned remote-sensing system based on a helicopter drone. The technology accomplished reaching specific destinations and acquiring multispectral aerial images. To identify and map cotton fields, Yang et al. (2010) assessed and did a comparative analysis of aerial multispectral (three-bands) and hyperspectral (128-bands) data. Primicerio et al. (2012) developed a six-rotor-based UAV to create a dynamic and efficient aerial imaging platform for vineyard monitoring. Based on the vegetation index, i.e. NDVI, classified maps were created and successfully mapped crop intensity over time. To extract good temporal resolution data with high spatial resolution, image fusion algorithms for high and low spatial resolution images are used, as suggested by (Singha et al. 2016). When the spectral properties are combined, varied crop types have different seasonal behaviours, captured by phenological behaviour.

Although aerial-based smart agriculture provides effective monitoring and management, there are limitations such as the cost of operation for individual farmers, which would be expensive and will need a skilled person to control.

12.3.3 GROUND BASED SMART AGRICULTURE

The Internet of Things (IoT) is a system of physical objects that are interconnected to other devices and networks over the internet via sensors, software, and other technologies. Due to the IoT, the sensors function as "smart sensors" and find effective use in a wide range of applications (Ratnaparkhi et al. 2020). The use of various types of sensors for monitoring and management of various environmental parameters, such as temperature, moisture, soil conditions, soil health monitoring, crop yield, pollutants, quality of air, ground water contamination, radiation, etc., has been included in agriculture applications over the past decade (Ullo and Sinha 2020).

Utilization of remote sensing imageries with sensors paved the path of implementation of Crop classification and management using Infrared thermography techniques in near-real time (Kayad et al. 2020). In another study on smart agriculture (Syrový et al. 2020), IoT based smart sensors to measure soil moisture are discussed. Further, employing temperature, humidity and soil moisture sensors are discussed in (Rodríguez-Robles et al. 2020) which assisted in implementation and monitoring for better crop yields.

It is significant to mention that ground based sensors along with IoT technology provides a cutting-edge platform for smart agriculture that has undergone proper testing and had performance assessed in the context of smart agricultural practises used in many nations. Using low-cost IoT-based platforms, crop quality, drought management, and drought-related loss estimation are done.

12.4 SUMMARY

The rapid growth of remote sensing and sensor-based technologies has facilitated better agricultural monitoring and progress. In this study, we examine various smart agriculture platforms and many agricultural domains in which they are needed. The rising global population makes food security a pressing issue for the modern world. As both farmland and the resources needed to sustain it are in short supply, the solution lies in the use of smart agriculture systems. Using various methods of collecting time series data, we can better comprehend the varying weather, water, and fertilizer patterns. Keeping tabs on the crop and figuring out what it is may be done with the use of satellite data. However, water, disease, and fertilizer needs may be identified and managed with the use of near-surface remote sensing. Time series data are kept alive with the use of ground-based sensors. The information below can be mined for further insights and patterns. Minimizing the need for human intervention in expansive areas is one use of the massive amounts of remotely sensed data already being used in machine learning and artificial intelligence. The time and money it saves will be much appreciated. Smart agricultural platforms have made inroads in India because to widespread smartphone use and lower internet costs. But the entry barrier is too expensive for the vast majority of India's farmers to afford these services. Lack of technical expertise is another major barrier to expanding these kinds of platforms in India. Indian farmers may better take use of smart agriculture's benefits by spreading the word, embracing new technologies, and joining the industry as private sector actors.

REFERENCES

Aghighi, Hossein, Mohsen Azadbakht, Davoud Ashourloo, Hamid Salehi Shahrabi, and Soheil Radiom. 2018. "Machine Learning Regression Techniques for the Silage Maize Yield Prediction Using Time-Series Images of Landsat 8 OLI." *IEEE Journal of Selected Topics in Applied Earth Observations and Remote Sensing* 11(12):4563–77. doi: 10.1109/JSTARS.2018.2823361.

Allen, Richard, Ayse Irmak, Ricardo Trezza, Jan M. H. Hendrickx, Wim Bastiaanssen, and Jeppe Kjaersgaard. 2011. "Satellite-Based ET Estimation in Agriculture Using SEBAL and METRIC." *Hydrological Processes* 25(26):4011–27. doi: 10.1002/HYP.8408.

Arumugam, Ponraj, Abel Chemura, Bernhard Schauberger, and Christoph Gornott. 2021. "Remote Sensing Based Yield Estimation of Rice (Oryza Sativa l.) Using Gradient Boosted Regression in India." *Remote Sensing* 13(12). doi: 10.3390/RS13122379/S1.

Burke, Marshall, and David B. Lobell. 2017. "Satellite-Based Assessment of Yield Variation and Its Determinants in Smallholder African Systems." *Proceedings of the National Academy of Sciences of the United States of America* 114(9):2189–94. doi: 10.1073/PNAS.1616919114/SUPPL_FILE/PNAS.201616919SI.PDF.

Cancela, Javier J., Xesús P. González, Mar Vilanova, and José M. Mirás-Avalos. 2019. "Water Management Using Drones and Satellites in Agriculture." *Water* 11(5):874. doi: 10.3390/W11050874.

Christiansen, Martin Peter, Morten Stigaard Laursen, Rasmus Nyholm Jørgensen, Søren Skovsen, and René Gislum. 2017. "Designing and Testing a UAV Mapping System for Agricultural Field Surveying." *Sensors* 17(12):2703. doi: 10.3390/S17122703.

Giovos, Rigas, Dimitrios Tassopoulos, Dionissios Kalivas, Nestor Lougkos, and Anastasia Priovolou. 2021. "Remote Sensing Vegetation Indices in Viticulture: A Critical Review." *Agriculture* 11(5):457. doi: 10.3390/AGRICULTURE11050457.

Goel, Raj Kumar, Chandra Shekhar Yadav, Shweta Vishnoi, and Ritesh Rastogi. 2021. "Smart Agriculture – Urgent Need of the Day in Developing Countries." *Sustainable Computing: Informatics and Systems* 30:100512. doi: 10.1016/J.SUSCOM.2021.100512.

Kamir, Elisa, François Waldner, and Zvi Hochman. 2020. "Estimating Wheat Yields in Australia Using Climate Records, Satellite Image Time Series and Machine Learning Methods." *ISPRS Journal of Photogrammetry and Remote Sensing* 160:124–35 doi: 10.1016/J.ISPRSJPRS.2019.11.008.

Kayad, Ahmed, Dimitrios S. Paraforos, Francesco Marinello, and Spyros Fountas. 2020. "Latest Advances in Sensor Applications in Agriculture." *Agriculture* 10(8):1–8. doi: 10.3390/AGRICULTURE10080362.

Klemas, Victor V. 2015. "Coastal and Environmental Remote Sensing from Unmanned Aerial Vehicles: An Overview." *Journal of Coastal Research* 31(5):1260–67. doi: 10.2112/JCOASTRES-D-15-00005.1.

Kogan, F. N. 1995. "Droughts of the Late 1980s in the United States as Derived from NOAA Polar-Orbiting Satellite Data." *Bulletin - American Meteorological Society* 76(5):655–68. doi: 10.1175/1520-0477(1995)076<0655:DOTLIT>2.0.CO;2.

Lelong, Camille C. D., Philippe Burger, Guillaume Jubelin, Bruno Roux, Sylvain Labbé, and Frédéric Baret. 2008. "Assessment of Unmanned Aerial Vehicles Imagery for Quantitative Monitoring of Wheat Crop in Small Plots." *Sensors* 8(5):3557–85. doi: 10.3390/S8053557.

Lilburne, L. R., and H. C. North. 2010. "Modelling Uncertainty of a Land Management Map Derived from a Time Series of Satellite Images." *International Journal of Remote Sensing* 31(3):597–616. doi: 10.1080/01431160902894459.

Lucas, Richard, Aled Rowlands, Alan Brown, Steve Keyworth, and Peter Bunting. 2007. "Rule-Based Classification of Multi-Temporal Satellite Imagery for Habitat and Agricultural Land Cover Mapping." *ISPRS Journal of Photogrammetry and Remote Sensing* 62(3):165–85. doi: 10.1016/J.ISPRSJPRS.2007.03.003.

Ministry of Agriculture and Farmers' Welfare. 1990. *Annual Report 2020–21*. New Delhi.

Nguyen, Thanh Tam, Thanh Dat Hoang, Minh Tam Pham, Tuyet Trinh Vu, Thanh Hung Nguyen, Quyet Thang Huynh, and Jun Jo. 2020. "Monitoring Agriculture Areas with Satellite Images and Deep Learning." *Applied Soft Computing Journal* 95. doi: 10.1016/J.ASOC.2020.106565.

North, Heather C., David Pairman, and Stella E. Belliss. 2019. "Boundary Delineation of Agricultural Fields in Multitemporal Satellite Imagery." *IEEE Journal of Selected Topics in Applied Earth Observations and Remote Sensing* 12(1):237–51. doi: 10.1109/JSTARS.2018.2884513.

Patil, K. A., and N. R. Kale. 2016. "A Model for Smart Agriculture Using IoT." In *2016 International Conference on Global Trends in Signal Processing, Information Computing and Communication (ICGTSPICC)*, IEEE, pp. 543–45.

Primicerio, Jacopo, Salvatore Filippo Di Gennaro, Edoardo Fiorillo, Lorenzo Genesio, Emanuele Lugato, Alessandro Matese, and Francesco Primo Vaccari. 2012. "A Flexible Unmanned Aerial Vehicle for Precision Agriculture." *Precision Agriculture* 13(4):517–23. doi: 10.1007/S11119-012-9257-6.

Ratnaparkhi, Sanika, Suvaid Khan, Chandrakala Arya, Shailesh Khapre, Prabhishek Singh, Manoj Diwakar, and Achyut Shankar. 2020. "WITHDRAWN: Smart Agriculture Sensors in IOT: A Review." *Materials Today: Proceedings*. doi: 10.1016/J.MATPR.2020.11.138.

Ray, Ram L., Sudhir K. Singh, Dorijan Radočaj, Mladen Juriši´c Juriši´c, and Mateo Gašparovi´c Gašparovi´c. 2022. "The Role of Remote Sensing Data and Methods in a Modern Approach to Fertilization in Precision Agriculture." doi: 10.3390/rs14030778.

Rodríguez-Robles, Javier, Álvaro Martin, Sergio Martin, José A. Ruipérez-Valiente, and Manuel Castro. 2020. "Autonomous Sensor Network for Rural Agriculture Environments, Low Cost, and Energy Self-Charge." *Sustainability* 12(15):5913. doi: 10.3390/SU12155913.

Singha, Mrinal, Bingfang Wu, and Miao Zhang. 2016. "An Object-Based Paddy Rice Classification Using Multi-Spectral Data and Crop Phenology in Assam, Northeast India." *Remote Sensing* 8(6):479. doi: 10.3390/RS8060479.

Syrový, Tomáš, Robert Vik, Silvan Pretl, Lucie Syrová, Jiří Čengery, Aleš Hamáček, Lubomír Kubáč, and Ladislav Menšík. 2020. "Fully Printed Disposable IoT Soil Moisture Sensors for Precision Agriculture." *Chemosensors* 8(4):125. doi: 10.3390/CHEMOSENSORS8040125.

Tantalaki, Nicoleta, Stavros Souravlas, and Manos Roumeliotis. 2019. "Data-Driven Decision Making in Precision Agriculture: The Rise of Big Data in Agricultural Systems." *Journal of Agricultural & Food Information* 20(4):344–80. doi: 10.1080/10496505.2019.1638264.

Ullo, Silvia Liberata, and Ganesh Ram Sinha. 2020. "Advances in Smart Environment Monitoring Systems Using IoT and Sensors." *Sensors (Basel, Switzerland)* 20(11). doi: 10.3390/S20113113.

Wardlow, Brian D., Stephen L. Egbert, and Jude H. Kastens. 2007. "Analysis of Time-Series MODIS 250 m Vegetation Index Data for Crop Classification in the U.S. Central Great Plains." *Remote Sensing of Environment* 108(3):290–310. doi: 10.1016/J.RSE.2006.11.021.

Xiang, Haitao, and Lei Tian. 2006. "Development of Autonomous Unmanned Helicopter Based Agricultural Remote Sensing System." In *2006 ASABE Annual International Meeting*. doi: 10.13031/2013.20893.

Xiang, Haitao, and Lei Tian. 2011. "Development of a Low-Cost Agricultural Remote Sensing System Based on an Autonomous Unmanned Aerial Vehicle (UAV)." *Biosystems Engineering* 108(2):174–90. doi: 10.1016/J.BIOSYSTEMSENG.2010.11.010.

Yang, Chenghai, James H. Everitt, and Carlos J. Fernandez. 2010. "Comparison of Airborne Multispectral and Hyperspectral Imagery for Mapping Cotton Root Rot." *Biosystems Engineering* 107(2):131–39. doi: 10.1016/J.BIOSYSTEMSENG.2010.07.011.

Zhang, Peng Peng, Xin Xing Zhou, Zhi Xiang Wang, Wei Mao, Wen Xi Li, Fei Yun, Wen Shan Guo, and Chang Wei Tan. 2020. "Using HJ-CCD Image and PLS Algorithm to Estimate the Yield of Field-Grown Winter Wheat." *Scientific Reports* 10(1). doi: 10.1038/S41598-020-62125-5.

13 Role of IoT Enabling Smart Agricultural Society

Satyam Mishra, Ravi Saraswat, and Sudhriti Sengupta
Galgotias University

CONTENTS

13.1 INTRODUCTION

A system of connected smart devices, a network of physical devices, technologies, items, animals, or people is known as the "web of things," or "IoT." Many essential research endeavors and examinations have been carried out to enhance technology through the Internet of things (IoT) [1]. This is essentially the concept of fundamentally connecting any device to the Internet (and/or with one another). This applies to almost anything that anyone can dream of, including telephones, coffee pots, dishwashing machines, headsets, lights, wearable technology, etc. In addition, there is the Industrial IoT, which uses similar concepts but in commercial settings and on items like manufacturing machinery. In addition, the device displays updated timetables and resource levels. We can prevent delays and alter routes before entering accident scenes by using the congestion alerts provided by maps to make it on time [2]. It is more complex and challenging to resolve safety problems affecting the trust connection between disparate entities, security communication, surveillance systems, and other security concerns. Numerous real-world challenges, including traffic congestion, city services, infrastructure prosperity, public participation, and public security and stability, are addressed through IoT applications. Examples of IoT in action range from a smart house that automatically changes lighting and heating to a digital workplace that continuously examines industrial machines for issues and then makes alterations to prevent failures [3,4] (Figure 13.1).

Examples of IoT in action range from a smart house that automatically changes lighting and heating to a digital workplace that continuously examines industrial machines for issues and then makes alterations to prevent failures. Before the IoT concept is widely adopted, many tough challenges still need to be tackled and both technological and societal knots need to be untied. Although IoT in business can take many different shapes, it frequently entails collecting intelligence on behavior,

DOI: 10.1201/9781003324720-16

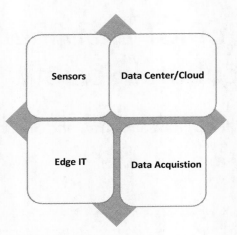

FIGURE 13.1 Components of IoT architecture.

protocols, and other factors. Many IoT devices can also act to fix problems. Organizations can easily determine their advantages and drawbacks according to the constant influx of big data, which enables them to spot usage patterns for their technologies [5].

13.2 ARCHITECTURAL VIEW OF IoT

This section briefs about the different components of IoT some components, which play a major role in the proliferation of IoT framework and its application in different domains. Irrespective of the domain and application, any IoT architecture will have the following components, viz, sensors, data acquisition system (DAS), Edge IT, and data center/cloud [6].

13.2.1 Sensors

In most IoT device architectures, sensors are used. Sensors are used to detect objects, machinery, and other things. A gadget that responds to a certain simulation is called sensor. Sensors must be linked to the data network in the IoT. A sensor is a device that can measure a physical characteristic and turn the data into an electrical or optical signal. Sensors with the ability to sense heat, weight, motion, pressure, moisture, and more. Normally, sensors are pre-programmed with precise instructions, but some of them can be set up to adjust their level of sensitivity or the frequency of feedback [7]. The sensitivity setting describes how much the output of the sensor changes as the quantity being measured changes. To detect the motion of people but not of dogs, for instance, a motion sensor can be calibrated. Sensor settings are changed using a controller, which may have a graphical user interface (GUI), either locally or remotely. Chemical levels including carbon monoxide, carbon dioxide, oxygen, methane, hydrogen, ammonia, and hydrogen sulfide are detected by sensors used in gas and oil mining. Some sensors used in the creation of applications for smart cities are pressure (for parking), dust concentrations, noise, crack displacement, temperature, humidity, and luminosity. For the development of IoT utilized in transportation, sensors monitor idle times, fuel usage, engine issues, and engine load. Sensors monitor soil moisture, leaf moisture, solar radiation, air pressure, and stem diameter in smart agriculture [5,8–11] (Figure 13.2).

13.2.2 Data Acquisition System

A data collection device collects and analyses real-time data to assist users in making machines smarter. It can communicate data in a structured and meaningful way thanks to IoT protocols. The key

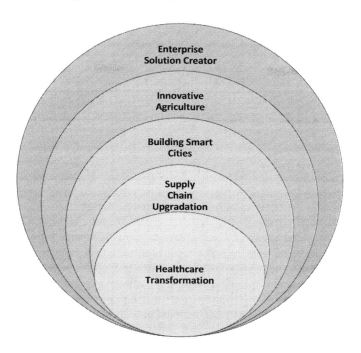

FIGURE 13.2   Functionalities in IoT.

building blocks of IoT technologies are data acquisition (DAQ) and protocols. A data collection device collects and analyzes real-time data to assist users in making machines smarter. It can communicate data in a structured and meaningful way thanks to IoT protocols. IoT protocols are programming languages that allow communication between user apps, gateways, sensors, devices, and servers [12].

13.2.3   EDGE IT

A network receives real-time data from sensors and devices at the IoT edge. Since processing is done closer to its site of generation using IoT edge computing and hence latency problems with the cloud are resolved. The IoT is a collection of networked smart devices that send and receive massive volumes of data to and from other devices, creating a plethora of information that needs to be processed and evaluated. Instead of sending IoT data back to a data center or cloud, edge computing, a technique for computing on site where data is received or used, allows IoT data to be captured and processed at the edge. IoT and edge computing work well together to quickly analyze data in real time. Edge computing is a method by which a business can scale centralized infrastructure to meet the demands of growing numbers of devices and data by using and distributing a shared pool of resources across a large number of locations [13].

13.2.4   DATA CENTER/CLOUD

To maximize uptime, improve energy efficiency, reduce operating costs, and guard against data loss and exposure, IoT for data centre infrastructure management offers a comprehensive view of the current environmental factors, resource utilization, and security. For long- or short-term applications, this layer stores data gathered from sensors and devices at the edge or in the cloud. The edge gateway provides features, such as sensor data collection, pre-processing of the data, and secure communication to the cloud IoT data is typically unstructured, making public cloud infrastructure a simple place to store it. On the basis of object storage technology, all of the major cloud providers provide affordable, scalable storage systems [14].

13.3   IoT ROLE AND ITS RESPONSIBILITY

By maximizing the use of alternative energy sources, we may reduce waste by using IoT-connected devices. IoT makes it possible for machine-to-machine, machine-to-human, and human-to-machine interactions that will affect how our device functions. IoT supports our welfare in the background while also enabling us to live smarter, work smarter, and take total control of our lives. The IoT has the potential to alter our world and is no longer just a "hype" or a "buzzword." Understanding why interconnection is so important to every IoT solution is not difficult. They all depend on an efficient, dependable internet connection. IoT technologies impress us while meeting our needs, thanks in part to their timeliness [15, 19–26].

13.3.1   IoT in Industries

Applications for IoT are still in their early stages. IoT usage, on the other hand, is quickly developing and expanding. In many different areas, such as environmental monitoring, healthcare services, inventory and production management, food supply chain (FSC), transportation, workspace and home support, security, and surveillance, numerous IoT applications are being developed or deployed. By utilizing the increasing pervasiveness of radio-frequency identification (RFID), wireless, mobile, and sensor devices, the IoT has presented a potential opportunity to develop robust industrial systems and applications [3]. IoT technologies, robots, equipment, software packages, cloud servers, and apps make up the Industrial IoT system. For specific applications, smart sensors are used at all stages of the production process. In industries, a network plays a very important role in the terms of web of the things which involve all the tasks that have to be done in a particular operation to get effective result the tasks are like communication, innovation [5] (Figure 13.3).

13.3.2   IoT in Smart Cities

International Smart City efforts are made possible by the new IoT applications. Through the use of vast real-time data streams, it allows for the remote monitoring, management, and control of equipment as well as the production of fresh insights and useful information. In the coming years, as populations and urbanization expand, many cities may look to technology and cutting-edge networks to assist them to manage resource shortages. Cities may increasingly use the IoT segment known as "smart city solutions" in particular. Cities must establish the circumstances for ongoing development, with urban infrastructure and buildings needing to be developed more sustainably and effectively as digital technologies become more vital [16] (Figure 13.4).

13.3.3   IoT in Security

There are currently billions of IoT devices spread around the globe. We shall discuss their inherent security vulnerabilities here because of the additional scrutiny they have received as a result of their increased involvement in our daily lives. Information security can indeed be particularly difficult because several IoT applications are not constructed with robust security in place generally, the maker's focus is on practicality, but instead of security, so the devices can be released rapidly [15].

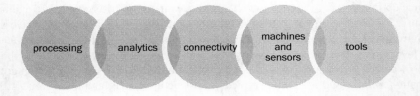

FIGURE 13.3   Component of industrial IoT.

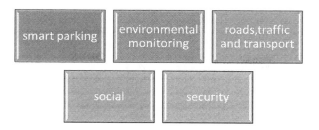

FIGURE 13.4 IoT in smart cities.

When using the safety level that best suits their application demands, a strong IoT security portfolio enables developers to shield devices from all kinds of threats. Smart homes serve as an example of how easily obtainable IoT devices are for everyday consumers. By purchasing such products, users can update their home's security system (using built-in sensors, Webcams, and motion sensors) or enhance their entertainment system [13].

- **Threats in security**: The enlarged attack surface of dangers that were already affecting networks makes IoT security essential. Insecure activities by users and businesses, who might lack the tools or expertise to properly safeguard their IoT ecosystems, constitute an additional concern [15].
- **Challenges**: This comparison helps explain why IoT and safety threats seem to be intertwined. It's simple to underestimate the risk that IoT infrastructure poses because it comprises several small, usually inexpensive physical endpoint devices, like sensors or switches. As a result, complete IoT security solutions must take into account all of these devices and offer a workable structure for resolving any vulnerabilities [17].
- **Solutions**: Most individuals continue with the router's name that was provided by the manufacturer and neglect to rename it. Your personal Wi-Fi's security can be compromised as a result. You have to be familiar with every feature your IoT device needs to work. The majority of modern technology, including televisions and refrigerators, may be connected to the internet. You should reconsider your password if you're still using "password" and "qwerty." For IoT devices, using a widely used and straightforward password opens the door to hackers [2] (Figure 13.5).

13.3.4 IoT in Healthcare

Applications of IoT in healthcare are advantageous to patients, families, doctors, hospitals, and insurance providers. IoT for Clients-Wearable gadgets like wearable and other connected directly medical equipment like glucometer and blood pressure monitors. While technology cannot reverse population aging or completely remove chronic diseases, it can at least simplify healthcare by providing users with affordable medical services. The focus of this chapter is not on pharmaceuticals, how IoT and AI aid in the cure of particular ailments, or advancements in particular fields like bionics and others [18] (Figure 13.6).

13.4 ROLE OF IoT IN AGRICULTURE

Connected devices have permeated every part of our lives as a result of the IoT increasing adoption, from smart cities and industrial IoT to health and fitness, home automation, automotive, and logistics.

IoT, linked devices, and automation have found use in agriculture and have the potential to significantly improve almost every aspect of it. This has helped smart farming technology spread more widely around the globe, along with the rising consumer demand for agricultural products. The IoT market share in agriculture grew to $5.6 billion in 2020 [1]. The term "smart agriculture" is typically used to refer to the use of IoT technology in agriculture. Farmers can use IoT sensors to gather

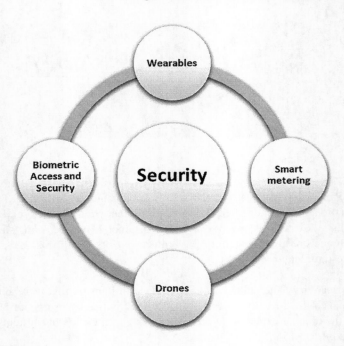

FIGURE 13.5   IoT in security.

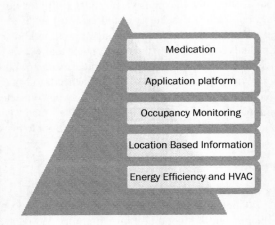

FIGURE 13.6   IoT in healthcare.

environmental and machine parameters, which will allow them to better manage anything from raising cattle to growing crops. Farmers can determine exactly how many pesticides and fertilizers they need to use to achieve maximum efficiency, for instance, by utilizing smart agriculture sensors to monitor the condition of crops. Some of the ways in which agriculture can be improved by IoT are:

- Smart agriculture sensors gather a ton of information, such as weather conditions, soil quality, crop growth status, or cattle health. This information can be utilized to monitor things like moisture levels and machine efficiency [2] (Figure 13.7).
- Lower production risks as a result of better internal process control is one of the aspects which can be done using IoT. We can plan for more effective product distribution if you

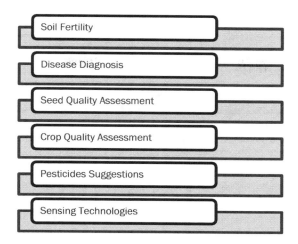

FIGURE 13.7   Solutions in smart agriculture [18].

can predict the output of your production. Farmers' output is less likely to be wasted if the quantity of harvested goods can be estimated.
- Due to the enhanced control over production, IoT in agriculture aids in cost management and waste reduction. It is less risky to lose produce quantity or quality if irregularities in crop growth or livestock health can be identified.
- By automating the production process, it is possible to maintain higher standards for crop quality and growth potential [16].
- The weather stations that incorporate numerous smart farming sensors are arguably the most well-liked smart agricultural technology. They are spread out around the area and gather various environmental data before sending it to the cloud. The measurements offered can be used to map the climate conditions, select suitable crops, and implement the necessary improvements.

To manage the greenhouse environment, farmers frequently require manual intervention. They can obtain precise real-time information on greenhouse parameters including illumination, temperature, soil quality, and humidity thanks to the usage of IoT sensors [17]. Weather stations can autonomously change the conditions to reflect the specified parameters in addition to sourcing environmental data. In particular, automation systems for greenhouses operate on a similar concept. Crop management tools are an additional IoT product category in agriculture and a component of precision farming. They should be set up in the field to gather information pertaining to crop farming, such as temperature and precipitation as well as leaf water potential and general crop health, just as weather stations. Using IoT, agriculturists can successfully stop any diseases or pests that could reduce crop's output, and also keep an eye on growth and any irregularities of cultivation [6].

13.5   CONCLUSION

The IoT keeps people's lives simple and satisfying. It has made people's lives much easier. However, with the rise of online of Things, the treatment for security and protection has also improved. Every connected item in the Internet of Things (IoT) transmits packets of data, which necessitates reliable communication, storage, and security. An organization's ability to manage, monitor, and secure massive amounts of data and connectivity from scattered devices is challenged by IoT. The potential for IoT in the future is limitless. Improved network agility, interconnected artificial intelligence (AI), and the ability to deploy, automate, orchestrate, and safeguard diverse use cases at hyper-scale will accelerate progress toward the industrial internet.

REFERENCES

[1] S. Tyagi and S. Sengupta. Role of AI in gaming and animation. *Lecture Notes on Data Engineering and Communication Technology*, 49, 259–267, 2020.

[2] M. Miraz, M. Ali, P. Excell and P. Rich, "A review on Internet of Things (IoT), Internet of Everything (IoE) and Internet of Nano Things (IoNT)", In *Proceeding of Internet Technologies and Applications*, Valencia, Spain, 2015.

[3] S. Higginbotham and M. Pesce, "Internet of everything: Macro & micro", *IEEE Spectrum*, 58(2), 20–21, 2021, doi: 10.1109/MSPEC.2021.9340118.

[4] Lavanya Sharma and PK Garg, *"IoT and Its Applications", From Visual Surveillance to Internet of Things*. Taylor & Francis, CRC Press, vol. 1, p. 29.

[5] L. Atzori, A. Iera and G. Morabito, "The internet of things: A survey," *Computer Networks*, 54(15), 2787–2805, 2010.

[6] M. Potkonjak, S. Meguerdichian and J. L. Wong, "Trusted sensors and remote sensing", *IEEE Sensors*, 10, 1104–1107, 2010.

[7] Lavanya Sharma, "Introduction: From visual surveillance to internet of things", Taylor & Francis, CRC Press, vol. 1, p. 14.

[8] Sharma, L. (Ed.). (2021). *Towards Smart World*. New York: Chapman and Hall/CRC, https://doi.org/10.1201/9781003056751.

[9] D. Miorandi, S. Sicari, F. De Pellegrini and I. Chlamtac, "Internet of things: Vision, applications and research challenges," *Ad Hoc Networks*, 10(7), 1497–1516, 2012.

[10] K. Voigt. China Looks to Lead the Internet of Things [Online]. 2012. Available: http://www.cnn.com/2012/11/28/business/china-internet-of-things/. Accessed on October 1, 2013.

[11] https://www.softwebsolutions.com/resources/7-must-have-sensor-solutions-for-iot-implementation.html.

[12] Lavanya Sharma and PK Garg "Block based adaptive learning rate for moving person detection in video surveillance", *From Visual Surveillance to Internet of Things*, Taylor & Francis, CRC Press, Vol. 1, p. 201.

[13] I. Bandaraand and F. Ioras, "The evolving challenges of internet of everything: Enhancing student performance and employability in higher education" In *10th Annual International Technology, Education and Development Conference*, vol. 10, pp. 121–131, 2016.

[14] What is Mirai Botnet? Accessed at https://www.cloudflare.com/engb/learning/ddos/glossary/mirai-botnet/ on 4 February 2021.

[15] S. Sen Gupta, M. Shad Khan and T. Sethi, "Latest trends in security, privacy and trust in IOT", *2019 3rd International Conference on Electronics, Communication and Aerospace Technology (ICECA)*, 2019, pp. 382–385, doi: 10.1109/ICECA.2019.8822178.

[16] D. Kohli and S. Sengupta, "Recent trends of IoT in smart city development", *Proceedings of the International Conference on Computer Networks*, 49, 376–3780.

[17] S. Sengupta and A. Rana, "Role of bloom filter in analysis of big data", *2020 8th International Conference on Reliability, Infocom Technologies and Optimization (Trends and Future Directions) (ICRITO)*, 2020, 6–9, doi: 10.1109/ICRITO48877.2020.9197859.

[18] A. Rustagi, C. Manchanda and N. Sharma, "IoE: A boon & threat to the mankind", In *2020 IEEE 9th International Conference on Communication Systems and Network Technologies (CSNT)*, Gwalior, India, 2020, pp. 114–119, doi: 10.1109/CSNT48778.2020.9115748.

[19] Lavanya Sharma, "Self-driving cars: Tools and technologies", *Computer Vision and Internet of Things: Technologies and Applications*, Taylor & Francis, CRC Press, pp. 99–110, 2022.

[20] Lavanya Sharma, "Computer vision in surgical operating theatre and medical imaging", *Computer Vision and Internet of Things: Technologies and Applications*, Taylor & Francis, CRC Press, pp. 75–96, 2022.

[21] Lavanya Sharma, "Preventing security breach in social media: Threats and prevention techniques", *Computer Vision and Internet of Things: Technologies and Applications*, Taylor & Francis, CRC Press, pp. 53–62, 2022.

[22] Lavanya Sharma, Mukesh Carpenter, "Use of robotics in real-time applications", *Computer Vision and Internet of Things: Technologies and Applications*, Taylor & Francis, CRC Press, pp. 41–50, 2022.

[23] Lavanya Sharma et al., "An overview of security issues of internet of things", *Computer Vision and Internet of Things: Technologies and Applications*, Taylor & Francis, CRC Press, pp. 29–40, 2022.

[24] Lavanya Sharma, "Rise of computer vision and internet of things", *Computer Vision and Internet of Things: Technologies and Applications*, Taylor & Francis, CRC Press, pp. 5–17, 2022.

[25] Lavanya Sharma, "Human detection and tracking using background subtraction in visual surveillance", *Towards Smart World: Homes to Cities using Internet of Things*, Taylor & Francis, CRC Press, pp. 317–329, 2020.

[26] Lavanya Sharma, "The rise of internet of things and smart cities", *Towards Smart World: Homes to Cities using Internet of Things*, Taylor & Francis, CRC Press, pp. 1–19, 2020.

14 Resilience of Digital Society to Natural Disasters

Haobam Derit Singh and Yaman Hooda
Manav Rachna International Institute of Research and Studies

CONTENTS

14.1 INTRODUCTION OF NATURAL DISASTER MANAGEMENT

Natural disasters can be defined as those catastrophic events which cause damage to property and fatalities, leading to a massive social–environmental disruption. These natural disasters have different origins and thus are categorized based on the same. The basic three origins of natural disasters include geological, atmospherical and hydrological sources [1–3]. Some of the examples of the natural disasters that often occurred worldwide and causes a humongous damage to the society are earthquakes, floods, cyclones, landslides, etc.

Natural disasters have a noteworthy effect on the different pillars of the society, including public health services, thereby affecting the well-being of the affected population. These adverse health impacts are categorized into two domains: (i) Direct and (ii) Indirect [4]. Direct impacts consist of injuries suffered by the population directly from the natural disasters and indirect impacts include all the secondary effects of the disasters, for example; Malnutrition and the rate of increase in any communicable disease. As the consequences of the natural disaster, these health issues may be intensified due to the harm experienced not only by the health systems but also by infrastructure related to water and sewage treatment. In view of an attempt to minimize the disastrous effects on the society, a system was developed, specifically focusing on the management of natural disasters.

A Natural Disaster Management System is a system of performing all those activities which aim in reducing the damage to the society caused by an event of natural disaster [1,2,7,15,20-27]. These risk-reduction activities are classified into three broad categories as:

1. Pre-Disaster Activities
2. Emergency Response Activities
3. Post-Disaster Activities

Pre-disaster activities include all the activities related to the prevention and preparedness before the event of natural disaster so as to minimize the potential losses of the same to society. Emergency response activities are the activities which take place during the event of natural disaster. These activities are most difficult as they have to be performed when any of natural disasters is taking place. The reconstruction and rehabilitation activities, which are incorporated after natural disaster

DOI: 10.1201/9781003324720-17

took place fall under the category of post-disaster activities. All these activities and their respective economic funding are now considered in every nation's development program around the world.

The successful application and monitoring of natural disaster management is based on four different phases as [5]:

1. Mitigation:
   The first phase of the natural disaster management is *Mitigation*. This phase focuses on the activities related in prevention or reduction of the source, effect and consequences of the disaster. Some of the examples under mitigation include:
   • Proper anchorage systems
   • Formation of water channels
   • Construction of levees and permanent barrier systems
   • Purchasing of insurance policies
2. Preparedness:
   The second phase includes all those activities of the natural disaster that cannot be mitigated such as educational activities, planning and training for the same. This includes:
   • Development of Disaster Preparedness Plan
   • Routine exercises including drills
   • Creating a list of all essential items which requires during a disaster
   • Identification of vulnerabilities of natural disasters
3. Response:
   The third phase, i.e., Response Phase, befalls just after the event of a natural disaster. During this phase, business and other industry-related operations do not function ordinarily. During an emergency, well-being and personal safety of every individual of the society; and the interval of this phase depends upon the preparedness level. Response activities may include the following:
   • Implementation of Disaster Response Plans
   • Conduction of Search and Rescue Plans
   • Activities related to self-protection, protection of family and members of the society
   • Spreading awareness about food safety
4. Recovery:
   In this phase, efforts related to the restoration occurred simultaneously with systematic activities and operations. "The recovery period from a disaster can be prolonged." These activities may include:
   • Avoiding stress-related illness
   • Reduction in the excessive financial burdens
   • Reduction in the susceptibility of future disasters
   • Repairing, rehabilitation and retrofitting of the damaged-existing structures; based on advanced information obtained from previous events of disasters.

The necessity of disaster management aims to ensure a coordinated and effective response system [6,7]. Some of the reasons for the importance of natural disaster management are as below:

1. Saving life and property
2. Improving community resilience
3. Reduction in poverty
4. Reshaping communities
5. Promoting social and economic stability
6. Promoting the protection of natural resources
7. Strengthening the borders security

14.2 BACKGROUND OF DIGITAL TRANSFORMATION

With the passing decades, different industries are showing interest in digitizing their systems by adapting and adopting the technological advancements experienced by the world at different stages for the purpose of automation [8,9]. At the commencement of Industry 4.0, the process of digital reformation in mainly all the sectors had been started and till now being implemented so as to keep the pace with "new" and "smart" mechanisms. Here are some of the technological innovations that are the possible reason for the digitization process.

With all the technological innovations mentioned above, the services of the various sectors of the society have been improved or new services had been evolved such as:

- Autonomous Vehicles
- Home Robotics
- Information-Collection and Target-Attack Robotics
- Healthcare Industry
- Construction Industry
- Air Traffic Management
- Disaster Management
- Manufacturing and Production
- Travel and Tourism
- Product Designing
- Security and Privacy Protection
- 3-D Printing applications

In spite of these explicit technologies, the digitization of the present era promises digitization which can unleash the unparalleled direction for the conduction of businesses and thus offering services and products, optimizing the beneficiaries' values and an organized management-relationship in all types of organizations covering, governmental, commercial, non-profit and public-based industries.

14.3 DIGITIZATION AND DISASTER MANAGEMENT

Digitization in the process of disaster management is a serious concern. As stated earlier, the cycle of disaster management includes four phases, and the digital reformation in each of the phase have to be carried out for proper utilization of the digital applications in disaster management [10]. For understanding the role of digitization in disaster management, the approaches are to be divided into two categories: (i) Opportunities and (ii) Challenges.

1. **Approach One: The Opportunities:**

    Approach one broadly focuses on the advantages, uses and opportunities of the techno-logical advancements which blend with each or all the phases of the disaster management cycle for improvising their individual tasks. The methodology proposed the applications of big data analysis, machine learning, data mining and sentiment analysis which provide an effective, strategic and timely recovery and response for every disaster [11]. The applica-tion of mobile cloud computing and Internet of Things (IoT) provides a platform for the creation of a system of optimum evacuation plan for rapid evacuation of largely populated societies for achieving shortened route length for evacuation, improving convergence rates and shortening of the evacuation time; with a balancing capacity in the shelter surround-ings. The invention of wireless technologies has improved disaster mitigation process and responses from disabled people.

    The applications of digital technologies of Smart Contracts, Blockchain and Building Information Modelling (BIM) develop an integrated, cyber-resilient, self-monitoring and self-regulating operations for providing automation in the building permit processes in the repairing, rehabilitation and retrofitting phase of the buildings after the occurrence of natural disasters [12]. "The clean innovations in the disaster mitigation strategies provides a rather inventive and effective solutions for managing social, economic and environmental challenges resulting from the post-disaster debris."

The applications of Big Data and Advanced Data Analysis in open-source solutions gave the agencies of disaster management irreplaceable understandings and actionable intelligence in the preparation and response towards natural disasters [13]. The technology for robotics, sensor networking and IoT improvises the response towards fire disasters in tunnels with the help of accurate detection, search operations and rescue skills in the domain of disaster response.

2. **Approach One: The Challenges:**

Many researchers examined the security concerns regarding the applications of wireless-sensors in the scenarios of disasters. It also focused on how these network- technology found solutions for the vital need in the exchange of real-time and sensitive information in muddles scenarios. Because of the lower or negligible digitization in remote areas, the awareness towards disaster mitigation strategies is low and thereby, can be proved to be unfavorable during the time of disasters. The discrepancy observed between the actual activity and the activity expressed on social media, by the citizens affects deeply accuracy of the information and thus, emerging to be a great challenge for the agencies of disaster management.

The telecommunication infrastructure plays an important role in transferring the information during and post-disaster scenarios [14]. Thus, failure of this network system leads to a huge loss, making the process of decision-making difficult by the government agencies in choosing a critical network system for the purpose of communication during disasters. Some of the studies examined that how digitization process in disaster management processes laid the route for the digital volunteering of the people as a fresh group in different phases of disaster management cycle. This would have led to the digital transformation in the dynamics of role and power in disaster management, philanthropical emergencies response, breaking the conventional restraints of media–aid relations by citizen journalism, and presenting fresh challenges towards disaster management.

Both of the approaches mentioned above have critical practical and theoretical contributions in managing the disasters, covering the following opportunities in detail:

- Phase-specific
- Technology-specific
- Task-specific

The challenges focused on an extensive strategy-based, long-term perspective of the organization for helping National Disaster Management (NDM) agencies worldwide in making a better-strategic plans, policies and procedures which aim in avoiding catastrophic loss of life and property due to natural disasters.

14.4 NATIONAL DISASTER MANAGEMENT AND DIGITAL TRANSFORMATION

The blending and application of digital transformation in different stages of National Disaster Management (NDM) can be recognized as a characteristic network of entity-relationship, which consists of planning and operation of National Disaster Management. The entity-relationship network for National Disaster Management can be easily understood with the following figure.

As shown, it is easily understandable that National Disaster Management incorporates a diverse array of stakeholders in response to the natural disaster and thus, protecting 3Ps, namely: Places, Property and People. For managing the disasters effectively, National Disaster Management collaborated and coordinated with private, public and governmental agencies and non-profit organizations such as NGOs.

FIGURE 14.1 Four phases of natural disaster management.

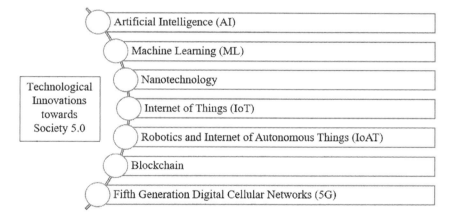

FIGURE 14.2 Technological innovations towards Society 5.0.

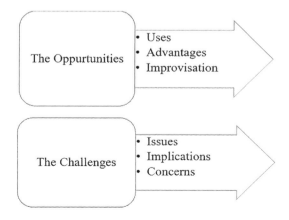

FIGURE 14.3 Approaches for digitization in natural disaster management.

FIGURE 14.4   Approaches for digitization in natural disaster management.

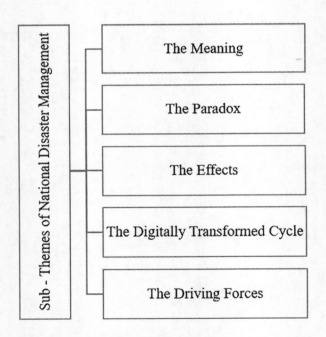

FIGURE 14.5   Sub-themes of National Disaster Management.

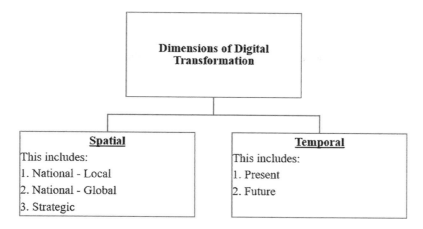

FIGURE 14.6   Dimensions of digital transformation in National Disaster Management.

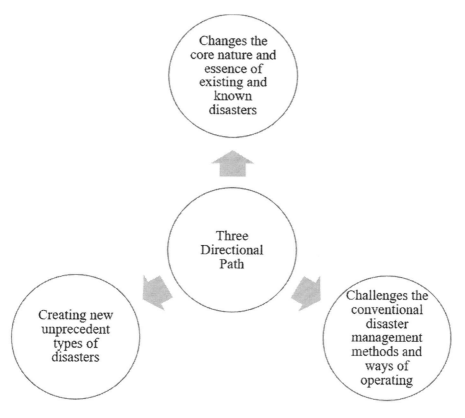

FIGURE 14.7   Three-directional path of digital transformation in National Disaster Management.

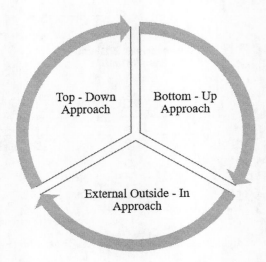

FIGURE 14.8   Approaches towards the driving forces for digitization in National Disaster Management.

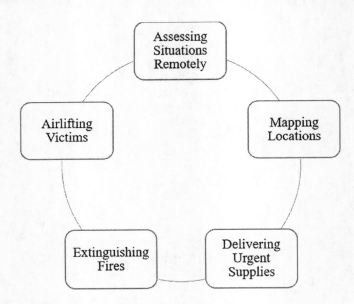

FIGURE 14.9   Applications of drones in natural disaster management.

Digital transformation is bringing reformation in the domain of understanding and defining the disasters. With reference to Society 5.0, the process of digital transformation is changing the methods and approaches towards which the disasters are mitigating, preparing for, responding to and recovering from. Giving an example of floods, the danger of flooding can be minimized by capitalizing on timely and on-site information, which can be collected with mobile data technologies, offering an improved way in understanding the behaviour and movement of people. Thus, proving the application of digitization in disaster preparedness in enhancing the awareness and sharing of information.

Also, digital transformation is shifting the serving approaches from traditional to modern approaches to the communities and their people of National Disaster Management. Presently, people are connected dynamically and connected in different ways, followed by the modifying the changes within the organizations. Due to emerging technological innovations, the observations, estimations and expectations of society are also changing rapidly. A huge portion of the population are expressing their requirements, thoughts, descriptions and noting emergencies and urgencies at various levels on different platforms of social media. The new generations of "Digital Natives" and "Born-Digital" are evolving. Digital transformation helps in reforming the means of communication among these generations by preferred sources, categories and arrangements. An effective monitoring system and understanding of the approaches enhance the decision-based responses of NDM.

The digital transformation in buildings and places is also enhancing the effectiveness of the resilient system of natural disasters. The applications of Internet of Things (IoT) and Augmented Intelligence (AI) are helping in the creation of a fresh topographical system of static, physical everyday objects and devices. AI and IoT give a way to devices for communicating wirelessly, receiving and sending on-site data, and can be monitoring and controlling the information gathered from minute areas over the internet. The concept of smart cities is creating sustainable, productive, transparent, competitive, efficient and highly well-connected cities with the role of governmental agencies. Thus, National Disaster Management requires to be understood, prepared and increase capitalization on digitization.

Many industries including NGOs and private sector organizations which are digitally reformed in their services and operations. The collaboration between different non-governmental industries and organizations is one of the many significant responsibilities of National Disaster Management for an effective and efficient response to the hazards. Still, the emerging digital age governs a major portion of the sustainable strategy of the cooperation and relationship mentioned [15]. Societal sectors like infrastructure, retail shopping, hotels and hospitality; and transportation are considering the digital reformation for redefining the business models internally and collaborations in their supply-chain management externally. All the industries mentioned and other sectors which are directly related to the society, are having direct implications, both strategic and operational, on National Disaster Management in the different phases of disaster risk reduction management. Also, the other collaborative organizations of National Disaster Management including industries from public sectors and government-undertaking, are also digitally reforming towards Society 5.0. Most of such organizations had already developed strategic plans and models in this direction. Considering the example of Government of United Kingdom, they had developed a Government Transformation Strategy [2017–2020], endeavouring specifications and methodologies towards a complete digital transformation in all governmental sectors. In the same way, the government of the nations worldwide are changing their operations and strategies dynamically and prioritizing to coping with the digital reformation. Thus, it is mandatory in the understanding the theoretical importance of digital reformation to National Disaster Management and ensuring that the systems under the government must remain efficient, effective and relevant in the emerging digital era.

14.5 IMPACT OF DIGITAL TRANSFORMATION ON NATIONAL DISASTER MANAGEMENT

For understanding the impact of digitization on National Disaster Management, one must consider the basic five sub-themes of the National Disaster Management.

1. **The Meaning:**
   The interactions with the various organizations and stakeholders discovered three important views or perceptions regarding the impact of the digitization and its concept and relevance in National Disaster Management, which are
   • The Acknowledger-Enthusiast
   • The Acknowledger-Moderator
   • The Acknowledger-Skeptical

The views of all of the contributors vary on the practical meaning of digital transformation in National Disaster Management, considering and acknowledging the probable influence of all the contributors towards digitization in National Disaster Management.

For an Acknowledger-Enthusiast, the process of digitization means a thoughtful real-time approach, which has to be considered by National Disaster Management in paying attention, understanding, reacting and capitalizing as the digitization progresses. The process of digital reformation improves the ability of disaster management in response to hazards and disruptions as it consists of different ways of enhanced communication with satellite and mobile communications and harnessing the technology in response to disasters including the applications of drone over disaster-affected areas.

For an Acknowledger-Moderator, the approach of digitization in National Disaster Management is taken to be an important-positive approach, considering the reserved perception in the way of making the same impactful in different stages of National Disaster Management. They believe that the impact of digital transformation relies on some detailed technological features and their significance in the principle operational-cycle of National Disaster Management [16]. Moreover, they also observed the impact (whether direct or indirect) relies on the temporal closeness of the technical advancements till the present scenario. The dependence on technical factors includes the difference between futuristic conceptual, under-development and already persistent technology.

For an Acknowledger-Skeptical, the process of digital reformation is perceived as either an intimidating approach or one which has negligible or low significance to National Disaster Management. One proclamation was based on the theory that even if the emerging technological advancements are providing solutions in every business, aiding in fulfilling all the necessary tasks towards Society 5.0, the method of obtaining solutions from the pen-and-paper approach remains the utmost resilient approach in all of the National Disaster Management work, thus making less meaningful the approach of digital reformation to National Disaster Management. These people believed that the increased application of technology is becoming a probable risk to privacy and security and thus, affecting the overall preservation of the national infrastructure. The response from the people specifies that the inclusion of more technological advancements in different sectors of society, making these sectors more vulnerable and thus creating a greater complication for National Disaster Management generally.

Thus, the outcomes from three different perspectives can be summarized as:

- The process of digital transformation is significant and inevitable for National Disaster Management and thus, must be understood and planned precisely.
- The leadership in National Disaster Management must be devise suitably since there is a difference in the perceptions among various professionals of disaster management background so as to navigate properly through the variation observed. One of the possible strategies is to begin the process by giving a platform for expert conferences and conversations, aiming the future of National Disaster Management towards digitization, keeping focus on the concepts of Industry 4.0 and Society 5.0.
- Both the dimensions of the digital transformation, i.e., Temporal and Spatial, must be well understood as it is a continuous journey and progresses parallelly with new technological advancement. Also, these dimensions must be controlled in a specific way for increasing the liveliness of National Disaster Management in the middle of both direct and indirect consequences of technological advancements.

2. **The Paradox:**

The paradoxical aspect towards the impact of digitization on National Disaster Management has two different directions, positive or negative. Every technological advancement towards digital transformation is equally having a challenging as well as rewarding perspective in the processes of National Disaster Management as the emerging technological advancements also bring fresh threats and opportunities. But, as per the researchers, the only best way to eradicate the threatening aspect of technology is the technology itself. Furthermore, the paradoxical effect can be observed in the process of gathering data and information, which again if pursued with the help of different means of digital technologies, can be beneficial or detrimental altogether. The volume of the information and data made available with the help of rapid technological advancements could either assist or hinder the power of decision-making and judgement of a layperson as well as experienced person of the organizations working with National Disaster Management. A different type of pressure on organizations is forming up so as to keep with pace and speed of the technological developments.

Overall, the paradoxical aspect brings both challenges and benefits. Considering the challenging aspect, National Disaster Management rapidly develops a positive methodology in understanding the implications of the new technological advancements, both directly and indirectly [17]. Beneficial aspect considering the implementation of strategies of digital transformation rightfully so as to improve the system of National Disaster Management.

3. **The Effects:**

The impact of digital transformation in its core components of "Disaster" and "Management" can be acquired by three different paths.

In the first path, the application of digital reformation modifies the existing disasters and thus, yielding reformed and complicated forms. This effect takes place with the addition to more variables, both positive and negative in nature, towards the state of affairs, and thus broadening the possibility of prevailing hazards, strengthening their consequences, or making dynamic changes of dependencies in the disaster scenarios.

The second path focuses on the application of digital transformation in creating new and unparalleled categories of disasters, which involve fresh methods in response as compared to the conventional way, recognized to National Disaster Management. This effect involves new and innovative disasters which use new technologies in its creation, resulting from the amplified digital interconnections or which can be created due to the failures of emerging technologies.

The third path encompasses the challenge offered by the applications of digital transformation towards the traditional methods involved in the system of disaster management. One of the many aspects consists of the unprecedented encounters that new technologies may impose on the structures of control and command in traditional National Disaster Management. Digitization challenges the existing the system of National Disaster Management by developing additional unconventional layers, which are to be accomplished at the time of disasters, for example social media platforms. A few examples of difficulties which can be brought to National Disaster Management include creating diversion for the people's attention at the time of disasters, persuading the perception of people, enabling random or uncontrollable contributions from spontaneous helpers. "Increased number of stakeholders and more data may obfuscate rather than ameliorate NDM protocols and procedures."

These three above-mentioned paths proposed a systematic methodology for determining and understanding the influence of digitization on National Disaster Management. The approaches of these paths are accounting, mitigating and capitalizing in the development of comprehensive, relevant, and well-rounded strategies for digital reformation in National Disaster Management. Proper understanding of these paths will allow the system of National Disaster Management in re-evaluating its current methodology and in deciding the important and unimportant areas of the system, the unimportant has to be eradicated before its invalidation with respect to the evolution of technology with time.

4. **The Digitally Transformed Cycle:**
   On considering the cycle of full disaster management, the studies discovered that there are some important areas in the disaster management cycle in which digital transformation has a substantial impact. The following areas may include the possibility of improvements:
   - Technologic-Specific Domains
   - Phase-Specific Domains
   - Task-Specific Domains

Digitization had been observed in different phases of the disaster management cycle and thus, can be summarized under three different sub-heads [18], which is explained below.

   a. **Modelling and Visualization:**
   The studies showed that the capability of modeling and visualization of the information and data collected is one of the prime benefits of the applications of digital reformation, that can be used in National Disaster Management. Digitized data permits improved exercising and training scheduling, enhanced early-warning systems, and better sharing of real-time awareness. With improved capabilities of modeling and visualizations, digital transformation offers various advantages such as better strategic prospective, enhanced decision-making and policy specification throughout the life cycle of disaster management.

   b. **Risk Control:**
   It consists of identifying, assessing and managing the risks related to the disaster management cycle. This phase is a prime component in all the stages of disaster management. With the help of digitization, the functions of risk control can be enhanced in preventing and mitigating phases, and also in dealing with the growing dangers during the phase of preparedness, response and recovery. In addition, a new set of risks may evolve due to the application of digital reformation, and thus must be taken care of with additional mechanisms of risk control. The studies expressed that digitization in risk control phase
   - Enhances risk prioritization and strategy building
   - Improving the risk management by blending of different technologies
   - Enriching awareness and knowledge of indirect and direct risks
   - Advance the numeration and depiction of risks and its consequences for better decision making.

   c. **Feedbacks and Learnings:**
   As obtained from the surveys, one of the most challenging and critical area is creating efficient feedback-lesson learning methodology in environment of National Disaster Management. The researchers concluded that the various stakeholders of National Disaster Management give emphasis on pre-disaster cycles of preparation, response and recovery; rather than on the various lessons learned and feedback obtained from field-specific professionals. The studies also proclaimed that the application of digital reformation in the phase of feedbacks and learning could be very impactful in enhancing the process of evaluation and assessment of the actions and decisions, learning the lessons in preparing for the following hazard and providing necessary improvements in the communication between agencies and government across various levels of organizations.

5. **The Driving Forces:**
   To conclude in better understanding the effect of digitization on the system of National Disaster Management, it is essential to understand about the potential or driving forces which would behind the effects. Three different approaches of the forces were studied by the researchers under:

The top-down approach focuses on all the forces from the level of forming strategies to the level of operations. The important decisions regarding digital transformation were taken by the leaders at the top level, followed by the people at the level of operations. This approach is useful in the development and installment of the technologies at different levels of the organizations for an effective and efficient communication system and thus bridging the gap between different stakeholders and agencies working under disaster management working environment. In bottom-up approach, the level of operations has the main driving force for adapting the concept of digitization in National Disaster Management. The factors working at the level of operations enhance the innovations and technical advancements, on the basis of their requirements to get fulfilled at the upper level. This approach is suggested on the justification of investment of proposals of digitization in natural disaster cycle and thus, proposed that the process of digitization stem at the level of operation will be more tangible on considering the investment outcomes. In the third approach of external outside-in, the external forces consist of the ideas of research and innovations from different science-based communities and industries; are the vital driven forces for the implementation of digital transformation into the systems of National Disaster Management. The forces under this category have to keep up the pace with the adaptation of technical advancements and implement the same in the processes and systems.

14.6   APPLICATION OF DRONE TECHNOLOGY IN DISASTER MITIGATION

The advancement in the technology of drone is finding applications in different domains of the society including inspection of infrastructure, construction industry, mining and agriculture. The applications of drone in the management of disaster cover the operations including monitoring, making of maps and assessment of damages due to natural disasters [19]. The applicability of drone in disaster management is growing significantly as they cover a large geographical area, aiming the drone as an aid in initial assessment of disaster management.

With the advancement in the drone technology, and in conjunction with Augmented Intelligence and Machine Learning, drones find extensive applications in the aftermath of natural disasters including landslides & rockfall, hurricanes, volcanic eruptions, earthquakes, floods, forest fires and even considering Chernobyl radiological disasters. Thereby, making the drone technology a significant shift in the disaster management systems from conventional systems, especially considering the two pillars of the society, i.e., Economic Pillar and Social Pillar. High-advanced drone systems provide efficient response-information system; which delivers high-quality images and aerial photogrammetric survey as compared to the satellite images. Drone finds effective in the assessment of flood and erosion due to the provision of continuous and detailed both two-dimensional and three-dimensional data with lesser time involvement on the site under consideration. Furthermore, these technologically advanced drones are proven to be more adaptable in data gathering for the resources in a time-efficient system. These drone systems gather and share information during the early stages of any disaster, through a web-based sharing system.

When any natural disaster happens, the most difficult areas which are to be assessed are the remote areas in which heavy instruments cannot be accessed. Drones are used in the assessment of building damage in such areas. Besides the assessment of damage and mapping, images from the drones are used in creating three-dimensional models of such disaster-affected sites using different software applications. A DEM model, commonly known as Digital Elevation Model, is an advanced three-dimensional model for the evacuation planning, which had been created with drone-based photogrammetry. This advanced drone-based technology is proving to be a supreme source for the data collection and data analyzing for the disaster management due to its capability of data collection in temporal and spatial resolutions. Light Detection and Ranging data, or known as LiDAR technology were used in the evaluation of the quality and the accuracy of the work done by DEMs.

The efficiency of the drones in the disaster scenarios can be improved with the application of a multi-propose drone, keeping in consideration the related equipment and mission plans, which have to be planned carefully so as to avoid collision with drone's trajectories. Deep learning algorithms and advanced photogrammetric techniques combined in the production of rapid results, in conjunction with accurate mapping of building damage. Drone-SFM technology is proven to be effective in the creation of high-quality digitized surface models rapidly. RTK or real time kinetic drones are significantly improving the accuracy of three-dimensional models, due to the development of advanced geo-referencing algorithms, which prove to be advantageous in disaster-related applications, the processing of a huge number of images can be done in a shorter duration of time. Several studies focused on the image processing in the creation of orthophotos from one platform of Photoscan to other platforms of DroneDeploy, which incorporates the algorithms on image segmentation, formulated on deep learning for the identification of burnt areas due to forest fires. With reference to the radiological mapping, a technological-customized drone was produced, can be launching manually and recovering with a parachute committed to airplane's end portion.

The main aim of National Disaster Management system is to safeguard the lives of people and properties when experienced by the natural disaster. Keeping the approach of 4th industrial revolution (i.e., Industry 4.0) and Society 5.0, the need for digital transformation had been increasing in the lives of people for living, interacting, working and managing their lives. Thus, it is unavoidable for the organization of National Disaster Management for considering the applications of digital reformation and how the same is affecting the prevailing working mechanisms and relations, and thus invent new methods for ensuring an effective working system, which is based on emerging technical-based era for maximizing its output in saving the life of the society.

REFERENCES

1. N. Kapucu, Collaborative emergency management: better community organising, better public preparedness and response, *Disasters* 32 (2) (2008) 239–262.
2. J. Lee, M. Azamfar, J. Singh, A blockchain enabled cyber-physical system architecture for Industry 4.0 manufacturing systems, *Manufacturing Letters* 20 (2019) 34–39.
3. G. Leeming, J. Ainsworth, D.A. Clifton, Blockchain in health care: hype, trust, and digital health, *Lancet* 393 (10190) (2019) 2476–2477.
4. J. Leigh, C. Vasilica, R. Dron, D. Gawthorpe, E. Burns, S. Kennedy, R. Kennedy, T. Warburton, C. Croughan, Redefining undergraduate nurse teaching during the coronavirus pandemic: use of digital technologies, *British Journal of Nursing* 29 (10) (2020) 566–569.
5. Lavanya Sharma, P K Garg *IoT and Its Applications, From Visual Surveillance to Internet of Things,* Taylor & Francis, CRC Press, (2021) Vol. 1, p.29.
6. Yaman Hooda et al. *Journal of Physics: Conference Series* 1950 (2021) 012062.
7. C. Lin, W.E. Braund, J. Auerbach, J.-H. Chou, J.-H. Teng, P. Tu, J. Mullen, *Policy decisions and use of information technology to fight coronavirus disease, Taiwan, Emerging Infectious Diseases* 26 (7) (2020) 1506.
8. A. Mamalis, *Recent advances in nanotechnology, Journal of Materials Processing Technology* 181 (1–3) (2007) 52–58.
9. A. Martin, *Digital literacy and the "digital society", Digital Literacies: Concepts, Policies and Practices* 30 (2008) 151–176.
10. Preeti Kuhar et al. *Internet of things (IoT) based smart helmet for construction Journal of Physics: Conference Series* 1950 (2021) 012075.
11. N.O. Martins, Technology and isolation: Clive Lawson on the impact of technology on the economy and society, *Real-world Economics Review* 125–133 (2018).
12. N.O. Nawari, S. Ravindran, Blockchain and building information modeling (BIM): review and applications in post-disaster recovery, *Buildings* 9 (6) (2019) 149.
13. D.N. Nguyen, F. Imamura, K. Iuchi, Public-private collaboration for disaster risk management: a case study of hotels in Matsushima, Japan, *Tourism Management* 61 (2017) 129–140.

14. T. Oliveira, M.F. Martins, Literature review of information technology adoption models at firm level, *Electronic Journal of Information Systems Evaluation* 14 (1) (2011) 110.

15. A. Ozsomer, R.J. Calantone, A. Di Bonetto, What makes firms more innovative? A look at organizational and environmental factors, *Journal of Business & Industrial Marketing* 12 (6) (1997) 400–416.

16. J.G. Palfrey, U. Gasser, *Born Digital: Understanding the First Generation of Digital Natives*, Basic Books, NY, USA (2008).

17. K. Panetta, What conventional companies can learn from organizations that consider digital technologies a core competency (2016) [online]. Gartner. Available from: https://www.gartner.com/smarterwithgartner/10-managementtechniques-from-born-digital-companies/.

18. S. Paul, S. Sosale, Witnessing a disaster: public use of digital technologies in the 2015 South Indian floods, *Digital Journalism* 18 (2019) 1–17.

19. N. Perkin, P. Abraham, *Building the Agile Business through Digital Transformation*, Kogan Page Publishers, London, UK (2017).

20. Gauri Jha, Pawan Singh, Lavanya Sharma, "Recent advancements of augmented reality in real time applications", *International Journal of Recent Technology and Engineering*, 8, 2S7, 538–542, 2019, https://doi.org/10.35940/ijrte.B10100.0782S719.

21. Akshit Anand, Vikrant Jha, Lavanya Sharma, "An improved local binary patterns histograms techniques for face recognition for real time application", *International Journal of Recent Technology and Engineering*, 8, 2S7, 524–529, 2019, https://doi.org/10.35940/ijrte.B1098.0782S719. ISSN: 2277-3878.

22. Lavanya Sharma, Annapurna Singh, Dileep Kumar Yadav, *Fisher's Linear Discriminant Ratio Based Threshold for Moving Human Detection in Thermal Video*, Infrared Physics and Technology, Elsevier, 2016 (SCI impact factor: 1.58, Published).

23. Lavanya Sharma, Dileep Kumar Yadav, "Histogram based adaptive learning rate for background modelling and moving object detection in video surveillance", *International Journal of Telemedicine and Clinical Practices, Inderscience*, 2016, ISSN: 2052-8442, https://doi.org/10.1504/IJTMCP.2017.082107.

24. L. Sharma, M. Carpenter (eds), *Computer Vision and Internet of Things: Technologies and Applications* (1st ed.). Chapman and Hall/CRC, 2022. https://doi.org/10.1201/9781003244165.

25. Lavanya Sharma, Pradeep K Garg "Artificial intelligence: Challenges, technologies and future", Wiley (In production), 2021.

26. Lavanya Sharma, *Towards Smart World: Homes to Cities using Internet of Things*, Taylor & Francis, CRC Press, 2020 (ISSN: 9780429297922).

27. Lavanya Sharma, *Object Detection with Background Subtraction*, LAP LAMBERT Academic Publishing, SIA OmniScriptum Publishing Brivibas gatve 197, Latvia, European Union, 2019 (ISBN: 978-613-7-34386-9).

Part IV

Challenges, Opportunities
and Novel Solutions

15 Society 5.0 towards Sustainable Development Goals in Technological Prospects and Social Applications

Shamita Kumar
Bharati Vidyapeeth Deemed University

CONTENTS

DOI: 10.1201/9781003324720-19

15.1   INTRODUCTION TO SOCIETY 5.0

Today we stand on the threshold of a transformative change in cutting-edge technology that is radically altering the way we live and work and interact with each other. The scale, scope and complexity of this transformation are unprecedented in human history. It has given rise to an increased collaboration resulting in new ideas, new businesses, and new ways of shopping, working and learning. It is against this background that Society 5.0 concept introduced first in Japan represents the fifth stage of the evolution of human society, following the initial four stages namely – the hunter–gatherer society, the agrarian society, the industrial society and the information society (Cabinet Office, Government of Japan, 2016). This society represents the next step in our evolution, a world where each individual can lead an enhanced quality of life through the integration of cyber and physical space guided by scientific and technical advances. It has given rise to a new dawn of human history, envisioning a human-centred world based on values of openness, sustainability and inclusiveness where technology enables a good quality of life.

The concept of Society 5.0 envisions solving social issues through the integration of big data, Internet of Things (IoT), and artificial intelligence (AI) to shape human actions and behaviour. It envisages an iterative cycle in which data are gathered through various means, analysed in the cloud, and then communicated back as meaningful information, based on which sound decisions can be taken for a range of social and other issues (Fukuyama, 2018).

It is characterised by five areas that include problem solving and creating value for its citizens, a diverse society with no discrimination and liberation in thoughts and ideas, a decentralised society providing opportunities to all, a resilient society and a society that is in harmony with nature. Thus, it is clear that such a society has the ability to address and resolve several critical issues facing humankind today ranging from poverty to gender disparity to environmental degradation and clean energy contributing significantly to the sustainable development goals (SDGs) (Holroyd, 2022; Shiroishi et al., 2018).

15.2   THE SUSTAINABLE DEVELOPMENT GOALS

All Member States of the United Nations at the United Nations General Assembly in September 2015, adopted the 17 sustainable development goals with the single agenda of transforming our world and ushering in an era where no one is left behind. These goals to be achieved by 2030 have 17 targets with 169 sub-targets that cover various aspects of our lives ranging from social to environmental to economic focussing on people, planet and prosperity. The goals are a blueprint for humanity, reflecting a new way of doing things through the cooperation of all sectors namely, governments, institutions, NGOs, businesses and civil society, reflecting a new way of doing 'development' using an overarching framework (United Nations Department of Social and Economic Affairs, 2015).

The SDG framework outlines a bottom-up approach towards a new society while Society 5.0 approach uses cutting-edge technology for ensuring inclusivity and a good quality of life, both however focussing on people, planet and prosperity thus complementing each other with Society 5.0 facilitating technological development for achieving the 3Ps.

15.3   SOCIETY 5.0 AND THE SDGs: THE COMMONALITIES

Society 5.0 leverages technology to facilitate the design and adoption of innovative solutions, to address social problems in order to build a prosperous and equitable human-centred society using a cooperative approach involving all actors of change, ranging from governments, industries, academic institutions, civil society, etc. through an inclusive process. It envisions a society where everybody has the opportunity to prosper.

The SDGs use a goal-based approach to usher in a new way of societal development benefitting the planet and ensuring social and economic prosperity for all through an inclusive and cooperative process involving all actors.

While many nations may not have adopted a Society 5.0 approach overtly, all of them have adopted the SDGs and have oriented their development process to a model where sustainable development is incorporated into the planning process itself through leveraging technology, thus inadvertently bringing in a synergy between the two concepts.

While the SDGs focus on leveraging technology for societal prosperity, Society 5.0 aims to enable a better quality of life envisioning a beneficial co-existence of machines and humans. It advocates the beneficial adoption of digital technologies. Both the SDGs and Society 5.0 have a common vision of creating a human-centric society where people enjoy and benefit from technological advances in a fair and equitable manner.

Both the concepts of Society 5.0 and the SDGs can only be jointly realised if the actors work together flawlessly solving more than one problem at a time; sharing best practices from around the globe. The SDGs are not mutually exclusive; one goal has knock-on effects on other goals making the adoption of digital solutions that can serve a number of goals simultaneously very crucial to their achievement.

The model of Society 5.0 as depicted in the figure begins with the identification of relevant social problems and then progresses to use a combination of frontier technologies such as AI, robotics, Internet of Things and big data with cooperation between all relevant actors to provide innovative solutions. These creative solutions are based on superior data from a multitude of sources that are analysed in cyberspace and communicated as personalised solutions providing a clearer insight into the problem and ensuring data-driven decisions both at the societal and individual level ensuring that we have a Society 5.0 that fulfils the p *Behind*.

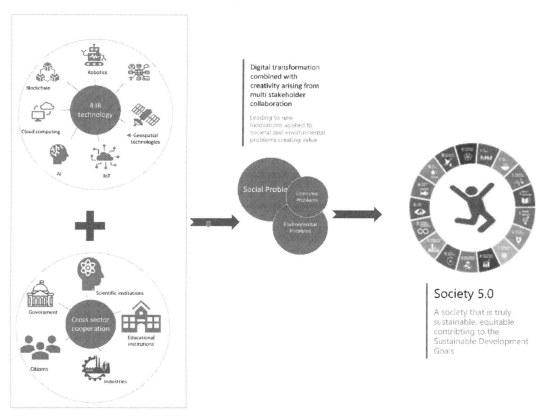

15.4   CAN IMPLEMENTATION OF THE SDGS BE ADVANCED BY SOCIETY 5.0?

Achieving the SDGs needs a multiple-pronged approach of enabling policies, technologies, education, skilling, etc. involving various actors from the government to industry to academia to civil society. Today we have a proliferation of frontier technologies such as machine learning and AI, DNA sequencing and 3D-printing, renewable energy technologies to biodegradable plastics, and new business models that present immense potential for achieving the global goals but are used in isolation of each other. On the other hand, in Society 5.0, the aim is to leverage technology and use it in an integrated manner to analyse a vast amount of data from various sources in cyberspace to provide innovative solutions to balance the resolution of societal problems with economic advancement. Prosperity for all with good health and longevity as well as environmental sustainability is thus achievable if we harness the full power of these innovations.

The outputs of Society 5.0, then, are the innovative technologies and systems that leverage vast amounts of data to develop problem-solving models. There is thus a synergy between the two with the outputs of Society 5.0 providing ways to accelerate progress in the SDGs.

Seventy per cent of the targets of the 17 global goals and their 169 targets have already been enabled through the deployment of the Fourth Industrial Revolution (4IR) technologies (World Economic Forum, 2020). These technologies include big data platforms that are today used in the implementation of all the SDGs, AI that is today key to the deployment of more than half of the applications being used as well as blockchain and IoT which are gaining increasing prominence in several applications related to the SDGs. Various combinations of these technologies are currently in various states of maturity (high, medium and low) in terms of impact given an enabling environment.

The report of the World Economic Forum states that these 4IR technologies have particularly played a critical role in the implementation of particularly three of SDGs namely- Goal 3-Good Health, Goal 7-Clean Energy, Goal 9- Industry, Innovation and Infrastructure given that these particular goals have strong links to private-sector markets. In contrast, the report states that Goal 1- No Poverty, Goal 5-Gender Equality, Goal 14 – Life below Water and Goal 15 – Life on land have the lowest adoption of 4IR technologies probably because they are linked to market failure or considered to be a public good (14).

However, this initial disparity is giving way to an overarching use of 4IR technologies that is progressing rapidly in almost all sectors covered by the global goals (Nair et al., 2021; Nanavaty and Goodwin-Groen, 2022) and contributing both to the creation of the necessary conditions for the realisation of many of global goals as well as offering innovative digital solutions for a truly sustainable society enabling progression towards Society 5.0 (Hoosain et al., 2020; PwC, 2018; Mou, 2019).

15.4.1   ENDING POVERTY IN ALL ITS FORMS

Poverty has many aspects and people who are poor experience many different forms of impoverishment at the same time, which can include not only a lack of wealth but a lack of educational opportunities and good health, exclusion from access to justice or networks, low living standards, insecurity, exclusion from the formal financial system, etc. which keeps many trapped in a vicious cycle of poverty. Access to financial services leveraged today in many different forms such as internet-based banking, mobile money, and electronic payments, powered by various new fintech apps has proved to be an enabler in lifting people out of poverty. The availability of these technologies for savings, credit and insurance availability as well as payments at very critical moments of distress play a catalytic role in minimising poverty and enabling people to weather the shock effectively which otherwise would end them spiralling down into poverty (UNSGSA et al., 2018).

Many 4 IR technology-based applications such as internet and AI-enabled digital footprint for credit access, insurance products that are enabled using satellite and drone data, mobile-based microfinance, crowd finance enabled through blockchain, shared and pay-as-you-go services in many sectors that leverage advanced demographic data analytics already have a high level of maturity and are in place in several countries across the world. COVID-19 has accelerated the use of digital money globally and spurred new models of service delivery and payment increasing per capita consumption. Digitisation in the financial sector has drastically lowered fees for remittances, directly helping to meet target 10.c of the SDGs that aims at the reduction of the costs of sending remittances which indirectly helps pull people out of poverty. Other technologies such as cryptocurrencies and bitcoin used for keeping digital transactions are decentralised systems. They have given rise to new business models with enhanced transparency and ease. The use of drones and machine learning in precision agriculture to decrease input costs, assess crop damage and increase yields and profitability, app-based e-commerce platforms such as e Mandi in India for negotiating fair deals and prices is assisting farmers in reducing poverty.

India has been a forerunner in implementing a system for large-scale digital financial inclusion. The country's digital ID system-Aadhar, interoperable payment systems (Unified Payment Interface), widespread use of mobile banking riding on the wave of mobile internet penetration, as well as supportive policies, have enabled new banking models and services empowering consumers. The outcomes are visible in widespread benefits derived from the direct deposit of social welfare payments to the poor across the country; new digital tools for savings, payments, insurance, credit, pensions, etc along with better ways to reduce inefficiencies and fraud in anti-poverty programs that plagued the country in yesteryears (Barik and Sharma, 2019).

These technologies in various combinations are addressing various aspects of multidimensional poverty and contributing to lifting people out of poverty through several innovative uses and applications arising from collaborations with various state and non-state actors truly addressing the various targets in SDG Goal 1 – No Poverty. They address several targets such as targets 1.1 and 1.2 which deal with reducing multidimensional poverty, target 1.3 that deals with the implementation of social protection systems, target 1.4 that focuses on equal rights to basic services, technology, ownership, and economic resources as well as land ownership among others.

15.4.2 Achieving Food Security, Improved Nutrition and Promoting Sustainable Agriculture

With our ecosystems and soil being rapidly degraded, we are seeing a tremendous loss of biodiversity that ultimately affects our food security. Coupled with climate change and the risks associated with it such as droughts and floods which have increased manifold, lack of food security is being amplified. The poor income from agriculture is thus forcing people to migrate to cities in search of better livelihood options bringing with it a new set of problems.

At the same time, we need to realise that the agricultural sector is unique in having seen quick adoption of the 4 IR technologies to design some innovative solutions. These have been game changers driving economic, social and environmental change in the global agricultural system to especially deal with threats from a rising population and thus hunger as well as a changing climate. The use of new 4IR technologies has in general achieved a reduction in the rate of use of fertilisers, herbicides, fossil fuel use and water coupled with an increase in crop production, easy access to markets and finances (Ullo and Sinha, 2021; FAO, 2019).

There has been a high level of adoption of four IR technologies across the globe. These include precision agriculture for early detection of diseases, optimising inputs and returns, use of agricultural robotics for process automation, optimisation of agricultural food supply and demand prediction through the use of AI and sensor-enabled prediction, indoor/urbanised farming solutions, including hydroponics and vertical farming which are low-emission technologies. Hyperlocal weather forecasting for agricultural management and prediction using AI has also enabled farmers to plan for harvesting and other agricultural practices (PwC, 2020).

In Australia, a country with very large farm holdings per capita, machine learning and AI are being deployed to predict weather conditions, temperature, water usage and soil conditions which have proved beneficial to farmers in managing their very large farms. Blockchain smart food card technology can be leveraged to ensure that appropriate state welfare schemes are leveraged by people who truly need them eg. Migrants, through simplifying logistics and eliminating the need to carry key documents and overcoming language barriers as they move across their own geographies in search of better livelihoods (Sung, 2018; David et al., 2022; Iaksch et al., 2021).

These new four IR technologies can bring about a reduction in agricultural production costs, enhancement of crop yields, improve the traceability of food and thus eliminate unnecessary wastage, optimise the food value chain from food production to processing as well as detect diseases in advance besides making life easy for the farmer in Society 5.0. This is turn has the potential to meet various targets such as reducing the prevalence of hunger, doubling the incomes of small-scale farmers, and developing resilient agricultural practices contributing to achieving the SDG Goal 2-Zero Hunger.

15.4.3 ADVANCING GLOBAL HEALTH FOR ALL AGES

The world has made significant progress today in reducing some of the common killers responsible for child and maternal mortality and thus increasing life expectancy. Access to clean water and sanitation has been enhanced, reducing tuberculosis, malaria, polio and the spread of HIV/AIDS. Much larger efforts are however needed to control a wide range of diseases including lifestyle diseases and address many diverse persistent and emerging health problems as we move towards a technologically advanced society.

Several novel technologies such as smart wearables, smart homecare, virtual healthcare assistants, tools to monitor and predict health metrics and disease, including smart implants, wearables, as well as smart hospital management that improves communication, collaboration and performance, use of drones for remote delivery of medicines, medical equipment and samples have a high maturity and are regularly employed for better wellbeing in major economies across the world. It is likely that within a short span of time we will also see large-scale deployment of practices that are today in the pilot phase. These include the AI-based prediction of spread of pandemics, smart healthcare access by citizens using blockchain-powered digital identity, improved surgical performance through the use of smart medical robotics and nanobots, and optimisation of large-scale, high-speed drug trial simulation using AI and digital twins. The technology of 3D printing is being experimented widely and 3D printing of body parts as well as lab-grown synthetic body organs is no longer a dream but waiting for a suitable policy environment to become reality (Fukuyama, 2018).

Based on an individuals' initiative and interest, data associated with their health can be used effectively to enhance their well-being. We see this is case of wearables which with their inputs about our movement and other body parameters enable us to take better decisions on our daily diet and exercise routines. In fields like health promotion and the prevention and treatment of disease, the use of digital biomarkers in people's daily lives is a useful tool for improving quality of life through appropriate interventions or by encouraging behavioural change. The health information collected for digital biomarkers includes both physiological (heart rate, pulse, blood pressure, electrocardiograms (ECGs), electrodermal activity, and blood sugar levels) and behavioral (walking, bodily movements, speech, and eye movement) indicators. Opportunities for using these indicators exist in health promotion including health management, driving safety, workplace safety, and sporting performance. Sleep evaluation beds, smart toilets incorporating stool analysis, non-invasive blood sugar analysis in the real time telling a person what and when he can eat safely, gait evaluation app, facial image analysis for assessing mental health of personnel, AI driven analysis with its ability to turn vital-sign data from wearables devices into individually customised diagnostics, will provide knowledge to the individual enabling smart decision making on lifestyle choices (Malomane et al., 2022; Fukuyama, 2018).

IoT technologies can help identify traffic accident hotspots, monitor driver health conditions, opening the door to ideas for transport safety that could help society eliminate traffic accidents altogether. Utilising collections of people's individual head shots and data points like weight, height, drinking preferences and smoking preferences, AI can even show people what they may look like if they maintain unhealthy lifestyles – an ability that would not only convey lifestyle disease risks on a more intuitive level but also make it easier for people enjoy the process of managing their health and prevent lifestyle diseases (Fukuyama, 2018).

These technologies will greatly enable better health promotion and disease prevention sectors by providing support for appropriate interventions and behavioural changes based on digital biomarkers measurement results truly leveraging the power of integrated cyber-physical-human systems to achieve good health and well-being. These advancements many of which are operational now coupled with the introduction of 5G networks will accelerate the achievement of targets such as reducing maternal and neonatal deaths among the poorest in society, fighting communicable diseases, reducing/preventing road injuries and mortality and at the same time providing universal access to healthcare and enhance early warning systems for global health risks helping achieve SDG Goal 3-Good health and wellbeing.

15.4.4 Ensuring Inclusive and Quality Education for All and Promoting Lifelong Learning

Obtaining a quality education is key to a better quality of life and underpins a range of fundamental development drivers. While globally basic literacy skills have improved tremendously, much greater efforts are needed to achieve the universal education goals and develop a generation with truly 21st century competencies. With very poor student teacher ratio in developing/emerging nations, besides quality concerns and overcrowded classrooms, access to quality education at the school as well as the vocational skills and university level is a growing concern. Gender disparities in education can seriously undermine the progress of nations. Short supply of qualified teachers is another serious concern (United Nations Department of Social and Economic Affairs, 2015).

The COVID-19 pandemic has accelerated the development in this sector by leaps and bounds. It is heartening to note that the education sector is seeing high levels of adoption of 4IR technologies. This is evidenced in smart and open educational resources that are today affordable as well as accessible, use of virtual reality to enhance remote learning and collaboration in learning and research. Some others such as 4 IR-enabled personalised learning lessons, including mass online open courses that are AI personalised are ensuring access to quality education to all. Natural language processing enabled voice assistants and speech to text for inclusive learning support is enhancing inclusivity, a key pillar of Society 5.0 as well as the SDGs (Leahy et al., 2019; Popenici and Kerr, 2017).

Education 4.0 through the provision of real and virtual world learning experiences prepares learners for a mixed reality future (Grodotzki et al., 2018). Besides aiming to develop the required literacy, numeracy, social, moral, digital, critical thinking creative skills as well as build problem-solving capacities; it focuses on nurturing emotional intelligence, and adaptability as well as foster the mindset of lifelong learning a key skill in the 21st century. It envisions a curriculum that is decolonised, non-linear, learner centered, interdisciplinary as well as personalised reflecting a paradigm shift in the way children learn (Arici et al., 2019).

The next step in this evolution would be the large-scale adaptation of immersive learning environments which are interactive and multisensory increasing student engagement, a key step in achieving universal access to education and creating a workforce that is truly in Society 5.0. Learning anywhere and anytime along with lifelong learning is a reality today and a crucial pillar of Society 5.0. The SDG Goal 4 – Quality Education underpins all the other goals and aims to ensure inclusive and equitable quality education and promote lifelong learning opportunities for all which is crucial for Society 5.0. The innovations in this sector achieved through technology will accelerate the achievements of SDG Goal 4.

15.4.5   FACILITATING GENDER EQUALITY

Gender equality besides being a fundamental human right is the bedrock for a peaceful, prosperous and sustainable world. When women and girls are provided with equal access to education, health care, decent work, and representation in political and economic decision-making processes, it catalyses the development of sustainable economies as well as the achievement of all the other global goals. Technology has levelled the playing field and brought economic opportunities for the underprivileged in many scenarios. Such progress is however much slower with this group.

Barriers to digital access, including physical such as device availability or internet connectivity, others revolving around insufficient digital training for women; social and cultural in certain other parts of the world are key hindrances in developing digital literacy among women (Taylor and Mahon, 2019). New avenues for the economic empowerment of women are today provided by digital access and have the potential to contribute to greater gender equality. In several economies around the world, there has been a high level of maturity in the uptake of several 4IR technologies that have benefitted women. The 'leapfrog' opportunities provided by the internet-based digital platforms, mobile phones as well as digital financial services have in many instances bridged the gender divide by enabling women to increase their employment opportunities, access knowledge and assert themselves with confidence (International telecommunication Union, 2017).

AI-enabled digital footprint for mobile money access targeted at women consumers and entrepreneurs, 4IR digital applications supporting women and girls for reporting on instances of sexual violence confidentially, 4IR-enabled educational platforms aimed at empowering girls and women are game changers. Empowerment of this one half of humanity is crucial to the success of Society 5.0 and will lead to the achievement of targets of ending discrimination against women, ensure full participation in leadership and decision-making, ensure equal rights to economic resources, property ownership and financial services achieving the SDG 5- Gender Equality in its true sense (OECD, 2018).

15.4.6   ENSURE ACCESS TO WATER AND SANITATION FOR ALL
AND SUSTAINABLE WATER MANAGEMENT

Very often clean water, which is a basic human need, that should be easily accessible to all is undermined by poor infrastructure, investment and planning, resulting in the death of millions of people, largely children from diseases associated with inadequate water supply, sanitation and hygiene. These are crucial issues that need to be tackled in our journey towards Society 5.0.

The widespread awareness regarding the precarious state of the world's water has resulted in the uptake of innovative technologies that have used 4IR successfully (Asian Development Bank et al., 2020). Climate change has necessitated adoption of technologies transforming the agricultural sector and ensuring wise water use. Some technologies such as AI-enabled precision and autonomous irrigation and nutrient prescription systems, use of robotics, sensors, drones and satellite technologies in agriculture for rationalising water usage, smart water-infrastructure predictive maintenance, AI-enhanced scenario modelling for water infrastructure risks and performance have a high uptake in developed as well as emerging economies. Some others such as AI- and IoT-enabled real-time water system insights for water quality and water availability, 4IR-enabled traceability to provide consumer transparency on water source, blockchain platform to cost effectively crowd-finance clean water infrastructure development and decentralised water systems with smart contract-enabled peer-to-peer water rights trading and dynamic pricing if mainstreamed will be game changers enabling decision making by the end user based on transparency (PwC, 2018). Targets such as provision of safe drinking water, increasing water use efficiency and ensuring fresh water supplies, implementation of integrated water resources management through active citizen involvement can be easily achieved leading to realisation of Goal 6 – Clean water and sanitation.

15.4.7 ENSURING ACCESS TO AFFORDABLE, RELIABLE, SUSTAINABLE AND MODERN ENERGY FOR ALL

Access to energy is central to nearly every global major challenge and opportunity and is crucial for jobs, security, climate change, food production or increasing incomes. Transitioning the global economy towards clean and sustainable sources of energy is thus a key challenge in the pursuit of Society 5.0.

In the sustainable energy sector, there has been a huge uptake of innovative 4 IR enabled technologies. These include decentralised and coordinated energy-grid management that include IoT, AI and smart infrastructure for operational efficiency and maintenance in terms of smart meters and smart grids; modelling and forecasting for optimised energy system demand and supply through harnessing AI and big data; financing mechanisms (e.g. blockchain finance platforms and mobile money) for alternate energy assets, AI-enabled virtual power plants for integrating distributed renewable energy sources and AI- and IoT-enabled predictive maintenance of energy infrastructure. Other innovations such as blockchain platform to crowd finance clean energy infrastructure development and 4IR-enabled peer-to-peer renewable energy trading are accelerating the achievement of the SDGs.

A smart grid that connects new electric vehicles, houses and communication systems such as smart meters, sensors, and remote control points and is thus the source of massive data. Such big data along with other technologies in smart grids enhances the efficiency of electricity delivery, along with a quicker restoration of electricity after power outages, reducing operations and management costs for utilities, which ultimately lowers power costs for consumers. These technologies also provide better customer service through efficient electricity consumption tracking and cost, by showing how much electricity the customer uses, when they use it, and how much it costs as well as the real-time pricing for wise electricity use. The future of electricity is defined by smart electric meters and smart, given the fact they engage active electricity management by having our smart devices connected (Lai et al., 2021; Talebkhah et al., 2021). Energy access has been amplified by pay-as-you-go by solar energy companies who have used digital finance to provide affordable and modern energy to more than 10 million people. With the development of local and decentralised power microgrids, Society 5.0 will supply clean sustainable power to everyone. The various targets including universal access to modern energy, increasing the global percentage of renewable energy, enhancing energy efficiency in usage, the SDG 7-Affordable and Clean Energy could be a reality by 2030 (World Economic Forum, 2020).

15.4.8 PROMOTING INCLUSIVE AND SUSTAINABLE ECONOMIC GROWTH, EMPLOYMENT AND DECENT WORK FOR ALL

The uneven economic growth across the world where having a job does not guarantee the ability to escape from poverty needs to change for a truly prosperous society. Achieving higher levels of economic productivity through technological upgrading and innovation and diversification including a focus on high-value added and labour-intensive sectors is the key to sustainable economic growth. This will need the overhauling of education systems and massive skilling. South Africa and many other economies today have huge focus on developing skills needed for this century.

Several four IR technologies are changing the labour market enabling access to opportunities created by the adoption of these technologies. Technologies involving AI-enabled digital support hubs for workers, AI-enabled remote work platforms to mobilise contingent workforce and AI, cloud, satellite and drone-enabled disaster risk insurance products and microfinance are game changers accelerated by COVID-19. The large-scale uptake of community-distributed marketplaces for goods and services, including peer-to-peer (P2P) trading and smart contracts, AI-enabled supply and demand 'matchmaking' for goods and workers will truly be a revolution in the labour market. Society 5.0 advocates a good quality of life in which access to decent jobs is crucial. The digital uptake in other sectors will have a spillover effect in the job market enabling the achievement of sustainable economic growth with a sustained increase in GDP, achieving higher levels of productivity through diversification, entrepreneurship, having a skilled workforce eliminating unemployment and most importantly providing access to financial services achieving SDG 8- Decent work and economic growth (International telecommunication Union, 2017).

15.4.9 BUILDING RESILIENT INFRASTRUCTURE, PROMOTING SUSTAINABLE INDUSTRIALISATION AND FOSTERING INNOVATION

Development and growth in a country are largely driven by building resilient infrastructure and through fostering innovation, promoting inclusive and sustainable industrialisation. On its own industrialisation facilitates economic growth, creates jobs, and increases income. While infrastructure provides essential connections for society and business, innovation leads to environmentally sound industrialisation. The promise offered by innovation in the current times is unprecedented. The manufacturing industry is currently experiencing an avant-garde technical advancement. An important element connecting the SDGs to technological innovation is the introduction of 4 IR technologies. This convergence of technology-development nexus has proved to be a game changer as industrialisation, development in infrastructure and technological innovation are the most viable means of achieving sustainable growth in the manufacturing industry and thus the goals of Agenda 2030 eventually leading to Society 5.0.

Previous industrial revolutions have come with immense costs in terms of unequal development and environmental degradation. Today innovations using AI, the IoT and blockchain have the potential to tackle many of the world's most pressing problems, accelerate economic development and bring value for societal development in the human-cyber-physical world. Some initiatives such as smart IoT-enabled infrastructure for efficiency and maintenance, robotics for automation of the manufacturing process, drones for remote goods delivery and remote infrastructure maintenance, next-gen satellite, drone and AI-enabled geospatial mapping, AR/VR visualisation for infrastructure planning, IoT-enabled tracking and optimisation of industrial machinery are at a high level of maturity.

Autonomous self-driving vehicles enabled by sensors, big data and AI, are being deployed for testing and will hit the roads soon. These have enormous potential not only in city transportation enabling route optimisation, automation of ride sharing, delivery and logistics services but also in agriculture with autonomous tractors and harvesting, in healthcare with autonomous ambulances, etc. Blockchain platforms are increasingly being used, offering the potential for traceability from source to store, thus building confidence as well as exposing illegal or unethical market trading, reducing administrative costs and at the same time enabling greater access to finance. The potential of a sharing economy that is already in place is accelerated by AI, combined with online platforms. This is evidenced by optimising the matching of customers with listings, price setting and detecting and eliminating fraud and misinformation. Anyone, even in the most remote locations with basic mobile infrastructure, can access P2P platforms to gain market access driving social inclusion.

In many emerging economies, inability to demonstrate a formal credit history is a huge barrier to financial inclusion for many individuals and businesses. Today new innovative methods that use non-traditional sources of data, such as mobile phone activity and other digital footprints, to evaluate creditworthiness along with machine learning have the potential to address exclusion from financial services (Ndung'u and Signé, 2020).

These innovations and adoption of 4 IR technologies by industries are paving the way for a society powered by technology benefitting its citizens enabling ease of living a key component of Society 5.0 and at the same time achieving the key targets of inclusive and sustainable industrialisation, increased access to financial services and markets, supporting domestic technology development moving towards achieving Goal 9 – Industry, innovation and infrastructure.

15.4.10   Reduce Inequalities within and among Countries

In spite of overall global development, there exist disparities between citizens both within a country and between countries. This disparity between haves and have-nots undermines the development of Society 5.0. An unequal world can foster a just and happy society. Most of the four IR technologies used for achieving the other goals have the potential to reduce income inequalities and promote social, economic and political inclusion, especially through technologies such as blockchain-powered digital identity for access to services, blockchain enabled digital voting, AI-enabled platform collating information on social services and policies, etc. This in sync with other technologies in other sectors will enable transition to Society 5.0 as well as the achievement of the key targets of Goal 10-Reduced Inequalities.

15.4.11   Make Cities Inclusive, Safe, Resilient and Sustainable

The world will add 3 billion additional citizens by 2050. As the global population becomes increasingly urban, cities will determine the success or failure of nations.

Society 5.0 is characterised by social processes and data distributed in a manner that would allow for developing smarter solutions for efficient resource use, management and consumption. The development of sustainable cities involves several SDGs, including that related to efficient water management and energy consumption as well as sustainable consumption of limited natural resources.

Several four IR technologies are already in place in many global economies for developing safe and resilient cities. Optimisation of resource use has been enabled through sensor-based grid and AI-based urban network management, AI-enabled urban mobility management, next-gen satellite, drone and IoT for detecting land use management, use of AI and VR/AR in optimising city design and planning, 4IR-enabled building-management systems, urban greening infrastructure (e.g. living buildings, pollution sequestration, graphene-based self-cleaning concrete), IR-enabled decentralised, peer-to-peer community energy and water grids, AI-led disaster prediction using automatic thresholds enabling early evacuation warning, etc. Some of these are widely adopted, while some are in the prototype stage (PwC, 2017).

The use of IoT sensors to relay environmental and other service data regarding waste collection, transport systems, etc. results in the perfect integration of human-cyber-physical space. Smart parking systems based on asphalt-embedded sensors, smart street lighting smart waste management already have a high uptake in many cities around the world. Their integration with open data platforms enhances citizen engagement as well as fosters innovation. Projects such as City Data Exchange, in Copenhagen is a marketplace for trading big data and are revolutionising the integrated use of the data to reduce the city's carbon footprint (Bjørner, 2021).

Engaging citizens to continuously facilitate bottom-up, grassroots initiatives is a key pillar of Society 5.0. The ready availability and use of social media data, geospatial big data and big data analytical tools will empower local communities to solve their issues besides making their lives more comfortable and convenient. These initiatives powered by technology will accelerate meeting the targets of safe transport systems, citizen-centric sustainable urbanisation, reducing the environmental impact of cities moving towards achieving SDG 11- Sustainable cities and communities.

15.4.12   Ensuring Sustainable Consumption and Production Patterns

The current pace of societal development will quadruple the global resource use within two decades. Integrated solutions to improve efficiency in terms of resource extraction, energy use, and waste management are crucial in taking action to stem this unsustainable resource use.

Smart cities across the world are using a number of four IR technologies to improve air and water quality, ensure efficient transportation and quick delivery of services (Kaginalkar et al., 2021). A number of four IR technologies using low-cost sensors, digital twins for lifespan performance optimisation, AI-optimised logistics and distribution networks to minimise costs, emissions and waste, four IR optimisation of recycling, including robotics for sorting and recycling, AI- and IoT-enabled consumption and production data analytics are being implemented as part of smart city implementation programs (International telecommunication Union, 2017; PwC, 2020). Other innovations such as newer biodegradable products/materials are in various stages of pilot implementation providing the needed technological impetus for Society 5.0. These technologies will see several outputs in terms of reducing waste, responsible management of chemicals and materials, encouraging companies to report on sustainability, a trend that we are already seeing across the world along with promoting a universal understanding of living sustainably moving the world towards achieving Goal 12 – Responsible Consumption.

15.4.13   TAKE URGENT ACTION TO COMBAT CLIMATE CHANGE AND ITS IMPACTS

With all the technological development come the challenges. Developmental activities have continued to accelerate the emission of greenhouse gases, advancing climate change. Since 1990 we have seen a doubling of global carbon dioxide emissions and they are now at their highest levels in the history of our planet. With the world's average surface temperature being projected to rise by more than three degrees celsius in this century, continuing with the 'business as usual' approach needs to change and is not a feasible option. Changing weather patterns, more extreme weather events, rising sea levels are being experienced globally and are serious impediments to achieving a Society 5.0.

There is an urgent need to enabling 'leapfrogging' to cleaner, more resilient economies that are based on renewable energy and energy efficiency. A host of measures that can reduce emissions, adapt to climate change and enhance resilience are today readily available for uptake. These include earth management big data platform, e.g. for monitoring carbon emissions and providing updates on air quality, smart and connected city planning and mobility systems for reducing vehicular air pollution arising from transport, large-scale AI-/drone-enabled, precision reforestation enabling carbon capture, 4IR-enabled decentralised clean energy grids, etc. Most of these have a high level of implementation maturity today. Some others such as advanced battery storage technologies, advanced materials for clean energy, generation and transmission e.g. semiconductors, solar coatings, which are rapidly advancing will hugely contribute to mitigating climate change in conjunction with the development of suitable policies and adoption (Sebestyén et al., 2021). These will be very crucial for Society 5.0 and their effective implementation will go a long way in achieving key targets such as strengthening adaptive capacities to climate-related disasters and implementing the UN Framework Convention on Climate Change addressing SDG-13 Climate Action.

15.4.14   CONSERVE AND SUSTAINABLY USE THE OCEANS, SEAS AND MARINE RESOURCES AND SUSTAINABLY MANAGING FORESTS, COMBATING DESERTIFICATION, HALTING AND REVERSING LAND DEGRADATION AND HALTING BIODIVERSITY LOSS

The world's oceans are a key lifeline, vital to our own future. Oceans contain over 200,000 identified species, the most prevalent source of protein – a major source of food for billions around the world. On the one hand, there are more than 3 billion people who depend on the oceans for their livelihoods, while fisheries directly or indirectly employ over 200 million people, and on the other hand, over 40% of the world's oceans are strongly influenced by human activities, including contamination, loss of habitats and livestock depletion. We both use and misuse the ocean more rapidly than at any other time in human history.

Habitat change from over harvesting natural resources for industrial production and urbanisation is one of the most important causes of biodiversity loss. We lose 13 million hectares of forests, which are habitats for approximately 80% of all terrestrial species of wildlife as well as subsistence providers for 1.6 billion people every year due to deforestation and desertification caused by anthropogenic activities and climate change.

While the ecosystem services and goods provided by these underpin our very existence, the innovation and use of 4 IR technologies in these sectors are limited given their service nature. It is however very crucial that this very bedrock of human existence be conserved as the foundation of Society 5.0. Some 4 IR technologies such as information for marine industries (fishing, shipping), real-time habitat and land-use monitoring and mapping, monitoring and detection of illegal activities, 4IR-enabled wildlife tracking, monitoring, analytics and pattern forecasting as well as real-time detection of disease, animal capture, etc. are being widely used today. Other technologies for monitoring and managing fishing activity using AI, the use of connected sensors for automated ocean health mapping, technologies for alternative financing such as cryptocurrency, reward platforms for sustainable fisheries and ocean conservation, earth management big data platforms as seen in the endangered species dashboard and rights codification, plant and animal disease identification and detection using AI are rapidly gaining maturity paving the way for conservation of these vital resources in a very efficient manner (Agrillo et al., 2022; Tampakis et al., 2022; Dąbrowski et al., 2021; Arribas et al., 2022). With this not only will we move towards a harmonious society that conserves its very bedrock but also fast track the achieving of various targets of Goal 14 – Life on Land and SDG 15 – Life below water.

15.4.15 PROMOTING PEACEFUL INCLUSIVE SOCIETIES FOR SUSTAINABLE DEVELOPMENT

Our journey to a truly sustainable society is fraught with many challenges - war, terrorism, local conflicts along with malfunctioning institutions and justice systems. Bribery, corruption, tax evasion continue to erode our social systems. Solutions to these issues is the backbone of Society 5.0. Fortunately globally there have been large strides made in moving towards a sustainable society through adoption of key technologies such as digital passport and visas for border security enabled with AI, low-cost biometric identification for last mile delivery, identity tax fraud identification through AI, cybersecurity systems enabled with AI, analysing public sentiment through real-time natural language processing to inform policy. These have been implemented in a majority of developed and emerging economies across the world. Some others such as blockchain and AI-enabled 'fake news' verification, corruption-reporting platforms will mature as the enabling policy is implemented across nations meeting the needs of SDG 16 – Peace, Justice and Strong Institutions besides laying the foundation of Society 5.0 (Hassani et al., 2021; Van Halderen et al., 2021).

15.5 THE PATH AHEAD

These truly transformative technologies have already begun to materialise as innovation processes, products in this century. New technologies will bring in sizeable and significant opportunities for achieving the SDGs. However certain barriers that are further discussed in Chapter 15 will need to be overcome. These include data availability, enabling policy frameworks, human capacity and insufficient infrastructure besides ethics involved in the use personal data as well as secure systems for the same. The risks that will arise especially related to data privacy will need to be carefully managed.

We are today at a critical juncture in our planets history where decisions are taken and policy and governance architectures developed to enable the digital age to deliver its full potential for humankind will impact the history of life on Earth. Purposeful and decisive action, collaboration, and coordination within multiple actors in society to leverage the true power of four IR technologies in developing innovations that are locale-specific, adaptable as well as transferable are key to achieving Society 5.0. The SDGs play a crucial guiding role in this process with the goals and targets serving as benchmarks in this new journey of humanity towards a truly sustainable world.

REFERENCES

Agrillo, E., Alessi, N., Álvarez-Martínez, J.M., Casella, L., Filipponi, F., Lu, B., Niculescu, S., Šibíková, M., Smith, K.E., 2022. Editorial for special issue: "New insights into ecosystem monitoring using geospatial techniques." *Remote Sensing* 14(10), 2346.

Arici, F., Yildirim, P., Caliklar, Ş., Yilmaz, R.M., 2019. Research trends in the use of augmented reality in science education: Content and bibliometric mapping analysis. *Computers & Education* 142, 103647.

Arribas, P., Andújar, C., Bohmann, K., deWaard, J.R., Economo, E.P., Elbrecht, V., Geisen, S., Goberna, M., Krehenwinkel, H., Novotny, V., 2022. Toward global integration of biodiversity big data: a harmonized metabarcode data generation module for terrestrial arthropods. *GigaScience* 11, 1–12.

Barik, R., Sharma, P., 2019. Analyzing the progress and prospects of financial inclusion in India. *Journal of Public Affairs* 19, e1948.

Bjørner, T., 2021. The advantages of and barriers to being smart in a smart city: The perceptions of project managers within a smart city cluster project in Greater Copenhagen. *Cities* 114, 103187.

Cabinet Office, Government of Japan, 2016. Society 5.0 society 5.0 council for science and technology. https://www8.cao.go.jp/cstp/english/society5_0/index.html (accessed 9.11.22).

Dąbrowski, P.S., Specht, C., Specht, M., Burdziakowski, P., Makar, A., Lewicka, O., 2021. Integration of multi-source geospatial data from GNSS receivers, terrestrial laser scanners, and unmanned aerial vehicles. *Canadian Journal of Remote Sensing* 47, 621–634.

David, L.O., Nwulu, N.I., Aigbavboa, C.O., Adepoju, O.O., 2022. Integrating fourth industrial revolution (4IR) technologies into the water, energy & food nexus for sustainable security: A bibliometric analysis. *Journal of Cleaner Production* 363, 132522.

FAO, 2019. Climate-smart agriculture and the sustainable development goals | Department of economic and social affairs. https://sdgs.un.org/publications/climate-smart-agriculture-and-sustainable-development-goals-33034.

Fukuyama, M., 2018. Society 5.0: Aiming for a new human-centered society. *Japan Spotlight* 27, 47–50.

Grodotzki, J., Ortelt, T.R., Tekkaya, A.E., 2018. Remote and virtual labs for engineering education 4.0: achievements of the ELLI project at the TU Dortmund University. *Procedia Manufacturing* 26, 1349–1360.

Hassani, H., Huang, X., MacFeely, S., Entezarian, M.R., 2021. Big data and the united nations sustainable development goals (UN SDGs) at a glance. *Big Data and Cognitive Computing* 5, 28.

Holroyd, C., 2022. Technological innovation and building a 'super smart' society: Japan's vision of society 5.0. *Journal of Asian Public Policy* 15, 18–31.

Hoosain, M.S., Paul, B.S., Ramakrishna, S., 2020. The impact of 4IR digital technologies and circular thinking on the United Nations sustainable development goals. *Sustainability* 12, 10143.

Iaksch, J., Fernandes, E., Borsato, M., 2021. Digitalization and big data in smart farming–a review. *Journal of Management Analytics* 8, 333–349.

International Telecommunication Union, 2017. *Fast Foward Porgress: Leveraging Tech to Achieve the Global Goals*.

Jenny, H., Wang, Y., Alonso, E.G., Minguez, R., 2020. Using artificial intelligence for smart water management systems. *Asian Development Bank*. https://doi.org/10.22617/BRF200191-2.

Kaginalkar, A., Kumar, S., Gargava, P., Niyogi, D., 2021. Review of urban computing in air quality management as smart city service: An integrated IoT, AI, and cloud technology perspective. *Urban Climate* 39, 100972.

Lai, C.S., Lai, L.L., Lai, Q.H., 2021. *Smart Grids and Big Data Analytics for Smart Cities*. Springer, Switzerland, AG.

Leahy, S.M., Holland, C., Ward, F., 2019. The digital frontier: Envisioning future technologies impact on the classroom. *Futures* 113, 102422. https://doi.org/10.1016/j.futures.2019.04.009.

Malomane, R., Musonda, I., Okoro, C.S., 2022. The opportunities and challenges associated with the implementation of fourth industrial revolution technologies to manage health and safety. *International Journal of Environmental Research and Public Health* 19, 846.

Mou, X., 2019. Artificial Intelligence: Investment Trends and Selected Industry Uses. *International Finance Corporation, World Bank Group* 1, 8.

Nair, M.M., Tyagi, A.K., Sreenath, N., 2021. The future with industry 4.0 at the core of society 5.0: open issues, future opportunities and challenges, in: *2021 International Conference on Computer Communication and Informatics (ICCCI)*. IEEE, Coimbatore, India. pp. 1–7.

Nanavaty, Reema, Goodwin-Groen, Ruth, 2022. How digital payments bring new economic opportunities for women in rural India. World Economic Forum. https://www.weforum.org/agenda/2022/08/digital-payments-economic-opportunities-women-rural-india/ (accessed 9.11.22).

Ndung'u, N., Signé, L., 2020. The fourth industrial revolution and digitization will transform Africa into a global powerhouse. Brookings. https://www.brookings.edu/research/the-fourth-industrial-revolution-and-digitization-will-transform-africa-into-a-global-powerhouse/ (accessed 9.11.22).

OECD, 2018. *Bridging the Digital Gender Divide: Include, Upskill, Innovate.*

Popenici, S.A., Kerr, S., 2017. Exploring the impact of artificial intelligence on teaching and learning in higher education. *Research and Practice in Technology Enhanced Learning* 12, 1–13.

PwC, 2017. The 4th industrial revolution for sustainable emerging cities - Report [WWW Document]. PwC. https://www.pwc.com/gx/en/services/sustainability/publications/sustainable-emerging-cities.html (accessed 9.11.22).

PwC, 2018. Building block(chain)s for a better planet 56. https://www3.weforum.org/docs/WEF_Building-Blockchains.pdf

PwC, 2020. 4 IR enabled technologies for the SDGs. https://www.weforum.org/press/2020/01/fourth-industrial-revolution-tech-can-fast-track-70-of-sustainable-development-goals/#:~:text=Over%20300%20use%20cases%20of,progress%20towards%20the%20Global%20Goals

Sebestyén, V., Czvetkó, T., Abonyi, J., 2021. The applicability of big data in climate change research: The importance of system of systems thinking. *Frontiers in Environmental Science* 9, 70.

Shiroishi, Y., Uchiyama, K., Suzuki, N., 2018. Society 5.0: For human security and well-being. *Computer* 51, 91–95.

Sung, J., 2018. The fourth industrial revolution and precision agriculture. *Automation in Agriculture: Securing Food Supplies for Future Generations* 1.

Talebkhah, M., Sali, A., Marjani, M., Gordan, M., Hashim, S.J., Rokhani, F.Z., 2021. IoT and big data applications in smart cities: Recent advances, challenges, and critical issues. *IEEE Access* 9, 55465–55484.

Tampakis, P., Chondrodima, E., Tritsarolis, A., Pikrakis, A., Theodoridis, Y., Pristouris, K., Nakos, H., Kalampokis, P., Dalamagas, T., 2022. i4sea: A big data platform for sea area monitoring and analysis of fishing vessels activity. *Geo-Spatial Information Science* 25, 132–154.

Taylor, S.R., Mahon, R., 2019. Gender equality from the MDGs to the SDGs: The struggle continues, in: *Achieving the Sustainable Development Goals*. Routledge, pp. 54–70.

Ullo, S.L., Sinha, G.R., 2021. Advances in IoT and smart sensors for remote sensing and agriculture applications. *Remote Sensing* 13, 2585.

United Nations Department of Social and Economic Affairs, 2015. The 17 goals | Sustainable Development. https://sdgs.un.org/goals (accessed 9.11.22).

UNSGSA, Better than cash alliance, UNCDF, The World Bank, 2018. Igniting SDG progress through digital financial inclusion.

Van Halderen, G., Bernal, I., Sejersen, T., Jansen, R., Ploug, N., Truszczynski, M., 2021. *Big Data for the SDGs: Country Examples in Compiling SDG Indicators using Non-Traditional Data Sources.*

World Economic Forum, 2020. Unlocking technology for the global goals. https://www3.weforum.org/docs/Unlocking_Technology_for_the_Global_Goals.pdf

16 Digital Reforms in Public Services and Infrastructure Development & Management

Yaman Hooda and Haobam Derit Singh
Manav Rachna International Institute of Research and Studies

CONTENTS

16.1 BACKGROUND OF DIGITAL REFORM

Digital reformation is a procedure of the application of the technologies in creating new or modifying the prevailing services such as business, education, culture, healthcare, social protection; the main aim being to satisfy the needs of the users and their experiences as per changing market scenarios. Digital reformation transcends the conventional roles of the society including customer services, marketing and sales. Perhaps, it commences and stops with the question of what a user might think and what are the necessary changes must be done in different phases of the society so as to meet their needs digitally [1]. The digital reformation in various aspects of the society lay the foundation for the development for Society 5.0, bridging the gap between the traditional ways and the digitised ways of availing the services, without compensating the basic requirements of the users [5,9,11-18]. The main objectives of digital reformation in any field can be listed as:

- To increase the efficiency of the services.
- To create/modify the existing models or systems of the services.
- To increase the collaboration between two or more than two services.
- To enhance the productivity of the systems.

The application of digital transformation in the society varies with its types, let us discuss various types of digital reformation as in Figure 16.1.

DOI: 10.1201/9781003324720-20

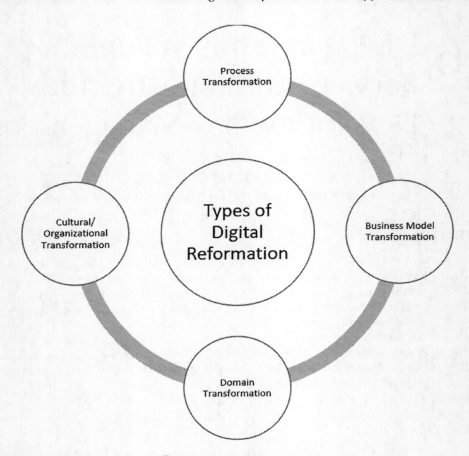

FIGURE 16.1   Types of digital transformation in a society.

1. **Process Transformation:**
   Process transformation includes the application of various technological approaches such as Internet of Things (IoT), Augmented Reality (AR), Data Analytics and Machine Learning (ML) in the services, re-inventing the service models; thereby reducing cost, improving the quality of the services and reduction in the cycle times of the services.

2. **Business Model Transformation:**
   Since the process transformation aims on the finite areas of the services, business model transformation emphasised on the foundational building blocks of the transformation of the services and its modes of delivery at user's end. With digitisation and keeping in consideration the needs of the users, organisations are reforming their service models from traditional methodology to modern technological friendly approach.

3. **Domain Transformation:**
   Domain transformation focuses on bring the reformation in the system of a particular domain of the services. It had been observed that due to the digital reformation in specific domains of any services, the efficiency and effectiveness of that domain had been increased, thereby giving a level of satisfaction to the users.

4. **Cultural/Organisational Transformation:**
   The digital transformation of any services depends on various factors including the mindsets of the users, processes of systems and most importantly, the capability of that service to be digitally reformed. With recent studies, the digital reformation in any service

requires a flexible system and a comprehensive decision-making process, with a considerable dependence on various service-based ecosystems.

The approach of the digital reformation in the public services are modifying the expectations of the citizens from the ability of the government in delivery of real-time, high-value services digitally [2]. In response to the emerging expectations of the users, the governments across the world are modifying their operational modes so as to improve the delivery of public services. Moreover, the government agencies focus on the digitisation of the public services proving to be effective and efficient in their designing and thus, achieving the basic objectives of the digital reformation covering satisfaction of the citizen of the society with inter-operability between the services and enhanced transperancy.

While framing the initial framework of the digitisation of the services, the basic four parameters on which it depends are:

1. The essential services that need the digital reformation.
2. The reasons behind which the digitisation of the services is required.
3. The extent to which the digitisation is required.
4. The advantages of the digital reformation in services.

The first parameter focuses on the essential services of the society that needs to have a digital reformation. These services are identified by making observation to the user-service interface, and thus framing a list focuses on the services which requires digitisation. The digitisation in these services may run simultaneously or concurrently, depending on the resources available. The second parameter covers the reasons for which the digital reformation is becoming a necessity in this society, providing an ease of access of operation of services by the users. The third parameter mainly deals with the extent of provision of digital reformation in the public services. Most of the public services are transforming their methodology and business framework from traditional way to the digitisation era, making the application and usage of the services by the users in an efficient manner. But the main question arises that whether the digital reformation adopted in the public services are being acceptable by the users, which fall under the fourth parameter. The main aim of the digital reformation of services is to provide the users a smart way to take the privileges of the services in the society. Thus, whatever the digital reformation that has to be introduced in services at any level, must be user-friendly.

A lot of discussion had been done on the implementation of the process of digitisation in any service, let us now study about various stages in the process of digital reformation:

1. Providing the services to the citizens of the society.
2. Experimentation at various levels in the system of service provider.
3. Formalisation of the results obtained from the experimentation stage.
4. Make a strategic plan.
5. Convergence in the application of digitisation into the services.
6. Innovation and adaptation.

16.2 DIGITAL REFORMS IN PUBLIC SERVICES

The intensive application of technologies presently can surely suggest that it had been a new benchmark established in the world. With recent advancements in the field of Internet of Things (IOT), along with AI (Artificial Intelligence or Augmented Intelligence) and DL (Deep Learning), every aspect of the life has been transformed [3]. With a proper blending with the information, it led to increase in productivity, efficiency and thus a more "connective" relationship worldwide at business, organisational as well as individual level. Being as a feature of "Information Society", it does throws light of the application of ICT (Information or Communication Technology) in every component of life; from education to health, economy and finance to governance. Society 5.0 relies on the bridge between the capability of manipulating the information (capital and skills) and the technological, spatial and occupational changes addressing the same.

In a broader sense, the most common public services that are offering to a society includes social care and healthcare, education and information, & protection services the digital transformation of the same is coined as "Digital Welfare". Digitisation of these welfare services opens a full world of opportunities for digital transformation in a radical manner. While digitisation today is an increasingly recognised tool for efficiency, few countries have yet turned to national co-ordination of the digitisation of welfare services across and between different sectors [4]. Thus, the absence of the approach of digitisation in public services refers to the fact that a huge number of benefits and savings for the society as well as its citizens are going in vain. Moreover, it refers to the fact that the considerable enhancements to the public welfare strategies, both in relation to the quality of the service provided as well as satisfaction by the user, hadn't been launched properly and thus, diminishing the overall efficiency of the services provided at large scale. Governments, both at state and central level, applies various patterns and models of public welfare services, which is being adaptive towards context on politics and delivery areas. Since the digitisation of the society towards the public services covers a significant portion in public spending, thereby covering a great portion of the societal workforce. With digital transformation, the funding related to different components of the public services increases due to demographic change with increasing the societal age.

The prime components of public welfare that experienced a significant portion obeying the phenomenon of digitisation includes Education, Healthcare Services & Social Care and Protection. In the domain of education, the digital reformation enhances the concept of learning via global communities and new blended teaching-learning approach is being applied in institutions at different levels. Emerging healthcare models including ease in excess of information, more independence, conduction of tests and collection of medical reports and telemedicine is the result of digital reforms in healthcare services at societal level. Social-care protection services categorised under three different domains as: (i) social care administration, (ii) in-home care and support and (iii) social protection (covering financial support). The digital reformation in all these three components are explained in detail in the following sub-sections.

16.2.1 EDUCATION

Since the people worldwide aren't mobile and thus, their surroundings hadn't been changed, different traditional ways of education are being followed by all the developing nations as well as some of the developed nations [5]. Its not wrong if said that the present traditions and schemes of education systems were settled at a time way beforehand the understanding of "advanced" or "accelerated" learning methods. The concept of "Accelerated Learning" is an approach which improves the learning processes and designing techniques. This had been recognised as a chosen learning methods by students, in conjunction with digitisation. Also, the approach of accelerated learning proves to be economical. The magnitude of innovation and research in higher education systems is found to be the average of that of primary and secondary education systems. Digitisation plays an important role towards the significant research projects and patents around the world. Because of the digital reforms in education systems around the worldwide, researches and innovations in methodologies of performing the same is observed to more than average, followed by innovations in product and service sector.

Due to digital reforms in educational sector, Massive Online Open Courses or termed as MOOCs emerges as a global revolution through online learning and teaching pedagogy. The commencement of radical digitised reform in education sector is online education. With the introduction of MOOCs in the education systems, the traditional cost structures of the universities are also changing, including the phase change of intensive labour learning experience to a cooperative and joint

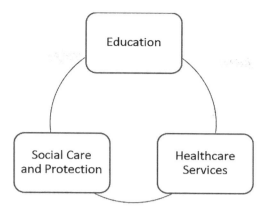

FIGURE 16.2 Prime components of public welfare.

online teaching pedagogy, which is scalable as a limited cost to high cost of the former. The basic advantage of digital reform from traditional education system to MOOCs is that anyone can learn any course of their choice, from one part of the world to another part. However, practices in educational systems such as submission of subjective-based assignments/exercises, conducting examinations and provision of study materials are still in mid-phase of the digital transformation.

With digital reformation in education society, the social interaction among the students, educationalists, researchers, academicians had been increased, thereby increasing both the quality and quantity of research and innovations in all aspects of educational domains [6]. With emerging application of IoT and AI in almost all the domains of knowledge, the products of the research studies as product development and patent filing had been increasing from past few decades, and thus contributing a large section in the development of Society 5.0. The credits earned by the students after successful completion of MOOCs from different platforms gives a significant weightage in their respective full-time courses. One of the most prominent advantages of MOOCs is that it gives a freedom to students to opt and learn the courses of their own interest, which may or may not be a part of their individual full-time course domain. One of the fundamental things that has to be consider in making efforts to bring the digital reforms in education is to think, predict and consider various developments that will be addressing by the same in different categories of educational services, summarised below.

Let just discuss these categories of Educational Services and the impact of Digital Reforms over the decades:

a. **School Administration and Management:**

From centuries, school administration plays an important role in the reformation of the education policies as time changes and management looks into the processes how these reformations are being implemented into the school administration so that it won't affect the teaching faculty members and students. Thus, the role of administration and management in a two-fold and both are dependent on each other on the proper functioning of their role. In this present era, all the stages in the school management such as application for applying in school at any level and submission of documents are being done online. The result of digital reformation in school administration also leads in ease of all the process related to examinations such as registering for it as well as getting certificate after being qualified. Some of the major universities and institutions worldwide make their all processes online mandatory. Also, for getting things done inside any institutional management, the digital reformation proved to be an efficient way. The work that took 1 week span of time, now takes just an hour to complete because of the digitisation.

b. **Communication between Main Institute and Its Co-Institutions:**

Using digitisations, the communication between different levels inside an institution or between two organisations are proved to be beneficial in work efficiency and productivity [7]. With the concept of cloud computing, the sharing of documents between teachers and students, and also parents is possible, thereby increasing the communication between them, may resulting in better performances of the students in their examinations due to the availability of study materials at a faster rate, as compared to the traditional way of communication and sharing of documents before the digitisation. Due to the evolution of collaborative platforms due to digital reformation, the institutions are saving their time by conducting the communication with the parent's ward online, showing the ability and ease of digital transformation of that institute, correspondingly matching the skills and accessibility with evolving technological trends in the society.

c. **Teaching and Learning Pedagogy:**

The traditional way of teaching and learning methods includes the applications of books and hardcopy notes. Teachers come into class and teach from the books or their notes; whereas students also make their notes from the books and notes taken down from the classroom. Both the faculty members and students are benefitted from the digital reformation in the teaching and learning pedagogy. With digital transformation, a huge content for every discipline of education is available, which are being used by the faculty members so as to increase their knowledge and impart the same to their students for better understanding of the topic. On the other hand, the application of this digitisation opens a door to many opportunities for students in their learning process. Students can download eBooks and study materials available online, thus increasing their dimension regarding their subject of interest. Also, as discussed earlier, the evolution of MOOCs gives an amazing opportunity, for both the faculty members and students, to not only grab knowledge about their own specialisation course, but can explore and enrol in other courses also which may be helpful in conducting research and innovation by proper blending of various courses of emerging technologies; proving to be fruitful for one or many aspects of the society.

d. **Mentor–Mentee Interactions:**

In simpler words, a student is known as a "mentee" and a faculty member is considered to be one's "mentor". On the basis of the observation made that most of the time, students share and want to communicate with mature people outside the family; an active "Mentor–Mentee" group has to be formed which is a safe space for any student to share one's feelings, which he/she hesitates or unable to express in front of their family members. The result of this approach leads to a decrease in the number of cases of depression among students. For keeping this view and as a fresh learning from the pandemic, these interactions can be conducted online. With one-on-one communication online, a mentee is able to freely talk and its mentor can resolve any query raised by the mentee. With digitisation, these interactions are being conducted online so that the communication between the mentor and its mentees remains stable, thereby forming a happy, depressed-free environment in the society, which may become a strong foundation to the psychological pillar of Society 5.0.

e. **Blended and Flip-Mode Learning:**

One of the most important components of the society that had been worst affected by the pandemic was education sector. With a different paradigm shift, from offline class learnings to online teaching, that time proved to be a challenging phase for teachers, students and their parents too. In the initial stage, it was difficult, but as time progresses, both the teachers and students were able to use various learning platforms to increase their respective domain of education. This is one of the results of digital reforms in technology. The meeting platforms that were used by corporates around the world are being used by every educational institution. Also, as the need increases, corresponding digital reforms had been taken into consideration so that the process of education and learning should not be hampered. With this, many institutions are focusing on blended or flip-mode classes, a methodology which deals with teaching and learning in both offline and online modes [8]. Some of the topics can be covered in class and some can be given to the students so that they can prepare the same with different study materials available online and then present them in the class. With the methodology, the courses related to laboratory experiments will be most benefitted. Sometimes, due to some reasons, the machines are not working in the laboratories. In these scenarios, students can learn and watch the methodology of performing the experiments usign virtual labs platform offered by the institutions or training centres. Teachers can share the online link of such platforms available to the students so that they can watch and observe the methodology of the experiment again for better understanding of the same.

Evolution of digital reformation and its applications in all the domains of public services gives a great emphasis on the design and layout of respective services and their accompanied procedures for better understanding and fulfilling the needs of users, and continuing on depending upon the skills of those components that plays a significant role in the delivery of the facilities. In the educational sector, with the digital reformation as per Society 5.0, not only the advancements are required with emerging technologies in the form of ICT tools and infrastructural developments, teaching skills of the teachers are needed to be improved so as to cater the changes; integrating the old traditional way of teaching with modern teaching techniques focusing on holistic development of students including curriculum as well as overall development and growth of the students for their better future endeavours.

16.2.2 Healthcare Services

One of the emerging issues in the healthcare services of both developed and developing nations is the proper functioning of their policies. These services are in direct relation with the citizen's interests and thereby, all the nations across the world are facing an alarming situation in economy due to the change in the demographic boundaries and an increase in the occurrence of harmful chronic diseases or as say, the world had suffered a major loss in life due to COVID-19. These aspects lay the foundation for improvement in the efficiency and effectiveness of the healthcare systems of all nations. With an increase in technological advancements, and digital transformations in particular, is proving to be a key agent in leveraging future policies for healthcare systems.

Every country has its own healthcare systems, simple or complex in nature, depending upon various factors such as its population, economic growth, environmental conditions and GDP. Various factors that affect the functioning of the healthcare systems include interests & values and responsibilities of different segments of healthcare policies, leading to a specific approach for the development of an integrated methodology and vision, that will require the process of digitisation [9]. Thereby, developing a digital transformation in healthcare services is a challenge, the biggest being adapting to the change by the people of the society.

With advancements in the technology, the healthcare units are changing their systems accordingly and with this digital reformation, the efficiency of the healthcare systems improves. Let us discuss various emerging trends in the healthcare systems that had been evolve due to digital reformations:

a. **Hospital Administration:**

One of the primary areas in which the digital reforms occurred in back-office administration. The basic advantage of this digital transformation is the recompenses of the health-related expenses, particularly in the nations which has a major portion of insurance–based healthcare systems and services. E-procurement for clinical equipments and medicine is also considered as one of the prominent applications of digitisation in healthcare systems.

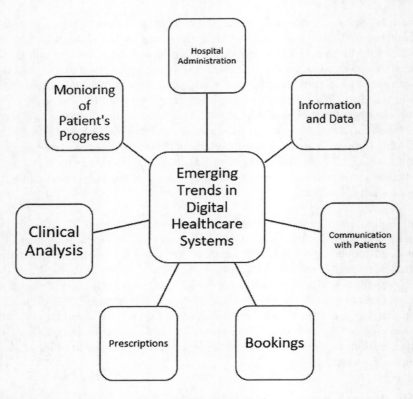

FIGURE 16.3   Digital education – categories of educational services.

b. **Information and Data:**

For the past few decades, the centre of the digital reforms in healthcare systems is maintaining the records of the patients electronically. Using electronically saved data, the health history of any patient can easily be fetched and can be treated well as per the data entered. Also, using this digital reformation, the stacking of the data in healthcare units proved to be more efficient rather than keeping the records of the patients in the files (hardcopy) and that too can lose or damaged due to some circumstances such as fire. The digitisation in healthcare units due to the application of AI and IoT still is a challenge for most of the developing nations [10]. Such countries are still struggling in creating suitable systems and also finding difficulty in maintaining such reformation to maximum capacity. Thus, these nations are actually exploiting and aren't utilising the benefits of the digitisation, resulting in lesser efficiency in the data collecting, interpreting and analysing comparatively.

c. **Communication with Patients:**

With digital reformation in the healthcare units, the communication with the patients becomes easier. Such communication with patients and their respective relatives are powerfully reinforced by various digital platforms. This makes every citizen of the society empowered by enabling the access to their personal data, allows the citizens for managing their respective data securely and autonomously.

d. **Bookings:**

With digitisation, online booking for hospitals and doctor's appointments has been increasing rapidly in past years. For example, hospital bookings via online were a part of *"National Program for Information Technology"* in health sector since 2002. In developing nations like India, online bookings are acceptable in major hospital chains, but still face difficulty in small-level clinics in rural areas.

e. **Prescriptions:**

The digital reformation in healthcare units does not only includes online bookings, but also the generation of prescriptions via online mode. The trend of issuing digital prescriptions is very common in developed nations and are being increasing in developing nations like South-East Asian countries. With the digital transformation from hand-written prescriptions to e-prescriptions, the discrepancies in buying the relative medical units had been reduced. Moreover, it reduces the time and error in transactions between pharmaceutical units, practitioners and hospitals and patients. Digitised prescription helps in improving the dosage, identification of drugs which can produce bad effects in one's immune system and also be helpful in minimising trafficking of medical units.

f. **Clinical Analysis:**

There is no doubt that doctors play a vital role in the analysis of patient's health; various components of the diagnostic system are increasing and segmented properly. The medical tests that are performed at one place and be analysed at other places so as to have proper consultancy. With the access of the digital data, the number of discrepancies in treatment is reduced.

g. **Monitoring of Patient's Progress:**

With the advancement in the technology and its application as digitisation, the patient care and monitoring had been widely increased, along with the treatments of the patients done online. Various services at the healthcare units are being sub-categorised as per remoteness and readiness. With digital reformation, various procedures had been redesigned or reconstructed as per the requirement. With digitisation, there is an ease for the patients to be interacted with the doctors sitting at any place in world, thereby increasing the monitoring of the health progress of a patient.

Healthcare systems in any nation, covering both public and private healthcare sectors are being moving towards the digitisation process as a part of Digital Government or E-Government. The initial step of the digital reformation any enterprise includes the adaptation of the digitisation in every procedure and channel of the healthcare units. But, one of the key points while adapting this digital reformation in the healthcare units is that the non-structural components of the healthcare units must be able to adopt these reformations and act accordingly. The staff members of the hospital and clinic units must be able to understand the digital reformation. Special training may be given to the existing staff members, who are not up to date with the latest technological advancements in the society so that the same does not hamper the productivity and efficiency of the healthcare units.

Development of a fully digitised system and its implementation are the key challenges in the healthcare systems presently. This may include proper understanding of the services as per the preferences of the users, developing products as per the needs of the user, scaling and elaborating different platforms for proper delivery of these services. Furthermore, these services may be integrating with the services and products of the other sectors which have a linear relationship between the former and the latter. From various studies across worldwide, it can easily be stated that for proper implementation of the digital transformation in the healthcare sector, a proper channel has to be established first, which focuses on the needs and services demanded by the users. The overall efficiency of this system only be optimum when both the users and the service providers act in the same direction, leading to a smarter way of dealing with the services related to health, thereby a "smart" approach for a "smart" society.

16.2.3 Social Care and Protection

The third pillar of public services, termed as *"Social Care and Protection"*, comes under the category of *Welfare Services*. These can further be categorised as Financial Support Services and Personal Support Services. The services fall under the domain of social care cover a wide variety

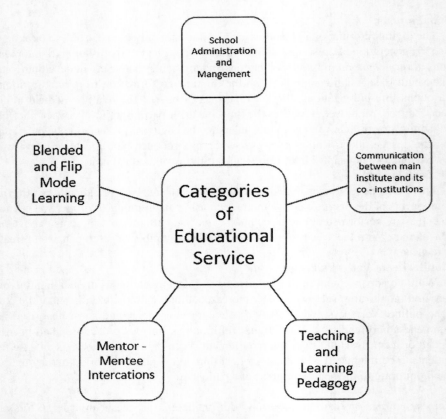

FIGURE 16.4   Emerging trends in digital healthcare systems.

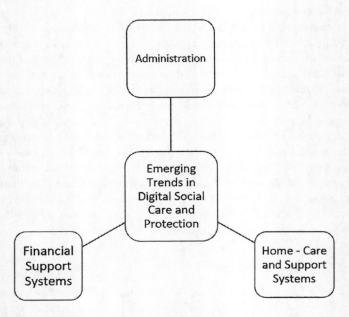

FIGURE 16.5   Emerging trends in digital social care and protection.

of home-support services for both young as well as elder people. Financial support services come under the domain of social protection services. These financial support services include pensions or supplementary economical dealing. Social protection services for working people consist of the domain in which they are unable to work in office due to some reasons such as any disability or medical conditions. Both the developed and developing nations are making progress in the digitisation of delivery of services. One of the most important domains in which digital reformation had been practiced and is proven to be successful is financial transfer. This financial transfer can be between two people or between two organisations or between person and organisation.

In comparison to the other two pillars of the public services, i.e., *Education and Healthcare Services,* Social Care and Protection proved to be a challenging task in the application of digital reformation as it will directly affects the cultural and social phase of the society. Let us discuss various components of this category in broader areas and how the digitisation influences its applications in real-time world.

a. **Administration:**

Digitisation is a case-improved management approach, having a wider impression of informing the individualised management on the end of the service provider, covering the coordination between different sectors. The impact of digital reform in such services enables a vast-integrated system of examination of the needs of user, determination and verification of the eligibility for the financial services and support. It also gives the user a choice to choose the best option from various care options, including both home-based as well as organisation-based care systems.

b. **Home-Care and Support Systems:**

The digital reformation in the home-care systems and its parallel arrangements proved to be beneficial for the society and can be considered as one of the emerging trends for Society 5.0. The blending of gathering and maintaining of data in form of records, along with network-based access for the support system gives user an easier way of operating such services. Some of the services which are become more efficient due to digitisation includes provision of providing the services for the people at their door-step, in conjunction with a specialised system of advices available using video links or online when required.

c. **Financial Support Systems:**

With digitisation in the financial transfers, there is an ease of transferring of funds, as compared to a lengthy, time-taking and hassle traditional way of money transfer. With an increase in the digitisation of the payment of transferring of funds, the rate of producing benefits from the payments had been increased, with proper consideration of verification, eligibility and calculation. This component of social care and protection built a cooperative relation between the private finance schemes providers and government.

The volume of the services enclosed within social care and protection towards the society suggested that the integration of the services which are strengthened and supported using digital reformation follows a more natural approach as compared to the other components of public welfare, i.e., Education Sector and Healthcare Services. Considering various scenarios from the user's perspective, where the users have a restricted capability towards leaving home to access services, the comparison between the services for determining a particular service is not useful towards social care and protection.

Expansion in the process of digital reformation of the services comes in the domain of social care and protection backs the all-purpose themes of digital government, by developing a relationship between the establishment and maintenance of user's greater engagement in the decision-making process, affecting them directly. This also includes an approach of maintaining all the emphasis on the needs of the users, resulting in the collective contribution of the same towards the shaping of different policies and agendas, which in turn provides necessary modification in designing of the

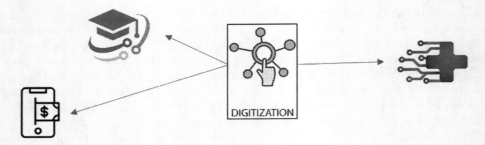

FIGURE 16.6 Components of a digitized society.

services; attaining a larger multi-sector coordination which are drawn upon various ICT platforms available for sharing of the data at a larger extent in support of improving the services which are delivered at user's end.

Discussing the approach of digitisation of protection and social care services at policy-making and implementation level, supports a normal re-evaluation of procedure of the provision of the organisation of the services, including the category of the services under consideration. using digitisation, the organisation and management of major life events in user's life is quite simple as comparative to the traditional methodology of the services, which requires a categorised system for each specialisation such as users' preferences, expected population and their needs and many such. This approach of "re-thinking" is not only considered as a major step in the digitisation of social care services, but also in healthcare and education sectors; and making a strong impression in the fields of policing and justice.

16.3   DIGITAL INFRASTRUCTURE

The reformation in the infrastructural sector is emerging as an equal or more significant necessity in comparison with the conventional infrastructural necessities such as provision of pavements, supply of water and electricity to the society. Relating the concept of Society 5.0 with the digitisation in the infrastructural development, it appears to have a direct relationship between the two. The approach of "Smart Cities" is the result of the applications of Augmented Intelligence and Internet of Things in the infrastructure sector. The pandemic, which was and still having disastrous effects on the whole world, emphasised on the need of the digital infrastructure, and that too in a well-defined system. Both the strong and weak economies across the world are transforming their systems of infrastructure. This digital reformation in the sector of the infrastructure includes the resources available physically for the application of data gathered, technology-based devices, advance and skills-adapting systems and methodologies, making the same more agile, resilient and futuristic. The digital reformation in infrastructure played a vital role in the functioning of the society and thereby, affecting the citizen's quality life in an efficient way.

The flexibility of a nation's digital reformation in infrastructure may be crucial in considering the adversities such as COVID-19 effectively. The digital reformation in the infrastructure faces a challenging situation while adopting increasingly the advancements in the frontier technology including Blockchain, AI and IoT. The continuous efforts of government of any nation towards making their cities "smart" and digitisation in the public services, it is a must now for introducing a digital reformation, which utilises these stative frontier technologies effectively for economic development, thereby affecting the overall development of a nation positively. Thus, the digital reformation in infrastructural development needs the digital technologies that provides the base for different operations and systems of information technology of any organisation.

Digital reformation in digital infrastructure aims to collaborate and develop an inter-connecting relation between both physical as well as virtual technologies. This relation depends on computer

FIGURE 16.7   Components of a digitized society.

systems, gathering of data, storage of data, network systems and applications in society. With recent researches, platforms like SaaS, PaaS and IaaS are being utilised to build the foundation of system of digital operations for any service-provider company. Hence, these services are being used to digitally reform the system at a global level so as to make an ecosystem which focuses on the needs of the users and thus, rebuilding their services and products so as to deliver them to the users in most effective and efficient manner.

Considering the infrastructural service development of any organisation, some of the areas in which digitisation is required for optimum productivity can be summarised under a well-efficient internet and broadband services, highly equipped data centres and networking systems, provision of cloud services, Application Programming Interface (APIs), Mobile Telecom and Digital Communication Suites, Operational Security and User-Identification and Data Encryption.

16.4   DIGITAL REFORMS IN INFRASTRUCTURAL DEVELOPMENT AND MANAGEMENT

As the technology advances, the traditional way of the development in the infrastructural sector had been changed and now considering the software applications in every aspect of their domain. An infrastructure may be defined as a system of basic services of a society including buildings, transportation, water supply, power supply and sewer systems. Getting the concept of infrastructure in detail, it can be divided into different sub-heads depending upon their functions in a society as described in Figure 16.8.

The digitisation of every aspect of the infrastructure is need of an hour, depending upon the increasing needs of the users. The main objective of digital reformation in the infrastructural sector is to have a long-term sustainable design life as well as an economic infrastructural design by a process of proper documentation, integration and analysation. The digitisation in the area of infrastructure consists of an extensive variety of business-process datasets, which consists the novel design, in-detail design information, fabrication & verification, commissioning confirmation, preventive maintenance & inspections, regular inspection of construction activities, repairing, rehabilitation and retrofitting and decommissioning of the facility. When blended precisely through an integrated-digital twin platform approach, these range of data sets can provide a complete knowledge and helps in determination of the analytical tools so as to maximise the investment return on their structure.

Let us now discuss the basic three crucial practices for digital reformation in infrastructural development:

a. **Technology Deployment:**
   The digital reformation in the infrastructural sector requires a successful deployment, configuration system and integration of the latest technology with traditional knowledge of building up the structure and society. For an efficient approach towards digitisation, a considerable focus has to be given to its three sub-heads, namely: (i) Business consulted process, (ii) Engineering consultation in selection and integration of the required engineering analytics and (iii) Digital reformation due to modifications in software needs and its integration as per the evolution of some specific technological tools/configurations so as to fulfil the owner's requirements. It also focused on broadening of the stakeholders in infrastructure for efficient engineering requirements. With a proper relation and delivery

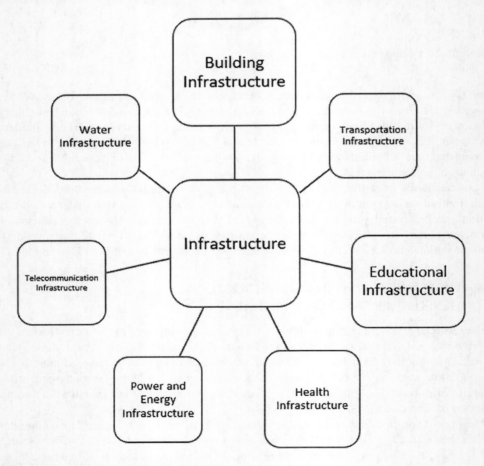

FIGURE 16.8   Components of a digitized society.

of all the above stative parts, a successful digital reformation in infrastructural sector can be established.

b. **Technology Platform:**

The investment required for digitisation in infrastructure is accompanied through a wider system of adoption and integration of the technology in the long-term application, followed by an efficient phase of maintenance and facility operations in designing and construction stages.

c. **Infrastructure Owner Leadership:**

For digitising infrastructure, the most essential approach is to install and mandate the application of technological advancements in infrastructure owner leadership. This leadership quality confirms that the stakeholders are trained in an appropriate manner for the digital reformation and also, are also capable of delivering a wide variety of services covering the stage of designing, inspection, fabrication, operations, maintenance and management. Moreover, this category ensures that the technological modifications (by the time) will be considered with proper operational support systems.

16.5 ROLE OF DIGITAL REFORMATION IN CONSTRUCTION INDUSTRY TOWARDS SOCIETY 5.0

As discussed earlier also, the need of the hour is to keep a shoulder-to-shoulder with the technological advancements. For digitally reforming the society as Society 5.0, there must be a consideration given to the aspects of Industry 4.0. With the evolution and adaptation of more software-related applications in technological-based engineering disciplines such as Computer Science & Engineering, Electronics and Communication Engineering, and Electrical and Electronics Engineering, the core engineering disciplines such as Civil Engineering and Mechanical Engineering are also now blending their fundamental principles with the computer applications.

Construction never stops, thereby making the construction industry one of the busiest industries in the world. The construction industry involves the construction of structures such as Residential Buildings, Institutional Buildings, Commercial Complexes, Hospital Structures, Railway Stations, Airports and many more. The beginning of any construction project involves the design and drafting of the plan. The traditional way of making building plans is paper and pencil, with the usage of mathematical instruments. With advancements, many software applications are available so as to make the building plans. With software applications, the time consumption in making plans is less, with more efficiency and precision. Also, it was difficult to make any plans other than line drawings.

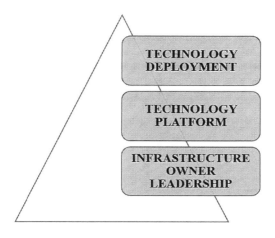

FIGURE 16.9 Components of a digitized society.

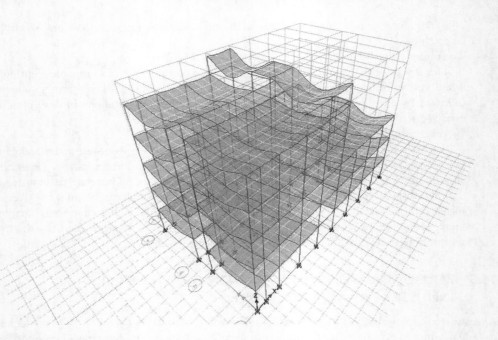

FIGURE 16.10 Analysis of structure by real-time software.

Digital reformation gives a platform for making plans for circular and elliptical-shaped structural elements such as Domes, Tombs and other irregular plans.

Not only in design, keeping pace with time and software-based applications, now the analysis of the structures becomes easier also. The traditional way of doing the analysis includes designing and solving the complex design and analytical problems on sheets of paper, using calculator. This would had been taken days to reach out to the optimum result. With digital reformation, various software platforms are available in which the designing and the analysis of all types of structures such as residential buildings, commercial buildings, Dams and reservoirs, bridge structures, piers and abutments have become less time-consuming with effective results. Also, these software applications provide the designing and analysis of irregular-shaped structures easier, with giving the user to modify the plans and calculations as per the users and architect's requirements. Its not false to comment that as the role of digitisation increase in the construction industry in coming decades, the civil and structural engineers will be able to present a unique approach of structures, which may be "smarter" and "technology-friendly", a step towards enhancing the concept of Society 5.0.

16.6   ROLE OF DIGITAL REFORMATION IN TRANSPORTATION

Society 5.0 does not only consider the digital reformation in just construction industry, but it also gives emphasis on the digital transformation in different modes of transportation such as roadways, railways, airways and waterways. But, the most important transportation domain which affects the everyday life of citizens of the society is roadways. The technological approach that blended digital reformation with the traditional manner of scrutinising the transportation activities is known as Intelligent Transportation System.

An Intelligent Transportation System, or commonly known as ITS, is a cutting-edge approach aims in providing ground-breaking services to the users, covering the domain of different modes of transportation and management of traffic. This technological reformation enables the users to get the information in an efficient manner, making the whole system safer, coordinated and "smarter" for the current and future generation. It can also be defined as a system which involves the applications

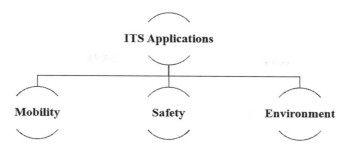

FIGURE 16.11 Types of Intelligent Transportation Systems.

of communication and information skills in the domain of road transportation, together with users and their vehicles & infrastructure; and in managing traffic as well as mobility. The basic aim of introducing ITS is to overcome the problem of increasing capacity of busy roads and thereby, reducing the time of journey.

Let us discuss the three broad applications of Intelligent Transportation System:

a. **ITS Mobility Application:**

ITS mobility applications are projected to deliver the mobility services including determination of the shortest path available between the origin and destination. Various factors which involve in this determination of shortest path are distance between the two points, time travel and the energy consumption. The shortest path determination is done on the information (data) gathered and collected by different ITS data collection strategies. This application provides the transportation management centres in proper monitoring and management of the performance of transportation system by providing necessary adjustments in traffic signals, management of transit operations dynamically and evolution in digital-based emergency maintenance system.

b. **ITS Safety Application:**

As the name goes by, these digitally reformed services in the transportation system only focuses on the safety of the users. For example, by giving a proper provision of a speed warning system on a slippery roadway or a curved section on road, the rate of the accidents occurred by crashing, slipping or skidding can be reduced. The ITS safety applications also include emergency management in the worst scenarios by providing the best emergency routes; and a monitoring system which focus on the monitoring of the safety of both the driver as well the vehicle. The information related to the traffic congestion helps the driver in making smart decision, thereby decreasing the environmental impact of the trips on daily basis. Either by taking alternative routes or rescheduling their journeys, the drivers actually avoid the condition of congestion, making the journey economical and eco-friendly.

c. **ITS Environmental Application:**

ITS Environmental Applications only focused on the systems based on the environmental conditions. With digital reformation and the application of the same in various environment-based systems, the drivers can now able to determine the weather conditions while moving from one place to another. These systems can directly connect to direst satellite-based systems, which directly gathered the information and then alert the users about the difference in the weather conditions, if happened.

All the three ITS application have different packages of stakeholders. Considering the parameter of variable speed limit, the stakeholders may include either (or both) private or public transportation agencies, vehicle drivers, emergency management services and law enforcement authorities.

TABLE 16.1
Data Sources and Data Users of applications of ITS

Type of Application	Name of Application	Goal of Application	Data Sources	Data Users
Mobility	Transit signal priority	To advance real-time transit system performance	Transit vehicle traffic signal	Transit management centre and traffic management centre
Safety	Vehicle safety monitoring	To detect critical elements of the vehicle and to alert the driver about any potential dangers	Vehicle on-board system	Vehicle safety monitoring system
Environmental	Environmental probe surveillance	To collect data from vehicles to infer real-time environmental conditions	Vehicle on-board system	Weather service, maintenance and construction management centre

A perfect cooperation among the stakeholders is required so as to have a successful system of designing, deployments and management of any or all the ITS applications mentioned. The crux of all the three ITS applications has been listed in Table 16.1, showcasing their illustration, mentioning their respective goals, sources of data and its users. The sources of the data consist of both infrastructure sources and vehicle sources, whereas its "users" consists of the system of people, centres and vehicles.

16.7 CONCLUSION

It's a necessity for the digital reformation in all the public services so as to keep a pace with the technological advancements and meeting the needs of the users. The digital transformation of all the public services has to be taken as all of them have a direct relationship with the ecosystem of the society. From the collection of data from different sources to gathering, analysing and employing these technological reforms (applications of IoT and AI), transforming the society into a "smarter" place to live in, following the basic fundamentals of Society 5.0.

REFERENCES

1. L. Sharma, P. Garg, (Ed.). (2020). *From Visual Surveillance to Internet of Things.* New York: Chapman and Hall/CRC, https://doi.org/10.1201/9780429297922.
2. Lavanya Sharma, (2021) *Introduction: From Visual Surveillance to Internet of Things*, Taylor & Francis, CRC Press, Vol. 1, p.14.
3. Lavanya Sharma, P K Garg (2021) *Block Based Adaptive Learning Rate for Moving Person Detection in Video Surveillance, From Visual Surveillance to Internet of Things*, Taylor & Francis, CRC Press, Vol. 1, p. 201.
4. Lavanya Sharma, P K Garg (2021) *IoT and Its Applications, From Visual Surveillance to Internet of Things*, Taylor & Francis, CRC Press, Vol. 1, p. 29.
5. Yaman Hooda et al. (2021). Emerging applications of artificial intelligence in structural engineering and construction industry, *Journal of Physics: Conference Series* 1950, 012062.
6. L. Sharma, M. Carpenter, (Eds.). (2022). *Computer Vision and Internet of Things: Technologies and Applications* (1st ed.). Chapman and Hall/CRC. https://doi.org/10.1201/9781003244165.
7. Preeti Kuhar et al. (2021). Internet of things (IoT) based smart helmet for construction, *Journal of Physics: Conference Series* 1950, 012075.

8. John Bertot, Elsa Estevez, Tomasz Janowski. (2016). Universal and contextualized public services: Digital public service innovation framework, *Government Information Quarterly* 33(2), 211–222.

9. Roberto Verdecchia, Patricia Lago, Carol de Vries. (2022). The future of sustainable digital infrastructures: A landscape of solutions, adoption factors, impediments, open problems, and scenarios, *Sustainable Computing: Informatics and Systems* 100767, ISSN 2210-5379, https://doi.org/10.1016/j.suscom.2022.100767.

10. Sakib M. Khan, Mizanur Rahman, Amy Apon, Mashrur Chowdhury. (2017). Chapter 1- Characteristics of intelligent transportation systems and its relationship with data analytics, Mashrur Chowdhury, Amy Apon, Kakan Dey (eds.), *Data Analytics for Intelligent Transportation Systems*, Elsevier, 1–29, ISBN 9780128097151, https://doi.org/10.1016/B978-0-12-809715-1.00001-8.

11. Gauri Jha, Pawan Singh, Lavanya Sharma, "Recent advancements of augmented reality in real time applications", *International Journal of Recent Technology and Engineering*, 8, 2S7, 538–542, 2019, https://doi.org/10.35940/ijrte.B10100.0782S719.

12. Akshit Anand, Vikrant Jha, Lavanya Sharma, "An improved local binary patterns histograms techniques for face recognition for real time application", *International Journal of Recent Technology and Engineering*, 8, 2S7, 524–529, 2019, https://doi.org/10.35940/ijrte.B1098.0782S719. ISSN: 2277-3878.

13. Lavanya Sharma, Annapurna Singh, Dileep Kumar Yadav, *Fisher's Linear Discriminant Ratio Based Threshold for Moving Human Detection in Thermal Video*, Infrared Physics and Technology, Elsevier, 2016 (SCI impact factor: 1.58, Published).

14. Lavanya Sharma, Dileep Kumar Yadav, "Histogram based adaptive learning rate for background modelling and moving object detection in video surveillance", *International Journal of Telemedicine and Clinical Practices, Inderscience*, 2016, ISSN: 2052-8442, https://doi.org/10.1504/IJTMCP.2017.082107.

15. L. Sharma, M. Carpenter (eds), *Computer Vision and Internet of Things: Technologies and Applications* (1st ed.). Chapman and Hall/CRC, 2022. https://doi.org/10.1201/9781003244165.

16. Lavanya Sharma, Pradeep K Garg "Artificial intelligence: Challenges, technologies and future", Wiley (In production), 2021.

17. Lavanya Sharma, *Towards Smart World: Homes to Cities using Internet of Things*, Taylor & Francis, CRC Press, 2020 (ISSN: 9780429297922).

18. Lavanya Sharma, *Object Detection with Background Subtraction*, LAP LAMBERT Academic Publishing, SIA OmniScriptum Publishing Brivibas gatve 197, Latvia, European Union, 2019 (ISBN: 978-613-7-34386-9).

17 Monitoring of Biological Pollution Index in Community Well Water

Vallidevi Krishnamurthy, Sujithra Kanmani, and Joe Dhanith
Vellore Institute of Technology

Surendiran Balasubramanian
National Institute of Technology

CONTENTS

17.1 INTRODUCTION

Water bodies in communities, such as wells and man-made lakes, are inhabited by small fish and other marine animals. It is also used as a source of water used by the dwellers of the community for multiple purposes such as drinking, domestic and residential, and possibly other economic uses. Polluted-water induced diseases and health issues, such as cholera, typhoid, and so on, make it of utmost importance to test the quality of the water before putting it to use [1].

The quality of water in wells in said communities will primarily be affected by the biological affluents in its environment as opposed to water bodies that are polluted by factory/industrial waste.

To determine the level of pollution in these wells as a result of and only of biological pollution, this chapter defines the Biological Pollution Index of water that measures the pollution level as a result of three parameters [11–14]: Dissolved Oxygen (DO), Temperature, and pH level [2].

This chapter collects parameter readings from the wells through respective sensors connected to the Arduino board and sends the same in real time to an Android mobile application that has been installed in the phone of the owner of the well. The NodeMCU WiFi-module [3], which is also attached to the Arduino, sends data to the Firebase from where the mobile application receives readings. The quality of water is classified into 'Under risk' and 'Safe' based on levels set by the Indian water quality standards. Such a system is ideally intended to alert the user if his well needs immediate attention to safeguard its quality.

17.2 WORKING OF THE PROPOSED SYSTEM

As shown in Figure 17.1, the proposed pollution monitoring system comprises three important components: the hardware module, the cloud module, and the mobile application.

17.2.1 HARDWARE MODULE

As shown in Figure 17.1, the hardware module consists of three sensors:

- **DS18B20 Digital Temperature Sensor:** This is a 1-wire digital temperature sensor, which has a precision of ±0.5°. It covers a range of −55°C to 125°C and provides 12 bits of precision [4].
- **DFRobotGravity Analog pH Sensor:** This sensor can detect water pH levels from 0 to 14 at water temperatures of 5°C–60°C with a precision of ±0.1 with very high response speeds [5].
- **DFRobotGravity Analog Dissolved Oxygen Sensor:** This sensor measures dissolved oxygen levels within a range of 0–20 mg/L with up to 98% full response within 90 seconds [6].

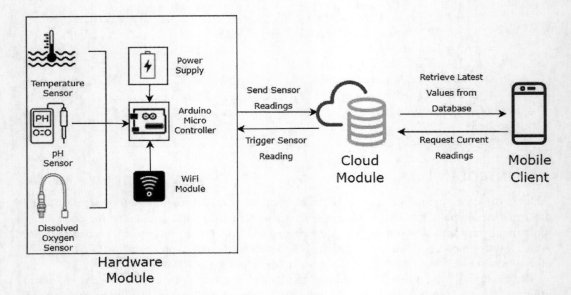

FIGURE 17.1 Water pollution monitoring system.

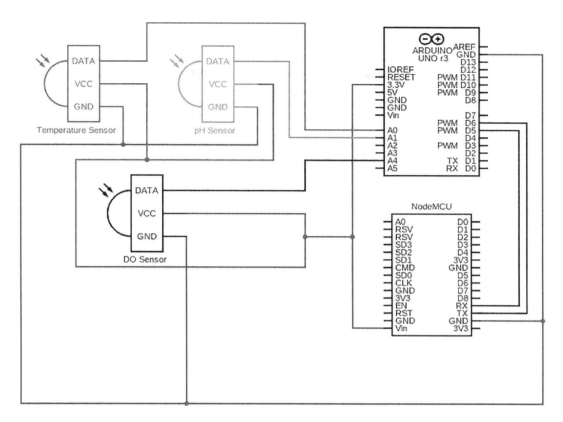

FIGURE 17.2   Circuit diagram for water pollution monitoring system.

The WiFi module is a NodeMCU, which is an open source IOT platform based on the ESP8266 (a low-cost WiFi microchip), with built-in TCP/IP networking software. This is used to enable data transfer using the WiFi protocol between the hardware module and the cloud database. These sensors and the WiFi module are connected to an Arduino UNO microcontroller based on the ATmega328P chip. This microcontroller can be powered by a USB cable or by an external 9-volt battery. As shown in the circuit diagram in Figure 17.2, the microcontroller integrates all the hardware components and provides the core computing power of the hardware module.

17.2.2   Cloud Module

The cloud database used the Firebase Realtime Database which is a cloud-hosted database where data is stored as JSON and synchronized in real-time to every connected client. Firebase has APIs for Android applications and can also be accessed through a REST API from the hardware module by issuing HTTP requests to Firebase's servers.

17.2.3   Mobile Application

This is the user accessible component of this system. Mobile applications have become a part of our daily routine and an average mobile user spends more time on mobile applications than a web browser. Hence, a mobile application provides a more real-time experience to the user than a web application. The mobile application also allows for more features like notifications. The application consists of a User Interface (UI) that presents the sensor readings in a comprehensible manner [7].

The hardware module is responsible for compiling the sensor readings and sending the values to the cloud database where it is stored with the timestamp of the reading. This process is done once every 12 hours. This data is then retrieved from the database and presented in the user-friendly UI of the mobile application. The mobile app has integrated security features by which a user can access the data about a particular water body only if they obtain the required permissions [8,9]. The mobile application also provides a mechanism to trigger the hardware module to retrieve current sensor readings.

17.3 HARDWARE MODULE

17.3.1 INTEGRATED COMPONENTS

This section proposes a hardware module that integrates the required sensors and the WiFi module required for data transfer as a single component.

17.3.2 SMOOTHING SENSOR READINGS

As shown in Figures 17.3 and 17.4, the hardware module calculates an average of ten readings. This is done to smooth out the values from jumpy or erratic sensors.

17.3.3 DYNAMIC WiFi CREDENTIALS

The connection credentials for the WiFi module are dynamically sent through an Access Point. This removes the need for fixed connection credentials.

17.3.3.1 Stable WiFi Connectivity

This system's hardware module maintains a stable WiFi connection by regularly monitoring the connection status.

17.3.3.2 Connectivity Status

The hardware module in this system provides a method to check the status of the WiFi connection of the device.

```
float do_avg=0;
for(int i=0;i<10;i++) {
  float do_reading=analogRead(A4);
  do_avg=do_avg+do_reading;
  delay(20);
}
float do_val=(float)do_avg/10;
float do_act = ((5.0* do_val/1024)*3.5)+offset;
```

```
float ph_avg=0;
for(int i=0;i<10;i++) {
  float ph_reading=analogRead(A1);
  ph_avg=ph_avg+ph_reading;
  delay(20);
}
float ph_val=(float)ph_avg/10;
float ph_act = ((5.0* ph_val/1024)*3.5)+offset;
```

```
float temp_avg=0;
for(int i=0;i<10;i++) {
  sensors.requestTemperatures();
  float temp_reading=sensors.getTempCByIndex(0);
  temp_avg=temp_avg+temp_reading;
  delay(20);
}
float temp_act=(float)ph_avg/10;
```

FIGURE 17.3 Reading sensor data with smoothing.

```
unsigned long epochTime = timeClient.getEpochTime();
int hour=timeClient.getHours();
int minute=timeClient.getMinutes();
struct tm *ptm = gmtime ((time_t *)&epochTime);
int date = ptm->tm_mday;
int month=ptm->tm_mon+1;
int year=ptm->tm_year+1900;
sprintf(timestamp,"%04d%02d%02d%02d%02d",year,month,date,hour,minute);
data_key=deviceid+"/Data/"+timestamp;
StaticJsonBuffer<1000> jsonBuffer;
JsonObject& root = jsonBuffer.parseObject(s);
if (root == JsonObject::invalid())
  return;
float data_do=root["DO"];
float data_ph=root["pH"];
float data_temp=root["Temp"];
String key_do=data_key+"/DO";
String key_ph=data_key+"/pH";
String key_temp=data_key+"/Temp";
Firebase.setFloat(firebaseData,key_do,data_do);
Firebase.setFloat(firebaseData,key_ph,data_ph);
Firebase.setFloat(firebaseData,key_temp,data_temp);
```

FIGURE 17.4   Sending sensor data to firebase.

17.3.4   MOBILE APPLICATION

17.3.4.1   Concise User Interface

The mobile application provides a simple and consistent UI that clearly separates various features of the system.

17.3.4.2   Communication with Hardware Module

As shown in Figure 17.5, the mobile application provides methods to check the hardware details like location of the module and the status of the WiFi connection.

17.3.4.3   Notifications

As shown in Figure 17.6, the mobile application provides a notification to the user if the most recently recorded value of Dissolved Oxygen, pH, or Temperature is not within safe limits.

17.3.4.4   Data Analytics

As shown in Figure 17.7, the application provides time line graphs of the recorded values to help the user get statistical knowledge about the water quality.

17.3.4.5   Access Data from Multiple Hardware Modules

As shown in Figure 17.8, the application is capable of accessing the data of multiple hardware devices from a single client. This helps the user monitor the water quality at multiple locations through a single application.

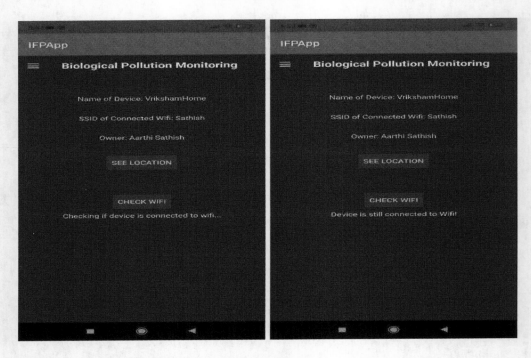

FIGURE 17.5   Mobile application WiFi connection status.

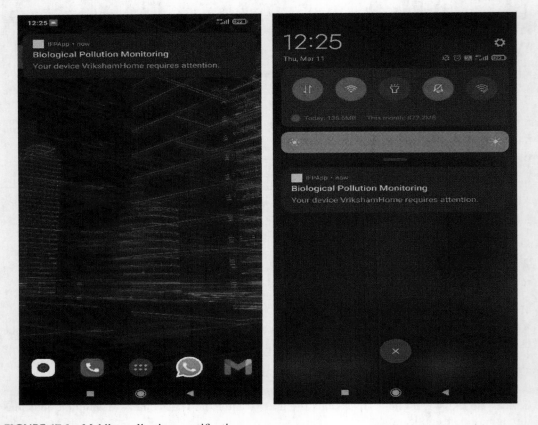

FIGURE 17.6   Mobile application – notification.

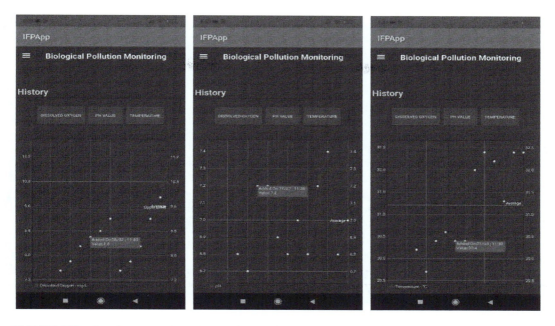

FIGURE 17.7 Mobile application – data analysis and graphical interpretation.

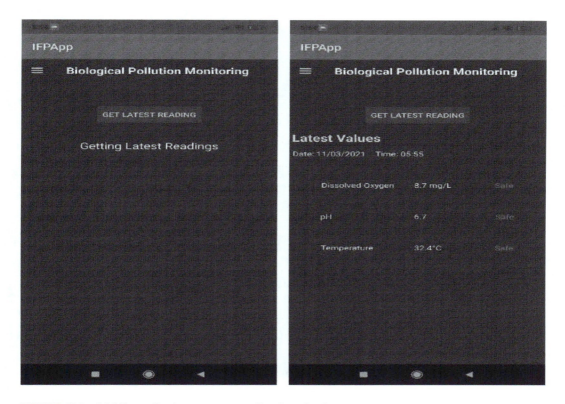

FIGURE 17.8 Mobile application – request reading from hardware setup.

17.3.4.6 Security Features

As shown in Figure 17.9, the system allows for waterbodies to be classified as private or public by the user. The interface for private water bodies can only be accessed by users who have acquired the permission from the owner of the water body.

17.4 RESULTS AND DISCUSSION

The three components are built and integrated by following the specifications described in the working of the proposed system. The hardware setup is built as shown in Figure 17.10. The system uses temperature, pH, and dissolved oxygen sensors to monitor the parameters in water bodies. The WiFi module enables data transfer every 12 hours between the hardware module and cloud database. Users can use the mobile application to login and with valid access permission to the water body, users can monitor the sensor information. The mobile application fetches information from the cloud database using REST Application Programming Interfaces (APIs) [10].

Figure 17.11 shows the user interface of the mobile application. The latest sensor values are displayed along with the timestamp of the data. A message about the value is also displayed. As shown in Figure 17.5, the mobile application can be used to check the WiFi connectivity status of the hardware setup. As shown in Figure 17.6, the mobile application notifies the user whenever the sensor value is not within the safe limits [11–15].

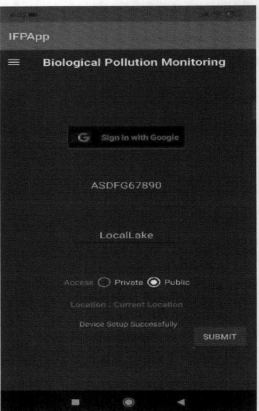

FIGURE 17.9 Mobile application – multiple devices.

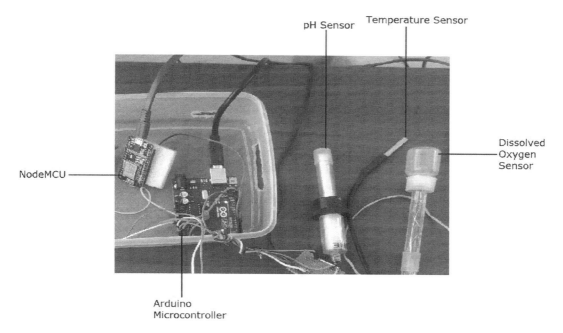

FIGURE 17.10 Implemented hardware setup.

FIGURE 17.11 Mobile application – display sensor values.

As shown in Figure 17.7, the mobile application displays time series graphs of the sensor values and provides insights about the average, maximum, and minimum sensor readings. As shown in Figure 17.8, the mobile application is used to request a reading from the sensors in real time [16,17].

The major advantage of the proposed system is the integration of the NodeMCU wifi-module. This module helps to receive information about the water immediately once a change has been identified. The disadvantage of our proposed work is the integration of firebase database. It takes time to transfer the messages [18].

17.5   CONCLUSION

In this chapter, a system that helps the user to monitor the biological pollution index of water bodies in a community is explained. The system alerts the user regarding alarming degradation or change in quality of water which helps the user to take efficient measures. The system provides sensor readings and time graphs to the users in a comprehensible manner to understand the state of water quality precisely. The data collected from the sensors can be used for future data analytics-related studies.

REFERENCES

1. Sitaram, DhaswadikarUsha. Study of the physio-chemical parameters for testing water: A review, *World Journal of Advanced Research and Reviews* 14(3) (2022): 570–575.
2. Tabrez et al. Water quality index, Labeorohita, and Eichhorniacrassipes: Suitable bio-indicators of river water pollution, *Saudi Journal of Biological Sciences* 29(1) (2022): 75–82.
3. Steephen, K., et al. An intelligent car parking using IoT with node MCU module, *International Journal of Communication and Computer Technologies* 10(2) (2022): 88–88.
4. Saha, Ramesh, et al. A working prototype using DS18B20 temperature sensor and arduino for health monitoring, *SN Computer Science* 2(1) (2021): 1–21.
5. Hartono, Rudi, et al. Improved data transmission of smart water quality sensor devices in Bengawan solo river with LoRa, *2022 1st International Conference on Smart Technology, Applied Informatics, and Engineering (APICS)*, Indonesia. IEEE, 2022.
6. Palconit, Maria Gemel B., et al. Multi-gene genetic programming of IoT water quality index monitoring from fuzzified Model for oreochromisniloticus recirculating aquaculture system, *Journal of Advanced Computational Intelligence and Intelligent Informatics* 26(5) (2022): 816–823.
7. Jan, Farmanullah et al. IoT based smart water quality monitoring: Recent techniques, trends and challenges for domestic applications, *Water* 13(13) (2021): 1729.
8. Jalbani, KhudaBux, et al. Poor coding leads to dos attack and security issues in web applications for sensors, *Security and Communication Networks* 2021 (2021): 1–11.
9. Sanyal, P., Menon, N., Siponen, M. An empirical examination of the economics of mobile application security. *MIS Quarterly* 45(4) (2021): 2235–2260.
10. Ahmad, Imam, et al. Implementation of RESTful API web services architecture in takeaway application development, *2021 1st International Conference on Electronic and Electrical Engineering and Intelligent System (ICE3IS)*, Indonesia. IEEE, 2021
11. Barzegar, R., et al. Comparison of machine learning models for predicting fluoride contamination in groundwater. *Stochastic Environmental Research and Risk Assessment* 31 (2017): 2705–2718.
12. Betrie, G.D., et al. Predicting copper concentrations in acid mine drainage: A comparative analysis of five machine learning techniques. *Environmental Monitoring and Assessment* 185(5) (2013): 4171–4182.
13. Betrie, G.D., et al. Predicting copper concentrations in acid mine drainage: A comparative analysis of five machine learning techniques. *Environmental Monitoring and Assessment* 185 (2013): 4171–4182.
14. Kong, X., et al. Real-time eutrophication status evaluation of coastal waters using support vector machine with grid search algorithm. *Marine Pollution Bulletin* 119 (2017): 307–319.
15. Manoiu, V.-M., Kubiak-Wójcicka, K., Craciun, A.-I., Akman, Ç., Akman, E. Water quality and water pollution in time of covid-19: Positive and negative repercussions. *Water* 14 (2022): 1124. https://doi.org/10.3390/w14071124.

16. Karydis, M. Critique on ecological methodologies used in water quality studies and coastal management: A review. *Journal of Marine Science and Engineering* 10 (2022): 701. https://doi.org/10.3390/jmse10050701.

17. Vappangi, S., Penjarla, N. K., Mathe, S. E., Kondaveeti, H. K. Applications of raspberry Pi in bio-technology: A review, *2022 2nd International Conference on Artificial Intelligence and Signal Processing (AISP)*, 2022, 1–6, https://doi.org/10.1109/AISP53593.2022.9760691.

18. Karmakar, P., Pal, S., Mishra, M. Arthropods: An important bio-indicator to decipher the health of the water of south Asian rivers. In: Patra, B.C., Shit, P.K., Bhunia, G.S., Bhattacharya, M. (eds) *River Health and Ecology in South Asia*. Springer, Cham (2022). https://doi.org/10.1007/978-3-030-83553-8_2.

18 Next Generation Digital Technologies in Smart Society

P. K. Garg
Indian Institute of Technology

CONTENTS

18.1 INTRODUCTION

In the 21st century, many countries require the best methods of capitalizing the scientific and technological innovations. Digital technology has given us a golden opportunity to connect to modern devices and "all things" through the internet. Advances in AI technology along with the 5G that connects various technologies have facilitated to predict, analyze, and optimize the information contents (Foresti et al., 2020). The advancements in digital technologies are expected to drastically change the setup of society. This transformation is called as "digital transformation" which is expected to enhance people's capabilities, enable the development of new products, and provide better and healthy living.

The use of advanced technologies, such as IR 4.0, 3D printing, Drone/UAV, 5G, IoT, Big data, VR/AR, AI and Robotics is rapidly improving the comfort and lives of people. Society 5.0, a human-centered society, is aiming to balance the economic growth and transformation of lives using next-generation technology. The age of AI, robotics, and digitalization creates new avenues and opportunities for governments, industries and organizations for the implementation of technologies to solve many problems, as shown in Figure 18.1. For example, early stage detection of disease and its treatment with effective healthcare can prolong healthy life expectancy of old-aged workers, and thus helps in increasing the productivity (Garg et al., 2022). Telemedicine will not only restrict

DOI: 10.1201/9781003324720-22

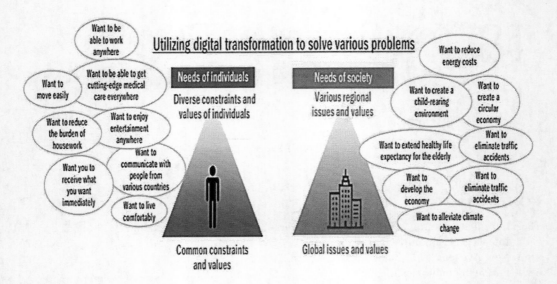

FIGURE 18.1   Digital transformation to solve various problems (Savaget et al., 2019).

the travel of patients but also offer good medical care in rural and remote areas that are inaccessible due to distance/terrain problems.

The next-generation technologies, such as the IoT, Big data, and AI, that integrate physical spaces with the cyberspace play a very important role (Narvaez Rojas, et al., 2021). Wireless sensor networks are required to be utilized to collect a large amount of data, which is subsequently analyzed by AI-based approach for real-time analysis and generate useful outputs. In addition, custom-based services can be provided to anyone, anywhere, and anytime.

18.2   IMPACT ON ECONOMIC GROWTH

Ever-increasing investments by government and private sector for expanding the services through digital platforms using geospatial technology have created several new geospatial applications. Satellite imageries, GIS/Spatial analytics, UAVs, GPS and Positioning, and 3D scanning, are very good input data sources for mapping, visualization and analysis of information required for better timely and decision-making. Various innovative geospatial applications are being developed to improve the efficiency and productivity, and thus making a greater impact on economy, worldwide. The modern economy, while required at producing wealth, has also resulted in widening the income disparity, skewed distribution of employment opportunities, and loss of jobs in traditional sectors, and thus bringing fundamental changes in economies, worldwide. As an example, Table 18.1 shows the expected benefits derived in terms of currency from the use of various innovative technologies in Japan.

Statistically, the data-intensive applications and activities can generate additionally approximately USD 13 trillion by 2030. The International Data Corporation's (IDC's) annual Data Sphere and Storage Sphere reports predicted that the creation of global data will grow at a CAGR of 23% over years 2020–2025, due to the use of cutting-edge and geospatial technologies (Rydning and Shirer, 2021). As per the European Data Strategy, European Commission estimated that the European Union's data economy is expected to rise between 2% and 6% of GDP in the next 7 years (OECD, 2022). The value of data economy will rise from EUR 301 billion in 2018 to EUR 829 billion in 2025, while the number of data professionals will increase from 5.7 million in 2018 to 10.9 million in 2025.

Westerman and Bonnet (2015) proposed a new economic model, related to digital tools, as presented in Table 18.2.

TABLE 18.1

Expected Benefits Derived in Terms of Currency by Using Various Innovative Technologies in Japan (UNCTAD, 2019)

Various Sectors of Society 5.0	Growth Opportunity by Year 2030 (Trillion Yen)	Market size by year 2030 (Trillion Yen)
Next-generation healthcare industry (as Japan's population grows older)	36.2	95.1
Robots (reducing the burden of nursing care)	11.0	30.0
Innovative drugs discovery	8.6	
Smart mobility	21.3	64.4
Automated logistics services	12.1	5.0
Service industry of manufacturing and 3D printing	28.5	108.0
Financial sector	8.6	20.0
Insurance sector	5.9	15.5
Next-generation energy sector	19.3	37.4
Smart living technology	18.9	45.9
Smart agriculture	7.0	15.1
New technologies, such as VR and AR	2.8	6.8
Cybersecurity	4.4	15.8
Accumulation all new technologies	250.0	760.0

TABLE 18.2

Challenges of Digital Transformation

Change in the Relationship with the Customer Experience	Change in Business Processes	Change in Business Models
Understanding the customer	Digitalization of processes	Digital transformation of Organizations
Segmentation analytical method	Improved performance	Increased products and services
Computerization of social networks	(productivity)	Transition from physical to digital
	New functionalities	Digital wrappers (digital network)
Growth of activities	Employee autonomy	New digital commerce
(turnover growth)		
Sales improved with digital tools	Working anywhere, anytime	Increased products and services
Predictive marketing	(telecommuting)	Redefinition of operational perimeters
Streamlining processes (integrated logistics)	Larger, faster, more agile working community	Redefinition of operational cycles
	Sharing knowledge and skills	
Point of contact with customer	Performance management	Globalization
Customer service	Operational transparency	Integration of firm with the world
Consistency of communication channels	Data-driven decision-making	Redistribution of digital power
		Sharing of digital services
Self-service		
Digital tools		
Unification of the market data and processes		Management numerical integration
Analytical capacity	Numerical integration of production process elements	New solutions for delivering products and services

18.3   NEW AVENUES

The aim of Society 5.0 is to increase the automation, which would provide the direction for future growth of AI technology to manage and control the cyber physical social systems. The essence of Society 5.0 is that it will become possible to quickly derive the suitable solution meeting the needs of most individuals. Ongoing advances in technology will enhance the linkage between physical objects through smart communications, enhancing the autonomy, safety and utility of CPS (Salgues, 2018). It will ultimately widen the scope of these systems in many applications, such as collision avoidance, robot-based surgery, search and rescue operations, air-traffic control, making energy-efficient buildings, and providing efficient healthcare services.

The modern technologies, such as cloud computing, IoT, and Big data require the latest IT systems, which include networks, cloud computing, and data centers established at the existing municipalities required for efficient management of energy, water, and transport systems. The development mostly requires high-speed connectivity throughout. In addition, it requires urban readiness to establish a link between users, IoT, Big data, robotics, and individualized services, as shown in Figure 18.2. Society 5.0, along with advanced technologies in different sectors and social activities, ultimately aims to make life safe, easier and trouble-free for everyone. In Society 5.0, new values created through innovations will minimize the gaps in regions, age, gender, and language, and provide the services customized to suit the individual needs. As the interplay between humans and machines is inevitable in future societies, it can be adopted and applied not only in one country (Japan) but also all over the world.

Society 5.0 uses digital transformation to meet the sustainable development goals (SDGs), as identified by United Nations. It also facilitates the utilization of innovative technologies, such as IT, IoT, robotics, AI and AR for making the lives and health of people better. Various technologies are used for the benefits of mankind, such as enhanced production, cost reduction related with old-age society, uniformity in wealth, control of greenhouse gases, increased food production, and balancing of regional disparities, as these could derive rapid socio-economic growth (Narvaez Rojas et al., 2021). The integration of technology, such as the use of drones, AI, Big data, autonomous vehicles, and robotics with the society is thus important in near future for the benefit of humanity. In general, the technological development in Society 5.0 aims to improve the living, but it could also impact the society adversely, such as unemployment, and unequal distribution of wealth.

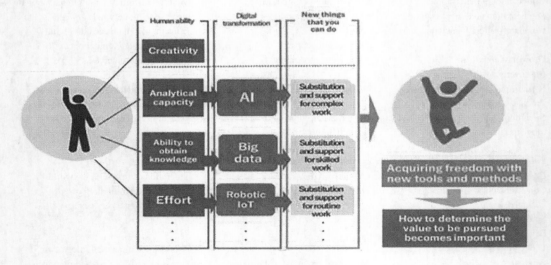

FIGURE 18.2   Creation of a relationship between users, IoT, big data, robotics, and personalized services (Scott and Rajabifard, 2017).

18.4 FUTURE TECHNOLOGIES

Innovations in Society 5.0 are expected to contribute to a modern society. All the countries should adapt Society 5.0 which may ultimately lead to achieving the SDGs, and helping various businesses (Zengin, et al., 2013). The innovations, thus created, would enhance the productivity and our working, as well as create improved goods and services to enhance the quality of life of people (Figure 18.3), and attain the goals of socioeconomic development. Over the next decade, IoT, AI, ML, blockchain, and VR/AR technologies will continue to develop their applications, as briefly given below.

18.4.1 GEOSPATIAL TECHNOLOGY

As digitalization is growing everywhere, geospatial industries are evolving geospatial-based solutions. These applications are further enhanced by advancing the geospatial innovations in the organizations. The technological developments, such as autonomous vehicles, smart cities, and urban development, will need enormous data, including high-definition maps. The navigational maps are required to show precise and detailed locational information. Geospatial data, such as LiDAR and remote sensing, are used to meet the increasing demands for such high-definition maps (Garg, 2020). Miniaturization of technology assets is important to drive the industry development. Today, sensors, LiDAR, drones, wearables and even small satellites, are offering greater avenues for data collection and analysis, as well as to make them more productive and accessible. For example, Building Information Modeling (BIM) in GIS is creating all-round development in smart constructions, urban development, smart cities, etc. The growth of LiDAR on UAV is largely due to high-precision data capturing and delivering highly accurate 3D models.

As true with any innovative technology, there is an acute shortage of skilled manpower to collect drone data using the designated flight parameters and the types of equipment as well as processing of software to ensure timely & reliable data collection. Geospatial technologies are also useful for creating the digital infrastructure and Digital Twin models. The geospatial technologies are the backbone for the development of Digital Twins used for socioeconomic development. From an innovation perspective, geospatial infrastructure, complemented by the AI, IoT, is accelerating the geospatial-enabled innovations. In digital age, geospatial technology/data and information, help driving the new business models.

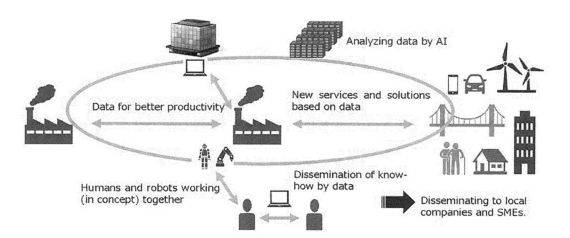

FIGURE 18.3 Connecting data and using data efficiently to encourage innovation, better productivity and dissemination of technology (METI, 2017).

18.4.2 Supply Chain 4.0

The COVID-19 pandemic has given us an opportunity to identify the existing gaps/problems for global supply chain. The absence of digital records and lack of data have impacted the existing supply chain system which was not adequate during the pandemic. The core technologies, such as Big data, cloud computing, IoT, and blockchain, can be used to establish a more robust supply chain network by improving the data quantity and quality and sharing the data.

18.4.3 Drones

Drones have been used earlier in geospatial science for collecting high-resolution data to create various kinds of maps. The drones are successful in collecting the data of disaster-affected sites and making action plans to save the life of flora and fauna (Garg, 2019). Later, these are used for delivering the goods and life-saving drugs. The COVID-19 has realized us that we can't completely rely on human interactions to make things work. The COVID-19 received a powerful push to deploy drones and robots for various kinds of work.

18.4.4 3D Printing

The 3D printing technology was introduced to mitigate the supply chain shocks and export restrictions on personal equipment. It provides flexibility in manufacturing, as the same printer can manufacture various items. The basic parts can easily be manufactured on-site without the need for a lengthy production process and long processing period. The 3D printing is an essential device to several modern industries, as it helps minimizing the wastage, reducing the risk, and creating lightweight and economical models for sustainable construction.

18.4.5 Autonomous Mobile Robots

Autonomous robots are working with GNSS systems for navigation. Several robotic systems employ GIS data to take decisions for navigation. Such robots provide solution which saves workforce. Autonomous vehicles make use of geospatial data, which is closely linked to defining the positions (coordinates), as well as situational awareness. Robots can be used to measure the distance of people and objects in real time, while the 3D sensor module provides useful data to be used in a large number of applications, such as delivery of goods, logistics, sorting and picking, etc. These robots use next-generation technology, the Time of Flight (ToF) sensors, to provide high-accuracy readings for near and far objects, as they generally perform the measurements a number of times and adopt the average value (Garg, 2020). However, for high-speed operation mode, such sensors calculate the distance with a single measurement. The ToF sensor along with a built-in edge noise reduction function enhances the reliably of objects detection, and thus reduces the chances of false detections. The ToF sensor can capture a sharp image for the detection of objects from any distance. It is expected that a lot of manufacturing workers will be replaced by machines in the future, new workers will be generated in the process at the same time.

18.4.6 Thermal Sensors

Thermal sensors have lots of useful applications. For example, Micro-electrical-mechanical systems (MEMS) are employed for accurately detecting the human presence to save electricity in houses, buildings, and industries. Accurate detection of human presence is very important in such cases. Modern thermal sensors allow touchless temperature measurement. The MEMS sensors with small weight provide ease of use, and higher accuracy in many applications, such as detecting the fever, saving the energy, sensing the motion, and monitoring the fluid levels in sophisticated equipment.

18.4.7 Virtual Reality/Augmented Reality

Virtual reality (VR) defines the objects in a virtual environment using a headset on a computer screen. The headset employs the head tracking technology that is used by human beings to move their head to look around the created virtual environment. The display provides a 360° view of the virtual environment. The powerful devices are required to create smooth VR. Handheld controllers are needed to track the hands' movements to provide a real experience.

Augmented reality (AR) allows to visualize the terrain around us using several digital images. The example includes playing a game, like Pokémon Go or using filters on Snapchat. Several AR headsets are available, but they are costlier than the VR headsets. However, without a headset, the AR can be created on devices, like smartphones and laptops. Several apps that use AR are also available. AR/VR can help developing virtual environments for sustainable smart city applications, such as reducing the carbon footprint. Both these technologies are developing very fast and will have a large number of applications benefitting the society.

18.4.8 5G and Information Technology

The technology trends are focused on reliable, high-speed, and economical internet. The 5G is being used in health monitoring and consultation in remote locations. The 5G implementation would be expensive as compatible devices and the data plan will also cost more. Addressing those issues to ensure inclusive internet access will remain a challenge as the 5G network expands globally.

18.4.9 Advanced Data Analytics

Advanced data analytics brings innovative decision-making in businesses. They use high-end techniques for data mining, and predictive analytics to study trends and patterns. As the data size increases, prediction accuracy of the models will increase. Advanced analytics tools support to analyze the cause of events, identify trends, and predict from the past trend. These tools facilitate analysis and operationalization of large quantity of data quickly for better decision-making. Some advanced analytics methods include; data mining, machine learning, cohort analysis, retention analysis, predictive analysis, complex event analysis, etc.

18.4.10 Quantum Computing

Technological growth in computing, particularly quantum computing, offers ample opportunities for processing the Big data. Although the quantum computing is still in the developmental stage, but its application is expected to drastically reduce the time to process the large unorganized datasets.

18.4.11 The Industrial Internet of Things

The Industrial Internet of Things (IIoT) includes networked sensors, equipment, and other gadgets devices connected for industrial applications, and manufacturing and energy management. The IIoT allows data collection & analysis, facilitates enhancement in productivity, and brings economic benefits. It is like a distributed automized control system that uses cloud computing to improve the control process. It is backed by various technologies, such as cyber security, cloud computing, edge computing, mobile technologies, machine-to-machine, 3D printing, advanced robotics, Big data, IoT, RFID, and computer vision. The cyber-physical systems (CPS) is the main technology platform for IoT and IIoT that connects the physical machines. The CPS integrates the physical processes with software and information, and thus offers modeling, design, and analysis techniques.

The IIoT architecture consists of various components, such as sensors, networking and gateways, device management and application platforms. Emerging technologies enable the easy establishment of a workable IIoT architecture. Manufacturing industry is most vulnerable with malware attacks industry, as it lacks to tackle with security issues. Smart industries can also face similar issues of malware, denial of service, device hacking, etc., that other networks face. These threats can result in serious damages and losses, especially to the IIoT.

18.4.12 VARIOUS OTHER BUSINESS MODELS

1. **X-as-a Service:** It is also commonly known as *Anything as a Service* business model which recognizes that the industries are aware about the benefits of delivering the products, tools and technologies as a service, over a network or as per the consumer's demand. The model is gaining popularity since business solutions need to be produced over a network on 24×7 basis. For example, the geospatial industry now is providing various kinds of "As-a-Service" models to provide the consumer-centric solutions.
2. **Infrastructure-as-a-Service (IaaS):** It is a building block for Cloud IT, as the Big data can be stored and shared with various stakeholders. For example, Amazon Web Services is an IaaS provider where geospatial big data can be stored and processed for developing the applications.
3. **Content-as-a-Service (CaaS):** It is a licensed data program which stores data, images, and updated maps, and is provided on demand to the users. The CaaS business model is based on the principle of sharing economy, like giving access to everyone.
4. **Platform-as-a-Service (PaaS):** In this model, the technology provider will deliver the applications over a network while hosting the user's hardware and software on its platform. This is the most preferred business model that drives innovation and brings transformation.
5. **Software-as-a-Service (SaaS):** It is a software licensing and delivery model offering a software as a service to users on a central platform. It is also considered as an on-demand software.

18.5 CONCLUSION

Society 5.0 is an opportunity which will shape the future. It is important to make use of the latest technologies for better future of mankind. A network of disruptive technologies is necessary for accelerating the innovations to achieve the goals of Smart Society 5.0. Technologies, such as Robotics, Autonomous vehicles, AI, ML; all will help us achieving goals of socioeconomic development (Narvaez Rojas, et al., 2021). Various sectors associated with Society 5.0 will use and develop innovative applications to enhance efficiency, thus making impact for socioeconomic development worldwide. New technologies, with huge data demand will require a modern digital infrastructure for automation and real-time delivery of information/data. To take full benefits of digital technologies, stakeholders of Society 5.0 ecosystem must strengthen the digital systems and improve upon data sharing and workflow processes (Foresti et al., 2020). It is also equally important to develop systems for public and private sectors to collaborate for the improvement of technological approaches for global use. In future, the geospatial data will be created using mobile methods, crowdsourcing, and social media platforms, which will facilitate real-time applications being demanded by the users.

Japan can now play a lead role in contributing to the goals of sustainable development embedded in Society 5.0. The main stakeholder in these will be the industry, and the entire process will dramatically change the businesses. At present, it is not possible to assess the impact of "Society 5.0" that is likely to bring revolution in the future. But what is important to us is to be one of the key players in bringing out this revolution, and therefore it is essential to work with modern tools and technologies to recreate the future. It is understood that such a society can't be achieved overnight, and the implementation of solutions will have lots of difficulties and problems. Japan has taken a lead to face the challenges and presented a model for future society, with the aim of being on top of the world.

REFERENCES

Foresti, Ruben, Rossi, Stefano, Magnani, Matteo, Bianco, Lo, Guarino, Corrado and Delmonte, Nicola, (2020), Smart society and artificial intelligence: big data scheduling and the global standard method applied to smart maintenance, *Engineering*, 6, 835–846.

Garg, P. K., (2019), *Introduction to Unmanned Aerial Vehicles*, New Age India International Pvt. Ltd., Delhi.

Garg, P. K., (2020), *Digital Land Surveying and Mapping*, New Age International Pvt Ltd., Delhi.

Garg, P. K., Tripathi, Nitin, Kappas, Martin and Gaur, Loveleen (Eds), (2022), *Geospatial Data Science in Healthcare for Society 5.0*, Springer Nature, Singapore.

METI, (2017), *Connected Industries Tokyo Initiative*, https://www.almendron.com/tribuna/wpcontent/uploads/2019/01/tokyo-initiative-2017.pdf.

Narvaez Rojas, C., Alomia Peñafiel, G. A., Loaiza Buitrago, D. F., Tavera Romero, C. A., (2021), Society 5.0: a Japanese concept for a superintelligent society, *Sustainability*, 13, 6567, https://doi.org/10.3390/su13126567.

OECD, (2022), *Economic Forecast Summary*, OECD, https://www.oecd.org/economy/euro-area-and-european-union-economic-snapshot/.

Rydning, John and Shirer, Michael, (2021), *Data Creation and Replication Will Grow at a Faster Rate than Installed Storage Capacity, According to the IDC Global DataSphere and StorageSphere Forecasts*, IDC, https://www.idc.com/getdoc.jsp?containerId=prUS47560321.

Salgues, Bruno, (2018), *Society 5.0: Industries of the Future, Technologies, Methods and Tools*, Vol. 1, Wiley & Sons, New Jersey.

Savaget, P., Geissdoerfer, M., Kharrazi, A. and Evans, S., (2019), The theoretical foundations of sociotechnical systems change for sustainability: a systematic literature review, *Journal of Cleaner Production*, 206, 878–892.

Scott, Greg and Rajabifard, Abbas, (2017), Sustainable development and geospatial information: a strategic framework for integrating a global policy agenda into national geospatial capabilities, *Geo-spatial Information Science*, 20(2), 59–76, https://doi.org/10.1080/10095020.2017.1325594.

UNCTAD, (2019), Value creation and capture: implications for developing countries, *Digital Economy Report 2019, United Nations Conference on Trade and Development (UNCTAD), Geneva, United Nations*.

Westerman, G. and Bonnet, D., (2015), Revamping your business through digital transformation, *MIT Sloan Management Review*, 56(3), 10–13.

Zengin, Yunus, Naktiyok, Serkan, Kaygin, Erdogan, Kavak, Onur and Topeuoglu, Ethem, (2013), An Investigation upon Industry 4.0 and Society 5.0 within the context of sustainable development goals, *Sustainability*, 13, 2682. https://doi.org/10.3390/su13052682.

Index